The Semiotics of
THEATER

Advances in Semiotics

Thomas A. Sebeok, General Editor

The Semiotics of
THEATER

ERIKA FISCHER-LICHTE

❑❑❑❑❑❑

TRANSLATED BY
Jeremy Gaines
AND
Doris L. Jones

INDIANA UNIVERSITY PRESS
Bloomington and Indianapolis

Originally published in three volumes as *Semiotik des Theaters* © 1983 by
Gunter Narr Verlag, Tübingen
Abridged English translation © 1992 by Indiana University Press

The paper used in this publication meets the minimum requirements of American
National Standard for Information Sciences—Permanence of Paper for Printed
Library Materials, ANSI Z39.48-1984.

 ™

Manufactured in the United States of America

Library of Congress Cataloging-in-Publication Data

Fischer-Lichte, Erika.
    [Semiotik des Theaters.   English]
    The semiotics of theater / Erika Fischer-Lichte ; translated by
Jeremy Gaines and Doris L. Jones.
        p.   cm. — (Advances in semiotics)
    Translation of: Semiotik des Theaters.
    Includes bibliographical references and index.
    ISBN 0-253-32237-5 (cloth : alk. paper)
    1. Theater—Semiotics. 2. Semiotics and literature. I. Title.
II. Series.
PN2041.S45F5713   1992
792'.014—dc20   91-24781

1 2 3 4 5   96 95 94 93 92

Contents

The Semiotics of
THEATER

Introduction

Theater as a Cultural System

❏ ❏ ❏   Theater is played in the widest range of different cultures: in the agrarian cultures or so-called primitive cultures based on hunting or fishing;[1] in the sophisticated ancient Middle and Far Eastern civilizations, such as those of Persia, Turkey, India, Malaysia, Japan, and China;[2] and in all of Western culture. Wherever there is culture there are forms of theater.

Research into other, unknown cultures has repeatedly confirmed just how widespread theater is as a cultural phenomenon, and its high profile has prompted a wide range of different attempts to interpret it. The existence of theater has been explained, for example, anthropologically,[3] sociologically,[4] and psychologically.[5] Viewed from the standpoint of the cultural sciences, theater appears initially to be one of many possible cultural systems. Theater can, like farming, hunting, housebuilding, tool manufacture, weapons, crockery and clothing, commerce, table manners, rules on clothing, the system of social relations, religious customs, language, law, myths, literary traditions, etc., form a constitutive part of that which, as the sum total of all such systems, we call culture. Yet, cultural studies must provide an explanation for the striking fact that theater is one of the unique constituent subsystems in almost all cultures known to us—especially striking because it is not one of the cultural systems that function to satisfy primary physical needs.

Theater is, on the one hand, a cultural system among others, i.e., it exhibits the same general feature as all the others, by virtue of which it can be defined as a cultural system in the first place. However, it is, on the other hand, a cultural system *sui generis*, one that is significantly different from other cultural systems because of the special functions which it alone fulfills.

Culture is understood here in quite a broad sense as something created by humans as opposed to nature, which has originated without human activity.[6] Everything which humans produce is "significant" for themselves and each other, because humans in principle live "in a signifying world,"[7] that is, in a world where everything that is perceived is perceived as a signifier which must be judged to have a signified, i.e., a meaning.[8] Every sound, action, object, or custom produced simultaneously involves the production of a meaning. The generation of meaning can therefore be regarded as the general function of all cultural systems; it is this function which allows them to be defined as cultural systems in the first place.[9] In other words, theater, understood as one cultural system among others, has the general function of generating meaning.

Cultural systems do not produce meaning per se—this would be a contradiction in terms—but always generate something that can be perceived with the senses as sounds, actions, objects to which a particular meaning is attached in the context of the culture in which they are produced. The production of meaning thus ensues via the creation of *signs*.[10]

According to Charles Morris,[11] a sign fundamentally consists of three nonreducible constituent elements: the sign-vehicle, something that denotes what is designated, and the interpretant. Morris derives three two-sided relations from these three elements: first, the sign's syntactic dimension, namely, the relation of the sign to other sign-vehicles; second, the semantic dimension, namely, the relation of the sign to the objects it designates; and third, the pragmatic dimension, namely, the relation of the sign to the user of the sign. Semiosis, the process by which a sign is accorded a meaning, occurs in all three dimensions; its product, meaning, can therefore only be adequately described and understood within this three-dimensional structure. Meaning arises when a sign is related by its user to something within a context of signs; the meaning can change if the sign is (a) inserted into a different semiotic context; (b) related to something else; or (c) used by another user. In other words, the meaning of the sign changes if one of the three dimensions changes. For meaning is a semiotic category.

This three-dimensionality provides an explanation for why it is that different people, and this is a well-known fact, can attribute different meanings to the same sign—whether it is a word, a drawing, a tool, or a building.

It can be assumed that within a culture the users of the signs of that culture attribute a meaning to them which contains a common, binding, relatively stable semantic component, i.e., the denotations and, furthermore, possible additional components of meaning, the connotations.[12] The latter can be commonly used by very different groups: they may be used by everyone in the culture; by individual classes or social strata; by a particular political, ideological, or religious group; by a group with a certain world-view; by other groupings; by the different subcultures; by individual families or other small groups. Indeed they may be valid solely for one individual, and they are, in general, subject to faster and more far-reaching changes than are the denotations.[13] Meaning is, in other words, always to be grasped as a complex composed of an "objective" element that is intersubjectively valid in the culture in question and of "subjective" elements that may differ greatly.

Both the denotative and connotative elements of meaning have their respective history: they are the product of what the members of the culture have experienced in the different roles they occupy—as members of the culture, of a social stratum, of a certain group, of a family, or as an individual. Meaning is always shaped by history and the course of people's lives—and this is naturally true above all of the connotations.

The meanings generated by the different cultural systems will exhibit a high degree of stability and homogeneity in a culture which, on the one hand, fixes and restricts the possibilities of experience within quite clear bounds for the different groups (e.g., children and adults, adults and old people, men and women, tribe and tribal chief, shaman and the non-initiated) and, on the other hand, successfully occludes outside influences. By contrast, a culture which either does not have strict regulations governing the possibilities of experience by the single persons and individual groups or permits—indeed even induces—frequent contact with other cultures, will be characterized by instability and heterogeneity in the meanings constituted in it. On the one hand, this latter culture will encourage the division of the complex of meaning into denotation and connotation, given that even it cannot get by without a minimum of mutually-accepted meanings. (This division is irrelevant in cultures with stable and homogeneous meanings, for the sign produced by a cultural system always signifies the whole complex of meaning.) Therefore, the culture will set off those situations in which in principle only the denotation and/or the denotation linked with certain connotations is to be granted validity from all conceivable situations. On the other hand, a certain number of meanings (understood here as a complex of denotations and connotations) will be selected that mean the same to everyone and are binding for them, for these are judged to be the pillars bearing the basic values of this culture.[14]

Both types of cultures—and all the "admixtures" which exist between the two—are characterized both by the meanings generated by their respective subsystems and by the degree of their stability and bindingness. Both these features are historically specific.

The meanings generated by a cultural system are not isolated, i.e., are not independent of one another, but rather form interrelated complexes; these are comprised either of various meanings taken together or, frequently, of combinations with meanings produced by other cultural subsystems. For these meanings are not produced arbitrarily, but according to certain rules,[15] on the basis of a *code*.[16] A "code" is understood here to mean quite generally a system of rules for producing and interpreting signs or complexes of signs. A culture always exhibits meanings shared by more than one person if its members all refer to the same code when constituting meaning; divergent meanings arise if different groups use different codes with regard to one and the same sign.

A distinction must be made between so-called internal and external codes. Internal codes are the basis of one respectively specific cultural system; indeed in extreme cases, such as autonomous artworks,[17] they are the basis of a product of that system; external codes are the foundation of several, and in extreme cases of all, cultural systems within a culture.

The internal code of a cultural system regulates: (a) which material products are to be valid in the system as units of meanings, i.e., as signs; (b) which of the units thus identified can be combined in what manner and under what conditions with each other, i.e., it governs a syntactic code; and (c) to what these units can be related and under what conditions (i) in connection with different possible syntagmas or (ii) in isolation, i.e., it regulates a semantic code.

Thus, the code of every language, English, German, or Chinese, regulates (a) which sounds are to be identified as the smallest units of meaning, i.e., as words of this language; (b) the possible combinations of these words in order to form syntagmas; and (c) the allocation of significations to these sound signs both as a lexical and as a contextual meaning. In other words, both the production and the understanding of utterances within a language function on the basis of a code that we shall term the internal code of the language. The same is true of all cultural systems: these regulate the process whereby meaning is produced on the basis of a respectively specific internal code on which the production or interpretation of all meanings is then based.

An external code is involved if, first, several of these codes are subordinated to another code as their hypercode in the sense that the generation and interpretation of their systems of rules are based on it, and second, the meanings produced by the individual cultural systems can now be understood in their function and meaning for the overall culture at a second level, as it were, namely, on the basis of a hypercode. Lévi-Strauss has shown that a commonly shared code is at the root of the structure of codes of such different cultural systems as, for example, language, family relations and marriage practices, eating habits, and the myths of various tribes indigenous to Latin America.[18]

The meaning of the signs and/or sign complexes generated by a cultural system can thus only be constituted comprehensively, given the application of both the system's internal code and the external code shared by it and other systems.

The codes on which cultural systems are based differ in terms of stability from one culture to the next. Thus, the syntactic code of language is quite stable in Western culture—it has only undergone minor modifications over the centuries. By contrast, the code regulating clothing habits—fashion—is particularly prone to change: it has been in a process of continual restructuring over the last few decades.

The potential instability of every code stems from its historical specificity, and this is expressed in the dialectical relation of code and message.[19] Meanings are generated and messages formulated on the basis of the code. The messages formulated in this manner can be of such a nature that they make it necessary to restructure the underlying code. This restructuring, in turn, enables new meanings to be produced, which themselves lead to the formulation of new messages, etc.

The early sixteenth-century European code for astronomy envisaged the possible message that the sun circled around the earth. This message was, on the one hand, drawn up on the basis of an internal code for astronomy and, on the other, was only possible against the background of the external theological code which structured the whole of social life at the time by decreeing it an iron law that humans, created in God's image, could only be placed at the center of the universe.

When a new message arose that was also based on the code for astronomy, namely, that the earth revolved around the sun, this initially led to a restructuring of the code. However, this process caused the internal code for astronomy and the external code of theology to contradict one another. Following vain retroactive attempts to annul the restructuring of the astronomical code, it became necessary to restructure the external theological code in such a way that it would be possible to uphold the validity of the message it insisted on, namely, that humans were created in God's image. At the same time, it was also necessary to revise the message which had previously been based on this and was now invalid, namely, that humans were factually and not simply spiritually the center of the Universe. The restructuring of the theological code that was subsequently effected led inevitably, in its capacity as the external code of other cultural systems, to a re-structuring of the latters' respective codes in such a manner that these were then able to generate new meanings that could be used to formulate messages. These subsequently resulted in the final instance in the theological system being stripped of its function as the external code for the whole culture in question.

The system of different codes present in a culture is, in other words, a dynamic structure in which changes can continually occur that cause a reorganization of the overall structure. Both the codes which function as internal or external codes for the cultural systems and the meanings generated by such codes can therefore only be adequately described and grasped with respect to their respective historical specificity.

Theater, understood as one cultural system among others, can therefore be con-strued as fulfilling the general function of generating meaning on the basis of an internal code. This code regulates (a) what is to be valid as a unit of meaning—as a sign—in theater; (b) in what way and under what conditions which of these signs can be combined with one another; and (c) which meanings can be accorded these signs both in specific contexts and, in part, in isolation. Furthermore, the theatrical code may depend on the rules of an external code with respect both to the production and to the interpretation of its signs and/or sets of signs. These conclusions, which touch on the question of the extent to which theater is just one cultural system among others, already provide the justification for suggesting that theater is a cultural system *sui generis*. For the internal code of theater con-stitutes itself precisely as an internal code, i.e., a quite specific code that is to be distinguished from all other codes of the culture. It does so by prescribing the use of quite specific signs and quite specific syntactic, semantic, and pragmatic rules during the process in which meaning is constituted.

Before, however, going on to describe, analyze, and discuss the details of the theatrical code's special nature, we shall briefly examine the fundamental differ-ences between it and the respectively specific internal codes of other cultural systems. It has thus far been assumed that all cultural systems function to generate meaning. The individual systems clearly fulfill this function in quite different ways, if one ignores the fact that they respectively fulfill it on the basis of a particular, unique internal code. I, for example, use the sound /hammer/ only as a sign, for instance for an object with which I can drive a nail into a wall. Yet I not only view the object "hammer" as a sign for the fact that I can hit a nail with it, but also actually use it in this function in order to drive a nail into the wall. I can use the hammer precisely for this function because the object "hammer" denotes a particular function on account of its specific material nature. Here the sign function serves, as it were, as the precondition for its utility function. I can, how-ever, hardly drive a nail into a wall using the sound /hammer/. For the sound can only be used meaningfully in its function as a sign and not in a utility function.

A fundamental distinction must therefore be made between those cultural sys-tems which deploy signs to denote a certain utility function,[20] and those in which signs do not have a utility function. Whereas the first type of system includes, among other things, clothing, food, utensils, tools, arms, and buildings, the second involves language, traffic signs, mimic signs, religious customs, painting, theater, etc.

It is, however, by no means the case that those cultural systems which involve signs that do not denote a utility function form one homogeneous group. Thus, for example, linguistic signs used in poetry are diametrically opposed to those used in all types of nonpoetic applications, and iconic signs in painting are opposed in this respect to iconic signs used in pictograms, traffic signs, etc. Likewise, mimic and gestural signs used in theater are the opposite of those mimic and gestural signs used in everyday situations. The meaning of these signs can change in non-aesthetic contexts to the extent that meaning quite generally is a semiotic unit, the constitution of which depends on the three semiotic dimensions—i.e., the syntactic, semantic, and pragmatic dimensions. However, the meaning can be changed to a far greater extent if the sign is used in an aesthetic application, for in this case the autonomous semantic dimension ceases to play a role as a stabilizing factor. Aesthetic meaning differs fundamentally from nonaesthetic meaning in terms of this potential intensification of what is in principle an ever-present capacity to change.[21]

The first differentiation made above must, in other words, be complemented by a second distinction, namely, between cultural systems which generate meaning on the basis of aesthetic codes and those which generate it on the basis of non-aesthetic codes.

The method used here, namely, distinguishing the different cultural systems from one another by viewing them as respective opposites with regard to the special way in which they fulfill their general function of generating meaning, leads us to a second question. Does theater—quite aside from the fact that it, like all cultural systems, follows a specific internal code—contrast in principle with the other systems which generate meaning on the basis of aesthetic codes? This question cannot be answered by referring to individual, possibly distinguishing factors, but rather only by taking into account a whole complex of such factors which relate to one another in a particular way and are relevant only as a whole—as a bundle of factors, so to speak. These factors refer above all to two sets of problems: (1) the ontological state of the artwork; and (2) the conditions for its production and reception.

The major feature of the network of signs which the cultural system of "theater" respectively produces—the performance—is that it cannot be separated from its producers, the actors. The material artifact[22] of theater does not—and here it is unlike a picture or the text of a poem—have an autonomous existence in isolation from its producers. The transitoriness of theater, as Lessing called it, is defined not only by its occurrence in time, like music or an oral reading, but also by the fact that its realization remains inextricably tied to its originator and has no transferable, repeatable autonomous existence.

A further important feature of theater arises from this, the specific ontological state of theatrical performance: namely, its complete contemporaneity. Whereas I can observe pictures that were painted many hundreds of years ago, read novels that were written in times long past, I can only watch theater performances that occur today, in the present. I can, as Steinbeck fittingly puts it, only involve myself theoretically, and not aesthetically, with past theater performances.[23] For the web of signs of the performance is indissolubly bound up with the actor who creates them, present only in the moment of their production. Nothing is changed by bearing in mind that some of the signs here—such as costumes, props, stage decor—outlast the process of performance. For what can endure are individual signs torn out of their context, but never the web of signs from which they originate. This cannot be handed down as tradition.

The specific conditions of theater production and reception are intimately connected with the special ontological state of theatrical performances as artworks. Given that the network of signs only exists in the process of its production, any reception of it has to occur at the same time: production and reception of a theater performance are synchronous. The moment an actor produces a sign by means of which he wishes to generate and communicate particular meanings, that sign is perceived by the audience who in turn produce meaning by attributing particular meanings to this sign. That is, in the case of a theater performance, we have to do with two aspects of the process of constituting meaning which occur simultaneously.[24]

This synchronicity points not only to the specific ontological state of theater performances from which it derives; it also magnifies another essential feature of theater as a cultural system. For a theater performance does not just produce a web of signs that *can also* be received in the process of its production. Rather, a theater performance that does not take place before an audience, i.e., cannot be received, is not a theater performance. The audience is in fact a constitutive part of theater—without an audience there can be no performance.[25] In other words, in addition to its specific ontological state, performances are characterized substantively by their public nature. Even if they take place before only one spectator, they nevertheless occur in public, for this one spectator represents the public in his capacity as a spectator. Theater always occurs as a public event.[26]

By virtue of these two features, each of which comprises quite specific factors determining the process of the constitution of meaning, theater as a cultural system contrasts fundamentally with all the other cultural systems which create meaning on the basis of an aesthetic code. For these two characteristics are not to be found in such a combination in any other artistic genre.

It can be concluded, then, that the cultural system of theater is based on two constituent elements that must exist if it is to be theater: the actor and the spectator.[27] These two constituent elements implicitly contain a third. For the actor is only an actor and not just person A, B, or C to the extent that s/he portrays someone else, X, Y or Z, i.e., plays a role. In other words, the minimum preconditions for theater to be theater are that person A represents X while S looks on.[28]

Now, in order to depict X, A (1) dons a particular external appearance, (2) acts in a certain way, and (3) does so in a certain space. Such a general description of the actor's activity does not provide a clear account of the differences between his activity and that of all other members of the culture. For these three characteristics hold for all people in all cultures: every person prepares his/her external appearance in a particular way and acts in a certain way in a particular space. On the basis of this general distinction all that could be said would be that the difference between what person A does as person A and what s/he does when portraying X consists solely in his/her donning a different appearance and acting in a different way in a different space. There is, however, a fundamental, qualitative difference between the two processes.

If person A in her capacity as person A prepares her external appearance in a special way, for example by slipping on a fur coat, then she probably does this because she is cold and wishes to warm herself. The fur coat denotes a certain utility function in which it is also used de facto. Furthermore, A may, if she is meeting other people when wearing the coat, perhaps put it on in order to show that she belongs to a certain social stratum, has a certain income, has a particular taste, etc. Everything for which the person's external appearance, in this case the fur coat, may be a sign is intended to be referred to the person himself: it is a sign for something that concerns person A as person A.

If A carries out an action as A, e.g., manufactures a jug, then she does so either because she wishes to use it herself or to sell it or give it to someone. She manufactures it for a specific purpose. If she has an audience while making it, then she may be manufacturing it in order to show others how skilled, how fast, how diligent she, A, is. If A cries, then we can assume that a certain emotion may be the cause: she cries perhaps because she is sad. If she cries in the presence of others, then this is a sign for them that A is sad. If A seeks out a certain spatial location, then she does so for a concrete purpose. Every space specially prepared by humans denotes a utility function, be it a living room, a stable, a church, a town hall, an office, a restroom, etc. A acts in such a space because she wishes to attain a goal connected with this space. The same is true if she seeks out a space not prepared by humans, such as forests, meadows, river banks, etc. In addition to fulfilling such utilitarian functions, spending time in a particular space may also be meant as a sign that she has something to do there or belongs there—a sign that is intended to say something about person A. In other words, if person A prepares her external appearance in a certain way as person A and acts in a particular way in a particular surrounding, then she does this either in order to attain a concrete end or in order to show others something about herself, person A.

If, by contrast, A prepares her external appearance in such a manner as to depict X—if, for example, she puts on a fur coat—then she does this quite clearly not because she is cold but in order to make a statement about X. Perhaps X is cold in this situation or—if X is Ferdinand in Schiller's *Love and Intrigue* and wears a present-day fur coat—X is a person with characteristics similar to those who wear such coats today, etc. A, in other words, prepares her external appearance not to achieve a specific end, but in order to say something about X. If A produces a jug while depicting X, then this occurs not in order to use the jug for some express purpose, but to generate a sign of something that concerns X: her ability to manufacture a jug, her skill, or her dire situation which forces her to make jugs, etc. If A cries while depicting X, then she does not cry because she, A, is sad. Rather, she cries in order to show that X is sad or that X is someone who cannot control herself, or that X wishes to appear emotional in the eyes of others, etc.

Everything that A does while representing X is done not to achieve a specific end—because everything which she does in this case is done not for herself, but for others, for the spectators. Nor does she do something in order to say something about herself as person A, but exclusively in order to show something that refers solely to X.

The space in which A acts when playing X is a special space to the extent that it denotes a quite specific utility function, namely, that of being able to signify different spaces. It may, on the one hand, be a space expressly built or decorated for the purpose—whether a proper theater building or merely a simple wooden stage made of planks that can be assembled anywhere. On the other hand, this special space may be situated in a space that denotes another utility function, such as a church, school, canteen, marketplace, fairground, meadow, railway station. Thus, that special space whose function consists of signifying a random number of other spaces can be realized in any space. For when A acts in order to portray X, then the space no longer denotes its original utility function, but rather the special space of the performance; in other words, it signifies whatever particular space X finds herself in.

A can act as A both in the presence of others and on her own. When A, by contrast, acts in order to portray X, then everything she does, the way she does it, and where she does it is related to the presence of spectators, for whom A's external appearance signifies that of X, her actions and behavior that of X, and the space in which she acts the space in which X acts.

To this extent the same underlying situation is to be encountered as is to be found in culture in general, in that both cases can be characterized globally as involving humans preparing their external appearances in a particular way and acting in a certain way in a particular space. However, whereas in culture, meaning is generated in general as a whole by the cultural systems activated by this process creating primary signs, in theater meaning is produced by generating signs for the signs created by the other cultural systems.

Thus, in a certain sense, theater involves the "doubling up" of the culture in which that theater is played: the signs engendered by theater respectively denote those signs produced by the corresponding cultural systems. Theatrical signs are therefore always signs of signs which are characterized by the fact that they may have the same material constitution as the primary signs which they signify—a crown can signify a crown, a nod of the head can mean a nod of the head, and a scream a scream, etc. It follows from this that an especially close connection must obtain between theater and culture. The signs of theater can only be understood by someone who is acquainted with the signs produced by the cultural systems in the surrounding culture and knows how to interpret them. Theater, in other words, reflects the reality of the culture in which it originates in a double sense of the word: it depicts that reality and presents it in such a depiction[29] for reflective thought.

Theater depicts culture to the extent that its signs signify those generated by the different cultural systems. It therefore places the culture at the scrutiny of a distanced and distancing gaze to the extent that the theatrical signs can only be generated with reference to the spectators. Culture is accordingly divided up in theater into a culture of those who depict it and a culture of those who watch it.[30] The audience as a public which represents the members of that culture as a whole can act as proxy for this overall number and thus, in the act of spectating, gain distance from the culture depicted and from itself. In this manner, theater becomes a model of cultural reality in which the spectators confront the meanings of that reality. In this sense, theater can be understood as an act of self-presentation and self-reflection on the part of the culture in question.

This specific characteristic of theater—which sets it off from all other cultural systems—may, from the viewpoint of cultural studies, be the reason for the wide-spread occurrence of the phenomenon of theater. For whenever a culture consti-tutes itself by generating meaning through the creation of signs with the help of various cultural systems, it has, in so doing, provided the signs which it needs to make theater possible. For theater does not require the invention of specifically theatrical signs if it is to come about, even if theater in various highly developed cultures deploys such inventions.[31] Rather, theater resorts to signs that are already present in the culture anyway. It takes up these signs without making use of the primary functions for which they were produced by the respective cultural systems in the first place. The new function given these signs in theater, namely, that of being signs of signs, enables the culture in question to take a reflective stance on itself.

In other words, wherever culture constitutes itself, it creates the preconditions for the constitution of theater. For the signs that theater needs are always available in a culture; the moment they are used in the above-mentioned new function, theater can be deemed to have come into being.

The Theatrical Code

The theater fulfills its general function of generating meaning not only under very specific conditions which place it in opposition to all other cultural systems, but also—as is the case with all of these cultural systems—in a very specific manner. For it does so on the basis of a code particular to it alone, namely, the internal code of the theater. This code regulates (1) which material creations are to apply as vehicles of meaning—in other words, as theatrical signs; (2) in what way and under what conditions these signs can be combined selectively with one another; and (3) which meanings can be attributed to these signs (a) in certain syntagma and (b) in some cases, as isolated elements. Therefore, in order to examine how the theater functions as a specific system which generates meaning, it is necessary to describe and analyze its code, i.e., the signs and the possible combinations and meanings of these signs.

This raises the question of which methodology should be adopted. For, as we know from theater history, the signs produced and employed by the theaters of different cultures, epochs, social strata, and genres are indeed completely different from each other, as are the various combinations and meanings of the signs they employ. Thus, there are forms of theater—such as the theater of Ancient Greece or Japanese Nô theater—that dispense with mimic signs because they prescribe the use of masks; or forms, such as pantomime, that do not utilize linguistic signs; and forms, such as the Elizabethan theater and various types of street theater, that do not require decoration. Forms of theater, such as opera, exist which demand the use of musical signs and others that make no use of them at all. Therefore, before attempting to compile the repertoire of theatrical signs, it must be made clear which type of theater is being referred to. Evidently, different theaters work with different signs; which is to say, in terms of the present definition, they function on the basis of differing codes. So it cannot be assumed that there is *one* and only one theatrical code per se—in the sense of a uniform system of rules. Rather, as obviously not one but many theatrical codes exist, these must be differentiated according to the various levels at which each theatrical code may be realized in a respectively distinct manner of its own.

The first step is to establish which signs, combinations of signs, and meanings are possible in the theater, both in general and in principle, and completely irrespective of whether in fact they have ever been or are being used in some performance at one time or another in some society. This level of investigation, which focuses on all those elements which can at some time or other become functional within a theatrical code, will be referred to as the systemic level.[32]

As a system, in other words, the theatrical code is not to be seen as the basis of any factual, historically verifiable form of theater; rather, the code contains all the elements from which each form of theater can draw, however widely it may differ from the others. Since the code does not correspond to any real form of theater, it must be regarded as a theoretical construct.[33]

Only a highly selective number of all the conceivable signs, combinations of signs, and meanings possible are realized in the theater of a particular culture, epoch, social stratum, or genre. A limited and limiting choice is made from among all the conceivable possibilities, a choice that lends sufficient definition and description to the theater through the constitutive elements which determine its specificity, i.e., that which makes it different and distinct from other theaters. Approached at this level, the theatrical code governs the creation of several actual performances of a particular form of theater. Thus, an examination is to be made of the theatrical codes which respectively determine Greek tragedy, commedia dell'arte, Elizabethan theater, the Baroque courtly opera, or the Viennese *Volkstheater*. This level of investigation will be termed the normative level.[34]

Because, as a norm, each version of the theatrical code underlies a number of performances—the actual occurrence of which can be historically verified—the code must be understood as a historical phenomenon. As a norm, the theatrical code contains rules that are valid for several different factual performances. However, each individual performance does not adhere to these rules alone, but also to a body of rules which, when put into effect, place the performance in opposition to all other performances that have taken place as realizations of the same norm. And this latter body of rules only holds for this one performance, for this individual, factual work. When investigating the theatrical code at this level, it is necessary to compile the complex of rules on which this one production is based. This level of investigation, which focuses on the code of a particular theatrical performance, will be called the level of speech.

Since the theatrical code as speech is the basis of one individual performance alone, it has to be studied by an analysis of that performance. At this level of the investigation, we must refer to one specific theatrical text,[35] whereby the attempt is made to understand this text on the basis of the method used for analyzing theatrical texts. The investigation of the theatrical code at this level can only be conducted in the form of an analysis of performances.

In other words, in order to be able to describe and analyze the theatrical code sufficiently and appropriately, it must be examined at the three different levels of system, norms, and speech. As each of these three levels is, in turn, based on different premises in proper theoretical terms, a different method has to be employed for the investigation of each level.

In examining the theatrical code at the systemic level, the focus will not be on phenomena that existed or exist in fact, but rather on the question of what is theoretically conceivable and possible, the purpose being to arrive at a theory.

At the normative level, on the other hand, attention will be focused on what is or was factually the case. It is a matter of looking at a series of historical phenomena and attempting to uncover and explain the specific characteristics which they have in common, the purpose being to reconstruct historical processes.

When examining the theatrical code at the level of speech, the object of investigation is one actual performance, an individual theatrical text; the purpose here is to analyze the performance's specific structure and to understand the text: this involves describing, analyzing, and interpreting the text.

Thus, if a semiotics of the theater is to examine how the theater functions as a system which generates meaning, then it must allow itself to be integrated as a subcategory of the three different areas of theater science: the theory of theater, theater history, and the analysis of performances. In order for the theatrical code to be sufficiently and appropriately described and analyzed, it must be accepted as an object of investigation in all three areas of theater science. In other words, a semiotic examination of the theater must be conducted in terms of all three classical areas of theater science.

I.

The Theatrical Code
as a System

If we wish to study the theatrical code at the systemic level, then we must first establish the complete repertoire of signs that are possible and conceivable with respect to theater. We stated above that theater occurs when a person A represents X while S looks on. We shall now attempt to derive the minimum and maximum repertoire of signs from this rudimentary definition of theater.

In order for A to be able to represent X while S looks on, A must (1) act in a specific way, (2) have a specific appearance, and (3) act in a specific space. Any number of possible signs can be derived from each of these three underlying factors.

(1) A *acts* in a specific way: A's acting can take the form of certain movements. These can be movements of either the head or the body. We shall term those signs generated by movement *kinesic* signs. Kinesic signs produced by the face, i.e., facial movements, include smiling, furrowing one's brow, opening one's eyes wide, turning up one's nose, crying, etc. We shall define the kinesic signs created by facial movement more precisely as *mimic* signs. Movements of other parts of the body may involve movements of the head, shoulders, arms, hands, fingers, torso, legs, or feet. These may be movements which are carried out in one place or can only be made by changing place, e.g., dancing, running, walking, etc. A further distinction can be made between movements carried out using an object—skipping rope, stubbing out a cigarette, knocking on a door, opening a window, etc.—and those executed without objects—nodding one's head, clapping one's hands, walking to and fro, etc.

With respect to *kinesic* signs produced by the body but not by the face, we shall differentiate between *gestural* signs, which consist of body movements without a change in location, and *proxemic* signs generated by movement through space.

In addition to the *visual* kinesic signs, whether mimic, gestural or proxemic, the actor's acting may, furthermore, generate *acoustic* signs: A can *speak, sing, make music and noises.* Unlike the visual signs, which were produced by the actor's body movements, acoustic signs can be perceived independently of the actor's physical presence: the audience picks up snatches of a conversation going on backstage; hears a bird's cry, which comes from behind a bush, perceives music and noises which emanate from sources that are out of sight.

By speaking or singing, the actor does not create meaning by means of one sign system; rather, there are *at least* two different sign systems involved in each case that relate to one another in a specific manner. In each of them the actor initially generates *linguistic* signs which introduce their lexical and contextual meaning into the theatrical situation. When producing these signs as vocal sounds, he utters them with a specific voice, a specific emphasis, pitch, volume, timbre, etc. We shall term the signs thus created *paralinguistic* signs. If, by contrast, the linguistic signs are produced in song, then we differentiate between spoken and *musical* signs. If the actor's action on stage consists of his speaking, the signs produced are *linguistic* and *paralinguistic* signs, and if it consists of his singing, they are *linguistic* and *musical* signs.

To summarize what we have said thus far, on stage the actor can in general produce the following signs: mimical, gestural, proxemic, linguistic, paralinguistic, and musical signs, as well as all sorts of sounds that function as signs.

(2) A acts *with a specific appearance.* We must differentiate between two groups of signs when enumerating the signs which are generated by the actor's external appearance: First, signs which are meant to refer to X's "natural" appearance, such as his face, his physique, his hair, and second, signs which involve X's "artificial" appearance and clothing, i.e., a deliberately fabricated appearance.

A adopts a particular shape when depicting X, e.g., he makes himself large or small, fat or thin, broad or slender, gives himself a straight or a hunched back; he uses no make-up or makes himself up "naturally," makes his cheeks white or rosy, dons a mask or does not. We shall subsume the appearance of both the figure and the face under the concept of *mask.*[1] In order to produce X's "natural" appearance, A must change not only his physical shape and face but also his hair: he selects a specific *hair style.* A puts on certain clothes to shape his external appearance further, i.e. he wears a specific *costume.* To summarize, the actor creates a specific external appearance by means of the following signs: mask, hair style, costume.

(3) A acts *in a specific space.* In this context, we must first distinguish with reference to the signs of theatrical space between the specific arrangement of the space in zones—for the actors, on the one hand, and for the audience, on the other—and the particular appearance of the spatial segment in which the actors move. We shall term that spatial arrangement which prescribes the manner in which the audience and the actors will relate spatially to one another—in other words, whether the audience is to be situated in a circle around the actors, or only on three, two, or one of four sides—the *conception of space.*

The appearance of the spatial segment in which the actors move is determined above all by objects that are present in it for a relatively long time and remain there without changing. We shall term the totality of these objects the set design, or, preferably, the *stage set*. Other objects, the location, shape and appearance of which may be altered by the actors in the course of their acting, can exist alongside those just mentioned. We shall term these *props*.

The appearance of the stage, however, is not just determined by the presence of specific objects, but also by a specific quality of light. We shall disregard natural light in this context and only consider light as a theatrical sign which is produced artificially as a sign, namely, *lighting*.

Spatial specificity is, in other words, created by the conception of the stage, stage design, stage decoration, the props, and the lighting.

Therefore, proceeding on the one hand from the minimum definition of theater, namely, that A represents X while S looks on, and, on the other, from the most general description of A acting in a specific way with a specific appearance in a specific space, we can list the following signs as possible theatrical signs:

Noises, music, linguistic, paralinguistic, mimic, gestural and proxemic signs; mask, hair style, costume, stage conception, stage decoration, props, lighting.[2]

These signs can be classified in terms of general categories based on the following oppositions: "Acoustic/visual," "transient/lasting" and "actor-related/space-related":

Sign	acoustic / visual	transient / long lasting	actor-related / space-related
Sounds	acoustic	transient	space-related
Music	acoustic	transient	space-related
Linguistic signs	acoustic	transient	actor-related
Paralinguistic signs	acoustic	transient	actor-related
Mimic signs	visual	transient	actor-related
Gestural signs	visual	transient	actor-related
Proxemic signs	visual	transient	actor-related
Mask	visual	long lasting	actor-related
Hair	visual	long lasting	actor-related
Costume	visual	long lasting	actor-related
Stage conception	visual	long lasting	space-related
Stage decoration	visual	long lasting	space-related
Props	visual	long lasting	space-related
Lighting	visual	long lasting	space-related

Theater does not make use of these signs in their original function, i.e., does not put them to the purpose for which they are/were generated by the respective cultural systems. Rather, it deploys them as signs of those signs produced by the cultural systems. Consequently, theatrical signs must, at least at the level of the system they form, be classified exclusively as iconic signs.[3] For all the theater's signs in turn denote signs. Usually, for example, linguistic signs function primarily as symbols—i.e., as signs which bear an arbitrary relation to what they signify in the sense that the relation is neither causal nor motivated by the wish to depict the signified. Mimic signs function originally as indices—i.e., as signs that refer to what they signify in terms of cause and effect. In theater, however, they are used primarily as iconic signs. In other words, the linguistic signs produced by A denote the linguistic signs produced by X, and A's mimic signs accordingly denote X's mimic signs. Theatrical signs are therefore not identical with the signs primarily generated by cultural systems, but rather portray these as iconic signs: they mean these. In other words, at the systemic level, the theatrical code contains only iconic signs, which can, however, also function as indices or symbols at the level of norms and, above all, speech.

If, having compiled a simple list of all the signs conceivable in theater, we now wish to create a corresponding catalogue of potential combinations of them and the meanings they may have, then we must go further than merely enumerating them and instead examine each sign system in detail in order to establish what it can specifically achieve for theater. We shall have to refer to the respective primary signs, given that theatrical signs denote those signs primarily generated by the cultural systems. For only if we establish clearly in what way the primary signs can be described, analyzed, and interpreted, can we then determine the achievements of those signs which, in their capacity as iconic signs, denote them in theater. A semiotics of theater must therefore also have foundations, for example, in a semiotics of costume, a semiotics of music, etc., in short, in a semiotics of cultural systems.

If the semiotics of theater is to be grounded in a semiotics of cultural systems— or, to put it differently, the cultural systems are to be studied in terms of how they function as systems generating meaning—then we must first ascertain which cultural systems produce those signs which are denoted by theatrical signs.

The theatrical signs produced by the actor's activities—linguistic, paralinguistic, musical, mimic, gestural, and proxemic signs—denote the corresponding cultural signs. We need to know the function and effect they have in culture as a whole if we are to be in a position to study them with respect to their specific function and effect in theater. Thus, it would appear meaningful to draw on a semiotics of language, music, mimicry, gestures, and proxemic movements.

We cannot, by contrast, draw any such clear and unequivocal connection in the case of those signs produced by the actor's appearance and the theatrical space. The costume certainly denotes clothing, the hair style a particular hair style, but to what signs does the mask refer? We stated above that the mask denotes X's "natural" physical shape and face, i.e., phenomena that are not engendered by cultural systems, but are given by nature.[4] They can, like all natural phenomena, therefore be interpreted as signs by cultural systems. Just as the weather, for example, functions as a set of signs for meteorology, and the animal kingdom as a sign for zoology, so too the figure and face can be interpreted as signs for medicine or physiognomy. The mask as a theatrical sign thus denotes signs which are generated by physiognomy or medicine as the interpretation of natural phenomena.

The same is true of the theatrical semiotic system of stage decoration. Stage decoration can either denote natural spaces or spaces created by humans—in which case it denotes signs of the cultural system of architecture in the broadest sense (architecture, interior design, landscape gardening, etc.). If a person is in natural surroundings, he refers to this only to the extent that in his mind it is a sign for something (for example, a sign for the opportunity to hunt; fish; gather berries, mushrooms or wood; to stay healthy, or to be particularly close to the gods, etc.). Stage decoration that refers to a natural space thus always also refers to possibilities given in the respective culture for interpreting this space as a sign. Thus, with respect to stage decoration, there is no need to differentiate between natural and "supernatural" spaces such as heaven or hell.

Props denote objects produced by the widest range of different cultural systems. Whereas these objects belong to different cultural systems within a culture, since the functions they denote in everyday practice are totally diverse, in their function as theatrical signs they belong to one semiotic system, for their various functions are irrelevant for theater. The focus in theater is on their function as objects for the actor's acting.

Whereas signs that are produced by the actor's activities can thus unequivocally be related to those cultural systems that generate the signs they respectively denote, such an allocation is not possible in the same manner with regard to the other signs. We shall take these differences into account when investigating the individual signs that play a part in constituting the theatrical code.

1. The Actor's Activities
as a Sign

❏ ❏ ❏   In this chapter we shall examine linguistic, paralinguistic, mimic, gestural, and proxemic signs. Although music and sounds can also be produced by the actor—above all, when he takes the stage as a singer—we shall deal with them in a separate chapter, since they are special in two respects: on the one hand, they are signs produced by the actor or at least are to be taken as being produced by the actor and yet, on the other hand, they are signs produced by special musicians and technicians in a way that precludes their being understood to be produced by the actor.

Language-based Signs

Linguistic Signs

No other semiotics is more advanced than the study of language as a system that creates meaning. More theories have been elaborated for this sign system than for any other, and no other can look back on such a long and uninterrupted scholarly tradition. For centuries, indeed for millenia, language theory, rhetorics, and poetics have been attempting to answer the questions how, by what means, and according to what rules language generates meaning. This is not surprising, since language is the most widespread, common, many-sided, and complex system of human communication; indeed, many theorists have emphasized that it is the precondition for culture in the first place. We are thus confronted by an almost impenetrable mass of theories, and consequently it will only be possible to make a halfway justifiable selection from among this mass if we refer to a quite stringent set of criteria.

Because the semiotics of linguistic signs has been taken as the model or at least the trend-setting point of departure for semiotic studies of all other sign systems, we shall only select those approaches from the wealth of studies and findings on the market that have since proved useful in the study of other sign systems.[1]

It is, above all, Saussure's definition of linguistic signs and his theory of the two structural levels of language that are important for our study. Saussure[2] defines the linguistic sign, the word, as comprising two parts which, like the two sides of a coin, cannot exist without one another: namely, the signifier, the sequence of sounds, and the signified, the notion connected with this sequence. Assigning a signified to a signifier is an arbitrary process, is the result of some agreement, and is thus a convention. As a consequence, it cannot be revoked by an individual: the assignation of a signified to a signifier is relatively stable within the framework of a given historical language.[3] This is one of the major factors presupposing language's ability to create meaning: the assignation of a signified to a signifier as regulated by convention is valid for all members of a linguistic community; it is, as lexical meaning, the conditio sine qua non of that community's linguistic communication.[4]

The theory of the two structural levels of language creates the foundations for language's function as a system that generates meaning by drawing on the different types of the smallest constitutive elements of language: namely, the smallest significative and smallest distinctive elements.

The phoneme is the smallest distinctive element of a language: in English, for example, the words /rice/ and /mice/ are distinguished from one another by the opposition between the phonemes /r/ and /m/, the words /dig/ and /dog/ by that between the phonemes /i/ and /o/. Every language exhibits a limited number of possible phonemes and a limited number of possibilities for combining these phonemes. Thus, the phonemes /t/ and /r/ are possible in English as are their combinations as /tr/ or /rt/, but not their combination as /trt/.[5]

Words, language's smallest significative units, arise from the regulated combination of the smallest distinctive elements, the phonemes. The number of words available to a language, that language's lexicon, is also limited. The smallest significative units, the words, can be changed according to rules of grammar and combined with one another according to rules of syntax.

The organization of language in two levels enables an infinite number of possible syntagmas, indeed an infinite number of meanings to be produced from a limited, finite repertoire of phonemes, words and rules. This two-level structure is thus the reason for the privileged position of language as a system that generates meaning.

These general procedures for the production of meaning—which are applied in the form of a determinate stock of phonemes, words, and grammatical-syntactical rules that differs from one language to the next—formed the basis from which the specific procedures for the generation of meaning have emerged. These have been examined, on the one hand, in textual linguistics, particularly through research into different types of texts, rhetorics, stylistics, and poetics, and on the other, by dialectology, sociolinguistics, and psycholinguistics.

In the sense of the basic functions Bühler discerns in language, namely, expression, appellation, and representation, the application of this specific procedure invariably results in the creation of meaning on three levels: the subject level, the intersubjective level, and the object level.[6] Everything that is said can, in other words, be understood as a sign both for the speaker and the specific factors presupposing his utterance, as a sign for the relation of the speaker to the one or more other parties to the conversation, and as a sign of a specific content (which may very well be the speaker himself, of course, or the relation between the parties to the conversation inasmuch as they function as the object of communication).

If we bear in mind that language, owing to its ability to generate infinite meanings, constitutes the most commonly used, most versatile, and most complex system of communication that exists in any culture, then it comes as no surprise that language's sign system is used in almost all known forms of theater, with the exception of pantomime and ballet.

The most important function of language in theater derives from its use by the actor: here, A's words signify X's words. This is the case regardless of whether A is visible to the audience, is hidden from view, or as in the special case of puppet theater, the words A speaks signify words spoken by X as denoted by a puppet.

The linguistic signs referring to X in theater can exert a function that corresponds to that which generally refers to A, B, or C in culture. They can be interpreted at the subject level as signs, for example, of X's place of birth, age, sex, social status, state of mind, general mood, emotional state, desires, will, and momentary mood. At the intersubjective level, they can be understood as signs of X's relation to Y, Z, etc., with respect to both the socially regulated relation between them (e.g., because of their position, social standing, age difference, etc.) and the special relation between them that stems from quite individual factors (e.g., Y saved X's life, or murdered X's only child, etc.). At the object level, they can be grasped as a sign of certain contents which can in turn clearly be related to both X and his relation to Y or Z, as well as to the plot sequence in the scene in question and the overall context of the theater performance.

With reference to the overall context of the performance, the words which X utters at point a can, due to a special poetological procedure, enter into a special relation to the words which either X, Y, or Z utters at points b, c, d, etc. Thus, with the aid of this procedure, a hypersemantic system develops over and above the semantic levels that refer to the individual figures X, Y, and Z, without this making it seem impossible for the performance to have an overall meaning.

In addition, because of its ability to generate an unlimited number of meanings, language can substitute up to a certain point for the other sign systems used in theater. If X talks about Y's lively mimicry, which Y cannot show because he is wearing a mask, then these factually nonexistent mimic signs clearly exist in the audience's imagination all the same, since they are present in X's words. If the audience is accustomed to a theatrical convention of this kind, then it will be prepared to "see" something which is not in fact present on stage, and yet which the actor's words mark out as being present.[7] When an actor talks about the appearance of the figure whose role he plays or that of someone played by another, referring to the figure, face, hair, and clothing in a manner that contradicts the factual appearance which we see—for example, because the actors are playing their roles without wearing makeup or costumes—then what counts for the audience is not what it actually sees on stage, but rather what it is supposed to perceive based on what the actors say. If the stage is an empty space that the actor states is a forest and subsequently refers to as a palace, a room, or a dungeon, then this empty space becomes the forest, palace, room, or dungeon in the eyes of the audience. If the actor's words refer to nonexistent objects as if these nevertheless existed, then they do in fact exist for the audience. If, in the actor's words, dusk draws in and the sound of the nightingale and the songs of farmers returning from the fields are to be heard, then all of this can still be seen and heard by the audience, even if the appropriate lighting, sounds, and music are not used, because the actor's words convey it to the audience's imagination as something that can be perceived.

Whatever can be perceived by the senses according to the actor's words can thus be perceived by the audience. To this extent, linguistic signs can replace all the other signs possible in theater.[8] Although this statement is true, it must nevertheless be qualified. This qualification is of exceptional importance and is to a great degree constitutive for theater. For we must bear in mind that, to the extent that our remarks apply to theater in general, and not just to a specific form such as the radio play (which, being a radio genre, cannot automatically be classified as theater),[9] linguistic signs can only be temporarily perceived independently of the person speaking them, because normally the actor is on stage when speaking. This presence necessarily implies that gestural signs are produced, for even if the actor stands in place without moving a muscle, this in itself counts as a gestural sign. Indeed, in many cases, proxemic signs are also created if the actor moves around on stage while talking. Since the actor speaking is factually present on stage as the producer of gestural and possibly of proxemic signs, these signs are factually perceivable; they cannot be replaced by linguistic signs. Language can, by contrast, function as a substitute for all other semiotic systems. Thus, for example, in classical Greek theater mimicry was replaced by language, since masks were worn, and lighting was also superfluous, since performances were carried out during daylight. Often in Elizabethan theater, in various forms of theater played by traveling troupes, and in street theater words were used to evoke and thus replace, either completely or in part, not only lighting but also stage decoration, whereas the other sign systems retained their respective functions.

However, since we are not focusing here on one particular form of theater, i.e., the realization of a specific norm, but instead are concerned with the system itself, it can be said that with the exception of gestural and proxemic signs, all non-linguistic signs used in theater can, generally speaking, be replaced by linguistic signs.

Language can be realized in theater not only in the words of X, Y, and Z spoken by A, B, or C, but also in graphic signs, i.e., in writing. Writing functions in this case either as part of the stage decoration—banners, slogans written on the walls, etc.—or as the stage decoration itself. For example, the signboard with the inscription "forest" or "palace" is a sign for the audience that everything which occurs on stage during the presence of this signboard is to be understood as happening in a "forest" or a "palace." Here, written language has a function comparable to that of spoken language which substitutes for stage decoration. Since such a signboard can signify not only the space in which the acting is taking place, but also the time, graphic signs can in some cases also replace lighting and to a certain extent even costumes. Thus, displaying the words "evening" or "morning" influences the audience to imagine the quality of light that corresponds to those times of day; "1610" or "Summer, 1789" conjures up the image of particular costumes, even without the actors (who may be wearing their everyday clothes or even dark T-shirts) actually having to be "in costume." In this case, however, we can speak only of potential, and not factual, substitution, since neither the lighting nor the costumes necessarily have to be presumed to exist solely on the basis of such a written display in the same manner as a forest indicated by a signboard.

As a result of language's ability to create an infinite number of meanings, it can in general take on the widest range of functions in theater, even if, de facto, it is not used in certain forms of theater and only plays a subordinate role in others.

Paralinguistic Signs

Paralinguistic signs are closely connected both to linguistic signs and to other nonverbal signs used in the course of direct communication to produce meaning, i.e., mimic, gestural, and proxemic signs.[10] Whereas we are accustomed to investigating linguistic signs in isolation from the communicative situation—and thus independently of the paralinguistic and kinesic signs that are simultaneously used—at the systemic level, this approach is relatively new in the case of paralinguistic signs. For here, no isolated smallest distinctive or smallest significative units can be discerned; rather, we are always forced to study a whole complex of characteristics. It is thus not surprising that the meaning of a paralinguistic sign is first perceived at the level of speech in terms of its interconnection with linguistic and kinesic signs, but not as the meaning of a unit that can be treated in isolation; this is, however, possible, for example, when addressing the meaning of a word as its lexical meaning.

This state of affairs is reflected in the state of research in this area to date, for interest in the problems of paralinguistic signs can look back on a millennia-old tradition, but not on a heritage of scholarly and systematic research. Thus, rhetoric in classical times developed not only as a canon of special linguistic procedures used in order to achieve certain effects, but also as a collection of prescriptions which laid down the precise manner in which paralinguistic and mimic-gestural signs had to be deployed so as to deepen or intensify their respective effects. Quintilian[11] and Cicero,[12] for example, teach not only how to use a specific type of language in speeches for the widest variety of occasions and purposes, but also the specific use of the voice and of the face and body as means of expressing oneself. Paralinguistic signs, like mimic-gestural signs, are understood here as a system which generates meaning in the sense that the meanings which the listeners (the audience) create while listening can be described as effects that are triggered in them when they perceive these signs. Since the various principles of rhetoric are always of a prescriptive, normative nature, it follows that the intended effects depend on the use of certain signs or the specific use of these signs (for example, in a given context). Thus, whoever wishes to move the audience, to make them feel sad or touched, to fill them with anger or excitement, or to satisfy them must deploy the paralinguistic (and mimic-gestural) procedures that are prescribed in order to achieve those effects in each case. By doing so, a meaning will be created that is communicated to the audience by triggering the effect intended by the speaker.

Classical rhetorics, in other words, endeavors to describe the procedures (a task which was subsequently pursued in a series of didactic texts on rhetorics and recitation for the theater)[13] that supposedly had to be used in order to achieve a particular effect. We, by contrast, are interested in the general question of how paralinguistic signs function as a system that generates meaning, i.e., the way in which paralinguistic signs help to create meaning, first in the communicative processes of a given culture and, second, in the theater of such a culture.

We must begin by defining more precisely what paralinguistic signs are. We understand them to be vocal sounds which cannot be produced as (a) linguistic signs, (b) musical signs, or (c) iconic signs for sounds of nonhuman origin (such as a dog's bark, bird song, the sound of a train, etc.).[14] Unlike linguistic signs, these signs cannot, as already mentioned, be divided into their smallest distinctive and significative elements. Rather, they constitute a complex of characteristics that is in turn composed of auditive features on the one hand and substantive features on the other. The former can be pitch, intensity, sound sequence, duration, articulation, emphasis, quality, rhythm, resonance, or speed; the latter, intensity, time, basic frequency, basic frequency sequence, formant sequence.[15] The rule here is

> the well-known but often overlooked fact that the relation between auditive statements and measured substantive features is by no means straightforward. For each auditive characteristic there may be a package or complex of all the substantive features that can be measured.[16]

For the auditive characteristics are perceptible simply by listening, whereas the substantive features have to be measured.

Unlike words—to which, being regular combinations of the smallest distinctive elements, a lexical meaning is allocated—no stable relation has yet been shown to exist between the complex of features of a paralinguistic sign and its meaning.[17] On the basis of experimental information available to date, we can clearly assume that in a given culture the meanings accorded to paralinguistic signs by members of that culture are relatively similar (e.g., what is meant ironically; sounds sad; expresses anger and/or is a question, an assertion, an order; etc.). Yet we cannot presume that a clear allocation of certain meanings to certain complexes of features exists. In addition, we must consider that a comparable meaning (e.g., irony) can be conveyed by different paralinguistic signs, i.e., by complexes of features that differ from one another.

In our context it suffices for us to proceed from the assertion that the members of a culture clearly accomplish the process in which meaning is constituted via paralinguistic signs according to the same underlying rules, or at least rules that are similar for the most part. It is not of importance that we are as yet unable to state specifically what these rules are.

Paralinguistic signs defined in this manner can be differentiated further according to whether they last for any length of time or are strictly of a transitory nature. All qualities of the voice come under the first group, and those that cannot be defined as pertaining to the voice under the second. We shall distinguish with regard to the latter between those paralinguistic signs that always occur in conjunction with linguistic signs and those that are not accompanied by speech. The latter category includes laughter and weeping as well as sounds that substitute for speech, e.g., "hmm." There are thus three different categories of paralinguistic signs, and it is these we shall now examine more closely.

The category of voice quality as we understand it here cannot really any longer, or at least not yet at this point in our discussion, be considered a paralinguistic sign. For voice quality signs are not produced in order to communicate; rather, they are qualities which—like the physique or face—are already given in that specific form, either by nature or by virtue of specific conditions. Consequently, they can function merely as indexical signs within a culture: the attentive observer can, for instance, draw conclusions from them as to a person's sex, age, health, body, mood, state of fitness, proximity, etc. In certain cultures, specific cultural identifications are made in addition to these physiological and physical characteristics, or are made at least in part on that basis. In European culture, for example, if a man has a particularly deep voice, this is considered an expression of masculinity, whereas it is unfeminine if it belongs to a woman. However, if this deep female voice is also somewhat husky, then it is perceived as being particularly seductive, as downright sexy. Bühler has shown in a number of studies that in Western culture a set of vocal qualities are attributed to particular character types. In other words, the voice is regarded and interpreted here not only as a sign for physical attributes, but equally as a sign for character traits.[18]

Whereas, in general, the qualities of a voice are not generated as signs, but are simply interpreted as signs, in theater the generation of voice qualities is itself a process whereby signs are produced and implemented. The actor can either alter the quality of his own voice in this process or deliberately make use of his natural voice as a semantic element. Thus, for example, a young actor can play an old man by transforming his own sonorous voice into the thin, timorous voice of an old man; by the same token, however, an old actor whose voice is in fact thin and timorous can also play the part. In the latter case, the actor's "natural" voice becomes a theatrical sign. If, in another case, an actress has to portray a man, then the manner in which she does this—regardless of whether she "disguises" her voice by lowering it to sound like a man's or uses her natural voice—becomes an element laden with meaning. It is then a sign that expresses something about the character being portrayed or about the relation between the actress and her role or about a particular concept of theater, etc.

Since the actor's voice always functions as a sign in theater, it can, of course, on the one hand always be used as that sign for features of the body or character that it can also signify in the culture in question, i.e., as a sign of certain physical and/or personality traits of character X. On the other, it can serve as a sign for something that cannot be related directly to character X. If, as in the example above, an actress plays a man without disguising her voice, which can clearly be identified as that of a woman, then—assuming that the use of other interpretative signs rules out the possibility that X is being portrayed as feminine or unmanly—the discrepancy between the masculinity of the character and the femininity of her voice becomes a sign. In a certain context, this sign can be interpreted, for example, as an expression of a certain conception of theater in which instead of illusions being created, the artificiality, which is to say, the semiotic character of the performance, is expressly emphasized. The meaning attached to the sign of the voice in such cases can only be assessed at the level of speech. At the systemic level it is only possible to point to a corresponding potential for meaning.

We stated above that the second category of paralinguistic signs to be investigated consisted of those which always occur combined with linguistic signs. Most paralinguistic signs belong to this group. Three different referential levels can be distinguished with regard to the paralinguistic signs of this group, as they can with respect to linguistic signs: object level, intersubjective level, and subject level.

Whereas the object level of linguistic signs is formed by the contents signified by these signs, paralinguistic signs refer to something that itself consists of the linguistic signs. Emphasis is, in this context, the most important feature from among the characteristics covered by paralinguistic signs. The linguistic signs are organized by means of emphasis—and pauses—in such a way that the organization can generate respectively different meanings for the linguistic signs. For example, in the sentence "He went down the street," a different meaning arises each time a different component is stressed:

He went down the street—a "he" as opposed to a "she" or another "he" who might have been mentioned earlier in the text.

He *went* down the street—as opposed to "ran" or "hurried" or "dashed" or even "crept," "crawled," "strolled," etc.

He went *down* the street—if "down" is emphasized, this may point to the fact that he neither went up the street nor zigzagged across it, did not stop after three strides, but rather headed for a particular point, perhaps a goal.

He went down *the street*—i.e., perhaps not across the field, through the forest, or down the garden path; what is important here is the fact that it is a street he goes down.

Emphasis, in other words, generates meaning at the level of linguistic signs. This meaning is only linked with the speaker to the extent that the particularity of his emphasis expresses something about him, and only refers to the other party to the conversation in so far as the emphasis indicates to the other person what the latter is supposed to consider important. The essential referential level is in this instance the object level of linguistic signs.[19]

The melody of the sentence, the intonation, is one of the most important characteristics at the intersubjective level. For intonation provides the hearer with information as to which speech act the speaker has performed with the respective utterance. Our example, "He went down the street," can be spoken as an assertion, as a question, or as an exclamation without any changes in the linguistic signs. In such a case, the intended speech act is not identified by the hearer on the basis of lexical or grammatical-syntactic features, but solely on account of the respective intonation which can be perceived either as terminal, as interrogative, or as progressive, depending on whether the pitch is declining, ascending, or regular. If the pitch is not altered, then this is a sign to the hearer that the speaker has not finished his utterance and that he should continue to listen, to wait with his answer, etc. Intonation thus functions not only as a sign of the speech act intended by the speaker,[20] but also as a sign regulating communication to the extent that it shows the partner in conversation when he can assume the role of speaker and/or that he should rather remain in the role of hearer. A sentence may well be an assertion in terms of its grammatical structure, yet if it is uttered not with terminal but rather with progressive intonation, this causes the hearer to understand that the speaker has not completed his statement. If the hearer accepts the rules of polite conversation, he will wait with his rejoinder until the speaker conveys to him by signaling terminal intonation that he himself has finished speaking and awaits his partner's answer. At the intersubjective level, the paralinguistic signs are thus, above all, used to regulate communication.[21]

We find the most varied paralinguistic signs at the subject level. The auditive features that are perceptible when a sentence is uttered are mainly understood as signs that can be interpreted as a statement about the speaker. We shall distinguish in this context between signs that point to the subject's membership in a group— such as accent, which can signify membership in a social stratum, a regional grouping, or a foreign country—and signs which refer to the subject as an individual. Research has shown that in a linguistic community there is a great degree of agreement in the interpretation of this latter form of paralinguistic signs. For example, a random selection of speakers (not actors) were asked to interject "aha" and to say the sentence "He's coming tomorrow" in as many ways as possible in order to express different intentions and then to state what the intention was. At a later date, this taped linguistic output was played to different hearers who then stated what intention they heard behind the respective utterances. The findings revealed an astonishingly high degree of agreement both among the different hearers as well as between the respective speaker and his listeners with regard to the interpretation of the paralinguistic signs, the meaning of which was described with expressions such as "friendly," "frightened," "angry," "ironical," "calming," "surprised," "sad," "annoyed," "obstinate," "indifferent," "determined," "unbelieving," "cunning," "disinterested," "doubting," etc.

We can conclude from this that intersubjectively accepted rules exist in a linguistic community for the production and interpretation of those paralinguistic signs that refer to the speaker as a subject. The signs in question are above all those of the speaker's mood, feeling, stance, etc., at the moment of linguistic production, but also of his attitude about what he says (e.g., ironical, indifferent, inquisitive) as well as toward the partner in conversation (e.g., bullying, beseeching, friendly, etc.).[22] These signs function as regulators of the communication process—in other words, as signs at the intersubjective level, inasmuch as they tell the partner in conversation something about the speaker's psychological frame of mind and his attitude toward the object of conversation and the other parties to the conversation.

Because these signs always occur in combination with linguistic signs, the two sets of signs are constitutive of meaning not only as two separate sets of elements, but also through the specific relation between the two sets. Thus, for example, the sentence "I am so unhappy" can be spoken with great sadness, punctuated by sobs, but can also be said ironically or even in a friendly tone of voice, or in turn aggressively, maliciously, or in a completely "neutral" way, with indifference or disinterest. The overall meaning of the expression is different in each instance, for it depends on the nature of the relation between the linguistic and paralinguistic signs.[23] This relation can be one of reinforcement or weakening, of neutralization, of modification or contradiction. It, too, is perceived and interpreted as a sign, as a semantic element.

Since the paralinguistic signs that are used in theater always denote the paralinguistic signs that X produces, they can also assume the respective semantic functions which they fulfill in the culture in question: they organize the spoken text in such a way as to suggest a specific way of understanding it. They show the audience what form of relationship obtains between the parties to the dialogue on the stage, and they also convey a certain knowledge of the inner processes of the characters who are being portrayed by speaking actors. The different norms of the theatrical code can often be differentiated according to the form these three functions take and how they are evaluated. Thus, the Weimar theater which Goethe directed is said to have practiced and cultivated the use of paralinguistic signs in a special way that was intended to enhance the interpretative organization of the spoken text, whereas the other two functions were taken less into account—they were on the whole accomplished by linguistic signs.[24] Stanislavsky's theater, by contrast, focused on the latter two functions. It significantly increased the repertoire of corresponding signs compared with those current in the culture of which it was a part. Thus, for example, one of Stanislavsky's actors was capable of saying the words "this evening" in forty different ways, ways to which the audience was, moreover, able to attach forty different meanings or nuances of meaning.[25]

The special arrangement and hierarchization of paralinguistic signs must always be related to the general intentions of the respective form of theater. This is, however, a problem which can only be solved at the level of norms, or of speech.

We have thus far presumed that theater makes use of paralinguistic codes which have taken shape and been applied in the culture in question, albeit with certain specific modifications and refinements. In this case an understanding of the paralinguistic signs used in theater depends on an understanding of the corresponding signs in that culture.

We must, however, consider the possibility of the theater's developing its own paralinguistic codes, which can only be adequately understood by those who have learned the rules on which these are based. French eighteenth-century tragic theater, for example, did not employ the terminal intonation constitutive of the paralinguistic code of French culture and the French language: the stress was not changed at the end of the sentence or was even slightly increased. The theater thus had a paralinguistic code of its own. The trinity of possible oppositional components so central to the intonation system was reduced in this manner to a duality, as only interrogative and progressive stress patterns were used rather than the generally usual terminal, interrogative, and progressive intonations. Due to this restructuring, the two stress patterns employed were imbued with a semantic function they did not exhibit in the culture in question, and, as a consequence, an understanding of the paralinguistic signs in theater was not guaranteed by a knowledge of the corresponding signs in that culture, but was the result of a specific didactic process.[26]

In many cases, paralinguistic codes are used in theater which differ from the corresponding codes of the respective culture with regard to the point at which meaning drops to "zero." A certain pitch, volume, resonance, and tempo are perceived as "neutral" in every culture, and every deviation from this so-called initial state is either used or interpreted as a specific element bearing meaning. Theater can proceed from a different complex of features and the meanings of the paralinguistic signs change accordingly. There have been forms of theater which took a trembling or a singing voice as the basic "neutral" voice, and forms of theater that were based on a particularly rapid or slow tempo, and others that considerably amplified the volume. A theater-specific paralinguistic code is created in each of these cases.[27]

The first thing that must therefore be assessed when studying the paralinguistic codes used in the different forms of theater is whether the code concerned is based on an existing paralinguistic code of the culture in question or rather involves the creation of a theater-specific paralinguistic code.

The third category of paralinguistic signs to be examined consists of paralinguistic signs not accompanied by speech, such as laughter, weeping, shouting, or even "hmm." For the most part, sounds such as "hmm" substitute for language; they could be replaced by linguistic signs such as "Yes, I understand," "I have my doubts," "not a bad idea," "I don't think so," etc., depending on the situation in question. The linguistic signs bring the respective lexical meaning they contain to bear in the situation, whereas sounds such as "hmm" can mean different things in different situations. The sound "hmm" signals that its meaning has to be culled from the whole complex of features; it is, in other words, a signifying sound without a fixed meaning which, because it can be employed to mean any number of things, can be used as a substitute for linguistic signs.[28]

By contrast, laughter, weeping, and shouting constitute a special case with regard to their capacity as paralinguistic signs that neither accompany nor replace speech.[29] They are signs that generate meaning above all at the subject level: they express inner processes, particularly the emotions, of the subject in question. A person not only conveys his own subjective emotions to someone else by crying, laughing, or shouting—assuming that he is in the presence of others and is not laughing, weeping, or shouting on his own—but also enters into a relationship with that other person. For his laughter may be an expression of his joy, but also of his wish to have the other share in his joy; or, it may be just the opposite, namely, malevolent laughter, or even laughing at someone. Tears may indicate sorrow, anger, annoyance, disappointment, or even a state of overwhelming joy; in addition, depending on the cultural tradition involved, the tears may express, for example, the weeping person's indifference to the other person's opinion of him as expressed in the former's not finding it necessary to control his feelings. Then again, it may also attest to a deep sense of trust and intimacy with the latter, to whom one is able to show one's feelings openly, etc. Laughter, weeping, and shouting are thus an expression of emotions as well as a factor regulating inter-action. In both cases, the signs of laughter, weeping, and shouting must not be interpreted only on the basis of the signs themselves, but also in light of the respective culture's rules for applying them. Such rules prescribe (a) in which situations unrestrained laughter, weeping, and shouting are possible; (b) in which situations they can be realized in a weaker or stronger form; (c) in which situations they cannot be realized at all; and (d) in which situations they must be replaced by other signs. The meaning accorded to loud and penetrating sobs will vary from one culture and situation to the next. It may, for example, be an expected, intensified expression of an affect without even actually feeling this affect (lamenting women) or, conversely, it may be an expression of strong affect that is not appropriate in public, a display of emotion that the others would do well to ignore if the weeping person is to be respected thereafter.[30]

The laughter, weeping, and shouting used in theater denote X's laughter, weeping, and shouting. They can assume all those meanings that would be attributed to them if they were fulfilling this function in the culture in question. A "correct" interpretation of laughter, weeping, and shouting must, in other words, not only take the signs themselves into account, but also the rules governing the application of these signs in that culture. Moreover, the laughter, weeping, and shouting used in theater may also function as signs in a way that contradicts the culturally valid rules of application. Whereas in some cultures, for example, the rule is that nobody may weep in public, or at least not loudly, this rule may become inoperative in theater if the strong expression of feelings is an important constituent factor in the theater form in question.[31] Here, laughter, weeping, and shouting must be related to a specific code of the dominant theater form of the day and not to the rules of application otherwise valid in society as a whole.

In summary, paralinguistic signs provide theater with a semiotic system with which manifold meanings can be generated. Since paralinguistic signs are produced in processes of direct communication, the manner in which their meaning is created can only be assessed if all other signs used at the same time are also borne in mind. We have already pointed out that the meanings of linguistic and paralinguistic signs that occur simultaneously influence one another and that the overall meaning of an expression can be established only if the specific relation between the two types of signs is also taken into account.

However, in addition to linguistic and paralinguistic signs, kinesic signs play a part in direct communication. The meaning of paralinguistic signs is, in other words, modified not only by the simultaneously produced linguistic signs, but also by the simultaneously used kinesic signs. This intercorrelation significantly increases the scope for potential meanings produced by paralinguistic signs.

Kinesic Signs

The concept of kinesic signs shall be used to include all facial and body movements. We shall subdivide kinesic signs into groups of mimic, gestural, and proxemic signs. All facial movements which serve to express primary affects will be considered to be mimic signs; all other facial movements as well as movements of the body that can be effected without changing location will be classed as gestural signs; and body movements which involve a change of place will be treated as proxemic signs.[32] We shall initially treat each group separately, even though in the vast majority of conceivable communicative situations a combination of signs from all three groups is used. Subsequently, the inquiry will focus on the specific correlation among the different kinesic signs.

Mimic Signs

> The human face is, irrespective of whether it is at rest or moving . . . of whether the person is speaking or is quiet, alone or with others, viewed externally or 'felt' from within . . . a dominating, complex and at times also confusing source of information.
>
> It is dominating because of its visibility and omnipresence. While sounds and speech can be interrupted, the face conveys information, in some cases even without moving. And it cannot be withheld from view—except by means of a veil or mask. . . .
>
> If we think of what the face can transmit, the information which it can contain, and the role it plays in social life, then its complexity becomes evident. Although there are but few terms to describe the different forms 'facial expression' takes (smiling, a furrowed brow, frowning, look askance, etc.), the facial muscles are so complex that they are able to produce thousands of different shapes for the face; and these muscles work so swiftly that all these shapes could be shown in the space of a few hours. The face is also a complex source of information. Observing a human face teaches us different things. It can inform us about such transient and sometimes fleeting events as feelings or emotions, or about the moment-by-moment fluctuations during a conversation.[33]

In other words, the human face incessantly produces signs to which the most varied meanings can be attributed. In the discussion on mimic signs we shall therefore concern ourselves only with those mimic signs which are perceived and interpreted as the expression of primary affects, this being the only group of mimic signs to which special studies have been devoted. The others are generally treated in connection with body language, i.e., with gestural signs, since the same criteria apply to an examination of them as do to a study of gestural signs.[34] Given that those mimic signs to which we wish to refer are signs that signify emotions felt by the subject making the signs, the subject level at which meaning is generated will be foregrounded in what follows. The intersubjective level will, nevertheless, be touched on to the extent that the expression of feelings in turn represents an important factor in regulating communication and interaction.

A discussion has raged ever since Darwin claimed in *The Expression of Emotion in Man and Animals*[35] (which appeared in 1872) that universal validity must be accorded the connections between facial expression and emotion, i.e., that human-kind conveys the same emotions with the same facial expression in all cultures. Strong cases have been made both supporting the thesis of universal validity and bearing out the opposite proposition, namely, that the link between facial expression and emotion is culturally specific. Judging from the research findings to date, it would appear that a more convincing case can be made for the position of universal validity.[36]

In order to be able to solve this problem we first have to examine a series of other problems that are of particular interest for our study. It is initially necessary to define emotion and compile a catalogue of emotions that can be expressed with the face. The different facial movements intended to express emotions must subsequently be described and analyzed. This approach serves to determine the repertoire of possible signs (facial movements) and the meanings attributed to them. Such a study must then be followed by inquiring how reliable the interpretation of these signs is, which is to say, the degree to which the interpretations of mimic signs coincide with one another both within a culture and among different cultures. A further question arises in connection with the reliability of interpretation, namely, as to the possible combinations (a) of two or more mimic signs and (b) of mimic signs on the one hand and gestural, paralinguistic, and linguistic signs on the other, as well as the question of whether interpretations are bound to a particular context. Since the answers to these questions are of decisive relevance to our problem, we shall review the individual research findings to date.

We cannot go into the details of the wide range of different categories of emotion put forward by the various researchers.[37] The variant developed by Ekman, which limits itself to a minimum of so-called "basic emotions," has proved itself to be the most manageable catalogue. Ekman proceeds from seven so-called primary affects which can all take on forms of varying intensity: happiness, surprise, fear, sadness, annoyance, revulsion, and interest. These seven emotions can be regarded as meanings, and in the narrow sense as denotations that can be attributed to certain mimic signs.[38]

In order to be able to find these mimic signs and describe them with precision, Ekman and his colleagues developed a trial procedure that divides the overall face into three zones: first, eyebrows and forehead; second, eyes and eyelids; and third, the lower face, cheeks, nose, mouth, and chin. Each observable movement in these three sections of the face is then evaluated. Using this trial procedure, they succeeded in distinguishing a set of facial movements in the three different facial sections corresponding to the primary affects listed; each of these sets is almost unequivocally accepted as the expression of the respective affect—or is at any rate initially in one, namely, American culture.

The following table lists the signs (sets of facial movements) allocated in this manner to the individual affects. The sets of facial movements listed here function as indexical signs for the emotions assigned to them.[39]

Even if we can allocate fixed meanings in the sense of denotations to these sets of facial movements, they can still not be compared with the smallest significative units of language, namely, words. For they do not constitute a combination of the smallest distinctive elements but rather a combination of sets that exhibit minimal complexity, i.e., sets that are generated by one of the three parts of the face studied. Now these sets can be combined with one another not only in the manner described—yielding signs for so-called emotions—but almost at random, e.g., the sad brows can be combined with the fearful eyes and the neutral mouth or the surprised brows and eyes with an angry mouth, etc. The meaning generated in this manner is either a weakened form of the same emotion (e.g., the combination of surprised eyes and brows and neutral mouth) or a mixture of feelings. We can conclude from this that the meaning created when the mimic signs listed in the table for the three parts of the face do not simply amount to emotion A or B but to both the exclusive presence of A or B and at the same time to a more intense form of it. For the presence of these emotions can also be signified by other signs (a combination of sets of facial movements from the three zones), either in a lesser intensity or as part of a mixture that includes one or more other feelings. In other words, it is not one single facial movement but rather a set of movements related to a part of the face which functions here as the distinguishing feature, but it does not function as the smallest element of distinction—although this is quite conceivable for the systematics of facial expression as a whole. These distinguishing features can be combined at random and each combination generates a different meaning with regard to the emotions involved and the intensity thereof.

Many scholars have pointed out that at this juncture the interpretation of these mimic signs would no longer seem to be reliable. For they question whether a mimic sign can be interpreted definitively in such a way that one can conclude from its realization that the emotion it denotes is in fact present. For "the face would appear to be the most flexible non-verbal communicator, and for this reason it is perhaps the most articulate liar; it is not only able to withhold information, but even to simulate the facial expression of a feeling that it by no means experiences."[40] In light of this, the question as to the reliability of mimic signs would seem, however, to have been posed wrongly. A reliable interpretation of signs in the sense demanded here can only be assumed and postulated for the interpretation of facts of nature that can be interpreted as signs. For example, if precipitation takes the form of snow rather than rain, then this can be taken as a reliable sign of the temperature; if red spots appear on someone's skin, then the doctor may take these as the reliable sign of a certain illness, etc. Signs produced as signs by people can always only be interpreted taking the problematics of hermeneutics into consideration, something that must also be borne in mind when interpreting

	Eyebrows/Forehead	Eyes/Eyelids	Lower face, including cheeks, nose, mouth and chin
Happiness	"normal"	Wrinkles under eyes; wrinkles at the outer edges of the eyes	Sides of the mouth pulled upward, mouth partly open, teeth visible; wrinkles extending from the nose to the outer edges of the mouth; cheeks drawn upward
Surprise	Raised brows; skin stretched under them; horizontal wrinkles across the forehead	Eyelids wide open; the white of the eyes clearly visible above, and at times below, the irises	Lower jaw drops, causing the mouth to fall open, but without tension in the jaw
Fear	Brows raised and straightened; wrinkles in the middle of the forehead but not right across it	Upper eyelid raised; the white of the eyes can be seen, the lower lid tense and raised	Open mouth, lips tense, baring the teeth or drawn tight
Sadness	Brows raised at the outer edges, the skin beneath them forms a triangle	Eyelids raised on the inside	Sides of the mouth pulled downward, lips tremble
Anger	Brows drawn together downward; vertical wrinkles between the brows	Upper eyelid tensed so that it cannot be drawn upward; lower lid tensed; the eyes stare and protrude slightly	1. Lips pressed firmly together 2. Mouth open as if to scream
Disgust	Brows lowered; pressing on the upper lid	Wrinkles appear on the lower lid	Nose is wrinkled (turned up), cheeks pulled upward; upper lid is raised; the lower lip is also raised and pressed against the upper lip or slightly lowered

mimic signs.[41] For, as is the case with all signs, each society has certain rules for the use of mimic signs, rules that can either be adhered to or broken. Both approaches function in turn as an element bearing meaning.[42] We can thus list four types of rules with regard to mimic signs that also lay claim to validity for the paralinguistic signs which express emotions: rules (1) of exaggeration, (2) of understatement, (3) of neutralization, and (4) which mask an emotion via a facial expression that denotes another emotion. These rules hold for almost all social situations; as a consequence, we learn during childhood who can use which rule under what circumstances; in other words, we learn in which way techniques for controlling emotional, expressive behavior are to be used.

These techniques of control depend on

a)   a person's static features (e.g., age, sex, height);
b)   the static features of the environment (e.g., ecological factors and specific social situation, such as funeral, marriage, job interview, waiting for a bus);
c)   temporary personal characteristics (e.g., social role, job acceptance); and
d)   temporary, regular occurrences during social interaction (e.g., "entry," "exit," transitional phases, periods of conversation, listening, etc.).

Rules for hiding one's feelings usually determine facial expression, so that such rules are more usually noticed when someone violates them than when they are adhered to.[43] As a consequence, the interpreter of mimic signs must assume that the person using the signs does not employ these exclusively in order to inform others of his actual feelings, perhaps does not even accord such a purpose priority, but rather deploys them in order to inform the others which feelings—and intensity of feeling—they are to presuppose he has. Mimic signs, which we have above all examined in order to assess how they generate meaning at the subject level, are essentially used at the intersubjective level as a means of directing and regulating the process of interaction. The strength of this function of mimic signs must not be underestimated when applied in all areas related to public life. I can, in other words, only understand the person using the signs in such situations if I at the same time consider all those rules for hiding one's feelings which are valid in the culture in question.[44]

The expressive function of mimic signs must naturally always be taken into account. They always dominate in cases where the person producing signs believes he is not being observed. The rules for hiding one's feelings cease to be valid in such a situation; here mimic signs can, with respect to prevalent emotions and their intensity, be interpreted in a relatively "reliable" fashion in the above sense. Yet, the interpreter must additionally take into consideration here that emotions can also be expressed by gestural, proxemic, paralinguistic, and linguistic signs— although this says nothing about which type of sign predominates. The sign system used as the most important bearer of meaning may differ depending on the cultural, social, and individual customs involved. Whereas A, when he is angry, makes a particularly angry face without otherwise moving, in the same frame of mind B runs around the room with clenched fists, while C sits and shouts or mumbles angry words to himself. The strength of an emotion expressed by a person who believes himself to be alone when producing the signs cannot, in other words, be assessed with complete reliability by exclusively considering mimic signs even if the otherwise valid rules for hiding one's feelings can be disregarded.[45]

This is, of course, all the more true in public situations in which the production of signs is oriented toward the parties present during interaction. Here, too, different sign systems may be deployed in a particular hierarchy: they may support or contradict one another, or even cancel each other out. The second possibility is of particular interest in our context. If, for example, someone with an angry face says to the person to whom he is talking that he is happy to see her, then the question arises as to which meaning should be taken as a fitting interpretation—that produced by the linguistic sign or that by the mimic sign. If the tone is also unfriendly, and the speaker turns slightly away from the person to whom he is speaking, then the interpretation would seem to be more straightforward. In this case, the paralinguistic and gestural signs back up the meaning generated by the mimic sign. What meaning are we, however, to assume, if, by contrast, the sentence is uttered in a friendly tone, and the speaker's body is nevertheless turned away? Mimic and gestural signs suggest annoyance, whereas the paralinguistic and linguistic signs hint at joy. In such an instance, only a completely accurate analysis of the given communicative situation enables a satisfactory interpretation to be made. The situation must be described (party, funeral, chance meeting on the street, etc.), as must the social and personal relationship between the two persons (employer/employee, friends, lovers, neighbors, etc.) and the particular frame of mind of the person producing the signs (e.g., general mood, occurrences experienced immediately beforehand, expectation of an experience that will immediately follow the conversation, etc.). The signs generated by the person can be interpreted adequately only if all these factors are taken into account and only then will the subject himself be understandable.[46]

What was true of paralinguistic signs also applies to mimic signs: we cannot assume here that they engender meaning by encoding an item of news which can then be decoded by the receiver in precisely the same way that it was encoded by the sender.[47] On the contrary, that large complex of hermeneutic premises and considerations—above all, the doctrine of the hermeneutic circle and of prejudice—must be applied in the interpretation of paralinguistic and mimic signs to an even greater extent than was necessary in the case of linguistic signs, which, due to their shared lexical meanings, guaranteed a minimum of consensus.[48] The signs can be interpreted adequately only if all the specific characteristics of the person generating the signs, the circumstances, modifications, rules, and the presuppositions on which the particular interpretation is based are taken into account. It is only possible to speak of a certain "reliability" in interpreting the signs, in understanding ("Verstehen") the person who produces the signs, if this precondition is fulfilled.

Taking these findings as a basis, we can now attempt once again to solve the problem posed at the outset, namely, the question of whether the link between facial expression and emotion is universally valid or culturally specific. Research in Western and non-Western literate cultures as well as in visually isolated, illiterate cultures exposed only to their own visual signs has shown that the mimic signs enumerated by Ekman and his colleagues are allocated to the respective emotions in all the cultures investigated. A high degree of agreement obtained with respect to the meaning of the production of signs and the interpretation of those signs— with the exception of signs for fear and surprise. With regard to the signs for fear and surprise, the degree of agreement was significantly lower[49] between the illiterate, visually isolated cultures on the one hand and the persons from other cultures, on the other.

We can assume with a great degree of certainty that mimic signs which serve to express emotions all mean the same emotions in all cultures. The differing forms of behavior actually to be observed among members of different cultures in comparable situations is thus not attributable to the fact that the same emotion is being expressed in different cultures using different signs.[50] Rather, each culture calls for different rules of application and rules for hiding one's feelings in the individual situations: whereas one culture prescribes loud weeping, screaming, and the unmistakable facial expression of mourning for funerals, another demands a serious, not clearly sad, and perhaps even joyful face, and indeed a third may prescribe a laughing, happy face. In other words, in each of the three cases we cannot interpret the signs solely by referring to them, but rather must also refer to their respective application in the context of the modalities of the situation in question. For the link between facial expression and emotion is universally valid to the extent that the specific facial expression is interpreted in all cultures unanimously as a sign for the same emotion, although culturally specific rules exist— those of application and those for hiding one's feelings—which prescribe the use of differing mimic signs in the respective situations.

In addition to these culturally specific differences, possible individual differences must also be considered. An emotion felt with the same intensity need not generate a mimic sign that is both the same and of equal intensity in all people, irrespective of whether they feel themselves to be watched or not. One person may only don a sad face whereas another may cry loudly and incessantly. These individual differences must be studied separately, to the extent that they cannot be derived from social rules (such as, for example, that a woman may show her feelings more strongly than a man, a member of the upper class must have himself more under control than a member of the lower class, etc.).[51]

Certain difficulties arise when attempting to transpose these thoughts onto the theater. We can establish that the mimic signs A generates denote the mimic signs produced by X, and to this extent all the above considerations can be easily applied to the interpretation of the mimic signs which denote X's mimic signs. The audience must take all the circumstances mentioned, all the rules and the individual features of character X, into account if they are to interpret these mimic signs adequately and to understand what a mimic sign used at a particular point is meant to signify. In this context, attention must be paid to a general distinction in the use of mimic signs in theater on the one hand and in the culture in question on the other. For whereas in culture such situations generally occur in which the sign-producing person generates mimic signs merely as an expression, believing himself to be alone or because he is in fact alone, mimic signs in theater are always produced with the audience in mind—and the latter are supposed to interpret these signs in a particular way.

This is precisely the point at which the difficulties arise, for in order to be able to interpret the signs, the audience must first be in a position to perceive them correctly. A film, for example, can make a mimic sign particularly visible to the audience via a close-up and can thus raise the face to the status of sole bearer of meaning for the duration of that shot, allowing the interpretation to concentrate in fact on the mimic signs presented.[52] In theater, however, the audience is always faced by an actor whose size stays the same and is standing at a distance which, in most cases, makes it almost impossible to perceive any of the mimic signs he produces with the same degree of precision that is possible when watching a film. For this reason, mimic signs can be perceived by the audience in a theater only within a fixed amount of space, e.g., in small studio or living-room theaters, and can be accorded a status as important agents of meaning only in such a context.

In large rooms or halls, theater has, by contrast, to resort to other means. Theater must either forego the use of mimic signs altogether and replace them with masks that emphasize the respectively important feature of the face and thus make it visible for the audience, as was the case in classical antiquity and in Nô theater.[53] Or it can forego using some of the mimic signs by employing half-masks that enable mimic signs to be produced somewhat clearly only in the zone around mouth and chin. Commedia dell'arte and all theatrical forms based on it have availed themselves of this opportunity. Another approach consists of producing exaggerated mimic signs so that they can be perceived from a distance: wild rolling eyes and a wide open mouth would be characteristic examples of this. This manner of implementing mimic signs was often reinforced by the use of a particular form of makeup that emphasized the eyes and mouth.[54] These two features were frequently in evidence among the traveling troupes in the baroque period. We can generally say that a close reciprocal relation obtains between making a mask of the face and the mimic signs deployed: a certain type of "mask" permits only a certain type of mimic sign.

The special nature of mimic signs allows for yet another approach to be taken. Since, as we have outlined above, on the one hand a universally valid link obtains between facial expression and emotion and, on the other, intersubjectively recognized rules of application and for hiding one's feelings prevail in a culture, the respective facial expression can be grasped without being clearly visible if the other sign systems that are used also function to support its meaning. If, for example, the paralinguistic, gestural, and proxemic signs A produces show X to be angry, then the audience will believe that it also sees an expression of anger in A's face, even if it is not possible to see his facial features clearly because of the distance involved. All forms of realist theater employ this mechanism: the actors may indeed produce the mimic signs in question, but since they know all too well that these signs can only be perceived inadequately, they do not make use of them as the dominant agent of meaning. Rather, they strengthen the other nonverbal signs produced—paralinguistic, gestural, or proxemic signs, or all of these—thus making them the most important agent of meaning in this context; in so doing, they suggest a suitable perception of the mimic signs.

Since mimic signs are as a rule of particular importance for conveying emotions, all those forms of theater which set great stock in the expression of strong feelings cannot merely treat such signs as trifles or simply accept that they are hard to perceive, if indeed they can be perceived at all. Such forms of theater will attempt to extricate themselves from this dilemma by choosing one of the above-described approaches.

If a small studio or living-room theater is involved, then the actors do not need to forego using mimic signs, but must rather aim to deploy them as the most important agent of meaning. Yet we must take into account here that the theater by no means has to abide by the culturally valid rules both for application and for hiding one's feelings, except, that is, if we have to do with a naturalist form of theater. In the latter case, any breach of the rules must be interpreted as if it were a breach in a nontheatrical situation.[55] Other forms of theater, by contrast, often invalidate the universally valid rules. Whereas it may otherwise be usual in a given situation to water down the mimic signs for anger, sorrow, or repulsion, in the theater of the same culture the rule may obtain that in all situations mimic signs must be used which lend intensive emphasis to the corresponding emotions. This separate rule for theater may in itself be significant, but given the contradiction between it and the rule that is universally valid in that culture it takes on real importance.[56] It therefore by no means suffices to establish what rule the theater follows without at the same time relating it to the other rules which are valid among the stratum of persons who support such a theater.

The theater can, in other words, quite clearly prescribe adherence to other rules for application and for hiding one's feelings than those advocated by the culture of which it is a part. It can clearly furthermore refine or over-intensify the mimic signs, and can yet again only generate those mimic signs of emotional expression which are universally valid. For the reason why both the exaggerated and the refined theatrical mimic signs can always be understood, to the extent that they are perceivable, is perhaps that these signs, for all their special shape, are nevertheless still a concrete form of those mimic signs which Ekman and his colleagues outlined in their studies, i.e., those mimic signs which are produced and interpreted as an expression of the corresponding emotions in all cultures. However, this does not mean that we can conclude that the theatrical mimic code is identical with the overall mimic code of the culture in question. This is only the case for certain forms of naturalist theater, although we must take a special situation into account here, namely, that in the culture in question mimic sign α may denote anger, whereas in theater mimic sign α produced by actor A denotes sign α generated by X to express that he, X, is angry. With respect to all forms of non-naturalist theater we must assume that the mimic code represents a specific theatrical convention which has to be learned by the audience.[57] This assumption is supported by studies made of lay audiences who attended a theater for the first time: they initially related the mimic signs they were able to perceive to the mimic code with which they were acquainted, with the result that they either admonished X for exaggerating things, rolling his eyes quite "unnaturally" or for behaving improperly when it would have been seemly to have his feelings under more control, etc.[58] Because in such cases recourse is had to a mimic code upon which the generation of mimic signs in theater is not based, the individual emotions signified can be understood, but not the meaning of the specific process whereby A realizes the sign at this point in this particular form in order to portray X. We can thus proceed in the majority of cases from a particular theatrical mimic code which the respective viewer must learn if he is to understand the performances adequately; this can be learned in the course of a performance because this code, despite the differences between it and the mimic code of the culture in question, nevertheless has its roots in that culture. The theatrical mimic code's deviations and differences must be related to that culture if the former is to be used satisfactorily in the production and interpretation of signs.

Gestural Signs

Gestural signs are of particular importance for theater: while theater is certainly possible without language, music or sounds, costumes, decorations, props, or lighting, no form of theater can completely dispense with the actor's physical presence, his gestural signs.[59] There are admittedly forms of theater which can get by temporarily, in individual scenes, without actors: a battle can, for example, be portrayed exclusively with music, sounds, and visual effects, and a chase can be evoked by means of voices, sounds, light, etc. However, a theater without actors—like a puppet theater stripped of the function of players playing—will always be a borderline case; it is difficult to say whether the performance in this case is theater or fine art. Such hairsplitting distinctions can safely be ignored for the purposes of our investigation here. If we proceed, as we have done, from the assumption that theater is constituted by A depicting X while S looks on, then we have to conclude that theater is not possible without A. Does this necessarily mean, however, that he has to be physically present on stage? Could the actor not be represented by his voice?

These are, essentially, purely academic considerations. For it may indeed be conceivable in theory that a theater foregoes using gestural signs and employs linguistic or paralinguistic signs, music and sounds, lighting, stage decoration, and props instead, none of which require the physical presence of an actor in order for them to move, assuming, that is, that stage technology provides adequate machinery. After all, factual examples of such forms of experimental theater are well known. Such attempts, however, are by definition experiments that continually seek to go beyond the bounds of the conventional notion of theater and thus to stake out possible new forms of representation for theater. They therefore have to move in that "murky zone" in which theater merges with other forms of art. Within this zone it is as a consequence difficult, indeed impossible, to demarcate the boundaries with any precision.[60]

If, however, we apply our thoughts to the overwhelming majority of norms that have materialized in the history of theater, then we will be forced to concede that they all depend on an actor who is physically present, indeed are to a certain extent exclusively created by and materialize via the agency of the gestural signs he produces, as in mime, pantomime, or *mime pure*. This importance of gestural signs, borne out by the facticity of the norms that have become reality, must therefore also be taken into account by studying them at the systemic level.

The concern with gestural signs has a long history that goes back as far as Aristotle.[61] Interest focused primarily on signs realized by the hands, which were treated in particular length in connection with paralinguistic signs by the discipline of rhetorics. The attempt was repeatedly made to compile the "natural" code of the hands' signs. The assumption was that gestural language, unlike its spoken counterpart, was universally valid, that it had the same meaning among all races. J. Bulwers's *Chironomica or the Art of Manuall Rhetorieke* (1644) is an especially impressive example of such attempts to collect and convey the "nature-given" meaning of such signs of the hands.[62]

What is especially noticeable in the millennia-long history of interest in gestural signs is that, irrespective of whether this was reflected in books on rhetoric, texts on the art of acting, or even in philosophical treatises, two specific characteristics of gestural signs are always stressed: their special ability to create expression and the repeatedly noticed ease and seeming directness with which they can be understood. These features would suggest that the language of gestural signs does not have to be learned and that the ways in which they can be combined and the meanings of such combinations are the same for all cultures, because, being part of human nature, they are available to all human beings in equal measure.[63]

This proposition that gestural language is universally valid went unchallenged for millennia and was the point of departure for subsequent scholarly research into gestures. Refutation of the proposition cleared the way for a systematic inquiry into gestural signs as a system for the creation of meaning.

The refutation was the work of ethnologists, in Germany particularly by Wilhelm Wundt in his monumental ten-volume study, "The Psychology of Peoples," published in 1900.[64] The second chapter of volume one, *On Language*, concentrates on "Gestural Language" and is probably the most important discussion of gestural signs prior to modern behavioral science and communications research; it is also the first attempt to provide a scientific and systematic classification of such signs. Wundt endeavors, by presenting convincing arguments and evidence, to show that gestures are culturally specific. Marcel Mauss's findings were equally pioneering in France, particularly as summarized and explained in his 1934 lecture, published the following year, on the "Techniques of the Body."[65] Mauss suggests that not only communicative or expressive gestures, but also techniques of the body, such as sleep, relaxation, movement, bodily hygiene, eating, etc., are treated differently in each culture because the gestures used to accomplish these functions are themselves culturally specific. *The fact that* humans eat, sleep, move, etc., is biologically determined; *how* they eat, sleep, move, etc., depends on the particular cultural tradition.

The third work which finally falsified the proposition of the universal validity of gestures was David Efron's volume, published in 1941, on "Gesture, Race and Culture."[66] In this pioneering work Efron attempted to disprove the claim made and disseminated by the Nazi's racist propaganda apparatus, namely, that the movements of Jews were different, indeed had to be different from those of the "Aryan" peoples solely on account of their racial origins. Efron studied gestures common among both the first and third generation of Southern Italian and Eastern European Jewish immigrants in New York. He was able to show that the respective five gestures were learned in the same manner as a language, in other words that they could by no means be attributed to some inherited inclination or deterministic programing. If, given these research findings, we can presuppose that on the one hand different gestural signs are used in each culture and, on the other, that the same gestures are used in different cultures with different meanings, then we must also suppose that each culture generates meaning with gestural signs on the basis of a specific code applicable only within its own domain.[67]

If we assume that a respectively specific code exists, then we must also inquire directly as to its structure, or to put it more precisely, as to the principles according to which a gestural code is structured and functions. We must therefore investigate the following: first, the nature of the units which function as the signs on which the gestural code is based; second, in what way these units can be combined with one another to form syntagma; and third, what meanings of these units can (a) be isolated and (b) be attributed to them in specific contexts.

The greatest problem is determining which are the units that count as signs in the gestural code. For everyone is undoubtedly in a position to accord a certain meaning to a certain sequence of movements—such as a nodding head, a shake of the hand, a furrowed brow, or stamping feet—in a certain context. Yet no one will be readily able to specify whether the sequence to which he has attributed meaning consists of one, two, or more signs or is to be understood as a single syntagm. Attempts have been made to overcome this difficulty by utilizing the criteria tried and proven in linguistics when differentiating between behavioral sequences; the main criterion involved, assumed hypothetically at the outset to be valid for and applicable to gestural signs, was that of the postulated structuration in terms of the smallest significative and distinctive elements. Ray L. Birdwhistell,[68] probably the most important proponent of kinesics, the science of gestural signs, has endeavored in a series of experiments conducted under laboratory conditions to isolate and specify kinemes, which, analogous to phonemes, are the smallest distinctive gestural units.

Birdwhistell has developed a notational procedure that enables the smallest change in movement to be recorded as a graphic sign—a precondition for the success of any differentiation between behavioral sequences.[69] It has proved to be expedient with regard to this procedure to divide the body into eight zones that are each examined individually: (1) the complete head; (2) the face; (3) the throat; (4) the torso; (5) shoulders, arms and wrists; (6) hands; (7) hips, legs, ankles; (8) feet. The informants were shown a set of movements for five seconds, namely, different initial positions for the different zones (e.g., left eye open, right eye shut, winking with the left eye, the mouth normal, nose lowered. One element in this set was subsequently changed (e.g., the right eye was open instead of the left, or the winking omitted, or a pouting rather than normal mouth taken) and the informant asked whether the meaning of the set had thus changed. Those elements which were cited by the overwhelming majority of the people questioned—if not by all—as the cause of the change were then taken as the smallest distinctive elements, as kinemes. By contrast, those elements which could be changed without this altering the meaning of the set were classified as allokines— in keeping with allophones in linguistics. In this manner, in the Anglo-American gestural code the position of the mouth was the decisive element causing changes, i.e., a kineme, whereas the switch from right to left eye was considered insignificant and thus classified as an allokine.

Just as the phonemes do not occur on their own but combine according to certain laws to form morphemes or words, so too the kinemes are combined to form sets which Birdwhistell refers to as kinemorphs or acts. Analogous to the formation of syntagms in language—in which words are joined to form constructions or sentences—several acts combine to form an action which is tied to a particular context, just as a sentence is positioned in terms of a context. This transposition of linguistic categories onto kinesics leads to the following analogies:[70]

Linguistics	Kinesics		
Sound	Muscular and skeletal changes		
Phone: Allophone 　　Phoneme	Kine: Allokine 　　Kineme		
Morph: Allomorph 　　Morpheme	Word　Kinemorph Construction Sentence		Act Action Action
Utterance in context	Action in context		

Whereas, however, words are defined as the smallest significant elements precisely by virtue of having a meaning irrespective of context, namely, a lexical meaning, there is no analogy here for acts. These never have a meaning in themselves, for their meaning always first arises in context. Every gestural sign can therefore take on the widest range of meanings: a clenched fist can, for example, be a sign of cramped anxiety or of anger; it can pose a serious threat or only mean the repetition of a threat; it can be a form of greeting agreed on beforehand, etc. The clenched fist, in other words, does not have a meaning in itself; the respective meaning it is intended to have is only constituted within a specific context. This is the most important, fundamental difference between linguistic and gestural signs.[71]

Movements of the body are something acquired as gestural signs in the process of social learning; this is the reason why the number and shape of gestural signs as well as the way in which they can be combined and their context-bound creation of meaning is culturally specific. As a consequence, we must assume that just as a historical language does not foresee all the possible phonemes and combinations thereof, so too a culture's gestural language does not permit all possible kinemes and combinations thereof, but rather always prescribes a certain selection from them. An examination of a culture's gestural codes must therefore start by drawing up an inventory of the kinemes and combinations thereof foreseen in that culture before being expanded to include the rules for combinations of acts and the context-bound creation of meaning.[72]

In addition to the fundamental difference between linguistic and gestural signs, consideration must also be given to two other important differences which result directly from the former. Given that words have a lexical meaning, i.e., that a conventional allocation of signified to signifier has occurred, linguistic signs can, in general, be interpreted as symbols. Gestural signs—acts—always function, by contrast, as signifiers; the attribution of signifier has to be effected anew with each new situation. Thus, as mentioned above, the clenched fist can be accorded the signified "greeting" in situation a, and functions as a symbol; in situation b, by contrast, it expresses anger and functions as an index; in situation c it is, as a threat, a sign of aggression and functions as an icon. The gestural signs can therefore refer to what they mean either as a symbol, an index, or an icon.

The lexically-encoded meaning of one group of words in particular, namely, conjunctions, enables language to make use not only of parataxis, but also of the more complex forms of hypotactical constructions, without which all complicated processes of thought and abstraction would be impossible. Acts, by contrast, can only be combined in paratactical form: one act follows on another, without the possibility of itemizing or expressing temporal, causal, final, or other relations or dependency for this sequence.[73] Gestural language can thus not constitute a possible sign system at a higher level of abstraction as it is bound to concrete, current processes.

Gestural signs can essentially be divided into two categories: either they are used in processes of commnication and interaction or they serve to fulfill an intention (e.g., the production of an object).[74] Gestural signs included in the former grouping can be generated and interpreted with regard to the object portrayed, to the person producing the sign, and to the relation between the parties in communication.[75] In other words, they generate meaning simultaneously at the object, subject, and intersubjective levels, even if one of the three levels is always foregrounded. A distinction must be made at all three levels between gestural signs that accompany language and those that substitute for it.[76]

Gestural signs accompanying language create meaning predominantly at the object level and are closely linked—just as are the corresponding paralinguistic signs—to the linguistic signs, the contextual meaning of which they co-shape and determine. Their function consists above all of (a) punctuation and (b) illustrating a point. The punctuation in the case of speech involves, in the majority of cases, accentuating or structuring gestures which emphasize, clarify, and underscore what is important at the level of linguistic signs. It also entails gestural signs that fulfill a syntactic function either by occurring regularly in connection with or as a substitute for certain syntactic sequences or by pinpointing certain combinations of nominal or adverbial constructions. Thus, for example, the importance of into-nation in a question can be supported by raising one's brows, hands, or shoulders, or by stressing the significance of a progressive intonation when uttering a sen-tence—that, according to all grammatical criteria, is complete—by keeping the other person's gaze and holding one's head in such a way that importance must be attached to the fact that it is not complete. By contrast, passing on to a new topic or point in the argument can be shown precisely by changing the position of the head, body, or feet. In keeping with these forms of constituting meaning, a close reciprocal relation obtains between such gestural signs and paralinguistic signs. Together they augment the degree to which speech can be understood by limiting the possible meanings of the linguistic signs to that manner in which they are presented.[77]

The gestural signs that serve to illustrate speech can indicate the direction thoughts are taking, signify a spatial relationship, point to persons present, designate physical actions, or "draw" a picture of that which the linguistic signs denote. These illustrative gestural signs, like their language-accompanying counterpart, enter into a close reciprocal relation with linguistic signs. Thus, for example, the words "he is quite big" may be supplemented by a corresponding hand movement; the nasty look which accompanies the words "the nasty look she gave me" reinforces what is said by giving it a visual dimension; and the gesture of the hand or head back over one's shoulder indicating the presence of someone else explains the words "it is what *he* always wanted" in terms of who the *he* is and also gives the words a definite derogatory meaning not expressed by the words themselves but unequivocally conveyed by the gesture, above all in connection with a specific emphasis.[78]

We must therefore study the gestural signs accompanying language, by means of which meaning is generated at the object level of linguistic signs, not just in terms of their relation to these linguistic signs, but also with respect to the relation between them and those paralinguistic signs that are deployed simultaneously. For these signs are, precisely owing to their interdependency, able to generate meaning at the object level of linguistic signs.[79]

The same can by no means be said of those gestural signs which substitute for language. They are used in order to convey meanings which can otherwise be created by linguistic signs. Gestures in the sign languages adopted by the deaf, the Trappist and Cistercian orders, and North American Indians have to perform a similar function.[80] This use of gestural signs is of special interest in the present context, for we may be able to ascertain the existence of universal features and characteristic forms of usage when studying them that can then be transposed—if with considerable modification—onto those forms of theater which are by defini-tion constituted exclusively or predominantly by the use of gestural signs, i.e., mime and pantomime.

In the first instance, gestures which serve as pointers function as gestural signs that substitute for language.[81] Using them, reference can be made to persons or objects that are present or to spatial contexts. Spatial demonstrative gestures are among those special gestures the meaning of which cannot be reduced fully to a function as pointer; the former include, for example, gestures which show size, gestures which point to a part of the speaker's body but not to these parts themselves and instead signify certain of their characteristics or functions, as well as finally gestures which point to all three spatial relations of the location at which they occur, to the way there, and to the future path leading away from there via the metaphorical meaning of the present, past, and future tenses.

The iconic gestural signs comprise the second important grouping; we shall distinguish here between iconic signs in the strict sense and connotative iconic signs. The iconic signs in the strict sense provide a picture of the object which they signify: for example, they represent a "house" by intimating a gable roof and walls, a "church" by adding the sign of a cross to that of a house, "smoke" by the spiral upward-moving turn of a finger, "speaking" by imitating lip movement, "hiding" by concealing the right hand under some article of clothing on the left side of the body, etc. In other words, one or more features which are held to be important with regard to the matter being communicated are imitated via characterizing gestures. These are readily understood by someone who knows the objects or the matter in question, and indeed can be understood immediately as long as that person can put two and two together tolerably well.

Connotative iconic gestural signs differ from these gestures by not reproducing the object in all its contours and characteristic features, but instead referring to some secondary, arbitrarily selected characteristic. Thus, in the deaf sign language used in West Germany "man" is designated by the gesture for taking off a hat—which derives from a quite coincidental feature, namely, that in Western culture the man wears a hat—and "woman" is conveyed by placing a hand on one's chest. The Cistercian monks, by contrast, designate "woman" by moving an index finger across their forehead, indicating the woman's shorter size. A corresponding gestural sign is also to be encountered among North American Indians. Such gestural signs are not even immediately comprehensible for someone who knows the object designated. Not only is a particular talent for combining disparate elements required, but the receiver must also have undergone a veritable process of learning in order to grasp the meanings of these signs.

This is true to an even greater extent for the third group of gestural signs which substitute for language, namely, symbols. The relation between what the gesture signifies and the signifier is a matter of agreement, of convention. Thus, for Southern Italians a dramatic move of the hand outlining a donkey's head means "stupidity," a hand describing a horned bull—the famous *mano cornuta*—signifies both "strength," "danger," and the "wish to be protected from danger." In order to communicate the notion of "a lie," the North American Indians move the index finger obliquely away from the mouth, and move it at a right angle to designate "truth." All these examples illustrate that the meanings of symbolic gestures can be constituted only by someone who has learned them. They are, as a consequence, not substantially easier to understand than are linguistic signs.[82]

If descriptive gestural signs are used not in connection with language, but rather instead of it, then they usually do not occur on their own but in a particular sequence: gestural signs then gel to form "gestural sentences," and the individual acts merge into actions. In other words, syntagma have to be generated. As we have seen, this can only occur in keeping with the principle of parataxis. We must therefore now investigate whether specific principles of syntagma formation via gestural signs exist over and above this general rule.

Some fundamental concurrent syntactical rules would appear to exist that are shared by deaf sign language and the sign language used by the North American Indians. Thus, in both systems mention is first made of the subject (S) followed by the gestural signs for the subject's attributes (A); next, the signs referring to the object (O) are given, followed by those for the subject's activity (V). If necessary, signs are then introduced describing adverbially the nature of the activity (A'). The following principle for "sentence" formation by descriptive gestural signs which substitute for language would appear to obtain:

$$S \quad A \quad O \quad V \quad A'$$

"The angry man beat the child severely" would thus be expressed in gestural signs as "man angry child beat severely." We shall therefore have to establish whether this rule for syntagma formation by means of gestural signs also holds true, for example, for pantomime.[83]

This type of syntagma formation can be regarded as the most common, the most frequently used, and the most widespread. Naturally, deviations from it are possible. If, for example, a person who is deaf and dumb is thirsty, he will perhaps first describe what he craves, namely, water, then the activity which he needs it for, and last of all himself, the acting subject: "Water drink I;" he would thus use the OVS sequence rather than the common SOV series. Here, the change in syntactic principle fulfills less a descriptive and more an expressive function: for it does not say anything about the matter in question—this is achieved by the gestural signs—but about the subject involved in this matter. The syntax of gestural language is, in other words, similar to that of spoken language in being able to take on an expressive function.[84]

Those gestural signs which predominantly fulfill a descriptive function, i.e., generate meaning above all at the object level, can in general express something about the subject making the signs. This is true to the extent that: (a) in the case of gestures accompanying language, the special nature of the accentuation, arrangement, and illustration of the sign-generating person's speech can itself be interpreted as a sign related to that person, as can, in the case of gestures substituting for language, (b) the contents—and in part even the form—of his description. A meaning can be produced by the gestural signs mentioned that in one way or another also conveys something about the person producing the signs.

Those gestural signs, by contrast, that are in the main used with an expressive function—that, in other words, create meaning predominantly at the subject level— are imbued with meaning by being related directly to the person producing the signs. These signs are intended above all to say something about the person. Although they can thus also provide indirect information about his relation to the parties to interaction or to some matter that they still have to find out, such concomitant information is not the primary function of such signs. The meanings that can be generated by stressing the gestural signs in this way can be related to the widest range of aspects of the person realizing the signs, namely, to the person's (a) age, (b) sex, (c) social status, (d) temporary role, (e) physical health, (f) mental state, (g) character features, and (h) mood.[85]

Every culture is acquainted with a series of gestures which it judges to be typical for a certain age. These include, on the one hand, gestures which are shaped by a special biological condition, such as the inability to sit or stand, the horizontal posture or crawling movements of a baby that result from this inability, the uncontrolled and in part uncoordinated movements of an infant, the occasionally gawky movements of an adolescent, the completely controlled and coordinated movements of the adult, and the gestures of elderly people who gradually lose all control and coordination. On the other hand, there are gestures which a culture permits only persons of a particular age group to make, e.g., gestures which cause offense if made by members of other age groups. We thus tolerate a child sticking out its tongue, tapping the side of its head with a finger, stamping with its feet, or rolling around on the ground. It is, by contrast, considered unseemly for an adult to use the same gestures. If an adult breaks such conventions, then either he will be considered lacking self-control or this breach will be viewed as an expression of his contempt for other people. Breaking the rules thus appears as a sign which has to be related to the person making it in terms other than those of age.

Just as each culture has developed a list of rules with regard to age, so too they have created lists or prescriptions with regard to sex which regulate the types of gestural signs that are suitable for and characteristic of men and women, respectively. To ignore these rules usually leads to the "perpetrator" being regarded derogatorily as "unmanly" or "unwomanly," as "feminine" or as a "virago." Some of the differences with respect to the gestures to be made may, to a minor extent, be rooted in biologically determined factors such as a different physique, which can be held to be the cause of the different ways in which a person moves him/herself. However, the rules which prescribe in detail how such gestures should be used and especially all regulations for gestures as a whole can be attributed exclusively to culturally specific notions of the differences between men and women.

In Western culture, for example, a man can lean back during the course of a conversation, fold his hands behind his head and stretch his legs out in front of him; in most cases, a woman who adopts a corresponding posture will meet with disapproval. One would, by contrast, regard a woman fluttering her eyelids, pouting, and repeatedly gently stroking her hair with her head on one side, as behaving in a quite typical feminine manner, whereas if a man did this it would hardly be tolerated. Gestures of dominance[86] are, in our culture, reserved almost exclusively for men and are permissible for women only in specially defined situations; other cultures have different rules in this respect. In other words, the culture ordains which gestural signs are valid as "typical" or "suitable" for each of the sexes.

Although differentiation between age groups and sexes in the context of the production of gestural signs can in small part be attributed to biologically determined differences, differentiation in terms of social status and profession is exclusively the product of culturally specific notions. Such differentiation is necessary above all in cultures that are founded on a strict social hierarchy, as a consequence of which the members of the different estates, classes, strata, and castes have to mark themselves off sharply from one another even in terms of gestural signs. Two different types of gestural signs exist that indicate the social status of the person using them: first, gestural signs which are different but which are used by the members of the different groups to generate the same meaning; and second, gestural signs that are reserved for the members of one particular group. The different forms of greeting belong to this first set of gestural signs: people greet one another in all estates, classes, strata, etc., but the greeting is not always the same. In most cultures distinctions are made among courtly, religious, military, and secular greetings; in some, even more precisely ordained forms of differentiated greeting exist.[87] Each social group uses respectively different signs to designate greeting—and the same is true in other areas; the use of these signs clearly identifies the members of the group, both for the members themselves and for other groups.

During the baroque period, for example, the gesture for commands,[88] which was reserved exclusively for the highest ranking person—and at court, for the monarch—belonged to the second set of signs. Of the gestures used in Western culture today, we should perhaps mention the hand raised as a sign of blessing, which is the prerogative of members of the priesthood alone. The production of such signs by members of other groups is understood as a usurpatory act in societies based on a strict hierarchy, an act that has to be punished. In societies based on a more egalitarian form of organization and in which such gestures have persisted as relics of certain traditions, these are, by contrast, interpreted as metaphors that must be assessed in terms of the specific situation.

Gestures would not be able to fulfill their function of distinguishing between the sign-producing persons in terms of age, sex, and social status optimally in all societies if they were not backed up by another cultural system, namely clothing. A simple linen smock and bast sandals cause and enable the person wearing them to walk, to hold himself, and to move his torso, hands, and head in a manner that differs from that of someone wearing a lace blouse, a brocade jacket with wide skirts, heeled shoes, a full-bottomed wig, and an ornamental cane. Furthermore, they determine the nature of the gait, etc., as well. Trousers permit a different positioning of the legs than do skirts, and short skirts a different stance than long skirts or a farthingale. Wearing sneakers causes one to walk differently from the way one does in high heels, and boots create a different stride than do sandals. Jacket or trouser pockets facilitate different arm and hand movements than does a dress with no pockets and a reticule. A tightly corsetted waist certainly does not permit the same movements of the torso as does a loose shirt, and a hat or a pigtail or full-bottomed wig allows different movements of the head than does natural hair that is not covered. This list could be continued ad infinitum. Yet it shows clearly that gestural signs, on the one hand, which distinguish the sign-producing person in terms of age, sex, and social status, and the person's clothing, on the other, intensify and support each other.[89]

The gestural signs that predominantly create meaning at the subject level also have the function of differentiating social roles. Thus, for example, a grown man who is playing with his little daughter will use other gestural signs than he would in his role as husband, as an employee reporting to his boss about his work, or in his role as a member of a club or as a patron in his local bar, etc. The gestural signs employed in the respective situation indicate which role the person generating the signs happens to have adopted at that particular moment.[90] In the case of these signs as well, the use of gestural signs that are not understood as being tied to a specific role in the respective society, by the same token, also generates meaning.[91]

Furthermore, gestures can provide information about the physical condition of the person with regard to both long-term and temporary states of health. A limp or hobble can, for example, be understood as a sign of a corresponding physical defect, whereas walking in a sprightly manner or jumping quickly up out of a chair can both be taken as signs of good physical health. Staggering or stumbling can indicate a state of tiredness or of drunkenness, while a swift glance or a rapid hand movement are expressions of concentration and acuity.

Gestural signs allow us to interpret the state not only of a person's physical health, but also of his mental health, indeed the attributes of his character. Uncoordinated, inappropriate movements may under certain conditions be interpreted as a sign of mental incapacitation; alternatively, slow, sluggish hand movements and a sleepy gaze may in certain circumstances be taken as a sign of a phlegmatic character, etc.[92]

Gestural signs fulfill a particularly important function at the subject level if they are intended to express mood, changes in mood, and feelings. The same rules for application and for hiding one's feelings, listed in connection with mimic signs, that served to express emotions are also valid for these gestural signs, namely the exaggeration, understatement, neutralization, and masking of an emotion by means of gestural signs that are meant to stand for a feeling that is not that actually felt. Whereas in the case of mimic signs these rules are culturally specific, although the different linkings of mimic signs and the emotion designated are not, in the case of gestural signs the linkages themselves depend on the culture in question. Each culture uses a different form of gestural behavior to express an emotion. Whereas, for example, the members of culture A beat their breasts, tear out their hair, and roll on the ground as a sign of sorrow, in culture B the same emotion may be expressed via a particularly slow, solemn gesture.[93]

Every culture has special techniques for controlling emotions which depend both on the static characteristics of the person (such as age and sex) and on the static features of the environment (such as, for example, social definitions of the situation at hand), as well as on temporary characteristics of the persons involved and temporary, regular occurrences during social interaction. Furthermore, along-side the socially required techniques of control we must also take into account the particular, different gestures the individual prefers to use to express emotions—above all, with respect to the intensity and strength of the feeling experienced. (A, for example, throws both arms into the air to express joy and runs around the room, whereas B only smiles briefly and strokes his chin in the same situation and under similar conditions, such as age, sex, social role.) If we bear these two facts in mind, then gestural signs which express emotions can be appropriately interpreted only by referring to these complex factors that condition them. It is only possible to establish in each concrete individual case which gestural sign expressing a feeling has what meaning in what context. For the adequate interpretation of gestural signs must take many more conditional factors into consideration than must the interpretation of signs which can be related to age, sex, or social status.

In the case of subject-related gestural signs, the distinction between signs which accompany language and those which substitute for it would appear to be mean-ingful only for the last group of signs mentioned above. For in all other instances, gestural signs fulfill their respective function regardless of whether the person produces linguistic or paralinguistic signs alongside the gestural ones. If, on the other hand, gestural signs that express an emotion are involved, then, assuming linguistic and paralinguistic signs are used in addition to gestural signs, the relation between these different signs must itself be analyzed as an element of meaning. For a gesture, such as a facial expression, can support the meaning of linguistic and paralinguistic signs, or modify, anticipate, neutralize, weaken, or even contra-dict them. If all four types of signs are produced simultaneously, then their overall meaning can be established only by a careful examination of the effect they re-ciprocally have on each other, a task we have already adumbrated using the ex-ample of mimic signs.

Gestural signs, which produce meaning predominantly at the subject level, al-ways indicate something that has to be related to the person generating the sign, for example his/her age, sex, social status, physical or mental condition, character features, mood, or feelings: all of these properties function as indices in relation to that person.

If these gestural signs are used in the presence of other people, they also function to influence and regulate the process of communication and interaction between the people involved. For any information as to the age, sex, social status, present role, physical and mental health, character, current mood, and feelings of the person producing the signs can be utilized as a factor that must be taken into consideration in some way in the course of interaction and understood as such. If, for example, a corresponding sign is used with the intention of unequivocally conveying to the others that the person producing the sign is in a mood that, should interaction ensue, will demand a certain behavior on the part of the others, then it is no longer generating meaning predominantly at the subject level but at that of intersubjec-tivity. In the given situation the sign's primary function consists of regulating the process of interaction in a particular manner.[94]

We can divide the set of gestural signs which create meaning predominantly at the intersubjective level roughly into three categories which reflect respectively different sequences of interaction: first, signs which are used during initiation of interaction; second, signs which regulate the further course of interaction; and third, signs which are intended to bring about the end of interaction.

Interaction is brought about on the basis of a certain initial definition of the situation. Factors that assist in defining the situation include, above all, time, place, and occasion of the gathering: a party, a conversation at the grocer's, a chance encounter on the street, and a panel discussion all represent different initial situations which demand a respectively different repertoire of signs in order for interaction to be initiated. When it is not clear whether the different parties to interaction share the same definition of the situation, signs first have to be produced which can be used to achieve a consensus as to the type of situation toward which all participants wish to orient their behavior. Should it not prove possible to define the situation in this manner, however, then an attempt will be made to reach a consensus by means of words.

Even if this results in a clear definition of the situation for all of the interactors involved, it by no means necessarily implies that all of the parties will refer to the same definition of the situation in the course of interaction. Even if they concur as to the general traits of a definition of the situation, the latter cannot force those involved to adopt a certain form of behavior. This is the root cause of the different ways in which misunderstandings can come about in interaction. The members of a family, a group, a stratum, a class, a society, or a culture may indeed concur as to the type of behavior generally to be considered appropriate in a given situation. Yet the individual forms this behavioral norm may take can differ to such an extent that they must frequently be grasped as forms of different behavioral norms.

Misunderstandings cannot be ruled out in the domain of linguistic processes of reaching understanding, although an intersubjectively accepted component of meaning generated by the denotative lexical meaning of words would appear to guarantee that understanding is reached, at least to a certain degree. Yet even greater attention must be paid to the possibility of misunderstandings arising in the domain of interaction, which is regulated by gestural signs, for the gestural signs used here lack any denotative meaning. If gestural signs are only accorded a meaning on the basis of their being embedded in a certain situation, and if a consensus as to the situation involved cannot be established in all cases beyond all doubt, then it follows that the process of interaction is especially subject to misunderstandings. It is not possible to rule out the possibility that each party to an interaction will refer the gestural signs to a different situation; if this occurs, then it would seem virtually impossible for understanding to be reached.[95] Even if this is an extreme borderline case that hardly ever arises in such a pure form in reality, it should nevertheless be borne in mind that the following deliberations are based on an *ideal* course of interaction which theoretically excludes the occurrence of such misunderstanding. To this extent, the ideal type also constitutes a borderline case, albeit diametrically opposed to the one just mentioned, for the majority of interactions by no means proceed "smoothly," but rather contain a wealth of possibilities for misunderstandings at all stages.[96]

The interaction is inaugurated by a particular form of greeting in line with the initial definition of the situation. We shall distinguish between different forms of greeting from a distance and greetings between people in close contact. Greetings from a distance may take the form of turning toward someone, greeting with the eyes, raising a hand, waving, etc.; greetings in close contact may involve a handshake, an embrace, rubbing noses, a kiss, etc. The signs that respectively produce a particular form of greeting can be interpreted with respect both to the situation and to the relationship that obtains between the people greeting each other.[97]

When interaction is initiated, signs are used following the signs for greeting which the interactor trusts will present him in a certain way. These are signs which are meant to provide the other(s) with information as to the manner in which the person in question wishes to be treated. If a person allows a sad expression to pass across his face and has drooping shoulders and yet, when meeting others, pulls his shoulders back and looks happy, he shows the others that they are not meant to ask about his troubles, but rather to behave as if they had not noticed anything out of the ordinary about him. Facial expression and posture are the most important signs used in self-presentation.

When interaction is initiated signs are used to indicate the current mood of the person in question to the interacting parties. Furthermore, other signs are also employed which are intended to establish a certain relationship between the parties concerned from the outset. These are signs which are used to activate courting behavior or dominance or submission.

In Western culture, signs used for courtship behavior by a woman and interpreted as such include, for example, a raised head, glowing eyes, a light tautening of the eyelids, offering an open hand, stroking one's hair, etc., and, in the case of men, great tension, pulling in one's belly, squaring one's shoulders, etc. We regard clenched fists, hands on hips, a threatening index finger, thumbs hooked in a belt as signs of dominance, etc.[98] These gestural signs function to clarify the relation between the parties involved during the initiation of interaction. They can, however, also be used in the further course of interaction and respecify the relationship that obtains.

A precise distinction must be made in the case of signs which demonstrate courtship, dominance, or submission as to whether real or only pretended courtship or dominance is entailed.[99] Real, albeit watered-down, forms of courtship or dominance are to be encountered in the inaugural phase of interaction, which focuses on the coordination and delimitation of the matrix of relations that are to be valid during the course of interaction. By contrast, in the further course of interaction—depending on the situation involved—forms of pretended behavior are more usual. Signs which designate the latter form of behavior are not primarily intended to establish the relations between interactors, but are instead used in order to facilitate other goals being reached, e.g., enabling a person to be allowed to say something or to continue talking, etc.

After the ritual exchange of greetings, the self-presentation, and the definition of the relationships, signs are produced that are intended to effect the formation of interactive groups. The signs involved are of body posture and position, i.e., the distance created and maintained or changed between the interactors,[100] the formation of the group as a circle, a triangle, as people standing next to or opposite each other, body postures that involve newcomers in the group or exclude them from participating, gestures which direct other persons toward specific locations, etc.

With the formation of the interactive groups the inaugural phase gradually dissolves into the first phase of actual interaction. Above all, gestures are now used which regulate the sequence and organization of speech and listening. These gestures are—like all others in this category—closely related to the respective situation. Different gestures are called for in the case of a lecture, a discussion with a list of speakers, an open discussion, an informal chat, a conversation, or a confidential talk with respect to being granted the right to speak or having it withdrawn, getting people to listen to you, or expressing your attentiveness or disinterest as a listener. In this context, we must also examine gestures which indicate that the speaker has finished speaking (such as a lowered or averted gaze, a change in posture) or wishes to continue speaking (holding the listener's gaze, certain hand movements), gestures which show that the speaker is too loud or too quiet, or is speaking in either a stimulating or a boring manner. Gestural signs that refer to the sequential arrangement of speaking and listening are utilized in all phases of interaction.

In the inaugural phase, those gestural signs are produced which clarify and specify the fundamental relationship obtaining between the participants. However, in the further course of interaction certain signs are used which qualify this relation in some way or other. Signs expressing emotions can function in this manner.[101] In this instance, their purpose is not to create meaning at the subject level, but rather to convey to the others the mood of the person producing the signs during interaction. This is particularly true if the emotional behavior changes in the course of interaction, e.g., sorrowful behavior becomes happy behavior, a good mood switches over into annoyance or anger, etc. The emotional behavior shown in each case defines the relation which exists at that moment more closely and thus regulates the further course of interaction.

Signs for sympathy (such as moving closer or touching the other person, etc.) and for disapproval (raised brows, a repulsed face, turning away, etc.) function in a similar manner. They can without exception be used and interpreted as signs that make a statement about the relation between the person producing the signs and the parties receiving the signs.

To a certain extent, those signs which convey to the others how they should understand what has been said and signs which lend expression to the seriousness or irony of the words accompanying them can also be included in this category. Examples would be laying a hand on your heart, twinkling your eyes, smiling, etc. These gestural signs only appear alongside linguistic and paralinguistic signs and modify in a quite specific manner the way in which the linguistic signs are understood.

Signs for courtship, dominating, or submissive behavior can also be used in the further course of interaction as signs that define the relationship more closely.

Signs that serve to persuade or influence the other(s) also constitute an important category of gestural signs. Signs of courting and of dominating behavior can also be deployed to this end. On the one hand, a wooing gaze and an open hand; on the other, arms folded behind the head and legs stretched out are both ploys to influence the partner in conversation to concur with the producer of the signs. This type of gestural sign was already analyzed in classical antiquity. Quintilian lists a whole series of gestures which can be used to influence listeners.[102]

So-called monitors constitute a specific type of sign produced to influence others. Such signs are employed when one or more parties to the interaction do not abide by the rules which the majority of the parties view as valid for the interactive situation in question. Gestural monitors function at a nonverbal level as a reminder that the rules are to be obeyed. In Western culture, certain glances are used as such monitors in order to prevent the person looked at from acting in a disapproved manner (such as picking his nose). Other signs include flinching (e.g., if music is too loud or expressions are out of place), holding your head askance, squinting, taking a step backward, furrowing your brow, glancing skeptically or in order to issue a warning, nudging someone, kicking someone under the table, etc. Frequently, the addressee expresses disapproval by paying close attention to his clothing, e.g., flicking imaginary specks of dust off his trouser legs or off objects in the immediate proximity. If the gestural monitors do not achieve their purpose of causing the person who provoked disapproval to return to behaving in a manner acceptable to all, then the result can be a scandal. The rebuke now has to be made explicitly, with words, so that the person rebuked can no longer revert discreetly to accepted behavioral norms. The interaction can now develop into a sharp discussion or an argument, or is simply interrupted. Whatever the case, the interactive situation must now be defined anew.[103]

The gestural signs which generate meaning at the intersubjective level discussed hitherto are used and interpreted by all concerned with reference to the situation at hand. In the course of interaction, however, other signs can be employed which are not related by the person producing them to the context of the situation and yet are interpreted by the others in terms of this context. If, for example, in the course of a serious discussion a participant to it digresses and focuses on an object that makes him smile, then he will refer his grinning to this object, whereas the others, who notice his grin, will relate it to the object of their discussion. Signs which are transcontextual in nature[104] can often be the cause of misunderstandings in interaction.

Signs used to bring interaction to a conclusion include signs that depict the end of an encounter or the end of attention: rubbing one's hands together, lowering one's eyes, standing up, going away, i.e., all the forms of a ritual of leave-taking.

Gestural signs that create meaning at the intersubjective level by regulating the course taken by interaction are usually accompanied by linguistic signs. This is the case even if the latter—as is above all the case with signs for courtship and dominating behavior, signs that further qualify the relationship involved and monitors—neither refer directly to the former nor interconnect with them. On the other hand, they cannot be categorized as signs that substitute for language, because touching someone with my hand during a conversation has a qualitatively different meaning than the words "I sympathize so strongly with you. Go on!" and the skeptical glance as a monitor fulfils its admonishing function in a different way than do the words "I find your behavior quite outrageous. You have evidently not realized what a tone of voice you are using." It would therefore appear not to be meaningful to divide this group of gestural signs here into those that accompany language and those that substitute for it.[105]

Since gestures in theater, i.e., actor A's gestures, denote character X's gestures, they can be described and interpreted as such by means of the categories just developed. To the extent that they signify communicative gestures they must be related to the object level of linguistic signs, or the subject level of character X, or to the intersubjective level between character X and characters Y and Z, or to two or even all three of these levels.

Attention should be paid in this context to the fact that our remarks with regard to the paralinguistic and mimic codes in theater hold particularly true for the gestural code in theater. They are clearly based on the gestural codes of the society or social groupings that call them into being and yet in most cases constitute specifically theatrical codes that differ from the former. The degree of variance can itself differ widely: it can range from the simple elimination of such nonsignificant gestures[106] as occur in all forms of nontheatrical communication, to the formation of complete unique codes with specific signs combined in specific ways and with specific fixed meanings.[107]

The above-mentioned form of theatrical code is employed by particular types of Far Eastern theater, such as Indian Kathakali dance theater and the Peking Opera in China. The Peking Opera makes use of a wide repertoire of carefully delimited gestural signs, each of which has specific meanings assigned to it: an actor enters a room by lifting his foot high over an imaginary threshold; he mounts a horse by taking a whip decorated with tassels from his companion and dismounts by giving the whip back.[108] The meanings of these signs cannot be understood from the context of the play by referring back to the gestural code of the culture in question, but only via recourse to the gestural code of theater. In such cases, the audience must be presumed to know it.

European theater, by contrast, remains more closely bound to the gestural codes of the culture in question when developing theater-specific gestural codes. In this case, the respectively different allocation of a signified to a signifier is based above all on particular forms of dominant formation. Since, in general, a communicative gestural sign can be interpreted at the object, subject, and intersubjective levels, dominants can be formed on the one hand with regard to these three levels; on the other hand, however, they may refer to the constitutive elements within one of the three levels.

The gestural signs which generate meaning above all at the object level will primarily constitute the dominant dimension of the gestural code in those forms of theater in which linguistic signs are dominant. For in these forms of theater the principal function of nonverbal signs is to reinforce the meanings constituted by the linguistic signs. From among all possible gestural signs, those signs that refer to the object level of linguistic signs are therefore to be accorded the greatest importance. Examples of such forms of theater are the French *tragédie classique* and Goethe's theater in Weimar.[109]

By contrast, forms of theater that focus less on representing a particular idea and more on expressing human behavior—such as the Enlightenment theater practiced by Ekhof, the Storm and Stress theater of F. L. Schröder, or Stanislavsky's theater[110]—will deploy those signs which generate meaning predominantly at the subject level as dominant gestural signs.

Finally, forms of theater which portray problems of interaction and communication, such as postwar American theater and certain forms of boulevard theater (popular French middle-class theater in the nineteenth century), give rise to gestural signs which refer predominantly to the intersubjective level in a special way.[111] In summary, each form of theater will develop dominants within the gestural code in line with its overall intentions and aims.

This formation of dominants can, as already indicated, not only have an impact on the differentiation of the three fundamental levels of the generation of meaning by communicative gestural signs, but also on the constituent elements within one of these levels. Thus, for example, it is quite conceivable that gestural signs which produce meaning at the subject level will be formed and used, signs, that is, which refer to age, sex, physical condition, social status, character, temporary mood and feelings, or to different combinations of these elements. In this manner, a set of gestures can be discerned in commedia dell'arte which is able to distinguish among a range of different characters.[112] Bourgeois theater from the Enlightenment to Stanislavsky, by contrast, develops and refines a set of gestures signifying the temporary moods and feelings of the individual persons.[113] Brecht postulates the formation of a set of gestures which describe and characterize the individual as socially conditioned, as a member of a certain social class.[114]

Moreover, the different formation of dominants influences not only the diachronic dimension of the sequence of theater of forms, but equally the synchronic level of the simultaneous existence of different systems of theatrical norms. Whereas *tragédie classique* predominantly uses gestures which serve to structure and accentuate the spoken text, at the same point in time and following in the wake of *comédie italienne,* Molière's troupe develops a set of gestures intended to mark the type of person involved in terms of both social status and character.[115] Bourgeois dramatic theater in the form it took under Stanislavsky devised gestures capable of depicting the finest nuances of a complex emotional life. The gestures, by contrast, that are used in the opera of the day make use of highly conventional signifiers for emotions, such as pressing a hand on a heart or wringing hands above one's head. In other words, gestures are involved which were formed as signs for these feelings in baroque theater and continued to be used in opera until the end of the nineteenth century and the beginning of the twentieth, because in such opera gestural signs on principle played a subordinate role.[116]

With reference to European theater, the meaning of gestural signs can thus also be understood solely via recourse to the gestural code of the culture in question only in the most infrequent of cases. To the extent that the theater has developed a code of its own, an interpretation of theatrical gestural signs can be undertaken only on the basis of a gestural code. An analysis of this theatrical gestural code can, in general, be made with the aid of the categories introduced at the outset. The special relationship between the gestural code of this form of theater and that of the social stratum that promotes it always also functions as an element bearing meaning.

The last group of gestural signs we must investigate are those which Greimas has defined as having a function fulfilling an intention.[117] The gestures concerned are those which are formed and utilized in the production, distribution, and consumption of material goods, i.e., those that are realized in interaction between humans and objects. These gestures have the primary function of either producing, repairing, maintaining, or caring for objects, or passing on, using, or consuming them. This primary function is of no relevance to theater. For if an object is produced, cared for, passed on, used, or consumed on stage, this does not occur with an aim to the object's actual production, distribution, and consumption, but rather as a sign that says something about character X producing something, passing it on, or consuming it. If gestures which are used in a culture for the production, distribution, and consumption of material goods are realized on stage, then they function at the subject level to generate meaning, for example, as signs of X's profession, special abilities, inclinations, or habits.[118]

In addition to their primary function, such gestures can also fulfill a secondary function in culture as communicative signs: (a) as signs that say something about the person, (b) as signs that refer to that person's relation to parties to interaction, and (c) as signs for his attitude toward the object in question. If, for example, a gesture is executed with particular dexterity or routine, then it can be interpreted as a sign of particular abilities of A, who carries it out; a sudden gesture, by contrast, can perhaps be taken as an indicator of A's character or current mood.[119] If such a gestural action is, moreover, effected in the course of a sequence of interaction, then, under certain conditions, the concentration on the object can, for example, express A's refusal to interact with B and C. Now, if gestures which fulfill an intention are used in a particularly caring or careless, concentrated or distracted manner, then they also function as signs of A's relation to the object he is using. Over and above their primary functions, these gestures expressing an intention can, in other words, also be used as communicative gestures which can produce meaning both at the subject and at the intersubjective levels. In terms of their secondary functions, such gestures can also be used in theater: the gesture A makes can be understood as a sign that says something about character X and his relation to Y and Z, who are parties to the interaction.

Gestures used in theater to fulfill intentions presume the use of props. Conversely, however, such gestures can serve as signs for the presence of such props. The actor can light a nonexistent fire in a nonexistent fireplace with a nonexistent stick of wood; he can take off a nonexistent hat, open a nonexistent window, etc.

In this sense, the gestures that are realized in order to fulfill an intention can also function as signs for objects at which the intention is aimed.[120]

They take on this function above all in pantomime; the interaction between pantomimer and the world of objects is realized predominantly using gestures that fulfill intentions. In this context, in a significantly high number of cases the pantomimer obeys the syntax that we have determined was characteristic of the sign language used by the deaf. He first introduces the person acting and the essential characteristics of that person, then presents the object to which the person's actions will refer, and finally uses gestures fulfilling intentions in order to show what these activities are.[121] Frequently, however, the phase of representing the object is omitted: the object is presented by carrying out the gesture that shows use of the object. To this extent, the group of gestures fulfilling intentions comprises the most important group of gestures utilized in pantomime; indeed, it is the gestural category which constitutes pantomime in the first place.[122]

The special capacity of gestural signs to signify and thus substitute for other theatrical signs is clearly visible in this function of gestures fulfilling intentions: gestures which braid nonexistent pigtails thus substitute for an actor's hair; the gesture which buttons up a nonexistent jacket and pulls on nonexistent trousers at the same time signifies the existence of these parts of a costume. By the same token, props and stage decorations can be signified by gestural signs alone, indeed, such gestures are to a certain extent able to replace lighting. Gestural signs can thus be realized in a manner which allows the audience to conclude that darkness prevails on that part of the stage where the actor is.[123] If gestural signs suggest that an instrument is being played or a song sung, then these signs must be believed to be present and accepted. Gestural signs can, in other words, substitute for other sign systems in theater, whereas they themselves cannot be replaced. A theatrical code without gestural signs is inconceivable. For gestural signs form the most important group of signs comprising it—without them, a theatrical code would not be able to constitute itself in the first place.

Proxemic Signs

It is difficult to classify proxemic signs and allocate them a place in the theatrical code because, on the one hand, they are realized as gestural signs and thus everything we have stated of gestural signs holds true for them. Yet, on the other hand, they constitute a separate category of kinesic signs because a meaning can only be attributed to them if they are referred to the space surrounding them. Proxemic signs can be divided into two groups:

(1) Signs that take the shape of the distance between the parties to interaction, i.e., as empty space, and as the change in this distance;[124] and
(2) Signs that take the shape of movement, i.e., movement through space.

The distance judged appropriate between communicating parties is strictly regulated in every culture, with respect both to the communicative situation and to the relation between the communicating parties. The distance deemed appropriate differs substantially from culture to culture. Intercultural comparisons have revealed that, for example, in Arabic and Islamic cultures the communicative distance kept in public between men who are friends is extremely slight, indeed that communication is only possible if the parties to interaction are so close to one another that they can easily touch each other. By contrast, in Anglo-American culture, the corresponding distance is approximately an arm's length, i.e., a distance that more or less makes physical contact impossible during the conversation.[125] The distance between parties to an interaction can, in other words, only be interpreted as a sign of the relation that obtains between the parties in the context of a particular culture. On this basis, for example, a minimal distance which permits frequent physical contact between the communicating parties can be understood as a sign of great intimacy in Anglo-American culture. Here, the interpretation must rest on a difference being made between the use of proxemic signs in public and in private. In general, the rule holds for private situations that the relation between the communicating parties is all the closer, the smaller the distance between them. In public situations, by contrast, this rule has to be modified. Here, distance serves not to indicate an emotional or family-related bond between the parties, but a social, hierarchical relation that rests on the structure of power relations in the workplace.

Thus, for example, a managing director will not receive another managing director, i.e., someone who is his equal, sitting behind his desk, but will get up and go to meet the guest, and then sit down with the latter; an exception would be made if the other was the representative of a much smaller company; thus a distance maintained in communication could be intended to signify this difference between the two companies concerned. Vis-à-vis a subordinate, a superior will increase the distance between them by remaining seated behind his desk. Moreover, if one of the two parties can arbitrarily reduce the distance, then this too is a sign of a superior position: for example, the superior approaches the subordinate from behind, going so close that he can look over the latter's shoulder while he works. The opposite is not permissible, namely for the subordinate to walk around the desk and look at his boss's work.[126] The distance between the communicating parties must, in other words, always be related to this distinction between private and public settings if it is to be interpreted at the intersubjective level as a sign of the relation between the interacting parties. On its own, however, this distinction does not suffice. The individual situations in these two settings must be described closely because respectively different rules may apply to them with regard to the distance between the communicating parties. That distance can be realized and interpreted as a sign generating meaning at the intersubjective level only if all these conditions are taken into consideration. It must also be borne in mind that precisely a breach of the rules which are generally accepted as valid itself constitutes an element of signification. The subordinate who enters his superior's room and does not stop in front of the desk but goes around it in order to stand behind his boss and look over his shoulder at the latter's papers or to sit on the edge of the desk may wish to use this rule-breaking alteration of the distance to indicate that he sees the relation between himself and his boss differently than does his boss or than do other people in general. The distance between communicating parties, either in line with the rules or in violation of them, can thus function as a sign at the intersubjective level.[127]

Theater can use the distance in a corresponding function as a sign. The distance between actors A and B can be realized and interpreted as a sign for the dominant relation between characters X and Y if one bears in mind the general rules accepted in the culture in question for the distance between communicating parties and the specific rules for the different situations in which they are applied.

In addition, the distance between the actors on stage may be laden with meanings that are not exclusively derived from the respective meanings in the culture in question but rather can first be created in terms of the specific meaning of the space of the stage and/or the characters. For example, if zones of the space on stage signify heaven and hell, dream world and reality, past and present, etc., then the distance between the actors who act in the particular zones, and any alteration of this distance, is instilled with a meaning that accords with these spatial designations. If, on the other hand, the characters are representatives of a certain world or idea, then the distance between them would suggest an interpretation related to such representation, etc. The distance between the actors can, in other words, be realized and interpreted as a sign within highly different semantic contexts.

Movement through space is—and this is its first decisive feature—accomplished as the realization of gestural signs. Everything stated above with regard to communicative signs also holds true for these gestural signs, to the extent that they can be allocated to the former group. If, for example, a person moves in a particular direction while talking, then the gestural signs that person realizes can be referred to the object level of linguistic utterances by one of the persons involved, to the subject level of that person, and to the intersubjective level between the persons involved.

The object level of linguistic utterances is not addressed if the movement is not made in the course of a conversation, but, for example, as the movement of at least two people toward each other, away from each other, or around each other, without linguistic communication ensuing. The intersubjective level is also not involved if the movement of only one person in the room is to be seen, without other people noticeably existing for him. In such a case, the gestural signs realized as movement can only be interpreted at the subject level. Thus, for instance, if the person in question drags himself across a certain space, then this can be taken as a sign of a number of things: of his great age or of a certain social status (perhaps that of a vagabond); of a weak body or of tiredness; of a phlegmatic character or of a lack of concentration; of depression or sadness; or that he is on his way to an unpleasant meeting. The type of movement will always be interpreted as a sign that creates meaning at the subject level.

Now, a movement across space is not only carried out in a particular way but also for a specific concrete purpose, which always lies beyond the horizon of the aims and purposes of a particular communication or interaction. It is movement toward a place, away from a place, around a place, in short, a movement that measures out a certain space. We can thus characterize it as a movement which serves to fulfill intentionality. Just as the gesture which fulfills an intention is first imbued with meaning by being referred to a concrete object—which is itself produced, cared for, distributed, and consumed with its help—so too the meaning of movement across space is first constituted by reference to the space which it has measured out. For in most cultures the primary function of such movement consists in covering specific distances of differing lengths.

Furthermore, the movement across space can also take on those secondary meanings which I outlined at the beginning; in other words, it can function as a communicative sign.

In theater, movement across space can just as little assume its primary function as can a gesture fulfilling an intention with regard to an object. For, if the actor crosses the stage from back right to front left, he does so in order to show that X, for example, goes from the harbor to the palace, or something else. The movement across space is thus always a sign realized with regard to character X and therefore has to be interpreted accordingly. If it is to be possible to interpret it, then it has to be referred to the concrete stage space in which it is realized. For the way a meaning can be attributed to the sign of the movement depends on the meanings of the stage space and its different zones.[128]

A's entrance or exit in any case signifies that X comes from somewhere to the location designated by the stage or leaves it to go somewhere. The locations therefore assumed to exist offstage can be designated verbally (e.g., "I'm going to my uncle's house"), or by means of parts of the stage decorations in the form of road signs, or by stage conventions (leaving the stage back right means going to the market);[129] whatever the case, they are assumed as givens the moment entrance and exit are accorded a meaning of their own.

In like manner, any movement across the stage that denotes a movement toward a goal first receives a meaning in relation to what the stage signifies; it is on account of these significations that movement becomes someone going to church, running around in a royal palace, strolling in a park, climbing to the balcony of one's beloved, falling sharply to hell, crossing over into the past, driving into infinity, etc. The manner in which these movements are carried out then says something new about character X and the relation between X and the goal he or she is striving for.

Theater makes use not only of goal-oriented movements across space, but also of movements that generate meaning by the way in which they divide up the stage space: movement diagonally across the stage, movement parallel to the apron or at right angles to the apron, symmetrical and asymmetrical sequences of movement, etc. Here, too, the meaning of the gestural signs can be established only if they are related to the space in which they are realized. However, they must not be related to that space as denotative signs of possible concrete space, but rather as signs denoting space itself, as space, i.e., as an abstract means of structuring space.[130] The stage space can exercise both functions at once. It can denote a certain place and simultaneously represent abstract space that is significantly structured by the movements. By his movements across space, the actor thus generates meaning by relating to that space as denoting both a concrete and an abstract space, i.e., space in itself.

Proxemic signs are used in all forms of theater; furthermore, in one theatrical genre they function as the signs that constitute that genre in the first place, namely ballet, dance theater.[131] Here, the relation that the dancer establishes to the space surrounding him or her is the signifying element par excellence: meaning only arises if and when the dancer relates to the space in a certain way, which is in turn different for each normative system of dance.[132] Only thus can the dancer's movement also contain communicative meaning, for example as an expression of the person the dancer is depicting, namely character X. The relation to space is therefore always the primary relation in this theatrical genre. As a consequence, we shall define the gestural signs used in it initially in terms of their functioning as proxemic signs.[133]

All the signs realized by the actor have now been addressed, with the exception of nonverbal acoustic signs (music, sounds) and a description has been given of what each essentially accomplishes. What has emerged in the course of our discussion is that these signs of the theatrical code can fundamentally be assigned only *one* meaning at the systemic level. For they all denote the corresponding signs produced by character X, e.g., A's voice denotes X's voice, A's gait denotes X's gait, etc. All other meanings—both lexical and context-related—can only be treated at the systemic level as possibilities of signification that can first be given actual form at the normative level, in particular at the level of speech. Thus, an actor's entrance can always in general be understood as "coming from a certain location"; at the level of the norms of the theatrical code of Greek comedy after the fourth century, if the entrance is from the right it quite specifically means "coming from the market or the harbor," and if it is from the left it means "coming from the countryside"; at the level of speech as the theatrical code in a performance of Thornton Wilder's *A Long Christmas Dinner,* the actor's entrance, by contrast, means "being born" if he comes from the left. The process in which the sign realized by the actor is assigned a meaning must therefore be investigated at the level of theatrical norms and of theatrical speech.[134]

The discussion thus far has treated the individual sign systems separately at the systemic level and has been restricted to pointing out that they are not usually used in isolation in a performance but rather together with signs from one or more of the other sign systems in question. The relation between signs realized simultaneously thus becomes an important factor in the process of the constitution of meaning. In conclusion, a few general observations will consequently be made on this specific relation.

In principle, the individual signs refer to one another in three different ways: first, the signs used simultaneously can reinforce and mutually support each other; second, they can contradict one another; and third, they can have no recognizable relation to one another.[135]

It should be borne in mind that only two, or three, or four, or all five sign systems outlined can be used simultaneously. Accordingly, the three possibilities just mentioned can be actualized in different ways, so that the cluster of signs has to be interpreted differently in each case. It is, furthermore, important to know when interpreting such a cluster of signs whether it occurs on the basis of a norm that prescribes a particular hierarchy among the signs generated by the actor. If, for example, the gestural or linguistic signs are the dominant bearer of signification, then the modifications of their meaning accomplished by the other signs has to be evaluated differently than would be the case if they had the same status as the latter signs.[136]

If a normative code or a performance code prescribes in principle the use of a certain sign system and yet in part dispenses with that use, then this process must also be regarded as generating meaning.[137] The meaning of the signs realized by the actor does not, however, depend solely on which signs are used simultaneously in relation to others and which signs are accorded dominance, but also on factors that cannot be subsumed under the issues bound up with the respective semic group. Just as paralinguistic signs take on a new meaning if produced by different voices, so, too, mimic signs may change depending on the face in question and gestural signs may be altered by the shape and clothing of the person realizing them.

This brings us to the second group of theatrical signs, namely those which make up the actor's appearance: the mask, costume, and hair.

2. The Actor's Appearance
as a Sign

❑ ❑ ❑ The moment an actor appears on the stage, the audience has already received information which allows it to identify the character being portrayed as a specific character. This identification may refer in quite general terms simply to the character's age and gender (old man, young girl) or more specifically to a particular position in society (king, beggar) and/or a social category in a particular period (medieval knight, a worker at the beginning of the twentieth century). Or it may refer to race or nationality (Englishman, Japanese, Indian), to a particular type (clown, funny old woman), to occupations (policeman, sailor), or even to individual figures in drama (Othello, Mephisto). The moment the actor appears on stage, we form a specific opinion about the character he is portraying and have certain expectations as to how that character will behave and what he will do. We have, so to speak, ascribed a temporary identity to character X by having identified him as someone on the basis of the specific appearance with which actor A represents X on the stage. The audience thus takes the actor's external appearance as a sign which can be allocated the meaning of character X's specific identity. Here, the actor's appearance quite obviously functions as a system that generates meaning, wherein the process of constituting meaning takes the form of a process of identification. Before analyzing the specific sign system of "appearance" in detail, we thus have to examine the question of what the conditions are under which we generally identify someone as a particular person—in other words, ascribe an identity to a subject.[1]

G. H. Mead describes identity as the product of a communicative process:

> The individual experiences himself—not directly, but only indirectly—from the particular viewpoint of other members of the same social group or from the generalized view of the social group as a whole to which he belongs. For he does not directly or immediately bring his own experience into play as an identity or personality, nor does he do so by becoming a subject for himself, but rather only insofar as he first becomes an object for himself, just as other individuals are objects for him or in his experience. He becomes an object for himself only by adapting the attitude of other individuals towards himself within a social environment or an experiential or behavioral context in which he is involved to the same degree as the others.[2]

In other words, Mead does not define identity as something which one could have for oneself and of itself, but rather as a variable which can take shape only in the course of communication processes. It is only when the individual can react to himself in the way that he does to others that he becomes a self. The obvious conclusion would be that identity by definition cannot be taken to mean an attribute for something which always stays the same. For if identity takes shape in processes of communication, it is the very product of a variety of personal relationships.

> We have many different relationships to different people. We mean one thing to one person and another thing to someone else. There are parts of the identity which exist only in the relation of the identity to itself. We split ourselves up into the widest variety of identities when we speak with our acquaintances. There is the widest variety of identities which correspond to the widest variety of social reactions. The social process itself is responsible for the appearance of identity; it is not present as identity outside of this experience.[3]

The individual may very well mean something different to different people, but these meanings are constituted from the context of the relevant culture in which certain patterns of language, action, and behavior are interpreted in a generally accepted manner. In other words, the individual initially acquires an identity from the fact that he belongs to a particular collective body and incorporates the institutions of this community into his own behavior.

On the other hand, however, identity is only possible if the individual sets himself off from the collective body of the others; he not only subordinates himself to it, but at the same time also asserts himself within it. In other words, he has to be different from the others in certain respects. Yet, he only has an identity by being a member of society, and thus the differences which are relevant to him also have to be recognized as such by the other members of society.

This condition can, in turn, only be met in the process of communication. Accordingly, Mead defines the use of symbols as the crucial prerequisite for the development of identity. For symbols help the individual to present himself both as a member of the collective body which generally employs these symbols and as an individual who sets himself off from the other members of society through the specific manner in which he makes use of the symbols. Mead concludes from this that the individual's physical presence has no function in that person's experience and development of his identity; identity can only be acquired through the process of reaching understanding through discourse—in other words, only in the medium of language.

It is interesting to note that the two conditions, the fulfillment of which Mead considers constitutive for the development of identity, namely, subordination in the community and distinction from the other members of the community, come up in a completely different context in the works of Georg Simmel on this subject. Simmel understands and explains these two competing principles which form the basis of all kinds of social existence in terms of their being the underlying reason for the creation and development of fashion. For fashion is, in his opinion, the imitation of a given pattern and thus fulfills the need for social borrowing. It leads the individual onto the track that everyone is taking and it supplies a general element which turns the behavior of every individual into a mere example. However, it is no less effective in satisfying the need for distinction, the tendency towards differentiation, variation, setting oneself off. . . . Fashion is thus nothing other than one special form of living among many others, by means of which the tendency toward social equalization merges with that toward individual difference and variation in a uniform action.[4]

Simmel thus describes fashion as a phenomenon which is based on the fundamental principles of social life and lends them expression. The effect of fashion essentially lies in its helping one person to signify for another that he or she is, like that other, a member of the same collective body, and that his specific attire shows that he is significantly different from all other members of this collective body. Fashion is thus assigned a function which Mead describes as typical of the use of symbols. According to this definition, fashion—in other words, the canon of rules governing external attire[5]—functions as a sign system which helps the members of a society to communicate with each other.

G. Stone makes this important insight the basis of his new definition of the concept of identity.[6] Stone first distinguishes between discursive and presentative communication. Whereas Mead considers only the discursive semantic context to be constitutive for the development of identity, Stone points emphatically to the role played by presentative communication in the course of identification processes:

Appearance, then, is that phase of the social transaction which establishes identification of the participants. As such, it may be distinguished from discourse, which we conceptualize as the text of transaction—what the parties are discussing. Appearance and discourse are two distinct dimensions of the social transaction. The former seems the more basic. It sets the stage for, permits, sustains, and delimits the possibilities of discourse by underwriting the possibilities of meaningful discussion. Ordinarily appearance is communicated by such non-verbal symbols as gestures, grooming, clothing, location and the like; discourse, by verbal symbolism.[7]

Stone thus defines appearance as being fundamental to the process of identification. The first thing we notice about a person is his appearance. It allows us to ascribe an identity to him before we have even entered into a discursive process of reaching understanding with him. The manner in which a person presents himself—makes himself up, wears his hair, dresses himself—announces to the others how he judges himself and wishes to be judged by others.

A person's clothing often served to establish a mood for himself capable of eliciting validation in the reviews aroused from others. The meaning of appearance, therefore, is the establishment of identity, value, mood, and attitude for the one who appears by the coincident programs and reviews awakened by his appearance. . . . By appearing, the person announces his identity, shows his value, expresses his mood, or proposes his attitude.[8]

For all members of a society can have recourse to a common canon of rules which is made the underlying basis for ascribing meanings to differing external forms of appearance. By presenting his external appearance in a certain manner, the person fashions an image of himself which is intended to be valid for himself and for others. External appearance thus functions as a sign, the meaning of which could be described as identity. Since every new and different form of presentation is capable of calling up a different image, the same person can mean something different in differing situations, depending on how he presents himself. For appearance is an aspect of the individual, a view of himself which is given in a specific perspective and points to him in his totality, yet without actually being that. Since this is usually the first thing we notice about a person, it is decisive in pre-forming our expectations with regard to how this person will act and behave in interaction. In other words, appearance is to be understood in symbolic terms; it functions as a sign which represents transcendental contents; it represents past and present action and conveys anticipations of future action. For as a symbolic complex, it evokes corresponding identifications in the subject as well as in the observer: for the most part, the meanings attached to the sign appearance coincide with each other.[9]

According to Stone, therefore, appearance is actually an essential factor determining the process of developing identity as Mead describes it. This process occurs in three phases, namely, investiture, dressing out, and dressing in. In the first phase, external appearance is imposed on the small child by the adults; to a great extent, the child's hair and clothing symbolize the identity which the adults want to ascribe to or nurture in the child. In the second phase, the child arbitrarily changes its own appearance, dresses up and plays in the costumes of various roles. It gradually acquires an identity of its own by playfully taking on the identity of many others in costume. In the third and final phase, the self emerges through the process of standardization and differentiation as an enduring identity: the external appearance is produced and interpreted as a sign of both what one means to oneself, and what one means to/for others.

Bearing these considerations in mind, we can now define the function of appearance in the theatrical process. Theater proceeds on the basis of the body as an a priori: without the actor, without his physical presence, theater as we defined it in the introduction is not possible. The actor's body is the condition, as it were, which makes theater possible. The body, for its part, however, cannot be thought of as anything other than a body which appears. Theater can thus only take place if we are confronted with the actor's appearance; the actor's external appearance is normally the first thing we notice about the actor. This initial perception causes us to make an identification of the character in the same way we attribute a specific identity as a meaning to the external appearance of a person.

The spectator then relates to the other signs produced by the actor—the linguistic and paralinguistic, mimic, gestural, and proxemic signs—to this identity

rarily been attached to him. They can supplement the aspect of
:sented by his appearance by confirming it, rounding it out, or
g it. The character's identity may have already been completely
ldience via his external appearance, but it may also not be con-
end of the performance, namely as the meaning of all signs that
the character has produced. In the former case we are dealing with a certain type,
and in the latter, with a multilayered, complicated character.

However, since the external appearance is in any case the sign which, on the
one hand, is the first to be received and, on the other, is perceived for a much
longer time than all other signs that the actor produces, the meaning attached at
the outset to this sign is of especial importance. Indeed, in theater it is first of all
the crown which makes the king, the uniform which makes the soldier, and the
cowl which makes the monk. The expectations we have of a character are initially
based exclusively on the actor's external appearance. To this extent, the character's
identity is sufficiently secured and validated for us by this appearance—at least in
the beginning and, so to speak, for our initial hypotheses about the figure.[10]

This capacity of the sign "appearance" or "external appearance" to provoke
an attribution of meaning attached as an identity when a person is first perceived
has been exploited in a multitude of ways by the theater. It has, for example, led
to the development of various conventions in the context of which a figure's
external appearance alone can bring to mind an entire set of expectations regarding
the figure's speech, action, and behavior. One need only think of the commedia
dell'arte, for example, which makes use of the external appearance of an
Arlecchino, a Dottore, a Capitano or a Pantalone, to provide failsafe forecasts for
the audience about the relationships between the persons who are acting and about
their behavior, the prognostic value of which is beyond any doubt. Based on the
prevailing convention, external appearance serves to establish and guarantee the
figures' identity conclusively for the audience.

We have thus briefly outlined the general function of the sign system
"appearance" in the theater and characterized it in terms of its basic elements.
In order to be able to describe and analyze this function in more depth, we will
now subdivide the sign complex "external appearance" into its three components—mask, hairstyle, costume—and discuss each of these elements individually.

Mask

We understand the actor's mask to mean that set of signs which denotes the
character's face and figure.

A certain need for clarification is implicit in this definition. For, one may at
first be inclined to say, the face and figure are not cultural phenomena; rather,
they are determined by nature. Whether someone is tall or short, has a long or
short nose or a straight or crooked mouth, is not attributable to culturally specific
conceptions and consensus, i.e., is not the result of a communicative process, but
of a natural, biological process. If the mask denotes face and figure, then it refers

to naturally given phenomena and not to cultural facts and processes. In this respect, it is unlike all other theatrical signs we have discussed thus far.

The meaning of facts of nature, unlike that of cultural facts which are signs by origin, cannot be constituted hermeneutically, but rather has to be grasped through diagnosis. This would suggest that the meaning produced with the sign system "mask" refers only to meanings which can be diagnosed. Wrinkled skin, for example, can be interpreted as a sign of aging, the bosom as a sign of the female gender, black skin as a sign of belonging to the black race, red spots on the skin as a sign of rash, etc. If this were the case, there would not be a very large number or wide variety of meanings which can be produced in theater with the sign system of the mask.

On the other hand, we have just shown how external appearance, which, after all, is largely determined by the face and figure, functions as a system of communication. If our explanations in this regard are correct, then the face and figure would have to be interpreted as cultural phenomena as well. It would follow from this that the mask as a theatrical sign does not denote natural facts, but rather cultural phenomena—in which case the possibilities for constituting meaning by means of this sign system would be infinitely greater.

Thus, before attempting to analyze the function of the mask as a theatrical sign, we should pursue the question of whether the face and figure can function as variables in communicative processes or whether their interpretation is exhausted de facto if subjected to scientific diagnosis.

Ever since classical antiquity, scientific-medical diagnosis, which is capable of identifying biological facts such as age, gender, race, state of health, has left something to be desired, and attempts have repeatedly been made to expand the application of such diagnosis to include the interpretation of character traits.

Aristotle assumed that there had to be a correlation between the constitution of a body and the constitution of the soul living inside it.

> For, as we said, the word substance has three meanings—form, matter, and the complex of both—and of these matter is potentiality, form actuality. Since then the complex here is the living thing, the body cannot be the actuality of the soul; it is the soul which is the actuality of a certain kind of body. Hence the rightness of the view that the soul cannot be without a body, while it cannot be a body; it is not a body but something relative to a body. That is why it is in a body, and a body of a definite kind. It was a mistake, therefore, to do as former thinkers did, merely to fit it into a body without adding a definite specification of the kind or character of that body, although evidently one chance thing will not receive another.[11]

According to Aristotle, the relationship between body and soul is one of analogy: in other words, a person's physical beauty is an indication of his or her inner beauty, whereas physical ugliness is an indication of moral depravity.

Aristotle thus formulated a view which was to have a decisive influence on physiognomy well into the nineteenth century. Given that an analogical relationship exists between body and soul, conclusions about a person's character can logically also be drawn from the person's physical appearance, i.e., the face and figure. Face and figure are thus construed by physiognomy to be more or less natural signs, the meaning of which is to be described as a character trait.

In the eighteenth century[12] Lavater conducted an experiment to justify the validity of physiognomy as a scientific form of diagnosis. Like Aristotle, Paracelsus, and della Porta, among others, Lavater also proceeded on the assumption that an analogy necessarily exists between body and soul.[13] In his view, however, any conclusions made about a person's character have to be based on more than a mere impression. Indeed, it is a matter of breaking the entire figure down into the various expressive zones that comprise it, of judging these individually, and then when making the final diagnosis, of taking into account the corresponding relationship between the meanings derived from the individual expressive zones. Lavater breaks down the head area, for example, into the following expressive zones:

(1) Face: Individual aspects: profile, complexion, "angle from tip of the nose to upper lip proper," proportion between the forehead and other parts of the face, wrinkles, lines in the face. Elements: forehead, span of the forehead, skin on forehead (position, color, folds, tightness), bones of forehead, eye, eyebrows, eyelid, set of the eyes, sockets, temples, nose, bridge of the nose, nose bone, transition from nose to lip, mouth, lips, cheeks, facial hair, chin, jaw, teeth, gums.

(2) Other portions of the head: Throat, neck. Back of the head, skull, cerebral basin, temporal bone, sinus cavities. Ears. Part in the hair. Hair (hair growth, baldness). Profile of the head.

In addition to the head area, bone structure, posture, proportions, constitution of the "flesh" (soft, loose, hard, pudgy, dry—i.e., muscle tone) and the hands also have to be taken into consideration. Of all the zones mentioned, Lavater considers the face to be the most important, since in his view the most reliable data for an accurate interpretation can be derived from its careful examination. For

> every feature many times repeated, every frequent expression on the face, or change in the face, ultimately leaves a lasting impression on the soft portions of the countenance. The stronger the feature, and the more often it is repeated, the stronger, deeper, more indelible the impression it makes (even, as will be shown below, on the boniest parts from early youth onward).
>
> A pleasant feature repeated a thousand times leaves an impression, and gives a lasting beautiful quality to the countenance. An ugly feature repeated a thousand times leaves an impression, and gives a lasting ugly quality to the countenance.
>
> In combination, many such beautiful impressions left on the physiognomy of a human being yield (all other circumstances remaining constant) a beautiful countenance; many such ugly impressions, an ugly countenance.[14]

The experienced physiognomist is thus in a position to "read" and understand the face and figure as a set of signs, the meaning of which he constitutes as a statement about the character traits of the person involved.

This procedure and the claims it made were already being criticized by Lichtenberg, a contemporary of Lavater's. For Lavater's theory of physiognomy contends that it can judge a person's character according to criteria that are intersubjectively verifiable, i.e., according to objective criteria. This implies that a positive or negative estimation of character has a validity that no one can question, which can have immeasurable social consequences.

> If physiognomy is out to achieve what Lavater expects of it, then children will be hung before they have committed the deeds that deserve the gallows. In other words, a new kind of initiation rite will have to be undertaken every year—a physiognomic auto da fe.[15]

Physiognomy, however, cannot justify these consequences if only because its findings are by no means capable of claiming objective validity, but are rather extremely dubious, since the procedure of physiognomics rests on false premises. For, as Lichtenberg sees it, the idea of an analogy between body and soul is not tenable on scientific grounds. "The above idea, which cannot be formally disproved here, and is hardly worthy of a serious attempt to do so in the first place, produced still another, namely, that of ultimately shaping the body to measure up to the ideals of Greek artists by beautifying the soul."[16] Whereas Lichtenberg declares the claim of physiognomy to be completely unjustified, he makes so-called pathognomy, namely the investigation of the language of mimicry and gesture, the focus of his observations. In his view this language points to the individual's human passions, feelings, and desires and can be interpreted accordingly.[17]

Although physiognomy has repeatedly been the target of serious criticism, it has undergone numerous revivals, even as recently as in our own century.[18] However, no one today any longer seriously supports its claim to being able to interpret the face and figure in their natural state as signs of character traits.

Be that as it may, this does not make physiognomy any less interesting for us here. For by pretending to teach us about the relationship between physical and character traits, it gives an insight into the repertoire of social stereotypes in Western culture, stereotypes which to some extent were a product of physiognomy itself, but which also served as a basis for its theories. After all, what is of interest here is not whether or not a high forehead, for example, allows us to conclude that someone is intelligent; what is relevant to us is the particular fact that in our culture it is generally assumed that a person with a high forehead (a lofty brow!) is intelligent.

Certain physical features are, as in this example, interpreted in most cultures with a view to specific character traits which differ in terms of social relevance. Consequently, these interpretations give rise to the social stereotypes taken as the basis for assigning values; this form of valuation allocates certain character traits expressed in specific physical features to certain social groups and thus plays a role in stabilizing the social hierarchy. In our culture, for example, a high forehead, a slender figure, a tanned complexion, or smooth skin are highly valued, because they are interpreted as signs of intelligence, fitness, health, and youth, i.e., as signs of characteristics which, as the expression of a high social prestige, enjoy particular esteem in our culture.[19] In other cultures, on the other hand, a flat forehead, a fat body, pale skin, or a wrinkly face are judged positively because they are indications of characteristics which rank high on the scale of social value because they, for their part, denote a high degree of social prestige in the hierarchies of their cultures.[20]

Since the members of every culture strive for recognition and esteem,[21] they will—to the extent permitted by society—make every effort in their power to bring their face and figure as much as possible into line with the ideals of their culture, the respective hierarchy of values, and the resulting rules of appearance that apply in the various social groups. As a consequence, however, the face and figure cease to be exclusively natural phenomena. Rather, their appearance becomes a social fact, a sign that communicates to others which qualities they expect of an individual, and which identity they can and ought to attribute to that person.[22]

A distinction must be made here between two modes of artificially altering the face and figure, according to whether the change they produce is temporary or permanent. Temporary changes are achieved in most cultures by applying paint or makeup. Form and color, on the one hand, and their local application, on the other, function here as elements which bear meaning. The application of makeup can bring about an extensive alteration: the use of ornamental painting can change the complexion, the number of wrinkles, the size of the mouth and eyes, the form and color of the brows; thus, regardless of a face's actual constitution, the respective cultural ideals, and the contingent rules that apply to making up the face to suit a specific social standing, the face can be transformed to the point where it is no longer recognizable.[23]

Tatooing and scarring,[24] and mutilation and deformation of individual parts of the body[25] are all known methods of permanent alteration. Moreover, in recent years plastic surgery has come into vogue, which cannot only create the impression of a different face—as can be done with makeup—but can actually produce an altogether different face.

It would therefore no longer seem justifiable to interpret face and figure[26] merely in the sense of natural facts as being indices for natural, biological givens such as gender, age, race, state of health. Rather they function as elements in processes of communication, which is why they can be adequately grasped only if they are interpreted with a view to social conditions. For face and figure may indicate the person's membership in a certain caste, class, stratum, or social group as well as an individual's attitude toward the hierarchy of values prevailing in this culture. They are therefore to be interpreted and valued in quite general terms as a sign of the position that a person assumes in society and of that person's identity in society.

The definition of makeup given initially can now be modified against the background of these explanations: actor A's mask denotes character X's face and figure in the sense that, as a sign, it is indicative of the signs employed in the surrounding culture. In other words, in this respect there is no contradiction between it and the other theatrical signs we have dealt with so far—they all function as signs of signs.[27]

Because the actor's mask denotes the face and figure of character X, it can be produced and interpreted as a sign of, first, X's age, gender, race, state of health; second, his social status; and third, his personality. In the latter two cases it is invariably related to the social stereotypes of the surrounding culture. Thus, for example, in our culture an innocent young girl is characterized by large eyes, even features, a relatively small nose, a straight mouth; a mean old woman, on the other hand, by a long, crooked nose, small, beady eyes, and a crooked mouth. A sensual figure will be given full lips, a philosopher, a high forehead. The characterization may contradict the social stereotypes, perhaps for the very purpose of pointing to the existence of these stereotypes and the lack of an objective justification for them—for example, by making up the philosopher with a "sensuous" mouth and giving the lecher narrow lips or a high forehead. It nevertheless still refers, albeit as an antithesis, to these stereotypes: an identity cannot be attributed to the character until the contradiction between the actor's appearance and the social stereotype, which prescribes other physical features to reflect this character's moral nature, is itself also understood as a sign and interpreted in relation to the character.[28] In this sense, the actor's natural appearance can also function as a mask. For his large or small eyes, his evenly cut or angular face, his lanky or plump figure are used as theatrical signs in the same way as are the corresponding artificially created attributes. If they are employed on the stage in unaltered form, it is not the fact of their being natural which is of interest, but rather the specific fact that they are employed for the purpose of characterizing character X. In other words, like makeup and artificial alterations of the figure, they function as signs which make it possible to identify the character.

In addition to the mask that refers affirmatively or antithetically to the social stereotypes of the surrounding culture, the theater has also developed its own mask code in isolated cases. This is especially true of the ornamental mask in Oriental theater,[29] in which the principles that apply to the creation of meaning through the use of makeup certainly coincide with the surrounding culture, but the meanings created in this way do not. Every line, every shade of color, every localization of the ornament here has a fixed meaning which provides detailed information for the audience about the character's social station and personality traits. The mask code specific to the theater has to be learned in order to understand these masks. Knowledge of the stereotypes which apply in his culture will not, in and of itself, enable the spectator to attribute the appropriate identity to the character based on the mask the actor is wearing.

The theatrical mask, on the other hand, not only refers to the prevailing social stereotypes of the surrounding society, but also frequently to other cultural codes, e.g., to a cultural historical code. It may thus be an indication of the context of a particular period from which the character is derived, or refer to a mythological code which governs the appearance of visionary figures such as that of death, the devil, angels, fable creatures, animals, etc.[30] We can only accurately identify the character if we take recourse to the cultural code underlying the character's mask. Although none of us has ever seen the devil, we will without a doubt identify the character who appears with horns and a pitchfork as the devil, whereas someone from a different culture which is not familiar with our image of the devil will hardly be in a position to assign an identity to this figure.

Aside from makeup, the theater also makes use of the fixed mask. We distinguish forms of theater which make use exclusively of the fixed mask—such as the Greek theater—from those forms of theater which employ makeup as well as masks for respectively different functions—such as Nô theater, the Peking Opera, and the Katakali.

Masks are generally used in a great many cultures.[31] Their use is invariably limited to clearly defined situations—to celebrations,[32] rituals,[33] public executions,[34] and crime.[35] The mask is always produced and interpreted as a facial sign. A specific relationship exists between the appearance of a mask and that of the human face. For,

> the morphology of the human face without a mask is a contrasting member of the pair formed by it with the mask; the mask can be adequately understood (within the given artistic and technological culture) only on condition that analyses of it (or its "reading") will be based on the knowledge of the normative morphology of the particular facial type. The mask represents in this manner a sign . . . of an ambivalent nature: in the mask is reproduced, to a certain extent, deformation of the traits of a human face (it can be said that in the mask they are 'quoted'), which conserves the general similarity between the mask and the face, although the entire appearance of the mask indicates that it must be understood simultaneously as another face, opposed to the human one.[36]

The meaning that can be attached to the sign 'mask' that is—being an imitation or distortion—thus always related to the human face can be described in terms of a binary opposition: The mask either signifies a human being or a nonhuman being (God or a spirit, animal, ancestor). In both cases its function is to transform the wearer into someone he is not. In the social life of a culture makeup, i.e., the painted or tatooed face, is intended precisely to indicate the identity which is assigned to that person in this culture—which is why it can be judged as a sign of the existing social hierarchy on the basis of which the individual's identity is secured.[37] By contrast, the fixed mask removes its wearer from this real hierarchy: It does not allow him to appear as the person he is for the others based on his position in the community, but rather as a different person who does not belong in a comparable manner to this community.[38] By robbing him in this way of his real social identity as verified by his "normal" appearance, it isolates him from the community[39] and juxtaposes him to this as a fundamentally different person.[40]

 Consequently, the wearer of a mask no longer acts as himself, but rather on behalf of another for whom the mask is a sign; it is, therefore, not he, but rather the person signified by the mask who is accountable for his deeds. The real social subject of the person wearing the mask cannot be blamed for them precisely because his identity remains concealed behind the mask. It is not possible to find out who is portraying the figure signified by the mask because the mask prevents the person from being recognized.[41]

This is the conditio sine qua non for the use of the mask both in cults and in crime. In the former case it is not important who is hiding behind the mask of the ancestor, spirit, or animal, since for the audience it is only the presence of the mask that vouches for[42] the presence of what is signified by it. In the latter case, however, the masked person wants to disappear behind the mask in order not to be held accountable for the consequences of the deeds committed while wearing the mask.[43] To this extent, the impossibility of identifying the bearer of the mask may be assumed to be a basic condition for any and every use of masks: Anyone who puts on a mask loses his socially recognized identity and becomes anonymous. In a society, in other words, the fixed mask fulfills a function that is both the opposite of and similar to that of the painted or tatooed face. It is its opposite insofar as it prevents an identification of the masked person as a particular member of society, and similar to the extent that it first enables what is being portrayed by the bearer of the mask to be identified. Whereas the painted face is produced and interpreted as a sign of the unity of person and social role, it is precisely the difference and distance between person and role which is constitutive for the meaning of the mask; for the mask is always indicative of two subjects, namely, the one it signifies and the one it conceals.[44] Thus, whenever a mask is employed, it functions as a sign of transformation: the masked person is no longer identified as the person he is, but rather as the person signified by the mask,[45] although without being equated with the latter; the consciousness of the difference between the subject of the bearer of the mask and the person signified by the mask is maintained.

This also describes the basic function of the utilization of the mask in theater. The actor who wears a mask is not identified by the observer as actor A, but rather as character X signified by the mask, yet without any possibility of their being mistaken for each other. Wearing the mask would appear in this sense to be the fundamental theatrical process par excellence: whoever dons the mask signals to the attending community by this very act alone that he no longer wishes to be identified as himself, but rather as the person signified by the mask, and does not at the same time wish to be equated as a real social subject with the subject signified by the mask. The difference between the two subjects is thus neither eliminated nor ignored. A does not become X; rather, A portrays X. To this extent, the mask functions not merely as a sign for the face of character X, but simultaneously as a sign for the realization of the basic theatrical phenomenon, namely, that one person (A) plays another (X).[46] In this context the mask can be construed as one of the very first signs that are constitutive of the theater.[47]

The mask is employed above all in order to characterize character X. In this respect, in theater—as opposed to the social life of the surrounding culture—there is no difference between using makeup and wearing a mask: both of them denote the face of character X.

Although the two types of theater mask fulfill the same basic function, they differ fundamentally when it comes to additional functions and definitions. For, in those forms of theater which traditionally make use of the fixed mask, the cultic origins are by no means insignificant, even if the connection to the cult is eventually lost in later periods, without this however invalidating the use of the mask. In these forms of theater, the mask originally functioned as a sign for the ecstacy of the person wearing the mask, for his renunciation of his own, individual personality in deference to the god in question (e.g., of Dionysus). Here, the human being is not speaking and acting for himself, but rather he functions behind the mask, as a medium of the god: the god speaks and acts through him.[48] For this reason, the identifiable person of the actor also has to disappear completely behind the mask: the actor is absorbed by the character, without actually being or becoming the character. For, the mask as a nonface, as a sign for the face, refers precisely to the lack of a face and thus to the difference between the actor and the role—between the human being and the god.[49]

At a later date, a practical function was added to the cultic function of the mask: masks made it possible for a single actor to play various roles in succession.[50] For, since the mask functions as a sign which allows the character to be identified quickly and conclusively, switching this sign in itself indicates a change in roles as well: if mask X is exchanged for mask Y, the actor can no longer be identified as character X, but rather is unequivocally identified as character Y.[51]

The opportunity to enable unequivocal identification afforded by the fixed mask has important implications: whereas makeup can be used as a sign and expression of a quite specific individual personality, the meaning of a fixed mask can invariably only be constituted as the identification of one type.[52] This by no means manifests a deficiency characteristic of forms of theater that employ masks;[53] rather, this peculiarity would seem to be a condition in order for specific modes of portrayal to be made possible. It is constitutive, on the one hand, of extremely conventionalized forms of theater and, on the other, of specific forms of comic theater.[54] In these forms of theater the mask serves as an important instrument of the continuity of tradition because a quite specific theatrical type is always passed on with the mask from one generation to the next, whether it is the various characters of the shite in Nô theater,[55] or the stock of characters in Greek-Roman comedy. The mask thus helps to ensure the continuity of a theatrical tradition.[56]

Makeup can be applied in such a way that, if combined at any rate with the appropriate use of the other theatrical signs, it suggests to the audience that the actor is completely identified with character X and one is, at least at times, inclined to equate the two—a phenomenon which can repeatedly be observed and has been maintained in the history of bourgeois theater of illusion.[57] However, such an identification between the actor and his role cannot be made if the actor is wearing a mask. For he cannot persuade the audience to believe that the mask is in fact his face—the presence of the mask itself points to the fact that the actor is hiding his own face in order to be able to portray another person. No matter how much he "becomes part of" the role and subjectively identifies with it, the audience will not for its part be able to make this identification. The mask itself reminds the audience that it should bear in mind the difference between the actor and his role.[58]

Since the expression on a mask is fixed by definition, the actor wearing a mask also does not have the possibility of changing his "facial expression" with mimic signs, a possibility which the actor always has with a made-up face, no matter how heavily the makeup is applied. Therefore, an actor wearing a fixed mask will make use of the other kinesic signs, gestures, and movements in a particular manner. In forms of theater where masks are employed this constellation frequently engenders specific types of movement: skipping around, hopping, jumping, etc.—as is typical, for example, of the Arlecchino in the commedia dell'arte[59]—movements which in many cases even become a form of dancing.[60] Such a style of movement calls attention to the typical, nonindividual, indeed even nonhuman element embodied by the mask,[61] thus supporting the process which is aimed at having the audience identify the actor as character X.

Hairstyle

We shall now discuss "hairstyle" as the second system of specific signs to be interpreted in relation to the character's identity. "Hairstyle" is understood to be the special arrangement of the hair on the head as well as facial hair, i.e., beards.

It may initially come as a surprise to find hairstyle set aside as an independent sign system, since hair is usually dealt with in connection with the mask to the extent that it is mentioned at all in studies of theater history. In the latter it is normally described as merely one of the elements on which the mask is based. While this approach may appear to be legitimate and thus meaningful for the presentation of the theatrical codes of many—or perhaps even most—cultures and periods, such an approach is not justifiable in relation to the theatrical code as a system.[62] For, although it can be assumed that in most cases the meanings generated by the individual component signs—mask, hairstyle, and costume—constitute the overall meaning of the complex sign "external appearance" by mutually reinforcing and supplementing each other, it is nevertheless generally necessary to allow for the possibility that one or even two of the three systems (mask, hairstyle, costume) will not be involved or that each of the three systems produces a meaning which has to be regarded as an independent piece of information about the identity of character X. The first possibility is given, for example, when actors perform in black sweaters without wearing makeup but do make use of wigs of different colors (and perhaps with different lengths of hair as well). In this case, the way in which "mask" and "costume" are used indicates that they are not functioning as elements that constitute meaning,[63] and thus hairstyle becomes the single distinguishing feature related to the external appearance: The character's identity is, so to speak, given and/or alluded to by the color of the wig.

The second possibility is presumed to exist, for example, in Dürrenmatt's *The Physicists*. The costume, makeup, and wig indicate that the Beutler character regards himself as an early eighteenth-century figure, namely, Newton, as is specifically articulated in language at a later point. Being a mobile hairstyle, the wig in this case permits the person portraying Beutler to indicate when Beutler actually

wants to be taken for Newton—by keeping the wig on—and when he takes the
wig off he proceeds from the unspoken premise that the others know as well as
he does that he is not Newton. The wig thus becomes a sign which supplies an
important piece of information about the identity of the Beutler character, which
is neither supplemented nor reinforced by the two other sign systems. Here, the
character's identity can be adequately grasped only when the meanings constituted
by mask/costume, on the one hand, and hairstyle, on the other, have been understood and related to each other. It would therefore seem necessary to assume that
hairstyle is an independent sign system at the systemic level of the theatrical code.

The treatment of this sign system gives rise to problems that are similar to
those of the system of mask. For like the face and figure, the hair is first of all
a natural phenomenon: Whether or not someone has blond or black hair, curly or
straight hair, fine or thick hair, a heavy or light growth of beard, is not the result
of a communicative process, but rather the consequence of a natural, biological
process. If the hair is to be conceived of as a sign, then it can in this sense only
be interpreted as a "natural" sign, so to speak, of age (white hair/blond, brown
hair, etc.), race (curly blond hair/straight black hair, etc.) and gender (beard/no
beard; medium-length hair/very long hair). Yet, as in the case of the face and
figure, in many cultures hair has been interpreted not only as a sign of natural,
biological features, but as a sign of character traits as well.[64] However, whereas
the face in our culture is interpreted in terms of a whole series of traits (e.g.,
cleverness/stupidity; industriousness/laziness; sensuality/asceticism; openness/
dullness, etc.), the hair is regarded above all as a sexual sign and as a sign for
the presence of moral qualities in terms of the "good vs. evil" opposition, and/or
of particular traits in relation to these qualities.[65] The distinguishing features which
serve as a point of departure for the corresponding process of constituting meaning
are (1) the amount of hair, (2) the hair color, (3) the texture of the hair, and
(4) the length of the hair.[66]

The history of European culture is full of examples of such interpretations of
the hair. Thus a heavy growth of hair was interpreted, on the one hand, as a sign
of savageness/wildness, animal instinct, even of evil in the human being—devils
are usually portrayed with a lot of hair—and on the other as an expression of
exceptional strength and potency.[67] Red hair, especially in women, was regarded
as a sign of evil—red-haired women were often discriminated against as witches.[68]
At the same time, it was imagined that they owed their magic powers to their red
hair, and consequently cutting off the hair was enough to strip them of these
powers.[69] The juxtaposition of blond and black hair is based on a further stereotype:
For centuries, blond hair was regarded as the sign of innocence, black hair as the
sign of badness in a woman—and was portrayed as such in literature, dating even
as far back as the old folk tales.[70] In our century another stereotype has emerged
in Hollywood movies: blond curly hair or wavy hair here is considered to be a
sign of the great seductress, the "sex bomb."[71] The length of the hair also took
on a special interpretation over the course of the centuries: whereas some (e.g.,
the orthodox Christians) regard long hair on the head or a long beard as a sign
of piety, of a life in service to God, others (e.g., the Catholic church) see it as

an expression of sexual depravity and a wanton lifestyle.[72] In the story of Samson and Delilah, on the other hand, Samson's long hair is interpreted as being the source of his extraordinary strength: when his hair is cut off, he is robbed of his powers. Only after it has grown back to a certain length is his strength restored; the length of a person's hair functions here as a sign of his or her measure of strength.

As an outgrowth of the development of such cultural stereotypes which, for their part, are already the result of a communicative process,[73] certain natural phenomena are ascribed an ethical, moral, or religious value. In this process, natural facts become cultural facts and thus factors which have an effect in the social life of a culture. Since every member of a community normally strives for recognition, i.e., to be held in high regard as a representative of positive values valid in the community, hardly anyone will resign himself to being judged negatively simply because nature failed to give him blond hair, for example, or a full beard. For hair can be dyed, curled or straightened, cut, styled, and even completely replaced by a wig or false beard. However, this makes it possible for a person to conform as he sees fit to the culture's hierarchy of values grounded in the particular interpretation of hair as a natural phenomenon: A person's hairstyle indicates to the others which values they are supposed to find in him, and which identity is to be ascribed to him. The artificial styling of the hair in accordance with the hierarchy of values set by the cultural stereotypes can, in other words, make hair a cultural factor, and a sign which is consciously employed in communicative processes. The use of "hair" as a sign is nevertheless by no means limited to those processes of communication which are related to the hierarchy of values fixed by the cultural stereotypes, but rather is generally widespread in all communicative processes in which identity is shaped and developed. Because all distinguishing features of this sign system—in other words, the growth of hair, color, texture and length of the hair—can be changed at random, the hairstyle as artificially arranged hair is particularly well suited to functioning as a sign within the social hierarchy of a society. It is therefore hardly surprising to see hairstyle being used in individual cultures as a sign for the widest variety of social relationships,[74] and in the following an outline will thus be given of the most important and/or most frequently used sign functions of this type performed by hairstyle.

Hairstyle can serve as a sign of the wearer's *membership in a particular class.* The history of European culture contains many examples of various rules that apply to the way hair is worn or arranged in individual strata: Members of the nobility, the bourgeoisie, the landed gentry were recognizable by special hairstyles which could only be worn by members of the respective stratum.[75]

Hairstyle can also indicate *social status.* Whenever the fashion in beards changed in antiquity, the rules for slaves changed as well: If the free citizen was clean-shaven, the slave had to grow a beard—and if the free citizen wore a beard, the slave had to shave.[76]

In many cultures, hairstyle also has the important function of distinguishing between the status of married women and that of unmarried maidens: Among the Eskimos, for example, married women wear two braids on each side, whereas the unmarried girl ties the braids up on each side. For centuries in Jewish culture unmarried girls wore their hair naturally, whereas married women had to cut it off and wear a wig.[77]

The hairstyle can also function as a "non-natural" sign of its wearer's *gender*, if the culture prescribes differing hairstyles for girls and boys, women and men. Whereas in our culture the only hairstyles that could respectively be worn by members of the male and female sexes were clearly identified until a few years ago, this function of hairstyle is becoming obsolete today: It often happens that the same hairstyle is worn by members of both sexes.

Hairstyles can also differ *in terms of the wearer's profession*. In nearly all cultures there are special rules, at least for priests and warriors, governing the arrangement of the hair.[78]

In addition, a person's hairstyle can be an indication of *nationality*. For the individual cultures have developed very different ideas and rules with regard to the way the hair is (traditionally) worn, and, as a consequence, it is very easy to recognize foreigners because of the particular way in which they wear their hair and beard.

Hairstyle can also function as a sign for a particular *regional* origin. Thus, for example, the traditional hairstyle of a Frisian girl will clearly differ from that worn by girls in the Black Forest or in the Bavarian Alps.[79]

The way in which hair is worn often indicates membership in a particular *religious community* if certain rules are prescribed for the hair. Thus, for example, the orthodox Jew can be recognized by the long curls of hair at his temples; the followers of Buddha by their shaven heads. The Catholic priest is beardless, with a shaven crown symbolizing the crown of thorns, whereas the orthodox Christian priest shaves neither his head nor his beard, allowing both to grow long. Since nearly every religion has well-defined rules as to how the hair should be worn,[80] the function of hairstyle as a sign identifying the wearer as a member of this specific religious community takes on a special meaning.

It may be surprising to find that the hair can also function as a sign of membership of a *political party*. However, in nineteenth-century Europe at least, it had to perform this function in very different ways. In August 1830, for example, the people of Brussels marched through the streets singing the popular song "Amour Sacré de la Patrie" from Auber's opera *La Muette de Portici*, and the men had glued false mustaches on their faces as signs for a national uprising. In July of the same year, false mustaches were already being worn in Paris as a demonstrative sign for revolt.[81]

It also bears mentioning here that the hair can function as a sign for *differing views of art*. On the occasion of the famous "Bataille d'Hernani" note was first taken that those who wore beards were advocates of Romanticism and they were then combatted. Victor Hugo writes the following about the meaning of the beard at this time: "The beard was declared ugly, stupid, dirty, unworldly, diseased, repulsive, ridiculous, antinational, Jewish, atrocious, abominable, hideous, and what was the ultimate insult, Romantic!"[82]

The way a person wears his hair can also be used to indicate a special *situation*.

For example, in some cultures a certain hairstyle is worn during wartime not only by the soldiers and/or warriors, but also by the civilian population. After the state of war has come to an end, people go back to wearing their hair as they always have. Moreover, the hair can also be arranged in a very specific way for certain festive occasions or in mourning. In Jewish culture of former times shaving the hair on the head and the beard was considered a sign of mourning. It is said of Caesar, on the other hand, that he once let his beard grow as a sign of mourning.[83]

In a variety of ways, a person's hair is also utilized to call attention to *deviant behavior*. After the French liberation following the Second World War, for example, women accused of fraternizing with German occupation forces had their heads shaved as punishment: A woman's bald head was an indication to everyone that she had been involved with the enemy. She was clearly marked—in this case, by the lack of hair.

However, an identity is not only fixed and assumed by the fact that the hair is arranged to adhere with the rules that apply to the respective social position and in some cases in accordance with the hierarchy of values based on cultural stereotypes; rather, the identity may be created by a violation of these rules or even by the specific manner in which the rules are followed. This manifests not only the "personal" but also the "social" identity. It comes to light especially in the alternative between conformity and violation, and in relation to this alternative, the respective concrete form a person has chosen.

Adherence to the rules and violation of the rules in a society are subject to different evaluations, depending on the culture: In cultures which are determined by a clearcut, rigid social hierarchy to which the hairstyle is clearly related, a violation of the rule is virtually unthinkable.[84] It would in any case have to be considered an expression of revolt, a sign for rejecting the community. In such cultures individuality can only be manifested by adopting a particular mode of adhering to the rules—for example, in the alternative between an orderly or disorderly arrangement of the hair, a simple or imaginative hairstyle, etc.[85] In a culture such as our own, on the other hand, in which there are no binding rules and only a few unspoken rules applying to the hair, nearly every hairstyle can be regarded as the sign of a completely individual identity. The hairstyle selected and its respective condition themselves tell us something about the person, his attitudes, values, taste, and perhaps even his particular moods. In the case of subject A, unkempt hair can be indicative of his values—A considers hairstyles secondary: if he were fixing his hair he would be wasting time which he could be using for something more worthwhile. In the case of subject B, by contrast, it refers to a state of mind—B normally assigns great value to a well-kept appearance, which is why the unkempt hair tends to indicate that he is depressed. Since in our culture the possibilities for a completely individual hairstyle are generally many times greater than in former periods or other cultures, the potential for individual meanings that can be taken on by hairstyle as a sign is considerably increased. The hairstyle can thus also always be interpreted as a sign of the person's individual identity.

Actor A's hairstyle denotes the hairstyle of character X. With regard to character

X the hairstyle is capable of fulfilling all of the sign functions mentioned. In this context, a distinction must be made between strongly conventionalized forms of theater and theatrical codes which are based on the codes applicable in the other cultural systems. In the strongly conventionalized forms of theater (Peking Opera, Nô, Kabuki) the individual features—growth of hair, color, texture, length of the hair, and kind of hairstyle[86]—and their possible combinations are assigned fixed meanings which the audience has to know if it wants to be able to attribute an identity to character X. The process of semantic constitution in Western theater, on the other hand, is grounded in the knowledge of the cultural stereotypes and of the other sign functions performed by the hairstyle in the culture in question. In this case, character X can have an identity assigned to him because every audience has recourse to the possible meanings he knows this sign can take in order to interpret the sign hairstyle. Thus, for example, white hair (or the white wig) of actor A is interpreted with reference to the natural sign 'hair' as being the sign for old age in character X. The blond hair of the actress portraying Käthchen of Heilbronn will be interpreted as a sign for Käthchen's purity and innocence[87] if one refers to the cultural stereotypes in force. If the actor has a shaven pate, the audience will identify the character as a monk or Catholic priest, depending on the costume, by referring to the social sign functions of the hair; if, on the other hand, the actor has short hair parted on one side with Brill cream or wet-gel, the audience will identify the character he is playing as a vain buffoon, a slick dandy, or a similar type by drawing on what they know from personal experience.

The initial, spontaneous process of identification in this case is always based on the culturally determined, everyday experiences and knowledge of the members of the surrounding culture. To this extent, hairstyle is capable of performing all of the same sign functions in the theater that it has in the culture in question. Moreover, in the theater it can also be assigned an "historical" sign function, as it were. The hairstyle in this case can function as a sign of the period from which the character comes. A baroque pigtail or full-bottomed wig, snake locks or an upswept hairdo make it easier to associate the characters on the stage with a certain period and thus facilitates their identification.[88] Aside from the functions already mentioned, the hairstyle can—like all other signs discussed thus far—also take on a *symbolic function*. Blond hair, for example, may not only identify its wearer as an innocent maiden, in accordance with certain cultural stereotypes, but may signify innocence as such. Such processes of symbolization are particularly common with regard to hairstyle, due to the reference to cultural stereotypes, which in many cases themselves harbor similar tendencies toward symbolization.

In Western theater, however, the "hair code" also does not by any means always coincide with the hair code of the surrounding culture. It is entirely possible for the theater to develop its own specific, theatrical hair code, the meanings of which cannot be constituted solely through recourse to the hair code which applies in the culture in question. To the extent that a hair code is "fixed"—which is to say, one which applies, universally and in principle, to a special theatrical norm—it is tied to the corresponding "mask code." Thus, for example, in Greek and Roman theater, certain wigs had to be worn with the individual tragic and comic masks, and the wigs differed significantly from one another in terms of color, length, texture of the "hair" and the way in which it was arranged.[89] I am not aware of any "fixed" hair code that is not linked to certain masks in the theatrical standards of Western theater.

In the twentieth century, on the other hand, it more frequently happens that in staging a production a specific hair code is established, the meanings of which can only be gathered from the overall context of the performance. If, for instance, to recall our introductory example, the actors are wearing green, red, blue, and yellow wigs and black T-shirts, without makeup, then the specific meaning of the individual wigs can only be constituted if the color symbolism that is developed in the course of the production can be decoded on the basis of the use of other signs—language, gesture, stage design, multicolored lighting, etc.[90] When the actor first appears on stage, in other words, the audience is not in a position to assign the character so much as a temporary identity; he will have to wait as the performance proceeds in order to derive the meaning of the red, green, blue, and yellow wigs from the specific combination of the various signs and to identify the respective characters. This is naturally an extreme example, not only because a specific theatrical hair code is given, but also because the hairstyle functions as the only sign constituting the appearance. This makes the matter of identifying the character more complicated.

In most cases, however, the performance of all these sign functions listed above for hair is supported by the signs makeup and costume. Consequently, the threefold perception of signs makes it possible to identify the character more easily and reliably. However, it is entirely conceivable—and a known fact—that there may be theatrical codes as well as individual productions in which one or the other of these three signs disintegrates, making it necessary to attribute diverse meanings to the signs which may very well be contradictory or which may appear at first glance to bear no relation whatsoever to each other. Thus, for example, the costume can assume the historical and social function—manifesting period, class, social status, etc., of the character—whereas the mask takes on a symbolic function—in which the two halves of the face are made up differently and thus point to the "two faces" of the character involved. Furthermore, hairstyle and mask may possess an individual sign function—to be understood as expressing the particular individuality of the character. Any number of other combinations are possible— examples of which can be found in practice in the history of twentieth century theater—two of which we have already mentioned in the introduction to this section. Complete identification of the character will, in any case, only be possible if all three elements and their specific combinations are taken into account.

Costume

Of all the elements which constitute the actor's external appearance, the costume is without doubt the most important component. For even though masks and wigs can be changed as easily and quickly as costumes, the costume is predominant, if only because it is easier to perceive in purely quantitative terms than makeup or hairdo. Therefore, as a rule the audience's first identification of the character is based on the costume: The purple cloak indicates that the actor is a king, a habit marks him as a monk, armor as a knight, the patchwork costume as a harlequin. Costume and role in this constellation are related to one another in a very special way.

The specific nature of this relationship already appears to be developed and ordained by the social meaning of clothing: The functions of theatrical costume largely coincide with the functions which clothing can fulfill in social life. Based on this characteristic finding, Laver comes to the conclusion that "it would not be far off the mark to say that all clothes for special occasions and stylized clothes of any kind are, in effect, theatrical costume. We are at least on safe ground in suggesting that all clothes are *in origin* theatrical costumes."[91] This assertion implicitly indicates the special relation between clothes and social role as the justification for concluding that all clothes are theatrical costumes in origin. For, "clothes for special occasions"—such as work clothes, leisure wear, ballroom gown, mourning attire, etc.—can be described more precisely as clothing for specific social roles. In order to be able to play a certain role within a society it is necessary to have a special type of clothing which identifies the person wearing it as playing this role: in our culture the uniform authenticates the policeman, the white coat the physician, the evening gown the opera guest, the black dress the mourner, etc. "Costume" and "role" thus also form a unit in social life.[92]

In many conceptions of identity the concept of social role is directly related to that of identity. Levita, for example, speaks of the "role character of identity"[93] and accordingly defines identity as a "specific package of roles."[94] Since he regards a person's role in a social system as the result of a status or a position which that person holds in this social system, the person's behavior in this role can be predicted with a relatively high degree of accuracy. Taking on a role or having it conferred on one thus gives rise to a whole series of specific expectations with regard to the behavior that the person will manifest in this role. Since the identity of an individual member of a society is never defined by a single role, but rather invariably by a variety of roles, namely, a set of roles,[95] his identity is fixed with the respective role set.

Gross and Stone define the role in a quite similar manner, "as a series of coinciding attitudes which are mobilized by an announced and confirmed identity in a certain social situation."[96] Identity can therefore only be acquired, on the one hand, if a role is adopted and, on the other, if a role is conferred.[97]

If identity originates in the reciprocity of adopting and conferring the respective role, it becomes particularly important for the establishment and confirmation of the individual's identity to announce in no uncertain terms to the others which role he plans to play in each case, so that they will be able to accord him this intended role and not some other role which he is not at all willing to adopt. In other words, he needs a clear-cut means of identification which puts the others in a position to recognize the respective role beyond any doubt.

Clothing in particular functions as one such means of identifying oneself, and Goffmann also refers to it in this sense as an "identity document."[98] For clothing informs the others relatively quickly and completely about the role that its wearer wishes to play and in this way gives rise to certain expectations with regard to his future behavior. The special relationship we have thus determined to exist between clothes and roles has its roots in a society in the specific functions fulfilled by the role in developing and conferring an identity. In a similar manner Stone characterizes the three stages in which an identity is acquired in terms of "dressing in," "dressing up," and "dressing out."[99]

In other words, clothes point to the respective social role assigned to the wearer and function in this way as an important variable in the process of establishing and/or stabilizing his identity. Analogously, the costume points to the respective theatrical role played by its wearer and functions in this way as an important variable in the process that serves to establish or develop the identity of this character. However, whereas the formation of a person's social identity depends on the adoption of many different roles, and thus various types of clothing,[100]—a character's identity can be indicated by a single costume; neither the figures of the commedia dell'arte nor the heroes in Greek tragedy ever changed their costumes. The costume which they wore for the entire course of the performance represented the means of identifying them and of certifying this identity for their role.[101] In other words, the external appearance constituted by the clothes could indeed serve as a clear-cut indication of the character's identity.

It is also possible of course in theater, just as in social life, to change costumes and thus their corresponding functions. For even the character's identity can in some cases be developed with the help of a large number of different roles to which various costumes—and not only various actions—may respectively correspond: thus, for example, Lear's transformation from the almighty ruling monarch to the helpless beggar is expressed and visibly documented by the change in his external appearance.[102]

In any case, the costume—regardless of whether it is changed or not—has the function of indicating the character's identity, just as clothes in social life have the function of referentially signifying the respective social role of the person wearing them.

Clothes and costumes can fulfill this general function because they are a specific system for the generation of meaning, the units of which are formed by material, color, and form.[103] With the help of these units, clothing and costumes can produce a series of different meanings which, however, are all related to the identity of the person and/or the character. It may be possible to establish and stabilize the person's identity, for which the clothes are intended to be a sign, with these meanings individually, severally, and as a whole.

Although, in line with Flugel's pioneering work on clothing in the psychological and sociological literature on this subject, the functions to be fulfilled by clothing are usually subdivided into three parts—namely, protection, decoration, and shame[104]—we shall proceed on the basis of a bipartite division into practical and symbolic functions.[105]

The practical functions that are served by providing protection against heat, cold, and damp, or even against malevolent spirits, are irrelevant for our study, since they lose their quality as practical functions in the transition to theater and are accordingly transformed into symbolic functions.

The symbolic functions with which we shall be exclusively concerned in the following discussion are defined as those which are intended to serve as a means of identifying the characters. In fulfilling these functions, clothing is capable of functioning as the sign for the natural phenomena of *age* and *gender*. In most cultures a clear-cut distinction is made not only between children's clothing and that of adults; rather, there is also a special type of clothing for very old people. The latter may differ from that of other adults merely through the use of a specific accessory or by reserving certain colors for them—for example, dark colors, which was customary in European culture until just a few decades ago and still persists in some rural areas—as well as certain fabrics or cuts of clothing.

In nearly all cultures clothing is designed to be strictly gender specific. Whereas it may be characteristic in some cultures for women to wear skirts and for men to wear trousers, precisely the opposite may be the case in another culture. In other words, there is no generally typical women's or men's clothing; rather, the differences in clothing for the genders are determined in different ways by each culture. Gender-specific clothing is therefore not attributable to natural, biologically given differences, but in each case to culturally conditioned differences.

Since every culture has its own clothing customs and dress codes, clothing can of course also be an indication of *nationality* and *regional origin*. It fulfills this function most visibly in the forms of clothing which are for the most part not affected by changes in fashion, namely, national and regional costumes. We recognize the Eskimo, Mexican, Bedouin, Dutchman by the clothes they wear, as well as the Texan, Amish, or Canadian farmer. As a rule, these national or regional costumes are able to fulfill a number of additional social functions as well, which, however, can only be recognized by people who come from this country or live in the respective region. For our purposes, the function that is most relevant for us in this context is precisely the one which allows outsiders—and in this sense the theater audience—to perceive and identify the wearers as belonging to a particular national or regional group.

Clothing frequently functions as a sign of the person's *membership in a particular religion*. While the Christian monk, for example, can be recognized by his brown and black robe, the Buddhist monk is identifiable from his yellow vestment. Corresponding differences equally apply to the priests of these religions and, in particular periods, also to their temple guards, knights of the order, etc., completely independently of their national membership. In situations where the demonstration of one's faith serves as the most important feature identifying a person, clothing has to be capable of visibly documenting this feature.[106]

Within many societies clothing serves to distinguish between the various *social classes, castes or strata*. In European culture of the Middle Ages a sumptuary law was applied which prescribed in detail the type of clothing which could be worn or had to be worn by members of the individual classes of society.[107] In this way, the members of the various classes were visibly marked as such for all to see, and this facilitated their dealings with one another insofar as the clothing indicated in each case which rules of conduct should be followed vis-à-vis the person wearing them.

This is also the purpose served in many cultures by the practice of distinguishing the *respective station*, with particular reference to the oppositions, e.g., free/bonded, married woman/single girl. P. Bogatyrev, for example, has shown that one can tell from the bonnet worn by women in a certain area of Slovakia whether the woman is married, unmarried, or a single mother. The bonnet informs all inhabitants of this region about the status of the woman wearing it and thus prescribes a specific form of conduct when dealing with her; the social role is ascribed by means of the clothing in a manner that everyone can recognize.[108]

One very widespread function of clothing is to pinpoint one's *occupation*, namely in the uniform, the clothing worn in the various skilled trades, and work clothes. In our culture, for example, policemen, railroad conductors, and mailmen are clearly recognizable by their uniforms, no matter where they may be. The white clothing worn by chemists, physicians, druggists, on the other hand, can only serve to identify them within a particular area, whereas the blue work clothes in many occupations only allow the person to be identified if, in addition to the context involved, the implements and objects employed in each case are also taken into consideration. These varied forms of occupational clothing differ from one another above all with respect to the degree of certainty with which predictions can be made regarding the role involved. Uniforms invariably permit the most precise prognoses, and indeed not only with regard to the wearer's occupation, but also in many cases with regard to the rank he holds in the relevant hierarchy: whereas the whole uniform marks the occupation, individual parts of the uniform, such as cap, shoulder pads, stripes on the sleeve, etc., are an indication of the person's rank. For this reason, uniforms are not only employed as occupational clothing, but rather are widespread in every kind of hierarchically structured *social organization*, whether fraternities and sororities or Boy Scouts, sports associations or political organizations, carnival associations or secret societies. Types of clothing that are comparable to uniforms are to be encountered everywhere.

Membership in the widest variety of *social groups*, whether political, social, artistic, or otherwise in nature, is often documented by clothing: neckscarf and Che beret, open-wing collar and trilby serve to identify their wearers as members of a particular group just as much as the clothes worn by outlaws or prisoners.

This function is closely linked to that of *delineating the situation*. In our culture various types of clothing are often called for in various types of situations. We have special attire for weddings and funerals, press receptions and discos, church and swimming pool, street clothes and clothes we wear to bed, etc.[109] In other words, the clothing provides information about the situation in which the wearer finds himself or which he has in mind. This clothing also functions for the most part as a regulating factor in the interaction. You would not, for example, tell a joke you have just heard to an acquaintance dressed in mourning clothes. If anything, you will avoid conveying your own good mood to him and instead conduct yourself in a more or less serious and dignified manner. For the clothes supply information not only about the anticipated behavior of the wearer, but also about the repertoire of potential behavior in dealing with him.

Clothes not only serve to characterize the overall social identity of the person wearing them, but can also signify the person's very special, *"individual" identity.* This individual identity can only be established in the context of a particular culture. In a culture such as that of the Hopi Indians, for example, who place the highest value on a "good heart," something which a person who is abandoned and without clothing is in the best position to prove, this individual identity will manifest itself in a fundamentally different manner than in a culture such as that of the Kwiakutl, whose highest values are beauty, physical strength, and wealth, which can be manifested above all by physical appearance, that is, by a specific manner of dress. For the culturally conditioned "body image" in each case not only influences the development of the general social identity, but equally that of the individual social identity.[110]

With regard to Western culture, Flugel attempted to compile and catalogue the individual differences that can manifest themselves in clothing as an expression of respective attitudes toward the generally valid values. He also attempted to differentiate among them in terms of the behavior manifested in clothing in terms of types—"rebellious," "resigned," "unemotional," "prudish," "dutiful," "protected," "supported," "sublimated," and "self-satisfied"—each of which fashions and produces a different body image that can generally be recognized from the clothing worn by that type.[111]

Individual differences that remain consistent over a long period of time apply not only to the attitude toward existing values, but also to personal taste. In addition, we have to take into account individual differences that only appear in the form of temporary phenomena, such as moods and emotions. With regard to the moods, Ethiopian culture has developed an intriguing system of communication: with the help of various drapings of the toga, the wearer signals whether his mood is sad or exuberant, self-confident or timid, downcast or happy.[112] In our culture, on the other hand, which does not have an equivalent system, the mood can only be gathered from the way in which one is dressed—which, however, can in turn be interpreted on "the basis of type." It seems that joy/happiness and fear/sadness in particular are manifested in clothing behavior: A happy, open, gregarious person will be more inclined to loosen his clothing or take it off altogether than will a person who is feeling miserable and abandoned.[113] "When we are miserable and depressed, we feel we need more clothes than when we are happy. Clothes are portable houses which have grown around us like the shell of a snail."[114] In other words, clothing can to this extent be employed and interpreted as a sign of passing emotions and temporary states of affect. It therefore functions also in this respect as an important factor regulating interaction processes.

The meanings the system of clothing is capable of evoking thus apply above all to the subject and intersubjectivity levels[115] and are all geared to establishing the wearer's identity.

Whereas clothing in social life can also always denote a practical function, it loses this quality when it becomes a theatrical costume. The theatrical costume always denotes the clothing of character X. From this it follows that in relation to character X it is capable of taking on and performing all of the sign functions that clothing fulfills with reference to its wearers in social life. Moreover, the theatrical costume is capable of exercising a whole series of additional sign functions.

Since the costume in theater has no practical function to fulfill,[116] wearing pieces of clothing which primarily serve such practical functions—such as a raincoat or winter or summer clothing—has a fundamentally different meaning here. They can, for example, indicate the climatic region or the season in which the dramatic work is set, or can be used as a medium for the characterization of the character. Thus, for example, light or heavy, warm or stiff clothing, in the context of the performance, is to be interpreted as a sign of a particular character type (in Flugel's sense) or a temporary psychic state in character X. The transformation of practical functions into sign functions in any case permits a multitude of possibilities for different applications and interpretations.

Aside from the so-called geographic-climatic sign function, the theatrical costume can also take on a historical function in many cases, for it indicates the period in which the relevant performance takes place. Consequently, it can clearly be maintained that a historical costume is capable of signifying the period in which the play would be situated, yet we cannot, conversely, draw the conclusion that a historical costume always has to fulfill the function of providing information about the period. For the historical costume can also be employed as a means of characterizing the character. Based on specific cultural codes, a historical type— such as the "Renaissance man," "Rococco doll," "turn-of-the-century entrepreneur," and so forth—is often equated with a particular type of character.

Furthermore, the theatrical costume can draw on mythological codes which govern the appearance of gods, angels, devils, figures from fables, and animals. A mythological costume of this kind is able to indicate, on the one hand, that the character is supposed to be a mythological figure—as was often the case in medieval and baroque theater—but on the other hand also that a character which does not portray a mythological figure has certain traits in common with the mythological figure involved. In other words, the mythological sign function can also be employed for a more precise characterization of character X.

The use of costume as a means of specific characterization was developed above all in Western theater in this century and in a special way. All of the sign functions at one's disposal can be drawn on for this purpose: if a young girl, for example, is wearing the dark clothes normally worn by old women, this can tell us something about the character of this figure in the same way that a woman's costume worn by a male figure has a particular meaning. National or regional costumes can refer to a character trait signified as a stereotype of the particular nation or region, or ascribed to the members of the given occupation, and so forth. The characterization of the role by means of such media usually concerns not only isolated qualities of the character, but rather all the contours of the conception of that role, as it were. Jessner's famous portrayal of Hamlet in the tuxedo, for ex-

ample, with which the tradition of a specific costume code of this type was founded
in our theaters, refers to the topicality of the character in that the tuxedo identifies
Hamlet as being a contemporary of those in the audience who are also wearing
tuxedos.

The cowhide cloak which Jocasta wore in Hans Neuenfels's Frankfurt production of *Oedipus* led the audience to see in this figure primarily the milk- and
life-giving mother animal, characteristics which necessarily had to be highly relevant, especially in view of Oedipus's relationship to Jocasta.[117]

In addition to the sign functions which are geared to establishing and developing
the character's identity, the costume is also capable of performing general symbolic functions which are not related exclusively to the character, but rather to
the entire performance. Through the use of similarities and contrasts in color, line,
or ornamentation, the costume can point to the presence of and changes in particular relationships between the characters or underline the meaning of a character. Thus, for example, the main characters might wear bright, colorful costumes,
whereas the so-called secondary or supporting characters are confined to wearing
"colorless," muddy tones.[118]

In addition, special links can be established between the costumes of the characters and the stage decoration—especially by means of the shade of color employed. These links can point to the overall atmosphere of the performance or
even particular ideas expressed or symbolized in it.[119] In all of these functions,
and they are all valid with regard to the totality of a performance, the theatrical
costume goes far beyond the functions exercised by clothing in social life.

The respective theatrical code of a period governs which of the sign functions
that theatrical costumes can perform in theory are in fact used, which of them
are to be considered dominant, and which are subordinate. This is a question, in
other words, which can only be answered at the levels of norm and speech. In
Greek tragic theater, for example, the dominant sign function the costume had
was to distinguish between the tragic hero, who wore a special garment that was
common only in the theater, and the other figures, who wore everyday Athenian
dress. In the religious medieval plays, by contrast, the costume served primarily
to differentiate between the biblical figures recognizable from specific and in part
liturgical dress and the "common" figures such as soldiers, merchants, etc., who
wore contemporary costumes. In the commedia dell'arte, on the other hand, the
dominant function of the costume was to characterize the various figures as types.
Nineteenth-century bourgeois theater emphasized the full-fledged social and historical function of costume—a development which had already begun in the theater
of Enlightenment, first reached its climax with the costume reform of Count Brühl
and was finally developed to perfection in the Meininger theater. The various
forms of avant-garde theater at the beginning of this century, however, primarily
developed the general, symbolic function of the costume.[120] The theatrical costume
is therefore entirely capable of fulfilling all of the sign functions mentioned, but
usually only a limited number of them are actually realized, and specific dominants
are at the same time formed.[121]

For this reason, the costume code of the theater does not in any way coincide with the dress code of the culture in question. The various forms of Oriental theater which have repeatedly been cited here have developed costume codes specific to theater which are completely distinct from the rest of social life. The color, ornamentation, and accessories of costume in the Peking Opera, for example, have meanings which cannot be grasped on the basis of a knowledge of the dress code of the culture in question, but rather have to be learned as special meanings, valid only within the theatrical code of the Peking Opera.

Even if Western theater has hardly ever developed a costume code completely integral to the theater, it nevertheless often draws on costume codes that, at least in part, are special—as we have clearly seen from our brief historical overview. The meanings constituted by it, however, can usually be grasped with the help of knowledge related to both general cultural codes and dress codes that are currently or were formerly valid in our culture.[122]

As already pointed out in the previous chapter, the costume stands in relation, on the one hand, to the two other sign systems that make up the external appearance, namely, those of makeup and the hair, and on the other, to the gestural and proxemic signs. For both the type of gesture and the type of movement through space depend on the costume. A distinction has to be made between movements which are imposed by the costume and those which are called for by the costume. A skin-tight dress and high heels, for example, do not permit any long strides to be made; a whalebone corset and farthingale permit only measured, upright movements. In contrast, an Empire-style dress will certainly permit big steps and quick movements in a bent-over position; however, gestures of this type would not seem appropriate in the social role signified by this dress. Such discrepancies are one of the many sources of comic effect on stage: the costume calls for a particular form of behavior in the role that, however, is not forthcoming in the gestural behavior.[123] The discrepancy between what is called for by the costume and the gestural behavior on stage, however, does not always serve to create comical situations, but is also frequently employed as a medium for characterizing the figure. Thus, the character's identity emerges precisely from the fact that the costume and gestural behavior are derived from different social or situational contexts, without its being possible to convey them in combination.[124] The possibility of a contradiction, or at least of a discrepancy between the identity signified by the actor's external appearance and his actions calls our attention to the presence of an additional, special problem grounded in the relationship between these two sign systems.

Until now we have assumed that the actor's external appearance establishes the identity of his character. This assertion, however, has to be modified and rendered more precise. For the external appearance only provides the outline of an identity, sketching the contours of a role that, in concrete form, arouses expectations which have to be met. This concretization is performed by the actor through his actions. The linguistic and paralinguistic, mimic, gestural, and proxemic signs he produces fill the role outlined by the external appearance with concrete, individual life. The character's identity, in other words, only takes shape in the course of a process in which the various sign systems related to the character enter into relationship with one another. Whereas the external appearance in this process represents the identity that can be separated from the actor's individuality and can be transposed to any actor embodying this role, the signs produced by the actor represent the identity of the character who is constituted by every actor in a different way that is tied to his specific individuality. For two different actors may very well—at least theoretically, and this would be an extreme case—try to develop the identity of a character not only with the same words, but also with the same emphases, pauses, gestures, and steps. However, since each of these actors possesses a different individuality, a different voice, and a different physical quality,[125] these accents, pauses, gestures, and steps, while practiced formally in a similar fashion, can never be the same in concrete terms.[126]

The identity of a character, in other words, is always developed as the product of a sign process, and indeed as that meaning that is constituted, on the one hand, with the help of the immutable signs of external appearance that can be reproduced in the same way, and on the other, by the signs which have the capacity for qualitative change, depending on the individuality of the actor who creates them through his activity. Consequently, a character's identity cannot be fully constituted if the spectator considers only the signs creating his appearance and produced by the actor's activity; rather, the specific relationships in which the two kinds of signs can come together also have to be recognized and interpreted as elements that constitute meaning in relation to the character's identity.

3. Spatial Signs

❑ ❐ ❑ In the introductory chapter we described and defined theater, reduced to its minimal conditions, as follows: actor A portrays character X, while observer S looks on. All of the signs we have discussed so far refer to the special relationship between A and X. The actor's appearance and activity function as signs of X's appearance and activity. Therefore, these signs also implicitly refer to the relationship between X and S, because, whereas the actor produces them in order to signify X, the audience interprets them in order to be able to constitute their meaning as character X. In other words, they are signs which apply, on the one hand, to the relationship between A and X and, on the other, to the relationship between X and S.

By contrast, spatial signs refer to the above theatrical triangle in a fundamentally different way. For they apply first of all to the general question of where A/X/S even takes place—in other words, the question of setting: is theater being performed in a church or in a market square, for example, in a pub or in a meadow, in a factory or on a farm, in a market hall or in a special theater building?

The second question involved in the issue of spatial signs concerns how the space in which A/X/S takes place is divided: how are the audience S and the actors A positioned in relation to each other? Is the space provided for A circular and that for S laid out in concentric circles around it, or is the space for A square, with three sides of this square set aside for S? In other words, are we dealing with an amphitheater or a Shakespearean stage, a proscenium or theater in the round?

Finally, the third question that arises in connection with spatial signs is that of the special segment of space in which A acts in order to portray X—the question of so-called stage space.

The spatial signs are thus related to the overall triangle A/X/S as well as to the relationship between A and S and also to that between A and X (and in this sense also to the relation between X and S). The first two questions hinge on an investigation of the problem of the way the theatrical space is designed, and the third calls for an examination of the elements that are fixed with the stage space, namely, decoration, props, and lighting.

Since spatial signs can signify theater in a wide variety of ways, it would seem to make sense to begin by looking into those functions of the architectonic sign system that theater is generally capable of performing, before going on to the second step of examining the specific variants in which these general functions may manifest themselves in the various areas of theater. In other words, we first have to clarify the two general questions of (1) how space functions as a system which generates meaning and (2) what the basic categories are to which the meanings generated by space can be related.

In order to be able to answer these questions, we shall first review the functions which space is in principle capable of fulfilling. Every space can be regarded as a potentially human environment, regardless of whether it is a "natural" space such as the sea or the forest or one which has been created by human beings, such as a building or square.[1] In this capacity it can be considered a potential field of human activity in that, like every spatial object, every space gives rise to or permits certain activities. One can enter a building through a door, climb stairs, look through a window, sit down on a chair, lie down on a bed, drink out of a glass, cut with a knife, and so forth. To the extent that a space or spatial object allows human activity to take place, it also refers to this activity. In other words, it can signify the activity made possible by it. Since we cannot list all of the activities that are in principle conceivable, we shall couch this observation in generalized terms by saying that a space or spatial object is capable of signifying those practical functions that can be fulfilled in it, on it, or with it.

I may, on the other hand, interpret the location of a school building next to the church to mean that, in the society in question, school as an institution is particularly closely linked to the institution of church. Alternately, I may interpret a Quonset hut as opposed to a comfortable brick house in terms of the social or economic status of the people who live there, or think I can recognize from the basic layout of a church or temple what religious ideas are involved. In such cases, I am understanding space not as a sign for the practical functions that can be fulfilled in it, but rather as a sign of symbolic functions which have in one way or another been performed there.[2]

Since spatial settings are established by society as a whole, by social institutions, or by individuals and/or groups of individuals, the symbolic functions fulfilled in the process can be related to the society as a whole, to the institution, or to the individuals or groups of individuals involved. To the extent that a spatial setting is interpreted with regard to society as a whole, it can be regarded as a sign of the values and ideas that apply and prevail in it: If, however, it is interpreted in relation to institutions, individuals, and groups of individuals, it functions as a sign of their status within society as well as of the values and ideas that are accepted and propagated by them respectively.

In a city, for example, the location, condition, and furnishing of the buildings which house the government and medical facilities can be interpreted with regard to the values "political power" and "health" or, as the case may be, "social responsibility" as well as their ranking in the respective hierarchy of values of the society living in the city.[3] On the other hand, the possible division of the city into "better" neighborhoods and slums, for example, reveals something about the productivity- or class-based ideology prevalent in this society.[4]

If the church is located in the center of a town, this speaks for the overriding status occupied by the church as an institution. By contrast, the division of the church, for example, into an altar area reserved for the priest and space set aside for the parishioners points to the special status enjoyed by the priest vis-à-vis the parishioners in this institution and thus to the specific form of interaction that is called for in this space. Finally, the idea of Christianity finds symbolic expression in the church's cruciform layout.

The location, design, and furnishings of a residential building can initially be interpreted as signs of the social and economic status of its inhabitants.[5] Moreover, one can also draw conclusions—especially from the interior furnishings and decoration—about the attitudes and values that prevail. The type of furniture and the way it is arranged, the condition of the rooms, and the way in which space is divided up provide information about the views of the people who live there. This data refers to their style of living, degree of comfort, order, cleanliness, beauty, preferred forms of interaction, etc., and testifies to the overall ideology on which their home environment is based.[6]

Rooms and spatial objects can, in other words, signify both practical and symbolic functions. At the same time, it can by no means be presumed that the meaning related to the practical function is the "actual," primary meaning to which those that are related to the symbolic functions may merely be added. The practical function of a Gothic cathedral, for example, lies in the possibility of holding religious services or meditating in silence there. One of its symbolic functions can be described as serving to signify "the Heavenly City of Jerusalem."[7] The symbolic function in this case has to be regarded as the fundamental, primary one because it is what provides the basis that makes the practical function possible. By virtue of the fact that the cathedral signifies "the Heavenly City of Jerusalem," the "house of God," one can pray and hold religious services there.[8] In other words, whether the meaning of the practical function or that of one of the symbolic functions is the primary meaning can only be determined on a case-by-case basis, especially in light of the fact that, as often happens in the course of history, functions can change and shifts in the relationships of the various functions to one another can take place.[9]

The meanings which space as a system that creates meaning is capable of generating may thus relate to both practical and symbolic functions of the space or spatial object in question. At present, however, there is no clear definition or consensus as to the units with which this system operates and functions.[10] Bernhard Schneider's suggestion that a distinction should be made between the topological, geometric, and morphological units seems plausible:

> The *topology* of constructed environment concerns the fixing of places and of the network of relations between these places in physical space and in the experiential space of a culture which is already structured as a semiotic system in pre-architectonic times. The topology contains syntagmatic and paradigmatic relationships, hierarchies of meaning, equivalencies and basic rules for pragmatic contexts.
>
> The *geometry* of a culture fixes the topological deep structure in constructional-spatial surface structures according to size and number. It contains theories of proportion and harmony, rules of sizing, modular orders and systems of standards, rules concerning perspective and other rules for the transformation of topological structures into constructional objects.

Finally, the *morphology* encompasses everything, from the building materials and the construction systems to the theories of form in ornamental art and the rules of the relationship between outside space and inside space (as 'transparency', 'closure', etc.), which has conventionally been summed up under the term 'style of architecture'. Even the 'treasure of acquired formulas', the rhetorical orders of architecture, belong in this category.[11]

With the help of these topological, geometric, and morphological units, space is capable of generating the meanings of practical as well as symbolic functions. Thus, for example, the location of individual parts of the building in the Christian church of the Middle Ages was assigned a specific symbolic meaning: the east section, the altar area, symbolized the firmament, the west section the region of hell, the place where the dead await the Day of Resurrection. The geometric form of the basic layout was also subject to a specific interpretation: the cruciform symbolized the crucified Christ, the circular form the perfection of God, the triangle the Holy Trinity, the octagon rebirth through baptism. Even the material of the church was interpreted as a sign in this sense, for the stones symbolized the devout, the cement that binds them, Christian charity.[12]

Not only the Christian churches, but also the temples, palaces, grave stones, and even the houses in many cultures were built and have been interpreted on the basis of corresponding symbolic codes.[13] They can therefore be understood as signs that are rich in symbolic meaning.

Neither the symbolic meanings nor the spatial meanings related to the practical functions are stable. As with all meanings, they are subject to historical change. The code according to which a structure was built or an object produced and originally interpreted may become invalid and be replaced by another that in turn assigns other meanings according to the structure or object in question.[14]

These changes can involve either the practical or the symbolic functions exclusively or both practical and symbolic functions. In any case, however, they result in a change of meaning: a castle built as the seat of a government may be interpreted as a symbol of feudalism, just as a church that was built to be a house of God can be regarded as the product of an architectural style, or a container made to hold snuff can be used as a decorative object. In other words, not only may the symbolic meanings change, but also the meanings related to the practical functions. For a space or spatial object only gives rise to activities which can be carried out in it or with it, but does not decree what they must be. A church can also be used as a barn, a school, or a hospital, a kitchen as a living room, a fork as a scoop, etc. In other words, space indeed makes activities possible, but without categorically requiring or even specifying them.[15]

Theatrical Space

When applied to theater, this quality of space acquires a special meaning and relevance. For a society may quite obviously erect special buildings in which the theater as an institution is to be domiciled, but without this excluding the possibility of performing theater in any number of other spaces that were originally created to serve entirely different practical purposes. Nearly all global practical functions that a space may signify,[16] in other words, can from time to time be replaced by the practical function of serving as the venue for a theatrical performance. This brings us to focus on the question of the symbolic functions potentially signified by the respective venue.

Since we are raising this question with regard to the theatrical code as a system, we are less concerned with the special meanings in Greek theater, the medieval traveling stage, or the courtly baroque theater, for example—which should all be examined at the normative level. Rather, we are interested in investigating a general field of meaning which it may be possible to distinguish from the others by resorting to various symbolic functions which have been performed in the history of theater.

In principle, we can distinguish between two kinds of venues: (1) those spaces which were set up expressly in order to serve as theater buildings and (2) those spaces which were created to serve a different practical function, but are used temporarily or repeatedly as a theater. In the first case the venue—the building specifically set aside for theater—can serve as the sign for all of those symbolic functions which we found to be fulfilled by architectonic signs in general. With the help of topological, geometric, and morphological units, it can constitute meanings which refer, on the one hand, to the society that erected it as well as to the values and ideas that are valid and prevail in it, and, on the other hand, to the theater as an institution and its status within this society as well as the values and ideas accepted and propagated by it. Thus, for example, the circular shape employed in Greek theater can be interpreted, among other things, with regard to the polis and its democratic constitution,[17] yet the location of the Athenian theater of Dionysus in the immediate vicinity of the sacred orchard of Dionysus, can be understood as a sign for the theater's origins in the cult of Dionysus and the meaning it thus had for the polis of Athens.[18]

Similarly, we can define the symbolic function signified by the theater building quite generally as the theater's social function. This can be fulfilled in a variety of forms, depending on whether the function involved is sacred, representative, political, pedagogical, entertaining, or compensatory in nature, etc.

If, by contrast, theater is performed in a space which was set up to serve other purposes, this space itself is to be taken less as a sign which could be interpreted with regard to the theater than as the specific fact that precisely this space is being used for the performance of theater.

The religious plays of the Middle Ages were not performed in a special theater, but rather either in the church—as was the case with the early Christian Easter celebrations[19]—or in the market square. Since the medieval church was interpreted as "the Heavenly City of Jerusalem" in which every section was, for its part, assigned a corresponding allegorical meaning, the Easter play in this case could only be practiced as a liturgical ceremony, as a part of the religious service: the church as a venue refers to the sacred function and meaning of the performance.

The market square, on the other hand, is the everyday environment of the town's residents. On this market square a simultaneous stage with various level platforms was set up which made it necessary for the actors as well as the audience to move around. It often happened that they even moved through the whole town.[20] In this way, the everyday environment took on a different meaning embedded in the history of salvation for the duration of the plays, which usually lasted several days. The town became the "Holy City of Jerusalem," and the town residents became its citizens. The everyday world and the sacred event formed a constellation of reciprocal signification here, for the everyday world was able to signify the sacred event because the sacred has always conceived of the everyday world as a part of itself. When it takes on such a form, the market square—and by extension, the whole town—can, as a venue, be interpreted as a sign for the specifically religious function of the play, and the social life of this urban society manifests itself as an element of the eschatalogical process.

In our century there has clearly been a tendency to move away from buildings set aside especially for theater and an increasing search for temporary or new permanent venues. This development took shape at the beginning of our century, when Max Reinhardt had his production of *King Oedipus* performed in the Schumann circus,[21] and reached its peak in the 1970s with, for example, Grüber's production of *Faust* in a Parisian church and of *Winterreise* in the Olympic stadium in Berlin.[22] In addition to the temporary conversion of spaces of this kind which were not specific to theater, in many cases an attempt is made to establish the theater permanently in such spaces: the Théâtre du Soleil transformed what used to be a cartoucherie into a performance site, and there have been plans to set up a theater in the old slaughterhouse in Bremen and in an old market hall in Hamburg.

The theater buildings that have been passed on for generations—especially those constructed in the nineteenth century—point to a social function of theater which can no longer claim validity today, namely, that of being a realm of the "good, true, and beautiful," removed from the rest of social life, in which the educated bourgeoisie was able to believe its identity was guaranteed. However, the theater of today has a need for the kinds of spaces that are able to fulfill its new social function. Since few appropriate theater buildings have been constructed, however,[23] all that remains is the search for spaces that, for their part, already have meanings that are able to an increasing extent to highlight the intended function of the performance in question. If the theater is no longer to be understood as a separate domain, but rather as a part of the social life of a society, A/X/S also has to take place in spaces which are related to this social life. Consequently, streets and squares, underground passageways and public parks, factories and the interior of market halls, shopping malls and sports stadiums can lend themselves as suitable venues—those places, in other words, in which vast sections of the social life of our society take place.

The space in which A/X/S takes place can, in this sense, generally be viewed and interpreted as a sign for the social function of A/X/S. The respectively specific relationship between A and S is also linked to the respectively different social function of the theater. In our introductory chapter we demonstrated how theater can be understood as the self-portrayal and self-reflection of a culture which, by the same token, is split up in the theater according to those who portray it and those who watch it. Whereas the one group, the actors, represent the role of those who act, the others assume, also vicariously, the role of those who watch.[24] The relationship between A and S is, in other words, a specific pattern of interaction, the meaning of which can only be ascertained in relation to the respective social function of the theater.

In Greek theater the circular-shaped section of space which is reserved for the actors is almost completely surrounded by the three-quarter circle set aside for the audience. Thus, the heroes and members of the chorus representing those who act in society act in the midst of the audience who in turn represent the public sphere. Since the "stage" as well as the "audience area" are cast in bright daylight, the audience also has to be present for the actors in this distribution of space, just as conversely the audience is not only able to see the actors, but also that part of the audience on the opposite side of the amphitheater. Those who act and those who observe are thus directly related to one another and form a complete unity which, for its part, represents the unity of the Greek polis in both a cultic and a sociopolitical respect.[25]

The religious plays of the Middle Ages, on the other hand, do not—in Germany at least[26]—make use of a fixed arrangement for actors and audience. The audience can surround the space where the actors perform at a very close range, and may even find themselves in the same space as the actors, in turn themselves becoming actors. Thus, for example, they may join the procession—more or less as citizens of the Holy City of Jerusalem—in bringing the corpus christi to the grave, and in this way they may become coactors.[27] There is no clear-cut division between the sphere of those who act and of those who observe; for they are all related in the same way to the history of mankind as the history of religious salvation.[28]

In counterpoint to the unity of those who act and those who observe, which is rendered and signified differently in ancient Greece than it is in the Middle Ages, the emergence of the proscenium juxtaposes actors and audience.[29] The section of space set aside for the actors and the section of space reserved for the audience meet in the middle to form a line of demarcation and are strictly separated from each other by an apron. The roles of A and S are not reversible.[30]

This sharp separation was rescinded to some extent by the courtly baroque theater and interpreted in a specific way inasmuch as, on the one hand, the space for the audience remained illuminated so that the audience in facing balconies could see each other and the actors could also see the audience, and, on the other hand, the actual actors in society, the members of the court, also had their places on the stage. Not only the actors representing those who act, but also the spectators representing those who act found themselves on stage and thus identified the action on stage as a representation of the baroque worldview. Just as the prince, the "divine creature," acts and suffers on behalf of humankind, the actor portraying him acts and suffers for his part vicariously. The role which one person fills on the stage of life is played by the other on the stage of the theater. By putting both in the same section of theatrical space, namely that of those who act and are thus juxtaposed to the rest of society—and by extension to the audience represented by it—this distribution of space is an emphatic reference to the special validity and meaning which the theatrical simile possessed for the baroque period.[31]

The box set stage of the nineteenth century, by contrast, finalized the complete separation of the two spheres. The stage space is on one side, where all of the light is directed, and the audience space is on the other, which is submerged in profound darkness. Consequently, the individual viewer in the audience cannot see any of the other viewers, nor can the actor see the audience. As a logical consequence, the actor performs as if no audience were present[32] and thus degrades the viewer to an indiscreet observer who invades the actor's sphere more or less without having the right to do so. As a result, however, the theater loses its ability to function as a form of the self-portrayal and self-reflection of society. For actors who no longer perform for an audience can also no longer represent those who act in this society, just as conversely the audience attending the performance, now being isolated individuals, has ceased to represent the public sphere. Theater thus becomes a domain removed from the rest of social life, a domain which has no recognizable relationship with the social life. For if the space for the audience is eliminated as the place allocated to the public social sphere, then the stage space can no longer function as the site of social life, but instead becomes the space into which the isolated observers project their inner world. This form of spatial arrangement is indicative of values of introspection propagated by the class in society which patronizes theater, namely the educated bourgeoisie, and of the status of social autonomy which was assigned to the theater just as it was to the other genres of art by the bourgeoisie of the nineteenth century.[33]

The withdrawal from nineteenth-century theater buildings that has been taking place in our century can thus also be described and assessed as an attempt to arrive at a new definition of the relationships between actors and audience, as an outgrowth of the new social function of theater.[34]

Forms are being tried out in which the audience surrounds the actors in a circle and moves from venue to venue with the actors; alternately, the actors play in the midst of the audience, etc. The idea is at least to blur and render flexible the boundaries between those who act and those who watch, if not to eliminate the boundaries completely.[35] Not only are entirely new venues sought for this purpose, but—since the meanings of the spatial signs are by no means stable and immutable and only suggest certain functions without determining them—existing theaters are also temporarily being redesigned in such a way that the space for the actors is moved to the middle of the space for the audience, as in Hans Neuenfels's Frankfurt production of *Medea* and *Oedipus*.[36]

The space in which A/X/S takes place, as well as the allocation of certain sections of space to A and S—in other words, the entire underlying use of space in a theater—can be understood as a sign for the social function of theater. This function becomes concrete, on the one hand, in the social status of the theater and, on the other, in the values and ideas propagated by the theater. As an indication of the social context within which the individual performance is carried out and should be appraised, the stage conception brings to light important, pragmatic factors on which the constitution of the meaning of every single performance depends.

Stage Space

We shall define stage space as that segment of space in which A acts in order to portray X. This means that the stage space need not be a place that is especially sectioned off, but rather is situated wherever A acts in order to portray X. This can be in the midst of the audience, on the steps leading to the area where the audience is located, on the lighting bridge, on a rope dangling above the audience's heads, etc. The location of the stage space depends, in other words, on the underlying overall layout of the space, and in particular on the space assigned to A and S and the resulting, set definition of the relationship between A and S.

Our definition of stage space implies both a practical and a symbolic function: it signifies (1) the space in which A acts, and (2) the space in which X is found. The stage space is thus defined both as the environment, i.e., the field of activity, for A and as the environment and field of activity for X. The actions and movements carried out by A in this environment signify actions and movements by X.

Like every form of space, stage space, because of its location (in relation to the space for the audience), its form and composition, also gives rise to certain kinds of activity which we shall initially limit here to certain kinds of movement: the sequences of movement that are possible in a circular-shaped stage area are different from those in a crescent-shaped area, those in a rectangular area differ from those in a square, and those in a trapezoid differ from those in an ellipsoid. A level stage floor allows for different movements than does one that is raised toward the back, and movements on a flat surface will differ from those on stairs. One has to step differently on cobblestones than one does on sand, and differently on a carpet than on smoothly polished wood floors; a large space that is sectioned off permits one to move differently than does a small set of stairs leading to the audience space, and one can move differently on a lighting bridge than on the arm of an easy chair standing in the middle of the audience space. However, since a space can only permit, but not determine, certain movements, the actor is, by the same token, not determined, but only stimulated, by the respective stage space in terms of the movements he carries out in it to portray X. He can thus make use of the possibilities provided by the space and can even execute movements that are not directly indicated by the space. However, to the extent that a certain movement can be performed in a stage space, the stage space can also be regarded and interpreted as a sign for the possibility of this movement. The stage space thus becomes a sign for the possibility of implementing certain proxemic signs which, produced by A, are meant to signify X.[37]

Since the actor, being a three-dimensional body, always needs room, the stage space also represents an irreducible element of the theatrical code. The signifying possibilities inherent in his person can thus invariably be presumed to exist.

Moreover, other ways in which the stage space can signify things through decoration, props, and lighting should be regarded only as potential, but not necessary, elements of the theatrical code as a system.

Decoration

Whereas stage space signifies the space in general in which X finds himself, the decoration can function as a sign for the special space in which X happens to be at that moment. The respective decoration identifies the stage space as the chamber in a castle, a forest, a dungeon, a garden, hell, the ocean floor, catacombs, and so on.

This description of the function of decoration entails a certain problematic issue. In the case of all of the theatrical signs discussed so far, we have assumed that theater may very well be able and is also usually accustomed to developing theater-specific codes for kinesic signs, for example, or the signs of external appearance. Yet we also assumed that a movement or a piece of clothing can, in principle, nevertheless always be employed and interpreted both in the social life and in the theater of a culture without any change in the substance of it and on the basis of the same code. In the case of signs of decoration, however, this possibility cannot, for obvious reasons, generally be presumed to exist or be taken for granted. For it is hardly possible to set up an actual castle on the stage if one wishes to signify a castle, or to plant a real garden if one wishes to signify a garden—unless, that is, it is a question of a baroque festivity in which the entire castle area is declared a "stage" and all of the castle's residents and guests act as actors.[38] In other words, we have to assume that as far as decoration is concerned, the theater is forced for fundamental reasons to develop a code that is specific to theater. The stage decoration may consist of a painted canvas or three-dimensional objects; it may portray all of the intended space or merely allude to a portion of it; it may work with stylization or true-to-life reproductions down to the last detail; it may take the form of decoration that remains uniform throughout as a typical setting or may change from one scene to another in line with the characteristics of the different "settings" or "backdrops."[39] Thus, signs are always involved which are capable of functioning in this way only as a system that generates meaning in theater.[40]

These signs can initially be interpreted with respect to the specific *location* at which X is situated. In *Faust*, for example, they signify the theater in which the prelude takes place; heaven; Faust's study; an open space outside the wall of a fortified town; Auerbach's Keller; the witches' kitchen; a street; Gretchen's room; the neighbor's house; a garden; a little summer house in the garden; a forest and cave; a square with a fountain; a narrow space between the town wall and the nearest houses; the inside of the cathedral; the Harz mountains near the towns of Schierke and Elend; a field; and a dungeon. The signs of the decoration, in other words, may point to interiors as well as exteriors, to buildings as well as to natural surroundings, to actual locations (such as Auerbach's Keller in Leipzig or the area near Schierke and Elend) as well as to "fictive" places (such as heaven or the witches' kitchen). Every possible type of space that is conceivable on the basis of a cultural code can be signified by the decoration as a place at which X finds himself. The decoration may be intended merely to suggest this place in vague terms or to characterize it specifically; it may stylize the location or include all of the authentic detail. The manner in which this function is performed in each case depends on the underlying theatrical code.

In both cases, however, the signs of decoration can also frequently be interpreted in relation to the *period* in which the play is set. A Gothic arch or an old cabinet, for example, can point to the Middle Ages, and ancient-looking pillars to the corresponding period, etc. In this sense, decoration can also function as a sign for the country in which the play is set. Paper walls and lanterns, for example, give a space the appearance not only of a room, but of a room in a Japanese house.

This possibility is, as it were, a special case which exemplifies the general function of decoration, which is to characterize the site at which X finds himself. The use of decorative signs to identify a period and country is usually closely linked with the use of costumes to identify the characters as belonging to a particular period and nationality.

The decoration that thus qualifies the location as a specific one at a particular time functions simultaneously as a sign for the *situation* or *an action*. For, since every space refers to a practical function which can be performed in it—a church refers to a religious service, a town hall to government and administration, a railroad platform to a train ride, a residential house to day-to-day living—the decoration, as the sign for a space, becomes a sign for the both practical and symbolic functions signified by this space. When employed and interpreted as the sign of the sign for a specific space signifying certain practical functions, it thus functions simultaneously as the sign for a situation or an action which could take place in this space as the realization of the practical functions concerned, e.g., a coronation, a meal, a battle, an hour of prayer, etc. However, since decoration is always put to a specific use, it is capable of characterizing not only the signified space more precisely because of its specific design, but also the action which might unfold in it. In other words, when signifying the practical function of the space it characterizes in this way, it simultaneously fulfills the additional sign functions which refer to a situation or an action.

Since a plot can be broken down in the course of performance into the actions of individual characters who, as a whole, constitute the plot for which the decoration provides the appropriate setting, decoration can also be employed and interpreted as a sign referring to the *characters*. In this connection, however, the relationship to the practical function of the signified space is different. For the practical functions of the decoration retain their validity insofar as they point to the activities which A can carry out in them or with them. A door on the stage can be opened; one can climb stairs; one can lean out a window, etc. However, since A does not do these things in order to accomplish a practical purpose, but solely to indicate that X is performing them, the signs of the decoration change their signifying quality in relation to the characters as well—albeit not in relation to the actors performing them. They are no longer signs of practical functions, but rather signs of signs signifying practical functions. As signs of signs they point to possible, intentional movements of character X. An object on the stage, the primary function of which lies in signifying a fountain, thus at the same time indicates the possibility that X can move to a fountain. If actor A crosses the stage and approaches the object concerned, then this sequence is interpreted as the character portrayed by A going to the fountain. In the case of stage decoration that involves an interior set, a chair, for example, gives rise to the signifying possibilities that X can sit down on it, go around it, stand behind it, stumble over it. The signs of decoration thus form a closely knit complex with the proxemic signs that can potentially materialize. They are what allows the audience to identify the actor's walking through the middle of the stage as the way to the door of a house, walking from backstage right to frontstage left as the way to get from the door of the beloved's room to the dungeon, and moving in a circle as walking around an altar. The proxemic signs produced by A can thus be interpreted as intentional movements by X by reference to the signs of decoration.[41]

This is naturally true especially for set decorations which are either related to particular spatial settings or can be related to particular, albeit changing, spatial settings.[42] If, on the other hand, the actors are performing on a large conveyor belt that runs across the stage or on an iron scaffold,[43] this decoration cannot identify the movements it enables character X to make and/or requires of him. Rather, it has to be understood as a specific rendering of the signifying possibilities generally provided for by the stage space. The conveyor belt, the iron scaffolding, or the stairwell postulate certain sequences and kinds of movements which must be interpreted with regard to character X. A set decoration of this type thus intensifies the concomitant function of stage space, namely the function of being a sign of the ability to give a shape to certain proxemic signs.[44]

In any case, however, the decoration can be defined as the environment of the character, and this environment predetermines a series of possible interpretations for X's actions. For the time being, we shall exclude those actions produced as gestural signs by A in order to be able to signify intentional gestures by X—such as the opening of a cabinet door, the shifting of a chair, etc.—and shall discuss them later in connection with props.[45] Instead, we shall limit our discussion here to those actions which are produced by A as proxemic signs in order to signify corresponding movements by X. In addition to those already discussed which refer generally to movement in the space or specifically to intentional movement, we should in this context take into consideration those proxemic signs that can be interpreted in relation to the interaction between various characters. For there is a close link between the arrangement of spatial objects and the forms of interaction that are possible in the surroundings so designed. A decoration which is supposed to signify a ditch, a wall, or something similar points to the difficulties which the characters who are positioned on various sides of these objects will have to overcome in order to come together. Chairs or other objects signifying "seating opportunities" that are arranged in a circle indicate a form of symmetrical group interaction, whereas a throne standing on an elevation or stairs refers to a certain form of asymmetrical interaction, etc. In other words, the decoration can be interpreted not only in relation to the characters' movements, but also in relation to the patterns and forms of interaction which may be applied by them. This does not mean that recourse has to be had to the models of interaction suggested by the decoration; rather, it is possible to create completely different models which may even be the opposite of those signaled by the decoration. However, the decoration also functions as a sign here, the meanings of which have to be related to the character because, for example, it serves to expose a particular character trait or to provide information about a decision taken by X or an action taken by X.

This brings us to a further sign function of decoration which is related to the characters: The decoration can also be used to characterize the character. Since the sign for space can generally be interpreted in relation to individuals and groups of individuals as a sign for their status in society and the values and ideas accepted and propagated by them in each case (in other words, for their attitudes, systems of value, views of the world), the decoration can also perform a corresponding function.[46] The books and apparatuses in Faust's study, for example, indicate that the person who lives there is a bookish man devoted to science, whereas the furnishings in Gretchen's room are to be understood both as a sign of the rather more modest social status of the person who lives there and of her high regard for the values of order and cleanliness.

Therefore, the decoration can function in relation to the characters as a sign which is capable of generating meaning both at the "object level" of the movements and at the subject and intersubjective levels.

When the decoration more precisely identifies the place in which X finds himself, no matter how this is done, it is able to fulfill a different, general function at the same time. A garden decoration that, for example, is limited to light shades of green and delicate shapes creates an atmosphere that is different from that of a massive gray cliff decoration. The creation of such a *mood* which may be characteristic for a single scene or even for an entire performance and predominate in it is generated by the decoration as a meaning which can be constituted only on the basis of general visual codes of the culture in question. In our culture, for example, light colors connote positive values such as joy, happiness, harmony, warmth, etc.; dark colors, on the other hand, denote negative values such as death, mourning, coldness, and fear. It is also on the basis of general cultural codes which assign meanings in this way that decoration is interpreted and attributed a corresponding meaning as an atmosphere which is "cheerful, lively," "depressed, sad," "horrifying, frightening," "excited, exalted," "coldly distant," or otherwise. In other words, the decoration not only functions as the sign for a particular space, but also as a sign for the mood that prevails in this space.

Based on the widest variety of cultural codes, however, the spaces and spatial objects that are given in a society are subject to additional interpretations that have to be related to the ideas or ideologies that are widespread in this society. We have already pointed to the fact that the churches were interpreted to be "the Heavenly City of Jerusalem" in the Middle Ages. Spaces which are traditionally imbued with rich symbolic meaning in our culture, however, include not only sacred spaces, but also caverns, the house, the forest, the sea, the cemetery, the "dungeon," the castle, etc. Indeed, there are corresponding spatial objects, such as the tree, the stone, the clock, the scythe, the scales, the horn of plenty, the scepter, etc. Depending on how it is specifically rendered, the decoration can engender in concrete form one or more of these *symbolic meanings* that are possible in the culture in question, or even introduce a new symbolic meaning until then uncommon for the corresponding space or spatial object. When the decoration constitutes a particular symbolic meaning of a space in this way, it points at the same time to the idea or ideology underlying this meaning. Examples would be the house as a peaceful, well-defined area of human activity unto itself; the house as an expression of constraint; the house as a sign for shelter; the house as a sign for the artificial separation from one's origins in nature; the house as a symbol for the inner realm, etc. Here, the idea or ideology is defined with regard to the individual scene or whole performance concerned as a signifying element and has to be interpreted accordingly. In this sense, the decoration can also be employed and interpreted as the sign for a certain *idea* underlying a scene or the entire performance. It can identify the world as a prison or a space of unlimited opportunities, as ordered creation or hopeless chaos, as a transitory illusion or a solidly built structure, as a labyrinth or a battlefield. When the decoration lends expression to a particular idea or view of the world in this way, it creates the context to which the performance has to be related and establishes the framework in which the other signs produced in it function and from which they have to be interpreted.

From the repertoire of possible meanings which can in principle be constituted with the signs of decoration, every theatrical code selects one or more with a specific predominant status, which it produces either primarily or exclusively. Thus, for example, Serlio's Renaissance stage made use in principle of only three uniform set decorations, namely, for the *scena tragica*, the *scena comica* and the *scena satirica*, respectively. Here the decoration was only able to convey a vague idea of the background against which the plot would take shape, and to intimate that the "basic atmosphere" was tragic, comic, or satirical.[47] The theater of naturalism, on the other hand, provided a detailed, as it were authentic, reproduction of actual interiors, which had the function primarily of portraying as precisely as possible the milieu that determined the actions, attitudes, values, and views of the world of the characters.[48]

The baroque set decoration, with its many changes of scene, conflagrations, volcanic eruptions, etc., was designed and conceived of as a visible allegory for the idea of the transitory nature of all being, for the theory of *vanitas*,[49] whereas the realist set decoration was primarily intended to specify the historical and geographic setting.[50]

Romantic theater took care above all to create a particular atmosphere with the set decoration and especially to enhance the symbolic meanings of the spaces—such as those of the abyss, the cemetery, the hut, or even, as in French romanticism, of specific parts of the city.[51] The avant-garde theater of a Meyerhold or a Tairov, on the other hand, specified that the most important function of decoration was its ability to provide the actor with a multitude of possibilities for the widest variety of usually highly artificial sequences and kinds of movement.[52]

The stage decoration is capable of forming the dominant element in a theatrical code, as, for example, in the case of relief stages, where every second element such as costume or movement is constructed as an integral part of the overall scenic effect. Yet it can also be completely replaced by other sign systems, as in the Elizabethan theater, where the decoration was created with linguistic media, so to speak, or in the Peking Opera and contemporary pantomime, where decoration is signified entirely through gestural signs.

The status of decoration in the hierarchical structure of a theatrical code and the selection it makes in each case from the repertoire of possible meanings that are available in principle can, for their part, only be interpreted and understood based on the overall context of this theatrical code and its specific accomplishments, goals, functions, and intentions.

Props

In a certain sense, props are difficult to categorize as a group of theatrical signs because the objects used to realize them can also function as elements of other theatrical sign systems. Thus, a distinction has to be made between props, on the one hand, and the signs produced by the actor's external appearance and the decoration, on the other.

Hair, ribbons, hair pins, etc., function as elements of the actor's hairstyle as long as they are attached to his head. Once the actor begins to rearrange his hair, braid it, put it up or pin it up, tie bows in it, take the pins out or put them in, then the hair, bows, and hairpins function as props. The gloves and swords an actor has donned or straps on are parts of his costume. If he takes them off on stage and uses them as objects which he manipulates, then they come under the category of props.

A table that has been set with everything that goes with it—a table, chairs, tablecloth, plates, cups, spoons, soup bowls, etc.—serves either as decoration, or at least as part of the decoration for a scene and/or a performance. If an actor moves a chair, sits down at the table and picks up a spoon or cup, then the chair, as well as the spoon or cup, is being used as a prop. In other words, props can be classified, generally speaking, as those objects which the actor uses to perform actions: as such, they are to be defined as the objects upon which A focuses his intensional gestures.[53]

An item used as a prop has the primary sign function of signifying a particular *object*. In fulfilling this function, it makes no difference whatsoever whether the item in question is a stylized or a faithful imitation of the object to be *signified*, nor whether it is itself a concretization of this object-species. Indeed, it is of no importance whether the item bears the slightest resemblance to the signified object or not: a medieval sword, for example, can be signified by either a simple club or an exact replica; by an authentic medieval sword—or, for that matter, by an old hat. If it is clear from the context that this object is a medieval sword, then it functions as the sign for a medieval sword.[54] Since the object signified can be understood as a sign of certain practical and symbolic functions, the prop should be interpreted as the sign of a sign: it is not only the sign for a signified object, but at the same time stands for the possible meaning it might have.[55]

On the other hand, precisely because the prop has been defined as the object on which A's intentional gestures are focused, and these are, after all, supposed to signify the corresponding intentional gestures of X, one or more of the meanings that the object may in principle have can be generated only by referring back to the character involved. Thus, for example, if a character holding a scythe can be identified as a farmer about to go out to the fields, then the scythe stands for the meaning of the practical function associated with this type of object, namely, that it serves as a tool for mowing. If, on the other hand, the character portrays Death, then the scythe signifies the meaning of the object's symbolic function: it points to the end of a life.

This brings us to the second major sign function of the prop, which is that of referring to the *character* who uses it. In this sense, it can function as a sign for that character.

A prop can be interpreted as a sign for the action that X can execute by doing something to it or with it, i.e., as a reference to possible intentional gestures: a cigarette implies that X can light it, stick it in his mouth, put it out, or drop it; likewise, a cup implies that X can drink out of it, throw it against the wall, put it on the table, or turn it around in his hands; and a flower implies that X can give it away, smell it, put it in a vase, or throw it away. In this way, every prop refers to the action which X can execute or has already executed in relation to the object signified by it.[56]

These actions often occur in interaction with other characters. As a consequence, props can also be interpreted as a sign of the relationship between the characters. If X passes Y a rose, threatens him with a sword, snatches his wallet, or forces a letter upon him, then in each case the action functions as a characteristic of the corresponding process of interaction. The prop has the task here of defining the respective relationship more closely. However, since the same actions can be accomplished using different objects, we must bear in mind that it is the respective correlation between a certain object and certain gestures that refer to the actions executed with it that allow us to interpret the prop as a sign of the relationship between the two characters. If X puts some medicine in Y's coffee, then this signifies a fundamentally different relationship between X and Y than would be the case if X had used poison instead of medicine.[57]

A prop can in this manner naturally also function as a sign that generates meaning with regard to the subject. The golden watch that X takes from his pocket may point to his being a rich man or, if in the previous scene we have verified that the watch is Y's property, may show him to be a thief. The money box that X caresses may show him to be a miser; the glass that he smashes may indicate that he is tempestuous, or angry, or determined. The Rosary that he prays may show that he is religious, whereas the newspaper he is holding upside-down while reading may show that he is distracted.

This sign function is of exceptional importance in the characterization of allegorical or type figures, for which an element of costume and/or a prop is predominantly employed. Thus, a scale and a blindfold demonstrate that the character is Justice, a triton characterizes Neptune, a basket of fruit shows the person to be Pomona, an hourglass and scythe characterize Death, a scepter and crown show him to be a king. They could to a certain extent be defined as part of the costume, as an element of the actor's external appearance.[58]

At the subject level a prop can thus point to both the general type or character of the stage figure, and to its social status, individual traits, feelings, attitudes, value judgments, and view of the world.

Props can accomplish this on the one hand in their capacity as objects or signified objects that are accompanied by a specific symbolic meaning constituted on the basis of a cultural code, as in the case of the representation of allegorical figures. On the other hand, they can achieve this only to the extent that note is taken of the specific correlation between the object signified and the intentional gestures aimed at it. It is the relation between a specific object and a certain action that can first be interpreted as the sign for the subject of the respective character or its relationship to other characters.

We can define props in this sense as signs that are able to generate meaning with reference to the character not just at the "object level" of the action involved, but also at the subject and intersubjective levels.

In connection with the actions carried out with it by X, the prop can refer to certain *actions* by other characters and to certain *situations*. For example, suitcases piled up at the door point to an impending departure; a laid table brings a coming meal to mind, and blinds let down may signify a secret conversation. If the oven is fed with wood and the fire fueled, this points to coldness; if a candle is lit, we may conclude that nightfall approaches; and a coffin carried onto stage points to a death, etc. This specific function of props as signs is, for example, used preferentially by the theatrical code of the Peking Opera: here, blowing out a candle signifies complete darkness on the stage; two flags painted with wheels held by servants on either side of a lady, for instance, function as a sign of a journey the lady has just embarked on, etc. In this manner, the prop becomes an important factor in the plot of a performance because the use of a certain prop immediately creates a complex situation or sequence of actions on stage, for it can signify these by pointing to them.[59]

The action accomplished with a prop may, furthermore, function as the sign of a *symbolic meaning*. Putting down a scepter and taking off a crown and purple gown is, for example, used as a symbolic procedure in baroque theater which signifies someone divesting himself of earthly power.[60] The ritual of washing one's hands is still used and understood in theater today as a symbolic expression of cleansing oneself of moral guilt,[61] and winding up an alarm clock is used to signify the beginning of a deadline,[62] etc. The prop constitutes a symbolic meaning on the basis of either a specific theatrical code or some other cultural code which can be presumed to be generally known. It may, however, be introduced for the first time as something new on the basis of the special context, i.e., of the special code of an individual performance.[63] By thus functioning as a sign of a symbolic meaning, the prop can also point to a general *idea, ideology* or *worldview* which may be at the heart of the scene in question or the performance as a whole.

Props are used in almost all theatrical codes, albeit in different functions and in differing degrees of dominance. In baroque, Romantic[64] and symbolist theater the constitution of symbolic meanings is prioritized. In realist and naturalist theater, however, preferential use was made of its function of pointing to the subject and to interactive processes. In theater in classical antiquity, above all in the comedies of Aristophanes, props were used very frequently,[65] yet in Goethe's Weimar theater, they were given a subordinate role.[66]

If the performance forgoes stage decoration as a system generating meaning, then the props can be used all the more intensively in those functions otherwise fulfilled by decorations, as in Peking Opera. Yet props can themselves be eliminated as a system creating meaning, such as is the case in the different forms of pantomime. Here, the sign functions usually fulfilled by props are effected by intentional gestures: they signify the object and the actions carried out with it, point to the character and to situations, assume symbolic meanings, and express an idea. Words can, of course, also substitute for props. If the language refers to a watch or flower, a glass or a book, then these objects are present for the audience.

In other words, no rules can be drawn up for the conditions under which props must be used more intensively, or used less, or not used at all. The prop functions preferentially developed by a theatrical code must always be related to the overall context of the code, as must the position of the props in the code. The description, analysis, and explanation of the sign functions preferentially realized using props and the position of the props in the code can therefore be provided only by an investigation of the theatrical code at the level of norms or speech.

Lighting

We have listed lighting as the third category of signs which are capable of adding to the possible significations of the stage space. Since "lighting" can refer both to the technical installations which produce certain kinds of light on the stage and the quality of light itself, we will in the following, for the sake of clarity, use the term "light" when referring to light in the sense of a specific sign system, and the term "lighting" for the technical facilities which serve to generate these signs in the theater.

Both natural and artificially produced light—like natural and artificially created spaces—can be interpreted in terms of their practical and symbolic functions. Making a space visible is, generally speaking, a practical function of light. Illumination of the space is what first allows the latter to become evident and to look like a room.

In addition to this basic, practical function—and usually as a consequence of it—light can assume a wide variety of symbolic functions that are developed, fixed, and regulated in the widest variety of cultural codes—such as religion, poetry, painting, astronomy, meteorology. Nearly every culture not only has learned to interpret light as a sign in relation to the time of day and season of the year, but has also developed a rich store of light symbolism which, in its earliest origins, can probably be traced back to the juxtaposition of day and night, light and shadow.[67]

In the theater light can be employed both in its practical function and as a sign for its symbolic functions.[68] It did not come to be used as a system which generates meaning until a relatively late date—in the case of Western theater since the 17th century—when the time of day at which theater performances were held was changed from the afternoon to the evening, and the location moved from open squares to an enclosed room. The introduction of light as a theatrical system that generates meaning did not, however, coincide with this change. For, to the extent that light was merely used in its practical function[69]—namely, in order to render the stage space and action on the stage visible—it was not possible to define it and understand it as a theatrical sign. It was not until the constant, unchanging lighting on the stage had been abandoned and the transition to more differentiated lighting had been accomplished—regardless of how this was done—that it became possible to assess and interpret the light on the stage as a theatrical sign.

In its quality as a sign employed in a given culture as well as in theater, light functions on the basis of the unities of (1) intensity, (2) color, (3) distribution, and (4) movement.[70] If one of these factors changes, the meaning of the light can also change. Thus, for example, intensive yellow light on the stage may signify noonday sunshine, dim yellow light afternoon sunshine, dim bluish light moonlight. Light distributed flooding the entire area can indicate an open space outdoors and light falling in rays, a forest. Light coming from the left may refer to the morning, and moving farther toward the back of the stage and from there to the right, the course of the day through midday to evening.

One of the fundamental sign-functions of light on the stage is to signify *light*: sunlight, moonlight, torchlight, candlelight, the light of a rainbow, neon light, and many others. By fulfilling this function, it can perform other functions at the same time that are related to the respective kind of light. For the light in each case has to be produced as concrete light that, for its part, may refer to meanings which have been developed in the widest variety of cultural—often poetic or icono-graphic—codes. Sunlight, for example, can be signified by bright yellow, muddy yellow, golden, or reddish yellow light, etc. This procedure may, depending on what is appropriate, define the sun as a ball of fire, an egg yoke, hair of the gods, or something of that nature; moonlight, as silver, bluish, greenish, or reddish light, depending on whether the moon is to be apostrophized as a silver ship crossing the heavens, the pallor of death, a drowned body, or a blood-red dagger.[71] The particular way in which the light constitutes the meaning of "sunlight" or "moonlight" thus already implies and suggests the various possible symbolic meanings which are to be assigned to sunlight or moonlight in the context of a given performance.

In denoting "light," light can also connote a large number of other meanings. In view of these possible meanings, we shall distinguish between sign functions of the light that can only be performed in relation to other theatrical signs such as mimicry, gesture, external appearance, decoration, or props, and independent sign functions, which are related to categories such as place, time, characters, etc.

The technology which has been developed to date permits effects to be achieved with lighting on the stage which were neither possible nor conceivable for hundreds of years in the theater. The film camera can focus on isolated individual aspects of the actor—such as his mimicry in close-ups, a particular movement of the arm in a waist shot, parts of the costume such as the hat or boots—or of the decoration and individual props and present them to the audience. However, on the stage the actor is always present in life-size, and the arrangement of set elements and props constitute a complex which can only be changed by the actor in the course of his actions or by the stage hands during scene changes. Lighting makes it possible to take such signs out of this complex and isolate them. The light can fall solely on the actor's face or his moving hand, or illuminate a single element of the set or a prop, and its position in the room can at the same time change. In film a close-up both declares the isolated element temporarily as the sole agent of meaning, and magnifies its dimensions, thus offering it to the audience with a special emphasis on its function as a sign to be interpreted. In theater, on the other hand, the stage space remains present in its entirety—albeit as a large black hole—regardless of which elements are isolated by the light, and the individual elements such as the face, hand, the cross on the wall, or the rose retain their original dimensions. The use of light to isolate elements of the stage space thus results in a modification of the signifying quality of the elements thus isolated. The nature of this modification cannot be defined in generalized terms, but rather has to be investigated on a case-by-case basis. It can be said, however, that isolation based on the use of light frequently actualizes possible symbolic meanings. The light thus becomes fused with the sign it isolates, which we can qualify in a certain way as a specific sign that is capable of generating new meanings not previously thought of. In other words, the light transforms the sign of a sign system into a different sign of this sign system and creates new possible meanings to be actualized by it. It brings about a change in the possible meanings provided for in the repertoire of the respective sign systems, without itself functioning as a distinct sign with its own meanings.[72]

If, on the other hand, light is employed as an independent sign, it can for its part constitute a multitude of different meanings. The light can signify the *place* at which X finds himself. Appia, for example, created the forest through which Siegfried goes with nothing other than a movement of light and shadow,[73] Gründgens created Faust's grave with an oblong beam of light on an empty stage. Thus, light can signify a room or a hut, the inside of a cathedral or a cave, and any number of other things, and can even completely replace set decoration.

Light can be used to indicate the *time of day and season of the year*. If the light denotes sunlight, for example, it connotes daytime—and, in addition, the kind of light often indicates whether it is morning, noontime, afternoon, twilight—and moonlight connotes nighttime. It can signify a hot summer day or a gloomy winter

afternoon, rainy or sunny weather. Moreover, it is able to indicate not only mete-
orological processes, but also both other natural courses of events and events in
human society—in other words, *situations* and *actions*. This function is usually
fulfilled by light in connection with nonverbal, acoustic signs, especially with
sounds. In this way it can indicate conflagrations and storms, volcanic eruptions
and meteors speeding through the heavens, trips in outer space and battles. Light
can, in cooperation with sound, even temporarily replace the actor: Flashes of
light and battle sounds can, for example, create the impression of a battle in which
enemy soldiers are attacking each other, without a single actor having to be present
on the stage.[74]

The light can furthermore constitute meanings that are related to the personal-
ities of the *characters*. It can identify a character as a saint or other luminous
figure or signify that a character is lonely by isolating the entire character on
stage, to name but two of them. When employed in connection with a character,
light is primarily used as a sign that is capable of constituting meanings on the
subject level. It primarily serves to make statements about their special status and
their particular constitution. It was widely used in this function in baroque theater,
especially in the apotheoses at the ends of the plays.

Light is one of the most important media for creating a particular *atmosphere*.
In order to perform this function, it will usually be necessary to go back to cultural
codes other than that of the theater, especially since one has to assume that specific
light codes are developed in the culture in question and function accordingly. In
our culture, for example, bright warm light is generally interpreted in relation to
a quiet, warm, friendly atmosphere, whereas cloudy or cold light is as a whole
understood in relation to an apprehensive atmosphere that provokes anxiety or
sadness. A certain kind of moonlight is felt to be romantic, a specific kind of
brightness—such as that of neon lamps—as obliterating feelings. If light in the
theater is to constitute a certain atmosphere as meaning, it will therefore be necessary to go back to the corresponding light codes which function in our culture.[75]

These light codes, however, are related not only to moods, but also to ideas.
Thus, for example, darkness connotes the realm of the evil, the demonic, whereas
brightness connotes that of the good, the divine.[76] If light in the theater is used
in a way that permits it to be related to such ideas, the light is also capable of
signifying *ideas*. For example, a stage flooded with light at the end of a performance can point to the victory of the divine; if it sinks completely into darkness,
the dissolution of the world in chaos. Such meanings can, of course, only be
constituted from the context of a certain performance or by laying the groundwork
of a corresponding valid theatrical norm.

Since it was first introduced, light as a system which generates meaning in
theater has been employed in a wide variety of ways and with various objectives
in mind. Whereas in baroque theater it was used primarily for the portrayal of
natural catastrophes and apotheoses in order to signify the association between
immanence and transcendence, its primary function in Romantic theater was to
create atmosphere. In the realist and naturalist theaters, on the other hand, the

objective was primarily to utilize light in its basic function—namely, to signify light—in a way that would create the illusion of a real room for the audience. In this case, light was supposed to be as "natural" as possible.[77]

It was not possible to exploit the full range of meanings which light can have in theater until the twentieth century, by which time the necessary technical prerequisites had been created. However, even in our century the various theatrical norms diverge considerably from one another in terms of their use of light. Whereas Appia declared it the dominant sign in his theatrical code and developed its utilization accordingly,[78] Brecht was determined to remove the sign system of light altogether from his theatrical code. Light was to be used merely in its practical function and to illuminate the stage space completely and evenly. When light was eliminated as a system that generates meaning, the fact of its elimination advanced to the status of a sign which was capable of signifying in a special way Brecht's rejection of atmospheric bourgeois theater.[79]

4. Nonverbal Acoustic Signs

❏ ❏ ❏ The underlying—denotative—sign function of the theatrical signs discussed thus far is invariably related, albeit in various ways, to character X: (1) the verbal and kinesic signs produced by A function as signs for activities performed by X, (2) the signs that make up A's external appearance function as signs for X's external appearance, and (3) the signs applying to the stage space function as signs for the space in which X finds himself, and in other words, as signs for X's spatial environment.[1]

This in principle covers all the factors that can result from the relationship between A and X. For, in order to portray X, A acts (1) in a certain manner, (2) with a specific appearance, and (3) in a particular space. Since it cannot be assumed that there is a further constitutive factor, the nonverbal acoustic signs, inasmuch as they are employed as theatrical signs, must therefore be subsumed under the factors mentioned—in other words, as signs to be employed and interpreted either for the activities or the appearance of X or the space in which X finds himself. Therefore, before going on to examine in detail the potential meanings of the nonverbal acoustic signs as theatrical signs in detail, we shall begin by clarifying to which of these factors sounds and music are in principle to be assigned.

Since nonverbal acoustic signs can be produced by A, they can also be defined as signs for X's activities. If A sings; plays a flute, fiddle, or harp; imitates animal voices; and creates intentional sounds through his actions, such as knocking, stomping, cracking, etc., these activities function as signs for X's activities. A's singing denotes X's singing, A's flute-playing denotes X's flute-playing, A's knocking, X's knocking, etc. The nonverbal acoustic signs produced by A are, in other words, to be interpreted as signs for X's activities.

On the other hand, sounds and music can only refer to X's appearance by negation. Since we have defined appearance as visual appearance tied to the physical presence, the actor's *Leib-apriori*, it can therefore also be denoted only by visual signs. However, to the extent that individual characters are to be introduced as incorporeal creatures—such as various spirits in Faust I and II—sounds and music function in addition to linguistic signs as the only conceivable signs with which such characters can be materialized as being present "in the flesh" and thus factually present in the theatrical space. The identity of the incorporeal characters can consequently be constituted only by means of acoustic signs.

In order to investigate the manner in which nonverbal theatrical acoustic signs are related to the space in which X is located, we should leave the theater for a time and first attempt to clarify the question of which relationship generally exists between sounds and music, on the one hand, and the surrounding space, on the other.

We have defined space as a potentially human environment. This environment is not constituted exclusively by visual signs, but also by acoustic signs. The forest, for example, appears as a possible human environment, a possible field of action, not only on the basis of trees, grass, reeds, flowers, mushrooms, berries, birds, wildlife, etc., but also on the basis of leaves rustling, water splashing, birds chirping, stags roaring, the sound of horns and dogs barking. A city can be described not only as a particular conglomeration of specific buildings, streets, squares, fountains, monuments, automobiles, trolleys, etc., but also as a particular acoustic complex comprised of the sounds of motors, bicycle bells, a mixture of voices, music from supermarkets and bars, the clattering of trains, and the noise of machinery in factories and offices, among many others. Thus, it has to be conceived of precisely in this respect as a relationship between visual and acoustic elements, and it is these that together form people's surroundings.

If the environment in which people live is constituted, on the one hand, by spatial elements and, on the other, by sounds and music, both components are directly related to one another and can, in principle, refer to each other. It can be concluded from this that sounds and music, to the extent that they are employed as theatrical signs, will form a closely knit relationship with the signs of space. They may therefore be employed and interpreted in relation to character X not only as signs for their activities, but also and above all as signs for the space in which they find themselves.

The nonverbal acoustic signs can generally function as a system that creates meaning on the basis of units of tone, pitch, melody, rhythm, and meter.[2] Music, however, has a smallest possible discrete tonal unit which can be joined together with other such units to form larger tonal syntagmas according to the rules of the respective tonal system. Yet it cannot be assumed that there is a minimal unit of differentiation for sounds. For sounds are in principle not produced on the basis of a tonal system that, by virtue of its specific structure, ascribes each note a particular value by the position it assigns, but rather represent an acoustic complex of features.[3] In other words, although the kind of units with which sounds as well as music function as systems that generate meaning may be the same, they nevertheless differ fundamentally owing to the respective manner in which these units are combined. This difference in combination, achieved in the former case as a musical syntagma and in the latter as an acoustic complex of features, represents the principal difference between music and sounds. This is a crucial difference, in that it means that music always has to be produced intentionally, whereas sounds may also occur as the product of natural processes or as the unintentional "byproducts" of other human activities. The sound of the ocean and the howling of the wind are no more attributable to an act intended to produce these sounds than the sound of engines running or the sound of footsteps. Even if the latter two can occasionally be deliberately intensified, this does not affect the correctness in principle of claiming that certain activities—such as walking or starting an engine—produce sounds, even without this being specifically intended by the source, that can only be avoided if a special effort is made to do so.

From this we draw the conclusion that it may appear to be necessary, and at least worthwhile, to treat sounds and music as two different types of nonverbal acoustic signs, even if we should discover later that they can assume similar functions as theatrical signs.

Sounds

Sounds produced deliberately—such as a policeman's whistle, screeching sirens, the clanging of a trolley car, the knocking at a door—are both created and interpreted as signs. However, sounds that are a natural effect and caused unintentionally should only be interpreted as signs, since they are not produced on the basis of an intention. The sound of rain drops hitting the roof can be interpreted as a sign for the fact that rain is falling, the sound of an engine as a sign for an automobile that is passing, the creaking of stairs as the sign for someone coming upstairs. Since in this sense all sounds can be interpreted as signs, they are also all capable of functioning as signs. Sounds that are employed in the theater in order to signify sounds are, for this reason, always to be judged as signs of signs.

For the same reason, however, all of those signs that appear on the stage, which have not been planned, but are rather the unavoidable result of certain actions—such as the sound of costumes dragging across the floor of the stage, the creaking of the stage floor, etc.—must not be regarded and interpreted as theatrical signs, but rather have to remain excluded from the process of constituting meaning, more or less as if they had not been perceived.[4]

The primary sign function of sound in the theater consists of signifying a sound. With regard to the performance of this function, it is totally irrelevant whether the sound is produced as a recorded reproduction of a corresponding "real" sound or as a stylized imitation. In the context of a certain theatrical code a choo-choo sound produced by a human voice backstage may be no less effective as a means of signifying the hiss of a steam locomotive than a recording of the actual noise created when such a locomotive leaves the station.[5]

The sounds that can be denoted in this way in the theater can essentially be divided into three large categories. They are (1) natural sounds referring to processes in nature, such as rain, thunder, wind, or referring to animals producing them: birds chirping, dogs barking, wolves howling, etc.; (2) the sounds of machinery that are automatically produced when work is being done with machines, such as clocks ticking, boilers churning, engines running; and (3) sounds which occur because of specific actions, such as dishes clattering when the table is set, glass breaking when a pane of glass is shattered, the sound of a door slamming, and many others.

Although a sound in the theater—regardless of what kind of sound is involved—denotes another sound, it at the same time refers to the process, the object, or the action that produced the sound signified, and functions in this way also as a sign for the respective source of the sound. To the extent that specific symbolic meanings may be assigned to the corresponding process, object, or action on the basis of various cultural codes, the sound can also be used as a theatrical sign to refer to these symbolic meanings. The sound of nightingales, rustling sounds in the forest, and the splashing of a waterfall or a well can be taken to mean signs for a natural space, which in Western culture as a *locus amoenus* has become a literary theme. The sounds which have the function of signifying this space can thus simultaneously also signify those notions which are traditionally associated with the *locus amoenus*. The sound of traffic of the widest variety, on the other hand, will refer to the space of a large city and in so doing also to those meanings of the large city which are provided for by the respective cultural code. Sounds used as theatrical signs may thus give rise to a wealth of potential meanings.

These meanings can, first of all, be related to space, and indeed in a multitude of ways. To the extent that they come from a certain direction, they indicate initially a spatial relationship. Engine noises that issue into the space occupied by the audience from above refer, for example, to an airplane passing over in the sky; engine sounds that can be heard from the front, far behind the stage, indicate an automobile going by there. Furthermore, if the volume or direction of the sound changes, it can indicate a movement of the object signified by it. The gradual amplification of engine noise can be interpreted as a sign for the slowly approaching airplane, which at its loudest is a sign for its position directly above the audience and, when gradually fading away, as a sign for its gradual disappearance.

Sounds may also characterize more precisely the place signified by the stage space. Bleating, mooing, and cackling identify it as a farm, the sounds of the ocean as a coastal region, the drone of machinery as a factory. Sounds can also be interpreted as telling time. Owls hooting indicate nighttime, cocks crowing point to daybreak, the chiming of a clock a particular time of day.

Sounds can be employed to describe a situation or action. The sounds of wind, thunder, rumbling, and rain splashing constitute the meaning "storm"; sables clanging, canons thundering, mines detonating, or the ratatatat of machine guns, signifies "battle," or also "battle in the Middle Ages," "battle in the twentieth century," etc.[6] The volume of these noises in each case refers to the distance at which the intended events are presumed to be taking place. If they are to be thought of as taking place on the stage, the sounds are usually accompanied by lighting effects.[7]

However, sounds cannot only be used to evoke the idea of a collective action—such as a battle or a sports event—but also to signify the actions of individual characters. In this case a distinction has to be made between sounds that are created onstage by A as a result of intentional gestures that function as signs for X's intentional gestures, and sounds that are produced offstage and refer to X's actions. If, for example, A throws a glass onstage and breaks it, the sound—even if amplified artificially—can only be interpreted as a sign supporting the intentional gesture with regard to the intensity of X's action.[8] If, on the other hand, X leaves the stage with a glass in his hand— pursued by Y or visibly upset—and at the next moment we hear a loud shattering sound, the sound functions for its part as a sign for the completion of the corresponding action and in this capacity in turn also as a sign for its intensity. In this sense, the sound produced offstage has greater importance, in that it not only represents a sign that accompanies the action, but also is the sign that in itself signifies this action. The meaning that sounds are capable of constituting with regard to the character are related in both cases to the object level of their actions. Yet, they involve both the subject and intersubjective levels only via the object level. The shattering sound initially refers exclusively to an action (throwing the glass), and only to the extent that this action for its part can be interpreted as a sign for the character and/or the momentary emotional state of X or for his relationship to Y does it also refer indirectly to these findings.

Since the sound as a theatrical sign not only signifies a sound, but, by denoting a sound, is also capable of connoting its cause and its possible symbolic meanings, the sound can frequently also be used and interpreted as a sign for such symbolic meanings. In every performance of Tennessee Williams's *A Streetcar Named Desire*, for example, this sign function has to be accorded a top priority. The clanging sound of the streetcar, produced in a particular way, refers to the streetcar and thus to the symbolic meaning with which it has been imbued in the context of this play.

Similarly, sounds can also be used—to a limited degree—as signs for moods. For the sounds which constitute the meanings "storm," "forest," "*locus amoenus*," "factory," "stadium," "large city," etc., complete this process in a concretization that is specific to each. This concrete form not only engenders the meaning of a particular space, object, or process, but also the meaning of a particular atmosphere that characterizes this space, process, or object more closely.

Our investigation of the sign functions that may be fulfilled by sounds as theatrical signs has yielded an interesting finding. It indicates that the sign functions that can be performed by sounds are indeed largely identical to those that can be performed by the spatial signs. The obvious affinity of the two sign systems— which are completely different according to material criteria—results in their especially close interaction and in their interchangeability in principle. Therefore, it can hardly be surprising on the basis of our discussions to discover that sounds can replace decoration—or parts of the decoration—as well as individual props or the intentional gestures geared to these props. They are, like the spatial signs, capable of signifying not only individual actions, but also complete action sequences, even whole complexes of action, by referring to them in this way.

Sounds are used—with varying degrees of frequency and emphasis—in most theatrical codes. Although the full range of possible meanings that can be achieved with sound could not be exploited until the age of technology, the stage techniques of former centuries had already devised impressive means of utilizing sound. In Greek theater, for example, the so-called bronteum was used to produce the sound of thunder, by allowing lead pellets to fall from a bronze jar onto a taut animal hide, or by pouring pebbles into a metal bowl. This technique was rounded out by the use of the kerannoskopeion, a reflecting bronze plate that was used to simulate lightning. This was employed to constitute the meaning "storm."[9] Similar instruments for the creation of sounds of thunder or wind are known to us in the theater of numerous periods.

Even if sounds possess many different possible meanings which have repeatedly been created in the widest variety of functions, they are not a necessary element of the theatrical code. For if theater, reduced to its minimal conditions, is determined by the fact that A embodies X while S looks on, sounds are by no means indispensable as theatrical signs for constituting the theater, but rather would appear merely to be a potential additional element that can be employed successfully and effectively under given circumstances, the use of which, however, can in principle be dispensed with.

Music

In the course of our investigation of the various potential theatrical signs, we have consistently begun with an attempt to ascertain the meanings that a certain sign system is generally capable of producing—linguistic, gestural, costume, sounds, etc. We have then gone on to distinguish those meanings that can in principle be constituted by the corresponding system of theatrical signs in each case. This approach is based on our definition of theater. For we have defined theater as a process in which signs that already exist in a culture and fulfill a specific function are not employed in this function, but rather as signs of signs in order to reflect on the corresponding culture in two ways. Theater is a reflection of a culture and as such presents this culture to its members for them to reflect on it consciously. We have therefore had to draw on the semiotics of the respective cultural systems, but not on a semiotic aesthetics of individual art genres. For if theater is not conceived of as a *Gesamtkunstwerk* made up of a complex of various forms of art that are its components—such as poetry, painting, performing arts, architecture, music—but rather as a specific complex of signs that signify signs of the widest variety of cultural systems, then the question of the aesthetic function cannot be raised at the systemic level. For an aesthetic function can only be accorded to an individual performance; it is, in other words, exclusively related to the theatrical code on the level of speech. In that case, however, it has to be assigned to the complex as a whole, and not to the individual sign systems that constitute it.[10]

These conditions give rise to certain difficulties when we turn to an investigation of the meanings that can be created with musical signs in the theater. For in most of the works on the semiotics of music it is not assumed that music is a cultural system with specific functions in that culture, but rather that music is an art, and in the stricter sense an autonomous art.[11] From this perspective the question of whether music is by nature a semantic or an asemantic art becomes the key issue.[12]

This question, on the other hand, can hardly be considered relevant in the context of our investigation. Since we know from the history of music and comparative musicology that individual periods in Western music history—such as Gregorian or baroque music—as well as non-European cultures—such as various oriental or African cultures[13]—even attach or continue to attach certain meanings to specific musical sequences, we can only direct our interest to the question of what the nature of those meanings is that can generally be created with music. This question does not involve the problem of a typology of musical signs. For the aim is not to examine whether music is constituted with the help of iconic signs (of the type which can be found in all musical onomatopoeia), indexical signs (as can be found, for example, in expressions of feeling in the music of Chopin or Debussy), or symbolic signs (as in Bach's Tritonus allegories).[14] Rather, we are concerned exclusively with the possible meanings that can be produced by music in general. In order to ascertain what they are, we will not assume that music is art, much less autonomous art, but rather begin by examining the general functions that music may perform in a culture.

Music is employed in most cultures—in concrete forms specific to each—in certain social situations, e.g., magic and sacred activities, celebrations (initiation rites, weddings, christenings, for example), various forms of entertainment, playing (dancing, for example), everyday work situations, deaths, and wartime processions, among many others. Each situation calls for a certain kind of music which is not interchangeable with any other. Dance music normally cannot be played at a religious service, a funeral dirge will not be heard at a wedding, and marching music is not performed at a ball. Such situations are also fixed in European culture as well and coordinated with a specific kind of music—the respective musical genres. In other words, since the musical genres are directly related to social situations, we can define the reference to these situations as their so-called "practical" function.[15] Inasmuch as they are capable, based on specific cultural codes, of referring to certain social situations, we can regard them as signs for such situations. The question of whether a motet or a funeral dirge can be a work of art while at the same time fulfilling this function is totally irrelevant in this context.[16]

On the one hand, European culture—like other cultures—makes use of such a correlation of social situations and musical genres. Yet, on the other hand, it also redefines two extreme situations in which music is employed, which ultimately contradict this connection. First of all, it introduces a situation which is determined by the function of exclusively serving the purpose of hearing music—the concert. The music performed here can come from any of the musical genres, without the connection between this genre and a particular social situation being relevant for the concert situation. In a concert all of music's "practical" functions are suspended. Its function lies instead in its fundamental lack of a function with regard to real social situations.[17]

The second situation newly introduced by our culture on the one hand represents a reversal in a certain sense, and amounts, on the other, to a consequence of the particular use of music in the concert. In our century—especially during the last twenty years—music has found its way into all kinds of social situations, but without being related to these situations in any particular way as defined by a specific cultural code. We are exposed to constant musical stimulation in the dentist's office, at the supermarket, on the street, in restaurants, etc., which—regardless of whether it is Beethoven's *Eroica* or the Beatles—is only capable of fulfilling the function of background, an environment of sound that is ubiquitous and cannot be shaken off.

Despite the prevailing tendency in our culture to relax, if not completely dissolve, the close tie between a particular social situation, on the one hand, and a specific musical genre, on the other, in our further discussion we will come back to this relationship, because in my view the use of music as a theatrical sign is possible and justified because of that relationship.

Music can only perform its "practical" function of referring in a specific way to a particular social situation on the basis of a symbolic meaning that music helps to constitute. Because it can signify mourning/sadness/sobriety, for example, it is used as a funeral dirge in a funeral procession; because it can connote courage/daring/aggressiveness, it is used on military occasions, etc. Symbolic and practical functions are thus closely related. Nevertheless, music can fulfill its symbolic functions even when it is not tied to any practical function—as in a concert, for example.[18]

We will therefore have to examine which kind of symbolic meanings can in principle be created with music in general, before we begin to explore and present their sign functions in theater. In the two Greek myths about the origin or discovery of music by the gods, two possibilities of symbolic meaning basically determined by it are articulated. According to Pindar's description in the twelfth Pythian ode, Athena discovered how to play the aulos in order to portray the heartbreaking, loud-sounding laments of Medusa's sister Euryale. She discovered music as the expression of subjective human emotion. According to Homer, on the other hand, Hermes has to be regarded as the inventor of music; for when he saw the shell of a tortoise he got the idea that he could create musical sounds if it were used as a resonant instrument, and in this way he created the lyre. He invented music by transforming the material world into a resounding reflection of space—music became the realization of *Weltharmonie*.[19] Whereas in Western music theory from Pythagoras to Kepler the second of these two possible meanings of music was considered predominant and music was accordingly viewed as the imperfect but audible reflection of the harmony of the spheres which could otherwise not be perceived by the human ear, and as the reflection of those inaudible sounds which were thought of as being attached to the planets, in subsequent centuries the first possible meaning became increasingly predominant. Indeed, in the first half of the nineteenth century music was defined and understood almost exclusively as the expression of human emotions.[20] Thus, according to these myths, the meanings which music may constitute are related either to the feelings of the human subject or to the space surrounding it.

In principle, all further schemes of classification can be traced back to these two potential fundamental meanings. In our context, however, a somewhat more detailed classification would initially appear to be more to the point. We therefore distinguish between (1) meanings of music related to space and movement; (2) meanings that are related to objects and actions in space; (3) meanings related to character, mood, condition, and emotion, and (4) meanings related to an idea.[21] Francès writes the following about the first three kinds of meaning:

> The coupling of the scheme of rhythm and melody with the gestural schemes that accompany behavior represents one of the fundamental elements of the expressive language of music. . . . The fundamental psychic states (calmness, excitedness, tension, relaxation, exaltation, depression) are normally translated by the gestural forms having a given rhythm, by tendencies and spatial directions (ascension, depression, horizontality), by the modalities of the organisation of partial forms at the heart of the global forms (obstinate repetition, diversity, periodicity, evolution). . . . The transposition of these rhythms, tendencies, modalities of movement at the sonorous level constitutes the foundation of the expressive language of music.[22]

These meanings naturally evolve—as do all meanings—on the basis of special cultural codes and are by no means to be understood as, as it were, determined as the "nature" of musical processes.[23] Whereas in our culture, for example, high-pitched tones are described as clear, cheerful, delighted, sunny, etc., and low-pitched tones as serious, somber, sad, celebratory, exactly the opposite connotations are attached to these sounds by the Jews, the Greeks, and the Arabs.[24] To the extent that the meanings of music are regarded as emotions, there are considerable differences with regard to their distinction even within our culture.[25]

The cultural specificity of the meanings to be constituted by music becomes evident above all when these meanings are construed as ideas. In oriental music, for example, the scales and notes are related to the prevailing cosmology, to the planets, and to the hours of the day. In a "sideric" scale of this kind the re, for example, means the moon; do, Mercury; si (b), Venus; la, the sun; sol, Mars; fa, Jupiter; and mi, Saturn.[26] In a similar manner, however, the portrayal of the divine, the revolutionary, etc., in European music history can only be understood in the context of the corresponding cultural tradition.

In music—at least as far as Western history is concerned—a fixed assignment of a meaning to a particular musical sequence in the framework of a prevailing convention can by no means be considered the rule, but is rather an exception to the rule—especially in European music of the last two centuries. We therefore have to take into consideration a specific peculiarity of the meanings constituted by music: they remain to a large degree undetermined. Whereas thunder and rain sounds, for example, may be interpreted with a large degree of correspondence as signs for a storm, it will not be possible, even within a given culture, to establish beyond any doubt the meaning of a musical rendition of a storm. Rather, it will remain open to many other—perhaps even contradictory—possible interpretations. We therefore have to proceed on the general premise that the meanings created with music generally have to be judged as vague and can hardly be defined more closely, above all when it is a question of "concert music" in our culture.

However, music is never employed in theater as "absolute" music, but rather always in particular functions which are related to the context of the other signs produced. Music's indeterminacy is therefore subject to a certain limitation here, and consequently it will be entirely capable of fulfilling distinctly separate sign functions.

With regard to music as a theatrical sign, we basically have to distinguish between two possibilities: (1) music that is created by actor A's activity and (2) music that is made by musicians in the orchestra pit or by musicians and technicians offstage. The activity that an actor performs to create music can be defined as (a) singing[27] and (b) music-making.

In dramatic theater the actor's singing denotes the singing of character X, whereas in musical theater it is a particular kind of speech by X. In this case, in other words, it takes on special sign functions which are performed by the paralinguistic signs in dramatic theater, and fulfills them in a particular way.[28]

This fundamental difference between dramatic theater and opera has to be borne in mind if we wish to examine the principal meanings which song can take on in the theater, because the respective modifications which these meanings may undergo in the specific theatrical forms will have to be traced back to it.

In both cases the musical signs are related on the one hand to the *object level* of the words sung, and on the other to the *subject level* of character X. To the extent that the meanings of the musical signs are geared to the meanings of the linguistic signs, the former can in a certain manner modify or reinforce the latter, contradict them, or even fail to appear to have any recognizable connection with them.

On the subject level, the musical signs of song are capable of creating meanings that are related above all to personality, the momentary mood, and the feelings of character X—even though they can also be interpreted to some extent as signs for X's position in the room and his movements. In Western opera specific types of voices are employed and interpreted as signs for various types of characters. The soubrette usually signifies a cheerful, uncomplicated, even-tempered person (often a servant), the coloratura soprano an extremely "dramatic" type, the "heroic tenor" the positive hero, etc.[29] The most important function of singing, however, can be defined as the expression of personal feeling.

> When a person feels joyful, he expresses this in words. When words are not adequate, he expands (sings) the words. When the expanded word is not adequate, he adds the instrumental orchestra to it. When the orchestra is not adequate, his hands involuntarily begin to sway and his feet stomp the floor.[30]

This two-and-a-half-millennia-old Chinese saying succinctly describes an insight into the graduated sequence in the use of media for the expression of human emotion, the validity of which is not by any means limited to oriental forms of theater. For they allow one to conclude that the musical signs of song take on those sign-functions of the paralinguistic signs that are geared to the expression of the character's mood and emotion and that they render in a specific way.

The meanings that the musical signs of song are capable of creating cannot be related directly to the intersubjective level, but only very indirectly via the meanings constituted on the subject level.[31] Whereas in opera by definition singing is part of the genre and to this extent the fact of singing itself cannot be regarded as a signifying element, in dramatic theater it has to be evaluated as such. For here the specific fact that X sings functions for its part as a sign that has to be interpreted either in relation to X's momentary frame of mind or in relation, for example, to the particular social situation.[32]

A's music-making invariably denotes *X's music-making*. With regard to this function the meanings to be assigned to the musical signs are directly related to *character X*, or to put it more exactly, they are related to the *subject level*. They can be employed and interpreted both as signs for X's position in the room, his movement, or his special skill in music-making, and as a sign for his personality, mood, and feelings.

To the extent that the musical signs are produced by A's activity and denote A's activity, their potential meanings always refer to character X. They thus put into practice the overall possible meaning music can have in referring to character, condition, mood, emotion—and thus its capacity to serve as the expression of subjective human feeling and yet do so exclusively in relation to character X. Because those general meanings are tied to a specific character, i.e., can be constituted only on the condition that they are constituted as X's character, condition, mood, and emotion, they lose the indeterminacy perhaps otherwise typical of them, and gain in terms of both individual shape and precision.

The musical signs that are produced by musicians in the orchestra pit and by musicians or technicians offstage can fulfill various sign functions. Their meanings may initially be related to *space*,[33] and—like those of sounds—in more than one way. The musical signs can refer to special *spatial conditions* as well as to *movements* of all the spatial objects and persons signified by it. This means at the same time that music in the theater can also constitute *spatial objects* as its meaning— regardless of whether this is done by means of a special leitmotif technique (sword motif),[34] musical onomatopoeia (cuckoo call), or even other specifically symbolic techniques.

Musical signs can also render the characterization of the *location* that the stage space is intended to signify more precise. Oriental temple music, Greek folk strains, Spanish guitar sounds, for example, allow the stage space to appear as a Japanese temple, Greek mountains, or the street of a Spanish city, whereas organ music characterizes it as being a church and electronic music as outer space,[35] to name only a few examples. Similarly, music can also signify the *period* in question. Baroque music can function, for example, as a sign for this period as well as generally for past periods, rock music as a sign for the present, electronic music as a sign for a distant future, etc.

The meaning of musical signs can also be related to a *situation* and/or *actions*. Music can be used to refer to processes in nature—such as a storm, tempest, etc.—as well as to processes in society—such as revolution, war, etc. It is particularly capable of constituting the latter meanings in that in theater the "practical" functions of music are transformed into symbolic functions. Horns sounding indicate a hunt, a funeral dirge a funeral, organ music a religious service, village dance music a village dance, minuets or waltzes a ball in the corresponding period, the trumpet signal military reveille, etc. As theatrical signs, the musical genres are thus capable of signifying action sequences and constellations of action by pointing to certain social situations.[36]

All of the above sign functions that music as a theatrical sign is capable of performing are shared in common with sounds in their capacity as theatrical signs. Unlike sounds, however, music cannot be used to provide a fairly clear-cut concrete representation of the object concerned, the place, the situation, or action, e.g., as a streetcar, the sea, a battle, or knocking on the door. Its wealth of possible meanings may, in principle, be limited to a certain degree by the reference to the respective stage space. Yet this does not involve the elimination or curbing of the possibility that its fundamental capacity to have potential symbolic meanings affords, namely to signify objects, places, and situations in one and the same musical act, and at the same time to signify an overall *mood/atmosphere*, an abstract *idea*, even if this is not its primary function. The musical sequences that are interpreted as signs for a storm can at the same time be regarded as signs of something terrible; those sequences which can be interpreted as signs for a rebellion can at the same time function as signs for the revolutionary element, etc.[37]

In other words, the sign functions performed by sounds are nearly completely identical to those functions of the spatial signs which are geared to concrete objects, places, situations, and actions. By contrast, those sign functions fulfilled primarily by the musical signs converge with those spatial signs that are intended to constitute their meaning as the creation of an atmosphere, as an indication of an idea. In this way, sounds and music can, in combination, assume all of the sign functions that would be performed by the spatial signs. Yet they are nevertheless geared to constituting distinct kinds of meanings. Whereas sounds refer to concrete things as their meanings, music tends to create meanings that are related to abstract elements.

The music produced in orchestra pits or offstage can, in addition, also be employed and interpreted—like the sign produced by A—as a sign for *character X*. In fulfilling this function it can be employed both as a general sign which—as a leitmotif, for example, assigned to a character—refers to the whole person of this character, even or precisely in the character's absence, and as a special sign for specific features or circumstances concerning the character and which can only be related to him because he is present on the stage. Music is thus capable of showing the character on stage as having a cheerful personality, for example, as being happy or carefree; as being a melancholy person, somber and depressed; as being aggressive and impulsive; or as being reflective, slow, etc. Or music may point to certain mental activities on the character's part. It can signify the characters' thoughts, ideas, dreams, memories; it can trigger them off or express his feelings, joy, happiness, love, hate and anger, sorrow, longing, and fear. The meanings that music is capable of constituting in this way in relation to the character thus apply above all to the subject level.

In addition, the meanings created by music can be related to the object level of the movements X executes in space. Music can signify his hopping, striding, climbing, jumping, running, etc., the kind of movement involved as well as the changes in position. The musical signs appear in this way to be most closely linked to the proxemic and gestural signs—in a similar manner as singing is related to the linguistic signs. Accordingly, the musical signs can modify the meanings created by the proxemic and gestural signs, may reinforce them, or may contradict them and in this way produce new meanings related to X.

This close connection between musical and gestural/proxemic signs constitutes a specific theatrical genre of a special variety, namely ballet, dance theater. Here the dominant vehicle of meaning is the respective special relationship between the two kinds of theatrical sign systems which form a unit and interpret each other within this unit.

If, in conclusion, we take another look at the most important sign functions listed here which music as a theatrical sign is capable of fulfilling, we can summarize by saying that, on the one hand, they overlap—as already mentioned—with specific sign functions of the spatial signs, but on the other hand, they also overlap with sign functions otherwise fulfilled by the signs which the actor produces through his activity, namely, verbal and kinesic signs. These are above all those sign functions intended to constitute meanings which can be described more closely as the personality, mood, or emotions of character X. In fact, music as a theatrical sign also actualizes primarily those two potential meanings which Athena and Hermes meant when they, each in their own way, invented music and bestowed it on humanity.

Music can in principle be employed in all genres and forms of theater as a theatrical sign. On the one hand, inasmuch as it does not add any new sign functions to the theatrical code, it does not represent an element necessary for the code's constitution. The theatrical process can take place without musical signs. Since music, on the other hand, fulfills those sign functions that it can have in the theater in a quite specific way, which is reserved for it alone, it then becomes a necessary element of the theatrical code under certain conditions and premises and in this way functions as a constituent of a specific theatrical genre—for the musical theater. To the extent that in many cultures—among them, the ancient Greeks, the Chinese, Indians, Africans—musical theater is regarded as theater per se because theater in these cultures has always taken the form of musical theater, music also has to be regarded as a constitutive element of the respective theatrical code. In medieval and modern Europe, however, theater primarily developed as spoken theater—albeit usually with musical interludes—so that here the dominance of music necessarily led to a special theatrical genre, namely, opera.[38]

The predominance of music in the theatrical code of opera—and this defines the genre in the first place—led to its theatrical code's being organized in a special way,[39] and it retained its validity into the first half of our century. It thus created a significant difference between the theatrical codes of postbaroque spoken theater and the postbaroque opera, respectively.

This difference exists not only with respect to the mimic signs which cannot be employed by the singer in all of their potential meaning functions because he or she is singing, but also in the area of gestural signs. Here the repertoire of expressive gestural possibilities, such as that developed in baroque theater, was retained and continued to be used.[40] Whereas the pre-avant-garde bourgeois spoken theater made an effort to create as complete an illusion of reality as possible, operatic theater contemporaneous to it abstained from such attempts. Since it originated as a nonillusionist theatrical genre in which a character's speech is denoted by A's singing, the opera hardly needed a set of gestures to fulfill the signifying functions inherent in it, gestures which for the most part coincide with the gestural code of the culture in question. Rather, it was able to draw on the traditional gestural code specific to the opera, a code that was comparatively meager in the meanings it afforded in that it expressed human thoughts and feelings primarily by means of musical signs. Indeed, these signs can in no manner address the problem of intersubjectivity, which was a key category for the fin de siècle theater of illusion and thus required the information of a corresponding gestural code.[41]

In Western spoken theater, music also often functions as an integrating component of the theatrical code. However, whereas in forms of theater which aim at creating an illusion of "reality"—such as Enlightenment, realist, and naturalist theaters—it has only to fulfill those sign functions which are related to certain social situations, in other forms of theater it is employed to perform the widest variety of sign functions. Just as its use in baroque theater, for example, was geared to the appearance of transcendence via immanence, in Romantic theater it was employed for the purpose of creating a specific atmosphere in each case; in Brecht's theater it even functioned as a medium of distanced reflection.

Music acquired a relatively dominant status in the theatrical code of the avant-garde. To a generation which wanted to create a new kind of theater that was totally anti-illusionist, it seemed that it was only possible to fashion such an innovation "from the spirit of the music"; not only Appia and Craig, but also Meyerhold and Tairov were convinced that in music they had rediscovered the basis of all that is theatrical and had found the factor determining the possibility of a truly "theatrical" theater.[42]

5. Theater as a Semiotic System

☐ ☐ ☐ In the introduction, the production of meaning was defined as the basic function of all cultural systems. However, since systems can in principle fulfill this function in different ways, they had to be differentiated further, and a distinction was made between nonaesthetic systems and aesthetic systems. In the group of nonaesthetic cultural systems, those cultural systems which served primarily to fulfill communicative functions—such as language, traffic signs, Morse code, etc.—were contrasted with those geared primarily to exercising practical functions, such as clothing, building, tool manufacture, etc. With regard to aesthetic systems, which are to be distinguished from their nonaesthetic counterparts by the fact that they overcome the dominance of the latter's respective primary function and replace it with a dominant aesthetic function, theater was juxtaposed to the other aesthetic systems. For, as has been shown above, theater is in principle diametrically opposed to all other artistic genres both in terms of the ontological status of the artworks it involves—the performances—and with regard to the conditions for its production and reception.

Furthermore, as described in a previous chapter, theater not only fulfills its function of generating meaning under those specific conditions mentioned that give it a special place among the cultural systems. Rather, like all cultural systems, theater fulfills this function on the basis of a special code intrinsic to it alone, namely, the internal theatrical code.

Having to a great extent outlined this internal theatrical code at a systemic level in the preceding chapters, we shall now focus on the question of whether the special position which we claimed was occupied by theater as an aesthetic system is reflected in the organization of the theatrical code, and, should this prove to be the case, whether an explanation for this fact is also to be uncovered in its organization.

The Specificity of the Theatrical Sign

All those signs that have been classified as theatrical signs function, as shown in individual cases, as *signs of signs*. It was P. Bogatyrev who first had this fundamental insight into the specificity of theatrical signs;[1] later semioticians of the theater have adopted the substance of this position without modifying it.[2] In the present context, however, the question arises whether this categorization of a property that sets theater off fundamentally from all other aesthetic systems can be upheld without being defined more precisely.

For the ability to function as the sign of a sign is a characteristic of all aesthetic systems: poetic signs or the signs of painting, musical signs or the signs of sculpture are not signs for objects but are to be understood as signs of the meanings posited with these objects—in other words, they too are to be considered as signs of signs.[3]

Nevertheless, there is a fundamental difference between theatrical and other aesthetic signs with regard to the specificity of the theatrical signs. For poetic or musical signs, for example, can only point to other signs in their capacity as linguistic or musical signs—i.e., they differ in terms of material from all the non-linguistic and nonmusical signs they may be intended to signify. Theatrical signs, by contrast, can in principle be materially identical with the signs they are meant to signify: a linguistic sign can signify a linguistic sign, a sign of external appearance can signify a sign of external appearance, a gestural, architectonic, or musical sign—each can signify the respective equivalent sign. Any random object that can function in a culture as a sign can, without its material nature being changed in any way, function as a theatrical sign for the sign it itself represents. Owing to this special ability, however, the specific characteristic typical of aesthetic signs, namely, that they are signs of signs, has a special bearing in the case of theatrical signs. For, if an object that is intended predominantly to fulfill a practical function in a culture, e.g., a chair, points in its capacity as a theatrical sign to the meaning potentially to be attributed to this object, then this act simultaneously highlights the character of the object "chair" as a sign. If the chair can be utilized and identified as a theatrical sign, then it will also be possible to conceive of it and identify it when it fulfills its practical function as a sign within that culture: for example, as a sign of these practical functions. The transformation of an object into a theatrical sign, which can occur without any alteration to its material nature, thus allows the observer to clearly perceive the character the objects in question have as signs, a trait they must in principle be assumed to have, and which is always implicitly given, as it were.

The great *mobility* of theatrical signs results from this capacity to function as a sign of a sign. As has been seen above, words, for example, can substitute for stage decor, props can be replaced by gestures, gestures by sounds, lighting by props, etc. As demonstrated in an earlier chapter, because these heterogeneous theatrical signs can partly substitute for one another, they can also be used interchangeably. Thus, rain can be signified by sounds, lighting, costumes, props, gestures, or words: a raincoat may fulfill the same function here as the sound of falling raindrops; a hand held protectively over one's head; dim, flickering light; an umbrella being opened; or the words "it's raining" being uttered.[4] A theatrical sign can, in other words, function not only as a sign of a sign that it itself depicts materially, but can in addition function as the sign of a sign which may belong to any other sign system at random.

It was the Prague structuralists who first observed this specificity of theatrical signs and studied it more closely, especially Honzl, Mukařovský and Bogatyrev.[5] It would, indeed, appear to be that special quality that fundamentally distinguished theater from all other aesthetic systems, on the one hand, and from the set of nonaesthetic systems, on the other. Since the other aesthetic systems can only be articulated using specific, homogeneous material, their capacity for generating signs is grounded in and limited by this material: the linguistic signs used in poetry cannot be replaced by pictures, objects, or gestures; sounds, architectonic, or paralinguistic signs cannot substitute for the signs of painting, etc.[6] Conversely, a culture's set of nonaesthetic systems is clearly characterized by its making all conceivable types of signs available, yet in the context of social reality these signs can only be interchangeable to a limited extent; indeed, in some cases they cannot substitute for one another at all. For the communicative or practical functions they are meant to fulfill cannot be adequately exercised by other sign systems: a traffic light cannot be replaced by a written description of its meaning, and the linguistic signs used in a philosophical lecture cannot be replaced by gestures. The trolley that I wish to board can be signified clearly by the sound of a trolley bell, yet the important practical function it fulfills for me cannot be replaced, just as the coat that I wish to put on cannot be replaced by the word "coat" or the picture of a coat or the gesture of putting on a coat. In theater, by contrast, I can in principle use any one sign instead of another. In this instance, an object can signify every other object and can therefore be replaced in its function as a theatrical sign by any other random sign. For, because the dominance of the primary functions valid in the rest of cultural reality—which prevents interchangeability— is repealed here, the sign can function exclusively as a sign of a sign, and because this function can be fulfilled by all theatrical signs, it can be replaced by other signs and in turn replace them.

The mobility of theatrical signs also involves their *polyfunctionality*. For a theatrical sign can substitute for other theatrical signs only to the extent that it can take on differing semiotic functions: a chair can, for example, be utilized to signify not only a chair, but also a mountain, a staircase, a sword, an umbrella, an automobile, an enemy soldier, a sleeping child, an angry superior, a tender lover, a raging lion, etc. The chair takes on those meanings which the actor's acting imparts to it.[7] Every theatrical sign can in this manner fulfill numerous functions and accordingly generate the widest variety of meaning.[8]

Structure and Hierarchy

Chapters 1 through 4 listed the heterogeneous material creations which can function as units of the theatrical code, i.e., as theatrical signs. The sign systems from which they originate were examined in terms of their specific ways of generating meaning. In this context, an attempt was made to describe the constitutive units of the respective sign systems by dividing the latter up into kinemes, sounds, or special complexes of features (as in the case of paralinguistic or architectonic signs).

If we define theater itself as a sign system, the problem arises as to the extent to which this system must also be subdivided into its smallest constitutive elements in order to establish the special way in which it functions as a system generating meaning. This brings the analysis up against the question of "the possibility of grouping the significant units in paradigmatic categories and determining the syntagmatic relations which unite them,'' as Corvin puts it.[9] This question is regarded by most theater semioticians today as one of the central problems of the field. There is hardly a semiotic study of theater that does not address this question at least in passing.

The structural principles suggested thus far can essentially be summarized in terms of two groups. The first group, put forward predominantly by French scholars, can be characterized by Roland Barthes's remark: "What is the relation between these signs, organized in counterpoint, i.e., signs that are at the same time both dense and expansive, both simultaneous and successive? By definition, they always signify the same thing, but use different signifiers."[10] Barthes, in other words, assumes that the individual units may be heterogeneous—with regard to both their specific ontological state and the duration of their presence on stage—but that the meanings they simultaneously generate are always the same, are always homogeneous. Theater, in this view, exhibits a high degree of redundancy, for multiples of every meaning are produced at the same time. It follows from this that one needs only resort to one of the systems involved in order to create the meaning, without running the risk of ignoring some factors that play an important role in the construction of meaning. In other words, the theatrical code cannot be broken down into homogeneous signifiers, but it can be divided up into homogeneous signifieds. Corvin[11] and Durand[12] are both also of this opinion, albeit with some qualification. The second group, championed especially by Polish theater semioticians,[13] presumes that the signs realized simultaneously may indeed generate differing meanings and that the overall meaning of all the signs produced simultaneously will therefore indeed differ from that of the meanings of the individual signs, for it is constituted precisely as a specific relation between these meanings.

A problem arises with this view, namely, how the overall course of a performance can be divided up into such smallest possible "simultaneous" units of meaning. Kowzan proposes the following definition: "The semiological unity of a performance is a slice containing all the signs issued simultaneously, a slice of a length equal to that of the sign with the shortest timespan."[14] Whereas this definition —and it is used with minor modifications by Brach and Osiński[15]—is adopted lock, stock, and barrel by Diez Borque,[16] Helbo, Pavis and Sławinska[17] charge it, to my mind justifiably so, with promoting an atomization of the theatrical code into a number of small individual units whose coherence is at risk of disappearing in the process, and the overall meaning of a performance can in no manner be constituted without recourse to this interconnection.

Ruffini provides an interesting variation on this position.[18] He divides theatrical signs into "segni partiali" and "segni globali": a *segno globale* is constituted by several simultaneously generated *segni partiali*. As a consequence, the course of the performance can be described as a series of such *segni globali*. The predominant task of a semiotics of the theater would then be to find and delineate the possible constitutive global signs. While Ruffini himself does not undertake to define theatrical global signs in such a manner, the suggestions made by Hamon or Jansen can perhaps be used to explain such an approach. Hamon wishes to take the *personnage* as the underlying theatrical unit, and he defines this as a sort of "doubly articulated morpheme which takes the form of a discontinuous signified, referring to a discontinuous signifier, that is, part of a paradigm originally constructed by the message (the system particular to the person of the message)."[19] Jansen, by contrast, suggests taking the situation as the smallest constitutive unit, and he defines it as

> the result of a division of the textual level into parts which correspond to closed groups at the scenic level. In other words, we shall posit the dividing line between two situations when analyzing a concrete text at that point where a person enters or exits, or alternatively where a change in location is effected by the stage decor.[20]

Prior to Jansen, Polti[21] and Souriau[22] had both attempted to divide the performance up into situations.[23]

Recourse to the characters as the smallest constitutive unit of meaning ignores the fact that by no means all theatrical signs can be conceived of as partial signs that can be subsumed under the global sign of a person in all instances, such as, for example, some spatial signs, some nonverbal acoustic signs, or those words and gestures by the actors that do not signify "person," but rather parts of the stage decor. By contrast, the subdivision into situations means that performances that do not involve a change in characters or location have to be understood as a whole to be the smallest unit. Pavis also reaches this conclusion when stating that "instead of a posteriori making a synthesis of the work out of its constituent elements, it would be in order to proceed from a notion of the work conceived of as if it were a sign that can be divided up into a number of subsigns."[24] If the performance is defined in this way as the "smallest unit," which is in turn to be structurally subdivided further, then the question as to the structural principle involved arises only at a different level. For, even if one can assume that "performance" is a global sign, it also has to be possible to define in general how the structure of this global sign can be analyzed.

Skwarczyńska takes a third approach.[25] She presumes that theater is by definition not possible without actors. Yet whenever the actor is present in person, a gestural unit is also produced. She therefore takes the gesture as the smallest theatrical unit. In this context, two things must be kept strictly separate. Theater can in principle not occur without an actor or the realization of the actor's function, yet a performance can temporarily dispense with the actor's active presence. If, as this would suggest, an actor does not need to be present during the overall course of a performance, then gestural units cannot always be assumed to exist. It follows that they cannot function as the smallest theatrical unit in the sense that theater can only be realized by means of them.

The insurmountable difficulties that face all attempts to subdivide the theatrical code into homogeneous units result on the whole from two basic circumstances:

(1) The theatrical code consists of many heterogeneous signs that stem from different sign systems and cannot therefore be analyzed in terms of homogeneous units.

(2) Since these heterogeneous theatrical signs can function as signs of signs and possess a high degree of mobility, different signs can take on identical semiotic functions. The constitution of a particular meaning thus does not depend on the use of a certain type of sign, but rather can be accomplished by means of various signs. The same meaning can therefore be generated using heterogeneous units.

In my opinion, only two conclusions can be drawn from this. The first is that the search for homogeneous units at the systemic level must be regarded as an approach doomed to failure, which should therefore be abandoned. Theater clearly differs from all other aesthetic and nonaesthetic cultural systems by virtue of its specifically referring to the respective culture in its entirety, not only in terms of the meanings it constitutes but indeed, prior to this, also by using a certain material, namely, heterogeneous theatrical signs. The fact that it does not use homogeneous units can be derived from this specific feature and thus justified by that fact. In this sense, Barthes's conclusion should be upheld, namely that theater "represents a privileged semiotic object, for its system is clearly original (polyphonous) compared with language (which is linear).[26] In fact, it is as polyphonous as the culture in which it is embedded.

The second approach is to accept the heterogeneity of the theatrical units, while at the same time insisting that, for practical reasons (for example, in order to facilitate the analysis of a particular performance), several heterogeneous units be merged into larger units. Yet it is necessary here as well to reject the call for homogeneous units. For only those categories will be able to function as larger units that have been pinpointed as being irreducible factors without which the theatrical process cannot ensue. In chapters 1 through 4 two categories were enumerated which had an indispensable function of this nature, namely, the character *and* the stage's space. For without space the character is a category of literature and without a character space is a category, for example, of sculpture.[27] If, in other words, one wishes to utilize larger units and to proceed from the heterogeneity of theatrical signs, then at least these two categories, to which all types of theatrical signs refer, must be taken into account. It is by definition impossible to delineate homogeneous units for theater.

Having thus established the pointlessness of any endeavor to divide the theatrical code up into homogeneous units, we will now attempt to draw up the general rules for the combination of heterogeneous theatrical units. We have become aware of such rules at various points thus far. These rules can refer, first, to the relation between the meanings generated by two or more simultaneously or successively realized signs, and, second, to the quantitative and qualitative valency of all the signs realized.

In the first case, two possibilities can be discerned: the meanings are either analogous, parallel to one another, or they are not. Analogous meanings support and reciprocally reinforce each other. Nonanalogous meanings either recognizably refer to one another or they do not. If the meanings recognizably refer to one another, then they may reciprocally modify or contradict each other; if no such reference is forthcoming, their meanings remain unaffected but may supplement one another. Various examples have been given in the course of the above chapters for each of these possibilities.

In the second case, each of the sign; systems used can either be accorded the same status or they can be deployed in terms of a hierarchical structure. If they are utilized with a view to their equal status, then the meanings generated by the different types of signs are also in principle to be treated as equal in standing, for no one sign can claim to have a greater importance than the others. However, if they are used in a hierarchy, one or more of the sign systems functions as the dominant one. The meanings these signs generate must in turn be conceived of as the signal meanings, and those constituted by the subordinate signs must then be related to them. Such a formation of dominants can be valid either for a single performance or for individual parts of it. The formation of dominant signs can, in other words, change within a performance.

The individual theatrical genres may be defined by the rule-based dominance of a particular sign system: dance theater is dominated by proxemic signs, pantomime by gestural sign, and opera by musical signs. By contrast, the norms realized in the course of European theater history are characterized by changes that take place in the formation of dominants, and consequently the way in which dominants are formed also functions as an element of meaning. If the formation of dominant signs in a performance deviates from that prescribed by the particular norm that is valid at the time, or if the hierarchy of components changes within the course of a performance, then this too must be conceived of as an element of meaning and investigated accordingly.

It is again the Prague structuralists who must be credited with having first drawn attention to the rule governing the formation of dominant elements. It was Honzl especially who concerned himself with this specific matter. In his study of the mobility of theater's signs he attempted to attribute the factual change of the hierarchy of theatrical elements precisely to theater's specificity with regard to mobility ("The changeability of the hierarchical scale of components of dramatic art corresponds to the changeability of the theatrical sign.")[28] In an essay on the hierarchy of theatrical means, by contrast, he attempts to outline the specific hierarchy of components used in ancient Greek tragedy.[29]

Neither Honzl nor Mukařovský, who also discussed the problem of hierarchy,[30] investigates whether there are homogeneous theatrical units; both conclude from a recognition of the specificity of the theatrical sign, its heterogeneity, and its mobility, that attention should be paid especially to the fact that a hierarchy is formed and to the respective type of elements given pride of place in the hierarchy.

Since the culture in question also represents a hierarchical system with specific elements accorded priority, the analysis of the theatrical code as a normative agency must take into account the relation between the elements characteristically accorded priority in the culture and those that are valid within the theatrical code. These are also signs that need to be interpreted. This step shifts the analysis onto the normative level.

The investigation at the systemic level of the construction of the theatrical code has thus been completed. The material creations of that code that function as its units have been enumerated, as have the significative potential of these and the general rules according to which they can be combined. All theatrical communication takes this code as its basis.

Theatrical Communication

In his 1970 essay "La communication théâtrale"[31] Mounin suggested that precisely the notion of "theatrical communication" was self-contradictory. Mounin takes up Buyssens's statement to the effect that actors in theater merely "simulate people communicating with one another; they do not communicate with the audience using the same system as that used to communicate among one another."[32] Mounin then tries to prove that no communication occurs between the stage and the audience. He defines the concept of communication such that "a sender (of messages) communicates with a receiver of these messages if the latter can respond to the former via the same channel, using the same code (or in a code which can be translated in its entirety into messages of the primary code)."[33] Mounin expressly highlights communication via linguistic signs as a model of such communication; the ability to switch between the roles of speaker and hearer as well as the dual structure of the code are thus declared to be the precondition and condition of all communication. It follows that, in light of the fact that, as was also shown in the previous section, theater cannot fulfill such requirements, it cannot by extension be considered or evaluated as communication. Mounin accordingly suggests that with regard to theater the concept of communication be discarded in favor of that of stimulation, for "the cycle initiated on the stage, and involving it and the auditorium, is essentially a (highly complex) circuit of stimulus and response."[34] Mounin's central hypothesis, namely that no communication occurs in theater, therefore clearly rests on his specific definition of the concept of communication.

Helbo attempts to disprove this suggestion by, on the one hand, pointing to the nonsensicality of the conditions on which it is based—communication with linguistic signs can be accomplished via various channels (e.g., by letter or telephone)—and, on the other, placing the concept of "decoding" at the center of his project. He writes that "we, for our part, shall retain that criterion, namely the option of coding/decoding."[35] He defines the concept of communication by means of these two notions and concludes from this definition that communication does indeed occur in the theater because "coding" takes place on stage whereas "decoding" ensues among the audience. The "competence of the theater audience"[36] is, in his opinion, manifested in this ability to decode; such a competence can only be acquired or demonstrated through a knowledge of the underlying code in question.

Helbo disproves Mounin's hypothesis by replacing the latter's concept of communication with a notion which permits him to subsume theatrical processes under it. The issue of whether communication occurs in theater or not can therefore be settled by concentrating on the specific concept of communication used.[37] For, whereas Helbo conceives of decoding as a constitutive element in the communicative process, Mounin classes the "interpretation" of a play as a noncommunicative process as it is not related to a purely linguistic message.[38]

The concept of communication to be used must therefore first be outlined if we are to continue to deploy the concept of "theatrical communication" in the present study. Communication between A and B occurs if, in order to constitute a meaning and by drawing on a code, A generates a sign to which B can attribute a meaning, using the same code. This definition by no means implies that communication takes place only if A and B constitute the same meaning—a case that, given the concept of meaning provided at the outset of the present study, would not appear to be conceivable. Rather, it would suggest that communication requires solely that partial agreement as to the meaning exist, whereby the degree of concurrence can vary. In a scholarly discussion it is regarded as absolutely indispensable that a wide-reaching agreement obtain, at least with respect to the terminology specific to the particular discipline. By contrast, a sequence of interaction between children playing can develop with a far lower degree of concurrence without this seriously jeopardizing the success of the communication.[39]

Whereas all forms of communication either related to a specific subject or based on a technical language tend to augment the extent of agreement, processes of aesthetic communication are characterized by a reduction of agreement effected with varying degrees of rigor. The ambiguity of the aesthetic sign, which by definition increases, will hardly allow for a higher degree of agreement, or at least will not bring such into being itself.[40]

Processes of theatrical communication must be thought of as constituting a special category of aesthetic communication. For signs are generated on stage in order to constitute meaning, signs to which the audience in turn attributes meanings that are in part those intended by the producers and in part different from these. The respective underlying normative theatrical code guarantees that a minimum of agreement exists, and a knowledge of this code must be presumed among both the producers of the signs and the audience attending a performance. Thus, the Peking Opera's normative theatrical code ensures, for example, that a candle being blown out is attributed the same meaning by actors and audience alike, namely, that the space signified by the stage is plunged into complete darkness; and that a foot being raised about a foot off the ground means that the character crosses a threshold. By contrast, other meanings that can be constituted by means of the signs "blowing out a candle" or "raising one's foot" within the framework of this theatrical convention may differ widely, depending on the actor, audience, or specific members thereof.

However, theatrical communication is not only a special case of aesthetic communication, but also, due to the special position of theater which we have repeatedly stressed above, an exception to some extent as well. For the conditions of theatrical communication differ significantly from those informing aesthetic communications in other artistic genres. Theatrical signs are generated and interpreted simultaneously; the constitution of meaning via the realization of signs and that via the interpretation of signs are completely parallel processes. It follows that, if communication is to be successful, at least the fundamental elements of a code shared by producers and recipients must exist prior to the beginning of the performance. That is, a knowledge of the underlying code selected by the producer cannot simply be acquired by the recipient in the process of interpretation, for example, by drawing on separate materials, comparisons, or extended reflection, such as is possible in the reception of poetry, a picture, or a statue dating from the past.

The various forms of theater fulfill the conditions for such a shared code in different ways. All forms of nonillusionistic theater, such as the Peking Opera, Nô theater, Italian opera, classical ballet, etc., do indeed presuppose a knowledge of a special, theater-specific code that has usually remained stable over a long period of time. Without such knowledge, theatrical communication cannot ensue successfully in any of the cases mentioned. These codes refer to a homogeneous audience that has learned the syntactic and semantic rules which constitute the respective code and knows how to apply these appropriately in the process of constituting meaning as receivers of the signs.

Illusionistic theater also depends on an homogeneous audience. Yet, here the homogeneity does not rest on a detailed knowledge of a complicated special theatrical code, but can rather be defined as the homogeneous experience of social reality. Illusionist theater counts on its audience's substantially belonging to one social stratum, or at least on their being at home in one and the same cultural domain. For the shared code is established here by both producer and receiver having recourse to a cultural code valid in this social stratum in order to generate and interpret signs; and it is to this code that the heterogeneous theatrical signs respectively refer. In this manner, a minimum consensus is also guaranteed in illusionistic theater, and thus the possibility of theatrical communication is secured.

The shared character of the code is, in other words, created either by the formation or tradition of a theater-specific code or by recourse to a cultural code universally valid and uniformly used in that social stratum. Mixed forms must be assumed to exist that utilize both of these approaches, which then alternately generate the shared nature of the code. The success of theatrical communication would appear to be in serious jeopardy should one or the other of these two conditions not be fulfilled.

Avant-garde theater at the beginning of the century was confronted with this problem when, negating the most extreme form of illusionistic theater, namely, naturalist theater, it expressly attempted to constitute an anti-illusionistic theater. For it was able to fall back on neither a homogeneous audience nor a valid traditional specifically theatrical code; rather, it was faced with the difficulty of first developing such a code and finding a corresponding audience for it.

Two possibilities avail themselves in this context, put into practice in exemplary manner by Tairov and Meyerhold, respectively. On the one hand, efforts must concentrate on forming a strictly theater-specific code which the audience can learn in the course of a number of performances. In this instance, realizing such an approach runs the risk that theatrical communication can only ensue with what is an elitist circle of cognoscendi; Tairov was consciously prepared to pay this price.[41]

On the other hand, efforts can focus on finding a nonhomogeneous audience, a mass audience. In this case, when forming a theater-specific code, resort must be made to elements and structural principles that stem from the cultural reality with which the mass audience is acquainted. Meyerhold believed he had found such elements and principles in the functionality of the world of work, for example, specifically in work clothing and the working rhythm of the person working at a conveyor belt. He based his development of the biomechanics of acting and of uniform stage costume on these. For Meyerhold regarded theatrical communication as only conceivable and meaningful in the form of "mass communication."[42]

These characteristic problems of avant-garde theater also confront that variant of post-avant-garde theater which wished to form an anti-illusionistic code. For neither had it proved possible to establish a valid theater-specific code, nor had a homogeneous audience formed. This is presumably the main reason for the fact that many producers in contemporary West German theaters often use signs, the meanings of which are to be constituted by resorting above all to comics, lowbrow literature, and B-films.[43] Clearly, they fear that without such recourse to a universally disseminated cultural code, the success of theatrical communication would be seriously jeopardized. For it is impossible to develop a corresponding anti-illusionistic theatrical code that is to be valid for one or more performances without incorporating elements and structural principles that the producers and receivers know beforehand. No matter how much opinion varies as to whether the type and source of such elements and principles should be assessed positively or negatively,[44] without such a code theatrical communication simply cannot take place.[45]

"Theatricality"

The special position occupied by theater among aesthetic systems and the specific organizational form of its internal code are mutually determining and each provides the basis for the other. The specificity of theater is constituted in this dialectic, namely "théatralité," as French semiotics have termed it, drawing an analogy with the notion of "litérarité."[46] Theatricality can consequently not be equated with aestheticity, even if it is always partially defined as aestheticity.

All aesthetic systems always refer to the culture in which they are embedded by virtue of the special fact that they generate signs for the signs produced by that culture. Other aesthetic systems realize these signs using a particularly homogeneous material, which can thus logically only be identical with the material of one of the nonaesthetic systems—such is the relation between the material of poetry and language, for example. By contrast, theater produces signs using heterogeneous material which can in principle be identical with the material of any cultural system: in the specific material quality pertaining to them, the human being and his total environment can therefore function as theatrical signs. Theater, in other words, not only interprets the signs generated by the culture, but in turn uses as its own precisely those signs made available by culture, utilizing them as the theatrical signs of signs. If, for example, the human body is used as a sign of a character—perhaps a demon, a mythological figure, an animal, a spirit, an ancestor or another person—then this process not only interprets the body as a sign, but also uses it as a sign: nature becomes a sign, existence becomes meaning.

This type of sign production is characteristic of all forms of theater; it is already to be found being implemented by theater forms linked to magical and ritual contexts, i.e., "pretheater"[47] (Leiris has shown this to be the case in exemplary manner with regard to the zar-culture of the Gondar Ethiopians),[48] and persists as the dominant feature in all forms of theater in advanced civilizations. If the body is not interpreted solely as a sign, but is also presented to others as a sign, then a theatrical process can be said to have occurred. For this means nothing other than that A embodies X while S watches. In other words, theater ensues in such instances in which the body and the objects of its surroundings are used in their given material form as signs.

In every culture, human beings and the objects of their environment always exist in certain communicative and practical, situative contexts and matrices that hardly permit a human being to be replaced by some other human being at random, an object to be replaced by another object at random, or even an object to be replaced by a human or vice versa. However, such mobility is the prevailing feature in the case of the human body and the objects from his/her surroundings being used as theatrical signs. Here, a human body can indeed be replaced by another body or even by an object, and an object can be replaced by another random object or a human body, because, in their capacity as theatrical signs, they can signify one another. For their material existence is of interest for theater with regard neither to its uniqueness nor to its specific functionality, but alone in terms of its ability to be used as a sign of a sign. What is crucial is not existence as such but rather the meanings to be created using existence as a sign. What is, therefore, constitutive of theater is the tension between existence and the signified, between being as nature or as objects and the character of signs. The difference that sets off theatricality from aestheticality emerges in this tension.

The various aesthetic systems have in common the specific way in which they accomplish the process of constituting the meaning of the work in its production and reception. This process allows a recombination and regrouping of the culturally generated meanings as signs of which the aesthetic signs are used and interpreted, despite the fact that those meanings form a hierarchical structure in the social reality of that culture that cannot be restructured without specific consequences. The product of this process is always the creation of a new matrix of meaning that by no means needs to harmonize with the web of meaning generally valid in the culture and usually accepted by its members, who accomplish the process of constituting aesthetic meaning. Owing to this specific form of constituting meaning, which has been defined as aestheticality here, aesthetic systems are able in a particular way to keep alive or to awaken for the first time an awareness of the opportunity for realizing semantic hierarchies that do not conform to that which is officially valid.[49]

Theater puts its aestheticity into practice in a particular way unique to it, something described by the term theatricality. For it enables a regrouping of meanings attributed to signs created by a particular cultural system in the everyday reality of that culture by using these signs—in other words, heterogeneous elements of cultural reality, such as the human body or objects from its surroundings—as its own, as theatrical signs. This means that theatricality permits a regrouping of the significative structure by undertaking in the stage space a quasi-factual restructuring of the material structure of signs in that culture and presenting this to the audience. Theater thus generates meaning by using the materiality of the signs produced by the heterogeneous cultural systems and in this manner changing, regrouping, and recombining these "primary" signs into theatrical signs according to its own rules.

Theater would thus appear to be the possibility forever latent in the "primary" signs of a culture of, as it were, an "originary" practice of sign generation that refers from the outset to the respective culture as a whole. For, by using the material products of that culture as its own signs, theater creates an awareness of the semiotic character of these material creations and consequently identifies the respective culture in turn as a set of heterogeneous systems of generating meaning.

II.
The Theatrical Gesture
as a Norm

□□□□□□

6. The Gesture in Eighteenth-Century German Theater

From System to Norm

❏ ❏ ❏ Whereas at the systemic level the theatrical code includes all those elements that could potentially take on a function, at the normative level it contains only those elements that have de facto been functional in a culture at a particular time, and, in certain cases, only within a particular genre.[1] In other words, as a norm the theatrical code always constitutes a specific selection from the possibilities afforded in general by the system. It is selective in terms of the (number of) sign systems involved and the particular form they have taken as well as the rules for combining them and the possible meanings to be generated. Since the selection is always made under specific concrete historical (i.e., political, social, cultural, and economic) conditions, it is clear that at the normative level the theatrical code in each case is a special, historically determined system for generating meaning. The step from system to norm can thus be regarded as a transition from systemic theater studies to theater history.

Whereas a systemic investigation with a semiotic thrust has the advantage of being able to lay claim to being self-evident, this is by no means the case in theater history. For unlike the theory of theater and the analysis of performances, theater history is the preferred area of activity in theater research to date. It is in this field that the great achievements in theater studies were made, and as a result, theater studios have often been equated with historical research on theater. Therefore, a semiotically informed theater history is explicitly obligated to legitimate itself and must clearly stake out the bounds of the special terrain in which it intends to undertake research.

It is, of course, able neither to generate new material nor to reconstruct, fully or even partially, concrete performances on the basis of existing material. Since such studies focus on theater as a historically conditioned system that produces meaning, they predominantly investigate the way in which the theater of a certain culture created meaning at a particular time and which factors determined this specific manner of generating meaning. It follows from such a strategy that semiotically oriented theater history must on the one hand describe and analyze the respective selection and examine this in terms of the principles of structuration on which the latter rests, and, on the other, relate the principles thus discovered to the principles for generating meaning prevalent in the culture in question at that time. In other words, theater history must first reconstruct the internal theatrical code, for which it can and must have recourse to existing material on the history of theater before proceeding, in a second step, to answer the question as to the relation between the internal theatrical code and a possible external code that dominates that culture as a whole. Since, as we have seen, the specificity of theater, its theatricality, has its foundations in a particularly close reciprocal relationship between a form of theater and the culture in which it is embedded, it follows that when studying *both* complexes recourse must repeatedly be had to the special conditions determining the culture in question.

We can thus define the task of semiotically oriented historical theater studies as that of rendering transparent the way in which and the conditions under which the theater of a specific culture functions at a particular point in time as a specific system for the generation of meaning.

If the theatrical code is studied at the normative level, then account must be taken of the fact that theatrical norms are subject to the same principles as aesthetic norms in general.[2] A theatrical norm can therefore only be accorded limited validity because its validity is circumscribed either by the simultaneous validity of other norms or by the genesis of a new norm. Thus, in a given society, several theatrical norms can exist alongside each other: the different strata of society, for example, or members of different generations, may grant validity to respectively different norms or put forward different norms for heterogeneous genres, such as tragedy and comedy. By the same token, it cannot be assumed that different theatrical norms are valid for the same length of time. Thus,

> norms, that have lodged themselves firmly in some sector or other of the aesthetic domain and in some social environment or other can . . . survive for a very long time. New arrivals among the norms continually take their place in layers alongside the existing norms, giving rise to the coexistence and competition of a great many parallel aesthetic norms. There are cases, particularly in the domain of folklore, where aesthetic norms survive for whole centuries.[3]

It follows from this that semiotically oriented historical studies of theater must focus not only on the functioning of a norm, but in certain cases on the simultaneous functioning of different norms and the processes whereby norms are established and dismantled. In other words, it must study theater as a system that generates meaning from both a synchronic and a diachronic viewpoint, and this includes analyzing the smooth functioning of an established norm that is generally accepted as valid, the restriction, alteration, and dissolution of such a norm, not to mention the establishment of a new norm. In this context, attention must be paid above all to the conditions which cause a valid and obviously functioning theatrical code to lose its ability to generate meaning adequately, so that it must of necessity be changed if theater is to remain a system that generates meaning within the culture in question. Semiotically oriented theater history thus proceeds from the presupposition that quite special relations obtain between theater as a system which generates meaning and the culture in question as a particular practice of generating meaning. These relations have to be illuminated by means of both synchronic and diachronic examinations and assessed in terms of how they function. Such a study therefore has the task of describing and analyzing a specific historical concretization of the universal systemic categories of theatricality and showing why it takes that determinate shape in each case.

These broad strokes paint a picture of the terrain that a semiotically based theater history must cover. In the following, a somewhat more detailed elaboration will be made of one of the manifold possibilities that have been outlined only rudimentarily above. This will enable us to differentiate clearly from other methods of writing theater history, in a concrete example, the particular approach taken by semiotics, thus providing the basis for a discussion *sine ira et studio*[4] of its advantages—and perhaps of its disadvantages as well.

Problems of a Semiotic Historical Reconstruction

We shall take the gestural code of eighteenth-century German theater as the object of study. This example would seem particularly well suited to our purposes for two reasons. First, there is an abundance of historical source material. In addition to various engravings of the individual performances and descriptions of the performances of individual actors, numerous textbooks of gestures still exist; these were particularly popular and widely published in the eighteenth century. Thus, relatively uniform material is available for the different scholarly approaches in theater studies to the object in question and the problematics involved. Second, studies of eighteenth-century theatrical gestures conducted by theater historians to date have left us with a number of questions and problems that they were not able to clarify or solve with the methods at their disposal. A semiotics of theater today can take up these inquiries and test whether the investigative instruments and lines of reasoning are appropriate to finding accurate solutions.

Ballhausen's[5] thorough and in many respects pioneering study has a twofold intention: on the one hand, to structure the art of acting in terms of whether the gesture is used for a characterizing or a decorative function, and, on the other, to relate the "physical movements of the actor on stage" to "forms of movement and life in his social environment."[6] Ballhausen takes Franciscus Lang's *Dissertatio de actione scenica* as his point of departure, a book that summarized the principles of the art of acting that had been developed for baroque theater and were valid in it at the end of that epoch. He defines theatrical gesture of early eighteenth-century theater as "rhetorical," i.e., as a purely conventional sign (of, for example, a particular affect) that has a predominantly decorative function. He relates this type of gesture to the fact that baroque courtly society was characterized by representation, viewing the behavioral forms of such a society as having been shaped decisively by, among other things, precisely such theatrical gestures.

By contrast, in the second half of the eighteenth century, a veristic form of theatrical gesture develops that has a strongly expressive function particularly suited to highlighting the individual nature and traits of the characters. Ballhausen believes that this type of theatrical gesture is directly related to "the ideal of introversion typical of bourgeois culture in Germany."[7]

Two questions in particular remain unresolved by the approach Ballhausen takes: First, he does not clarify the manner in which the gesture, deployed as a purely conventional sign in a decorative capacity, should be able to achieve the effect which Lang lauds as the highest aim of the art of acting, namely to "excite/arouse/provoke/induce affects" in the audience.[8] Second, if "the actor's own private gestures are . . . made to serve the immediate ends of the role,"[9] and his gestures are thus defined as spontaneous, natural, and individual expression, then it is hard to explain the function of the general rules which Lessing, Lichtenberg, Göz, and Engel all insist must be adhered to when devising theatrical gestures.

Owing to the strict division he makes between two fundamentally different types of theatrical gestures, one for the early eighteenth (and late seventeenth) century and the other for the second half of the eighteenth century, Ballhausen is not able to consider or explain the properties shared by both types of gestures (their affective impact or their generation in line with given rules). By contrast, Dene Barnett[10] emphasizes above all the second common property and in so doing obscures the substantial differences that exist. He divides his study of theatrical gestures in the eighteenth century into five chapters: (1) Ensemble Acting, (2) The Hands, (3) The Arms, (4) The Eyes, the Face and the Head, and (5) Posture and Attitude. In each chapter he quotes extensively from the respective passages of the textbooks of gestures. He thus places, without any explanatory comment, parts of Lang's book alongside quotations from J. J. Engel's *Ideen zu einer Mimik*, ideas that were characteristic of theatrical gestures in the late Enlightenment or alongside quotations from Goethe's "Rules for Actors," in which a form of acting is propagated via recourse to certain baroque rules that grants the spoken word a dominant position. Thus, we are given the impression that the most important characteristic of theatrical gestures throughout the eighteenth century was that they were produced in accordance with rules, without any indication (e.g., by means of an investigation of the work of Lang, Engel, or Goethe) of the substantial differences that existed among the gestures generated in this manner.

In other words, a method must be adopted that will allow us to arrive at a precise description of both the common properties and the differences, and which moreover provides a satisfactory explanation of them.

If the actor's gestures are—like all other theatrical media—conceived of as signs, and defined as such, then they can be assumed to be constituted according to the general principles that are universally valid for the constitution of signs in the epoch in question. The foundations for those principles of sign constitution that were valid for almost all of the eighteenth century had been laid in the seventeenth century.[11] They were based on the conviction that the signs that human beings needed in order to know and represent the world did not readily exist in the natural world—as was commonly believed in the sixteenth century—but first had to be invented and devised by humans for their special purposes.

Leibniz defines such a sign, a "signum," as something one perceives from which one then derives something one does not perceive.[12] The sign, in other words, consists of a signifier and that which is signified and requires the existence of a subject who refers the one to the other. Leibniz limits this general definition, which initially includes natural signs—such as smoke as the sign of fire—to clearly indicate that he understands only artificially created, i.e., invented, signs to be signs in the narrow sense. Thus, something can only function as a sign if it is consciously produced as a sign by a person.[13]

Here, the relation the subject has to establish between the signifier and signified is by no means construed as already implied or as arbitrary. Signs are accordingly defined as follows in the Port Royal logic:

> If you regard an object on its own and in its own existence, without allowing your intellect to address what it may represent, then the idea that you have of the object is the idea of a thing. . . . However, if you view an object only as representative of another, then the idea you have of it is that of a sign, and the first object is called a "sign." . . . To be exact, the sign contains two ideas, one of the thing which represents and the other of the thing represented; it is the nature of the sign that it encourages the first idea by means of the second.[14]

The signifier, in other words, refers to the signified by virtue of the representation, i.e., on account of the capacity the signifier has for representing the signified. This capacity is not to be encountered in the material existence of the signifier, but rather in the idea it represents. For it is the idea alone that is capable of representing the idea of that object which the signifier is supposed to stand for.[15]

The late seventeenth century and most of the eighteenth century thus understood, defined, and utilized the sign neither in the sense of a semantic relation governed by convention nor as a natural expression, but rather as representation throughout. As a consequence, in the period in question theatrical gestures can also only be suitably described and defined as representation.

However, this undermines an important argument put forward by Ballhausen. For early eighteenth-century gestures and those in the second half of the same century cannot be juxtaposed as conventional signs on the one hand and natural expression on the other, and by extension as paradigms for two fundamentally different "structural types of theatrical gestures."[16] Rather, both are to be conceived of uniformly as representations and can only be distinguished from one another with regard to what they represent and in what particular way they accomplish this. Since the relation between signifier and signified in the representation is neither already implied nor arbitrary, certain rules have to be drawn up for the construction and production of signs. It is this specific character of representation that is the basis for supposing that rules must be upheld and obeyed when developing and enacting the actor's gestures, something to which Lang and Lessing, and indeed Engel, continually refer so emphatically.

The signs structured in this manner subsequently have to be combined with one another if they are to express some complex state of affairs, that is, an order.

Ars characteristica is the art of forming and ordering symbols so that they reflect the thoughts or have the same relation to one another as the thoughts. To express a thing is to merge the symbols which depict the object to be expressed. And the following is the law of expression. The expression for the object must be assembled from the symbols of those things, the ideas of which go to make up the idea of the object to be expressed.[17]

The principles for the combination of gestural signs in theater can be derived from this law, which Leibniz drew up for the combination of signs in general. The first important principle is that the individual signs must not change their meaning when combined with others. Rather, it is precisely by virtue of the meaning enscribed in what they represent that they can enter into meaningful combination with one another. A theatrical gesture thus cannot at one point represent emotion A and then later emotion B; rather, its use always points to the same emotion. The second principle refers to the combination itself. The individual signs must be combined with one another in such a way that their successive sequence or simultaneous spatial arrangement depicts the order to be described point for point. An actor's individual gestures may therefore follow one another only in the particular way in which, for example, the emotions or feelings they represent are construed as succeeding one another. This means that rules also necessarily have to be laid down for the combination of gestural signs.

The consistent use of general principles for the constitution of signs is the reason for the fundamental similarity between theatrical gestures in the early eighteenth century and those in the late eighteenth century. Both types of gestures must be construed as representations that are constituted and then combined with one another according to generally valid and, to this extent, binding rules.

Both types of theatrical gestures drew not only on the general principles for the constitution of signs, but also on the general principles of an aesthetics of effect (*Wirkungsästhetik*). Indeed, both types were conceived of and generated in the context of a theater the primary purpose of which was to trigger an emotional response in the audience. In baroque poetics, the assumption had been that the stage was able to evoke the complete canon of eleven affects; consequently, the highest aim of theater was "ad sublimes affectus in spectatorum animis excitandos," in order to thus transform the audience into "viri perculsi."[18] Lessing was admittedly still of the conviction that "there is no better principle to aid the production of tragedies than: tragedy must excite the passions."[19] Yet he limited the affects triggered in the audience by tragic theater to one single emotion: pity. "Tragedy can be defined as follows: it is meant to expand *our ability to feel pity*."[20] In other words, both baroque and Enlightenment theater endeavor to make an emotional mark on the audience, even if the reasons for this and the goals involved are significantly different in the two cases. If there is agreement that theater is to be able to fulfill an emotional function with regard to the audience, then it can be assumed that in both cases theatrical gestures are intended at least partially to exercise this function. Early eighteenth-century theatrical gestures can thus be compared with those of the second half of the century to the extent that both (1) are conceived of as representations and (2) are intended in that capacity to fulfill an emotional function in the sense of their having an effect on the audience.

The Gestural Code in Eighteenth-Century German Theater

Preconditions: The Gestural Code of Baroque Theater

The meanings for which theater in the baroque era tried to find suitable representations in the form of theatrical signs were preordained by a code external to theater. This code held for the overall culture of the day and interpreted the world and human life from the viewpoint of religious salvation and redemption in terms of the tension between immanence and transcendence. In this context, the principal meanings for which the different cultural systems of the time had to find respectively specific signs were: the illusory and transitory nature of the world and of human life; the strong ego which asserts itself despite all changes of fortune; and the weak soul who adapts to meet changes in fortune or perishes because of them. We have already alluded to the "theatrum mundi" or "theatrum vitae humanae" as the dominant theme of the age.[21] Theater with its numerous sign systems thus appeared at the time to be particularly well suited to form signs for these meanings, signs that were generally accepted as being capable of representing the meanings appropriately. Theater developed special signs for the meanings "illusoriness and transitoriness of the world" above all in the systems of decoration, props, lighting, sound effects, and music. By contrast, it constituted signs for the meanings which referred to the character predominantly using the systems of costume (mask and hair), mimicry, gestures, proxemic movement, language, and music.[22] Only if this is borne in mind is it possible to evaluate the development of the gestural code that was to remain valid until well into the first half of the eighteenth century.

A basic posture is prescribed for the actor as the initial stance for all roles. Hips and legs, arms, elbows, and hands must all be arranged in terms of the contraposto principle, and the fingers slightly bent.

> This positioning, however, does not involve the fingers being kept in one and the same position, as if they were wooden or could never be moved and held differently; rather they must be bent in different ways when moved, by bending them in, extending them or (otherwise) changing them, here a bit more, there a bit less.[23]

A certain positioning of the feet is obligatory, and this has become known as the "crux scenica."

> When the soles of the feet touch the ground . . . care must be taken to ensure that they never point in the same direction, but rather point considerably away from each other on the boards; indeed they must be positioned in such a manner that whereas the toes of one foot point in one direction, those of the other point in the opposite

direction, ... and the one foot shall be set slightly in front of the other, the other drawn back slightly behind the first.[24]

Movement across the stage was permitted only in terms of this highly artificial positioning—it was the only one allowed and one that took a great deal of practice if it was to be accomplished effortlessly.

> This gait on stage is executed with three or four steps, whereby the actor must step in such a way as to keep within the crux scenica at all times; attention must be paid to this . . . The foot that was in front . . . shall be drawn back and then moved forward again, and placed further forward than it was before. The second foot shall then follow it, and be placed in front of the first; yet the first must not stay behind, but in turn be moved forward in front of the second.[25]

Taken as a whole, the contraposto stance of the torso as well as the arms and legs, crux scenica and passus scenicus, constitute an obligatory initial position for the actors, irrespective of the character they are going to play. This physical stance can only be adopted after much practice and if the rules are followed to the letter. Ballhausen judges that the stance is decorative on account of the high degree of stylization involved and its extremely artificial nature. Yet if the stance is viewed in the framework of the pregiven meanings, then it would appear apposite to interpret the initial contraposto position adopted whenever the actor has a deter-mined bearing in which all parts of his body are involved as the suitable repre-sentation of an Ego who wishes to draw attention to himself when in the presence of others. This form of physical stance can be produced and understood as the sign of a controlled, self-confident, dominating Ego.[26]

Whether or not this Ego is held to be a strong character or instead ultimately proves to be weak is something that first comes to light when the character is bombarded with emotions. If the character withstands the barrage, then he has proven its strength, and if he succumbs to them, his weakness is patently manifest. In other words, a suitable representation of the character requires not only the basic stance, but also signs for the different emotions. Baroque theater found such signs in Quintilian's[27] works and developed a differentiated repertoire of gestural signs in which each emotion was judged to be signified by a specific gesture, or by a combination of signs. For example:

> 1. We admire by lifting both hands and moving them close to the chest with the palms pointed towards the audience. 2. We show disdain by turning the face to the left and, with extended and slightly raised hands, repel the object of our disdain, pushing it away from us. When showing that we despise something we do the same with the right hand alone, bent slightly towards the wrist and simultaneously shooing, using a repeated shooing and defensive movement. 3. We implore either by raising or lowering or linking both hands with the palms turned towards each other. 4. We suffer anguish or grief by interweaving the hands like joined combs and either raise them towards the breast or lower them to the waist. The same is conveyed by mod-

erately stretching out the right hand while at the same time turning it towards the breast.[28]

We must take issue with Ballhausen and stress that these gestures were not intended solely to support speech, but also functioned as independent signs, as representations of the different emotions. It was possible to give a full-fledged portrayal of the characters being bombarded by the various emotions by making use of a combination of numerous such signs precisely because each of these gestures and/or combinations represented a specific, delimited emotion. We should bear in mind here that the emotions were not understood as psychological processes in the way we understand them today, but rather as hypostatized entities on the strings of which the individual was suspended like a puppet.[29] As a consequence, the combination of gestures that represented the emotion did not have to follow some law of psychological probability; on the contrary, the rule here was that mutually contradictory emotions had to succeed each other if the emotional bombardment was to be portrayed in a particularly effective manner.

If the character of the dramatis persona is a strong Ego capable of controlling the emotions descending upon it, then the actor must abide exactly and uncompromisingly by the given rules with regard both to the basic posture and to the portrayal of the emotions. The character has not yet irretrievably succumbed to the emotions bombarding it as long as the basic posture is retained. The emotions described in this physical stance must therefore be considered as moderate or at least as controlled.

A breach of the rules, by contrast, is an appropriate sign indicating that the character represented by the role is so weak that he succumbs to the emotions without further resistance. Lang accordingly states the following with respect to the switch from normal to immoderate anger:

> As soon as it starts to flare up, as long as the person is still in control of himself, one normally wrinkles one's forehead, presses the lips together, takes sudden steps forward, executes frequent hand and arm movements; here, speech becomes more excited, occasionally interrupted and distorted by pauses. Wild glances are then cast at the hated person if he is present; if not, then one, as it were, flings bitter words through the air at him, gesticulates wildly, punches one hand into the palm of the other, gnashes one's teeth and does similar other things which express the passion of anger. This refers to normal anger. If the anger exceeds the usual measure and erupts into rage, then the portrayal must likewise be immoderate. Thus, someone raging must be permitted to do things not befitting a reasonable person.[30]

The actor may, in other words, ignore the bounds of the stage and the prescribed gait on stage if he wishes to show that the character of the dramatis persona he is depicting has fallen prey to certain emotions. Indeed, the actor may run across the stage, beat his head against a wall, writhe on the floor, raise his arms well above his eyes and head with fists clenched, grimace, roll his eyes, rant and rave, or shout—in short, he not only may, but in fact should, break all the rules mentioned. For obeying the rules shows strength, whereas violating them, by contrast, shows weakness.

For this reason, the switch from obeying rules to violating them must be viewed primarily as one of the factors capable of prompting an emotional response on the part of the audience. For the transition from the one to the other demonstrates, as it were ad oculos, to the audience the impending danger of loss of identity in a shocking manner. In other words, in the period in question it was not just acting in line with the rules which was able to transform the audience into "viri perculsi"; rather, in order to do so, such an approach had to alternate with a form of acting that broke with the rules, which was capable of depicting someone being ruled by his emotions in a threatening and deterring manner.

A breach of the rules must not, however, be interpreted only as a sign for someone succumbing to his emotions, but rather more comprehensively as the sign of a loss of identity. It is therefore also employed when portraying a constantly vacillating character determined by changes in fortune. For example, the comic figure is distinguished precisely by the fact that the person portraying it more or less ignores all the rules which are valid for the other actors. Tomfool and Merry Andrew therefore often take the stage "screaming and shouting," running—without keeping to the stage gait—across the stage, clenching their fists and using obscene gestures, and all too often they let their hands gesticulate well below the belt. Thus, if rules are broken, but not as a result of overly strong emotions, then this can be understood to represent an indecisive character, as is typical of a comic figure, and can be employed to the same end.

Furthermore, gestural signs are also an excellent means of representing an impostor. If, for example, the prescribed basic stance is conveyed in an exaggerated manner or is exposed as presumptuous behavior through words spoken beforehand or afterwards, or is shown to be deceptive by a subsequent comical breach of the rules—as is often the case with Falstaff or Mrs. Trollop—then the sequence of rules obeyed and rules broken can signify the pretenses of the character who claims to be something other than he or she in truth is.

Gestures in baroque theater must thus be treated as representations of emotions or, as in the case of more complex gestural combinations, as representations of the character (steady, emotionally uncontrolled, unstable, an impostor, etc.). They accordingly represent historically determinate meanings that can be derived from the specific theological code which dominated seventeenth-century German culture, and their use as theatrical signs mirrors the particular ambivalent attitude the baroque had toward signs as a whole. On the one hand, signs were considered the only means of representing not only things not immediately accessible to the senses in a manner that could be perceived and grasped by the senses, but also the true order of the world, something that was located behind sensorily perceptible objects. On the other hand, the signs, as representations that could be perceived by the senses, had themselves to be subject to the same verdict and/or were suspected of something that applied to all sensorily perceptible matter, namely, that it was both transitory and capable of deceiving the senses. Theater was especially well suited to represent and signify precisely this ambivalence. For the "true" signs constituted in theater were mere pretense and also showed themselves to be such in that they were produced and presented by an actor in order to signify a character other than his own. The "false" signs constituted here, however, are equally true, for only by means of them can the pretenses of the character in the role be represented and exposed as such on stage. Whereas in social life the observer is never sure whether the signs he is presented with are indeed true representations, he can always accurately interpret the signs produced by the actor, because he is left in no doubt as to their pretense, i.e., he knows that pretense is their conditio sine qua non from the outset. The signs which the actor uses as representations therefore possess a greater truthfulness for the spectator than those presented to him in real life in society, for, although they admittedly deceive his senses, they never attempt to deceive his intellect.[31]

Changes in the Baroque Gestural Code during the Early Enlightenment

As we have seen, the external code imposed certain meanings on theater and the baroque theatrical code developed its own specific representations for these meanings. Since the interpretation of the world and human life in terms of religious salvation and redemption was gradually ousted from its position as the code dominating culture at the end of the seventeenth century, the early eighteenth century saw changes in the internal theatrical code.

Whereas in the seventeenth century the divine order of the world was presumed to be perfect, and it was assumed that humans were only able to know it to a limited extent because of human imperfection, at the beginning of the eighteenth century this view gave way to the optimistic conviction that Man could quite clearly understand the order of the world.[32] For the faculty of reason, as an organon for cognition of the world, which God gave Man, corresponds to the rational construction of the world. In this context, the world is not to be thought of as an empirical order to be perceived by the senses, but rather as an a priori order, i.e., a universal system of general truths, which, as Christian Wolff elaborates, can therefore only be cognized as an order of rules with the aid of reason.

> If one views the interlinking of things in such a manner that the truths can be connected with one another without drawing on some statements from Experience, then Reason is sincere. By contrast, if one draws on statements from Experience, then Reason and Experience become mixed with one another and we do not completely perceive the interconnections of truth.[33]

However, in order to be able to link the truths with one another without resorting to experience, reason must be furnished with special signs that can function as representations of these truths. For the rational linking of truths would appear to be possible only as a rule-bound combination of signs independent of experience.

The tasks and functions taken on and fulfilled by art, and in particular theater, change accordingly. The general postulate for art is that it obey an *imitatio naturae*: art must imitate nature in the sense of that a priori order, and the individual artwork must be created as a depiction of this order.[34] "For all is interlinked in Nature, because everything has been made as part of an order; this must also be the case in the Arts, for they are imitations of the former."[35] In order for art to be able to imitate nature, it must consequently follow those rules which reason has recognized to be fundamental for the order of the world. The "rules of art" which the artist must follow are, in other words, "derived from Reason and Nature."[36] By basing his creation of the artwork on them and methodically following them, the artist depicts them in the artwork. Now, the individual work of art is able to depict the order of the world perfectly; in other words, it functions as an adequate representation of it to the extent that the order of nature and that of the artwork are based on the same rules. The imitation of nature called for here can thus be described as the appropriate representation of the order on which nature is based.

Imitation defined in this manner has a series of individual consequences which, in the final analysis, lead to the dissolution of the baroque theatrical code. If the artwork is intended to imitate rules of reason *a priori*, anything contradictory, and in this sense improbable, has to be excluded. In this context, whatever violates the rules that regulate natural and social life is considered improbable.[37] "The disorder and improbability which come from violating rules are also so tangible and disgusting in Shakespeare's works that probably no one who has ever read something reasoned will be able to find enjoyment therein."[38]

Gottsched's verdict on the improbable applies by the same token to the compendium of magical and miraculous devices used by baroque theater and which helped turn it into a *theatrum mundi* with a universal appeal. Since apparitions, ghosts, devils, angels, and saints are to be assigned to the supernatural and thus to the irrational, they must quit the stage: theater returns from the vertical plane that stretches from "heaven through the world down into hell" to the horizontal plane of the mundane world as the axis of reason. The call for probability excludes those essential elements that constituted the uniqueness of the baroque theatrical code from partaking in the future of theater.

The second requirement made of art's imitation of nature refers quite directly to the gestural code—the requirement that the artwork reveal good taste. Taste, in turn, was believed to be bound up with the rules determined by reason. "And Taste has invented and proposed Rules, precisely so that a Choice can be made with greater certainty."[39] The rules themselves, however, are "inalienably" grounded "in the exemplary model of nature."[40] Such normative good taste functions as an agency of aesthetic judgment and is able to determine whether the imitation is objectively correct by virtue of the fact that it relates the imitation to the pre-given criterion of decorum.[41] Gottsched thus defines as "good Taste" that "which agrees with the rules that Reason has set down, in the way of things."[42]

All of those kinds of scenes that typically entailed a violation of the rules were bound to conflict with good taste if defined in this manner: scenes involving a jester, the comic figure of the Merry Andrew, the buffoon and the harlequin, or those involving cruelty or madness. They thus had to disappear from the stage. In the process, the important element of opposition between gestures that obeyed the rules and those that violated them—a principle so central to the constitution of the unique baroque gestural code—was eliminated. All that remained were the gestures that obeyed the rules, and these were adopted by the theater of the early Enlightenment and in turn declared to be the exclusively valid norm.

Since the baroque theater's gestural code provided for the use of specific rules for facial expression, posture, gestures, and movements, the signs generated in this manner could be viewed as the product of adherence to rules. It was thus possible to understand them as imitations of nature in Wolff's or Gottsched's sense. Whereas it was the opposition between obeying and violating rules which had defined the gestural code in baroque theater as a particularly suitable system of generating meaning, in early Enlightenment theater, by contrast, only those signs were permissible which were produced according to the rules and by means of measured and seemly signs. Furthermore, it followed that such signs could be interpreted as the appropriate representation of the rational order of nature, because they were produced in line with the rules. Stripped bare of those gestures which violated rules, the gestural code of baroque theater could be retained, for it was possible to give it a new function and reinterpret it in light of the a priori concept of nature adopted by early Enlightenment rationalism. It was precisely the measured, seemly gesture generated according to the rules of "Reason and Nature" which now appeared to be particularly suited to depicting humans as beings determined and guided by reason, and theater was intended to provide the spectator with an exemplary model thereof to follow in his own life. For as long as the notion of nature as an a priori order was predominant, baroque theater's gestural code in its reduced form was more than able to imitate nature and thus to convey the aims of the bourgeois theater of early Enlightenment. These aims can essentially be summarized as the intention to instruct the spectator with regard to the fact that human nature was determined by reason and thus to improve the spectator morally with that in mind.[43]

The Genesis of a Gestural Code for Bourgeois Illusionistic Theater

A development is to be discerned in Germany from about the middle of the eighteenth century onward that led to a change in the concept of nature valid in the early Enlightenment; this change undermined the retention of the gestural code still further. With the influence of English sensualism, it was increasingly believed that the faculty of human reason could not conceive of anything unless it stemmed from sensory perception.[44] The rationalist concept of nature, which defines nature as an a priori order, gave way to an empiricist concept of nature that presumed that nature could be perceived with the senses and was based on an investigation of it: according to Linnaeus, *naturalia* are to be distinguished from *coelestia* and *elementa* precisely because they are destined to be directly accessible to the senses.[45]

It follows from this position that the order of nature cannot be cognized with the aid of certain logical operations, i.e., exclusively by reference to the organon of reason. Rather cognition must be based on careful observations which permit identities and differences to be discerned between the different creatures and thus allow for their classification. And it is this presentation of the totality of such classifications that can first be conceived of as the presentation of the order underlying nature. The signs necessary for such a presentation must thus be capable of representing the elements observed in nature appropriately, and it must also be possible to combine them with one another to depict the visible order.

Because art, furthermore, is called upon to imitate nature, the change in the concept of nature and the new functional definition of the constitution of signs that resulted from this change invariably had an impact on the artistic production as well as the art theory of the Enlightenment period. They also inevitably had an impact on theater's gestural code. Now that empirical nature was taken as the point of departure, the gestures and movements created on the basis of the baroque gestural code appeared to be highly unnatural, artificial, and thus derisory. The development of a new gestural code that was geared toward empirical nature therefore became necessary and indispensable if theater was to be able to continue to function as a didactic and, above all, a moral institution.

This development was set into motion and furthered by the discussion of those problems that can also be regarded as having been constitutive for art theory in general. In this context, interest focused in particular on arguments that had already been voiced in the corresponding debate in France, which had gotten underway at a much earlier date.[46] The task at hand was to answer above all the following questions:

(1) What sort of signs are gestural signs? What natural objects can they best depict?[47]

(2) Which of these objects are they meant to depict and in what manner? (a) Should only those objects be selected which can be considered "beautiful nature"? (b) Should "nonbeautiful" objects be rendered more beautiful and the imperfect objects more perfect by use of the signs? (c) Which of the characteristic features they are intended to imitate should one choose?

(3) In what way and/or with what method can one best and most exactly produce those gestural signs that, after answering the above questions, have been adjudged most suitable for imitation?

It was believed that theoretical deliberations on these questions would lead to a clarification of the problems they raised and that this would lead to the constitution of a new gestural code for German theater. The assumption was that those gestural signs necessary to trigger the desired effect in the audience had to be found by theoretical means, then carefully distinguished from one another, described, and prescribed with regard to usage. Otherwise, according to the opinion of the day, there might be a danger of the play's effect being undermined by a rather more random use of unfounded, and thus ambiguous, signs in the negative sense of ambiguity.

Diderot first raised the question quite baldly as to the specificity of gestural signs in his *Lettre sur les sourds et les muets*, which was published in 1751. The German audience became acquainted with the book via a lengthy review which Lessing wrote on it the same year. In a comparison of linguistic and gestural signs carried out empirically in concrete communicative situations with deaf-mutes Diderot came to the conclusion that both types of sign were suited in the same way to expressing actions, concrete objects as well as those ideas which it was possible to depict by metaphorical description. He found that whereas it was almost impossible to describe an abstract complex using gestural signs, they were more suitable than linguistic signs when expressing extraordinary feelings and extreme emotional conditions. "The sublime gestures" were able to describe these in a way which "the most articulate of speakers could not emulate."[48] Furthermore, gestural language had the advantage of being easier to understand than verbal language, because it knew "no established signs" and its syntax was known directly by all, for it was "suggested to them by nature."[49] Diderot accordingly construes the language of gestures in this manner as a "natural language."[50]

For Lessing, who investigated the specificity of gestural signs at a theoretical level, it was the latter distinction which was crucial. In *Laokoon* he introduces the difference between "natural" and "arbitrary signs," a distinction that was of relevance for the discussions in art theory in general and was taken up in this context by later theorists such as Engel. He defines those signs as "natural signs" which are instilled with meaning by virtue of resembling the object signified.[51] Whoever knows the signified objects must therefore "naturally" be able to understand the signs signifying them.

To the extent that gestures were to be classified as "natural signs,"[52] it appeared logical that they were suitable for the imitation of all those objects to which they could be related by resemblance. Since gestural signs occur both across space— such as signs in painting—and successively in time—such as the signs of poetry—it followed that they are also able to evoke the "true sensuous impression"[53] of objects which either exist alongside each other and/or exist in a sequence. They were, in other words, suited to imitating bodies and actions alike.[54] They imitated bodies that move and change, or the actions carried out by particular bodies, precisely because they were thus related to both types of objects. As a consequence, owing to their specificity, gestural signs were especially suited to depicting human bodies, actions and movements.

To Lessing's mind, the universal principles according to which the concrete objects to be imitated by gestural signs were to be chosen, namely "truth" and "beauty," both derived from the specific positioning halfway between signs in painting and signs in poetry.[55] For:

> the art of the actor is halfway between the applied arts and poetry. Admittedly, beauty must be the law the actor's art obeys before all others, as it is visible painting. Yet, as transitory painting it does not always need to give its stances that air of tranquillity which makes old artworks so impressive. It can, indeed must, allow itself more than once to indulge in the wildness of a Tempesta, in the cheekiness of a Bernini; the expressiveness so characteristic of the latter is retained without the insulting nature it has when made a feature permanently present in the applied arts. However, the actor's art must not tarry too long in such expressions, must gradually prepare the ground for them with prior gestures and dissolve them into the general tone of due

and proper behavior by means of the movements that then follow, must not give them all the strength with which the poet can instill them in his work. For although the actor's art is speechless poetry, it wishes to make itself directly comprehensible to our eyes.[56]

Thus, those gestural signs had to be chosen which, as Engel was later to demand, were at the same time "the most beautiful and the most true."[57]

The ideal of beauty—and all the theorists of gestures from Lessing via Lichtenberg to Engel are united on this point—can be put into practice only by carefully following the rules on which executing Hogarth's "line of beauty" rest, Garrick's adherence to which Lichtenberg praises so highly.[58] Acting must by no means consist "of nothing more than the description of such beautiful snaking lines,"[59] because "every movement . . . must be meaningful."[60] Nevertheless, it must follow the "fundamental aesthetic laws,"[61] and always adhere to the "line of beauty" whenever it is possible to do so without violating the second, more important requirement, namely that acting be true. Since the "line of beauty" will only be encountered in a minimum of real cases, it follows that the actor's gestures cannot be generated as a slavish copy of the gestures observed in reality. Rather, the gestures must be shaped in line with special, purely aesthetic laws and the rules derived from them, so that "our eyes" are not "insulted."[62] In other words, and this contradicts Ballhausen's findings, the decorative function of gestures continued to be upheld during the Enlightenment.

The principle of beauty was, however, clearly subordinated to that of truth. The most important demand to be made of gestural signs was that they had to be "true" when expressing feelings and emotional states as well as when referring to a person's individual character or membership in a stratum of society. Unlike the French theorists, who limited themselves on the whole to discussing the signs expressing feelings, all the theorists involved in the German discussion concentrated on gestures which depicted feelings or the individual character. Yet Lichtenberg's was the only study to include gestures that refer to social strata. The reason these were otherwise usually neglected in theoretical deliberations—although not in the various descriptions that focus exclusively on them—may be that it was impossible to derive such gestures from a natural law as was generally and unanimously assumed to be the case with the aforementioned gestures. Models for the form such gestures should take on stage could, by contrast, only be gleaned from a study of social reality. For such gestures were believed not to be determined by human nature, but rather exclusively by a certain social hierarchy and order. In his *Vorschlag zu einem Orbis Pictus*, Lichtenberg listed a series of such gestures that pointed to membership in a social stratum and recommended that the actors study them carefully. He started with a corresponding characterization of male and female servants. For

observing the lower class of people, which anyone is free to do, does, on the other hand, indeed make the matter at hand more straightforward. Yes, I believe that the higher classes cannot be studied well without a knowledge of the lower class. The mob class contains the eccentric originals on which our ossifications of the higher world are based.[63]

The close link between these gestural signs and the particular costume or parts thereof can be clearly seen from the instructions that Lichtenberg then gave for an actor who was to play a servant:

> He enjoys plucking feathers from a hat and chases flies with the energy of someone about to die, spins his hat around his navel like a windmill. These must be used sparingly. Polishes buttons with his sleeve, or brushes his hat with the same, or one sleeve with the other. . . . If he wears silk stockings, he kills flies on his calf with great propriety. Grasps his comrades by their coat buttons while telling a story.[64]

Lichtenberg regarded gestures that make use of props or involve the use of props in the same manner as that to be observed in social reality as being particularly well suited to serve as signs for the respective membership in a stratum of society and the specificity of the character derived from it.

By contrast, it was possible to refer gestural signs that expressed feelings or pointed to the individual character of a person to human nature in general. For the general assumption was that a relation of similarity obtained between emotional and physical changes, a relation which was in fact investigated and claimed to exist by physiological research of the day.[65] To the extent that this analogy of feelings and physical expression was presumed, it was taken as a fact on which all else had to be based. However, there was disagreement as to how widely applicable the principle was. Physiognomists believed that the principle could also be applied to the relation between the fixed shape of the body and the character of a person.[66] Lichtenberg, however, sharply rejected such an approach, regarding it as pseudoscientific, and wished instead to limit the applicability of the principle of analogy solely to the relation between psychological and physical movements and changes.[67] Lessing and particularly Engel, on the other hand, were prepared to accept the validity of the principle for the relation of certain poses and stances preferentially adopted by a person to that person's character. Thus, Lessing implicitly presumed the validity of the analogy in his fragment *The Actor* when putting forward "walking with stiff feet stuck out forwards" as the natural sign of a "proud and vainglorious" person.[68] Engel expressly refers to the principle of analogy and accordingly assumes that the bodily stance, gait, and posture are to be interpreted as signs of the person's character. For, "just as the different character traits are never erased from the peaceful surface of the face, and can perhaps be recognized with the greatest certainty and accuracy in this state of tranquillity, so, too, noticeable traces of the individual character remain even in the more peaceful stance and position of the body."[69] Thus, the truth of a gesture with reference to the character of the *dramatis personae* consisted of the gesture being shaped according to this principle of analogy. Because, for example, the proud person was believed to regard himself as larger and more important than the others, the gestures used to describe him also have to make the actor appear larger and more spacious (e.g., head raised up high, chest puffed out, one leg always put out further than the other). Since a lazy-bones had to be thought of as emotionally languid, the actor had to depict all the parts of the body as hanging limp, etc. The gestural signs thus used to describe the *dramatis personae* were, however, substantially supported in this function by the use of masks, hairstyles, and costumes, something that Engel admittedly overlooked, or at least did not mention, whereas Lichtenberg expressly stressed them in his description of the different roles acted by Garrick.

These poses and stances used to characterize a person functioned as the basic positions to be adopted by the actor which correspond with the character he plays and on which he then based his acting. Consequently, they took the place of the basic position in the gestural code of baroque theater that Lang had described as being the only position possible for all "characters." The basic position thus no longer functioned to signify an Ego which wishes to center attention on itself or, quite generally, the rational constitution of the human being, but rather to point to a quite specific individual character who was clearly distinct from other characters.

All the theorists of the day, English, French, or German, agreed that gestural signs had a particular capacity to express feelings, and that there was thus no need for this assumption to be given specific theoretical foundations. For this capacity had to be taken as the basis of all further deliberations, as a fact of human nature, to the extent that it was to be observed in people of all ages, classes, and nations. The assumption was that all human beings tended to express their feelings through physical changes.[70] If the actor's gestures were to fulfill the same function, it followed that they had to imitate the signs of that "involuntary language of gestures that is spoken throughout the world by the passions in all their varying degrees."[71] The art of acting thus required the "whole semiotics of emotions or the knowledge of the natural signs of changes in feelings."[72]

This raised a special problem, one that Lessing explicitly referred to in his extensive review of Remond de St. Albine's *Le Comédien*, which appeared in 1747.

> Monsieur Remond de Sainte Albine implicitly assumed throughout his oeuvre that external modifications of the body are natural consequences of the inner state of the soul which occur effortlessly. It is admittedly true that every person can, for better or for worse, express the state of his soul without training by the use of signs which we can perceive with our senses; one person does this, another that. However, in theater one wishes not just to see opinions and passions expressed for better or for worse, not just in the imperfect manner in which an individual person would express them if he really found himself in such a state, but rather to see them expressed in the most perfect form possible, in such a manner that they cannot be expressed better or more completely.[73]

Lessing stated something similar at a later date, namely in his *Hamburgische Dramaturgie*, as did Diderot in his *Observations sur une brochure intitulée Garrick ou les acteurs anglais* and in his *Paradoxe sur le comédien*, and as did Engel in his *Ideen zu einer Mimik*. Since the natural language of gestures is not completely capable of generating perfect expressions of feelings, it was impossible for the gestures the actor used to imitate them to measure up effortlessly to the criterion of truth. With regard to the passions expressed with its aid, the gestural code developed by nature was by contrast so lacking "in clarity and stress"[74] that it had to be corrected by the actor. In Lessing's opinion there was "no other means" of finding the gestural signs which respectively describe the passions in the "most perfect manner" other than the actor's "acquainting himself with the special ways in which they are expressed by him or other persons and to assemble a general type from this picture he has, a type that will appear to be all the more true because everybody will discover something of himself in it."[75] Gestural signs intended to meet the demands of the criterion of truth could therefore not be produced as the one-to-one imitation of gestures encountered in reality, but rather arose as the result of a complex process of observation, registration, selection, and synthesis. The method St. Albine propagates for producing such signs, namely for the actor himself to feel the emotions to be described, was to be rejected irrevocably. The "correct" gestural signs had rather "to be learned in a certain mechanical manner, but in a way that is based on immutable rules."[76]

Whereas even in his later writings Lessing did not discuss these rules in any detail, Engel attempted both to provide general justifications for them and to find an individual wording for each. He took as his basis the "law" or "rule of analogy" mentioned above, according to which physical changes occur analogously to emotional changes. It follows from this that the "correct" gestural signs, i.e., those that measure up to the criterion of truth, can only be generated given a comprehensive knowledge of the emotional processes on which they are based. For the individual parts or elements of a gesture had to be perfect analogies of the individual sections of the psychological process they imitated. Thus, in Engel's eyes the first stage in constituting a gestural code was to classify the states of the human soul. He constructed them as a binary system and ended up with the order shown on page 164.

This classification claims to take all the simple emotions that are not the product of combinations into account. All those which are not listed must thus be considered to be mixtures—in other words, combinations. Engel provided a detailed description of each state contained in the classification and, by means of the principle of analogy, derived from each a description of the gestural sign best suited to providing a perfect expression of the state. Thus, for example, he described anger as "the desire to remove, to destroy an ill," a desire which is "one with the desire to punish and take revenge":[77]

all Nature's energies stream outwards in order to transform the joy of what is Evil into Fear by the terrifying sight of it, into Pain by its destructive effect, and, by contrast, to turn our own bitter Annoyance into a pleasant feeling of our Strength, the Terror we instill in others.[78]

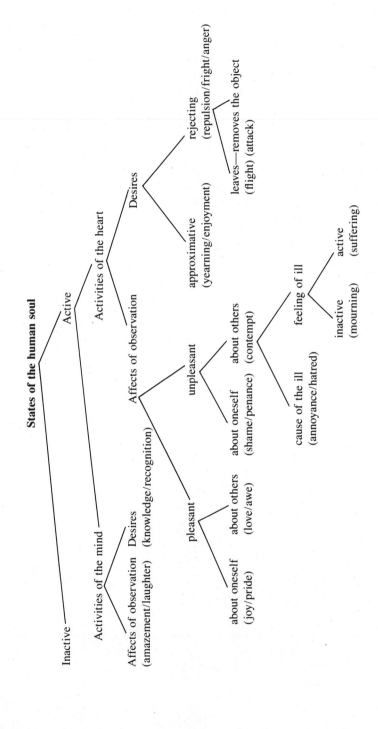

The corresponding physical expression followed analogously from this state:

> Anger equips . . . all the external limbs with strength; pre-eminently arming those who are destined to destroy. If the external parts, overfilled with blood and juices, brim over and tremble, and the bloodshot, rolling eyes shoot glances like fiery daggers, then a certain indignation, a certain disquiet is also expressed by the hands and teeth: the former are clenched convulsively, the latter are bared and gnashed . . . all movements are jerky and of extreme violence; the gait is heavy, forced, shattering.[79]

Each individual physical change, in other words, was held to have its cause in a certain emotion and thus pointed back to that cause. Taken together, all these changes formed the gestural sign for anger and consequently described the expression of the respective emotion perfectly. Whereas the corresponding modifications generated by real anger were, if taken together, to be understood as an indexical sign that pointed to the feeling that caused them, those gestural signs produced on stage according to the rules Engel drew up constituted an imitation that perfected them. The result was iconic signs, the suitable and perfect representation of the indexical signs of reality. They were neither a spontaneous expression of the feeling nor an arbitrary, conventional sign thereof, but rather adequate representations of the gestural sign observed in reality, a sign which had arisen as the spontaneous expression of the respective feeling.

Since the theater of the day described not only simple, noncombined feelings nor merely series of individual feelings, it followed that the gestural code could first be considered complete once it also possessed rules according to which the signs for individual, simple feelings in the repertoire could be combined with one another in order to depict both mixed feelings and a sequence of feelings.

In this context, it was the "Continuity of Playing" which was considered to function as the general rule for successive combinations. In other words, signs had to be generated in uninterrupted succession, since there were no pauses in "the play of gestures" as there are in speech: "every glance in every moment is laden with meaning, be it by the expression of a certain affect or by calm, indifference, distraction."[80] Since there can be no pauses in the generation of gestural signs, it follows that particular care had to be taken to ensure their "correct" successive combination. Three different possibilities were, in principle, distinguished here: first, the linking of several peaceful activities; second, the transition from a peaceful to an affective state and back again; third, the combination of several impassioned movements.

It proved possible, in all cases, to derive the rules for combining gestural signs according to the principle of analogy, i.e., they followed from the regularity of psychological processes. Thus, only those signs could be combined with one another that signified emotional states that would naturally directly follow one another. "Mimic" knowledge stems here from psychological knowledge. The rules governing the combination of signs could thus only be drawn up assuming that "the moral being is of just as much value to the observer as a polyp to Trembley or an aphid to Bonnet."[81] For each successive combination of gestural signs had to depict the sequence of different emotional states in a way that appeared possible in terms of human nature, which was presumed to hold equally true for all persons.

The combination is able to provide such a description because each of its signs has a fixed, immutable meaning. Placing the signs in a sequential series therefore initially means only the precise sequencing of the individual emotional states the signs signify, without this causing the slightest modification of the meanings of the individual signs. If this combination is, in turn, regarded as a complex sign, then the meaning of it can logically only follow from the sequencing of the meanings of the individual signs that go to make it up. Since gestural signs are generated continuously, the super-sign combining them all is delimited by the beginning and end of a scene. To the extent that each combination is oriented toward psychological regularities, toward the "nature of the soul," it must conversely be possible to interpret it, too, as a sign of these regularities. The meaning of the combination is consequently to be defined as that psychological regularity which governs the sequence of the different emotional states signified by the individual gestural signs. The sum of these regularities was held to constitute the underlying order of the human soul, an order which manifested itself in the visible order of the gestural signs that followed each other in reality. Thus, it was only possible to define the continuous combination of gestural signs in theater appropriately in terms of its being the perfect depiction of that order of the human soul which was preordained and fixed by nature.[82]

Gestures in Theater as a Representational System of Meaning in the Discourse of the Epoch

Each of the different shapes the gestural code of German theater in the eighteenth century took developed in specific relation to those trends and notions which can be shown to have played a dominant role outside of theater in different social domains and different cultural systems. This interconnection may not be as apparent elsewhere as it is in the case of the gestural code of baroque theater, which had already arisen in the course of the seventeenth century. For, as is intimated by the theme of the *theatrum mundi* and *theatrum vitae humanae* that dominated the epoch, the theater and the world, i.e., human life, were conceived of as two quantities fundamentally related to one another, two quantities which could only be characterized and grasped adequately in terms of their mutual referentiality. Theater as "the complete depiction and perfect symbol of the world,"[83] on the one hand, corresponded to a far-reaching theatricalization of courtly life, on the other.[84] In theater, the gestures—words, costumes, decorations, props, lighting, and music were constituted as representations of pregiven meanings—and the task was to perceive these meanings and interpret them correctly in that light. In like manner, the phenomena to which the gestures pointed—human life and the world—were in turn to be conceived of as signs that were of importance not in terms of their material existence, but solely with reference to their immaterial, eternal meaning. For the opinion was that the world and human life were, just like theater, to be comprehended as a complex of signs which pointed to the divine order of the world and thus had to be interpreted with a view to their eternal meaning in terms of religious salvation and redemption. In this context, the gestural code of theater is indeed to be understood as a constitutive and representative element of the "large theater of the world."[85]

During the Enlightenment, a new gestural code for theater came into being under fundamentally different conditions. It arose parallel to developments and hypotheses in those sciences that had specifically undertaken to research human nature: anthropology, ethnology, psychology, and physiology. And it borrowed from these. The latter two disciplines could at that time already look back on a long tradition, and the task at hand was to reformulate that tradition in terms of new research objectives—one need think only of the doctrine of the affects and that of the temperaments. By contrast, the genesis of anthropology and ethnology in the real sense is indebted to the specific scientific interests of the century.[86] The aim was to replace theology's dogmatic definitions and determinations of human nature once and for all, placing in their stead intersubjectively verifiable statements gleaned or derived from observation and comparison. The formulation of such statements could only occur as the result of lengthy and arduous research processes. For "the science of human beings is also a natural science, a science of observation."[87]

It thus comes as no surprise that the new gestural code of theater was developed in clear reference to developments and hypotheses in the sciences mentioned above. After all, on the one hand, a gestural code relies on certain assumptions about human nature, and, on the other, the sciences in question attributed particular significance to the study of gestural signs, as can be seen in the much-discussed question as to an ur-language.[88]

However, the gestural code of theater was not created in direct dependence on the activities and results of the aforementioned sciences, if only because of the differences and timelags.[89] The assumption that the two developed parallel to one another appears, by contrast, quite plausible. The fundamental upheavals and changes that occurred in the course of the eighteenth century have an impact in particular on the notions of "Man," human nature, and human destiny valid until then. This process, on the one hand, made it necessary to research human nature scientifically using empirical means and thus prompted the formation of new sciences or the specific alteration of existing sciences, and, on the other, triggered a need for a new artistic depiction of human beings that was appropriate in light of these changes.[90] Seen in this light, the gestural code of theater appears to be a specific system of meaning which developed on the one hand as a consequence and on the other as a constitutive, and at the same time representative, element of that epochal discourse which characterizes and dominates the second half of the eighteenth century.

The gestural code constituted during the Enlightenment provided a theatrical paradigm that was to remain valid for bourgeois illusionistic theater until the advent of the avant-garde movement in the early twentieth century. Shortly after the turn of the eighteenth century, theater admittedly relinquished its claim to improving the spectator, to perfecting him morally and instructing him, and thus ceased to function as a moral institution. Indeed, its objectives and functions changed fundamentally in the course of the nineteenth century. Nevertheless, the basic traits of the gestural code were retained and developed further. For three of the substantive principles on which its constitution during the Enlightenment had rested continued to function as "guiding principles" of theater:

1. Theater was intended to create an illusion of reality. Not only did this statement, the postulate of Enlightenment theater, continue to be valid, but the illusion created on stage was perfected to an ever greater extent, even as far as the famous "fourth wall": life took place on stage, a life the audience watched, without notice apparently being taken of it. The illusion created by the stage using Stanislavski's method was perfect in this sense.[91]

2. Acting took psychological states and emotional processes in the bourgeois individual as its object. Whereas during the Enlightenment the feelings the actor expressed were conceived of as the depiction of universal human properties—for the immutable human nature common to all was portrayed—increasing psychologization in the course of the nineteenth century took the form of lending expression to the specific emotional condition of the bourgeois individual. Portraying the most minor of emotions such that it could be perceived by the audience became the highest aim of acting. In this respect, too, Stanislavsky put the ideals of bourgeois acting formulated during the Enlightenment into practice with an almost unsurpassable degree of perfection.[92]

3. The human body was by nature capable of and suited to perfectly expressing emotions. In line with this axiom, further developments in the art of acting focused on finding a "natural" gestural sign, natural in the sense that it was readily understandable by the spectator, a sign for every emotion that was experienced, for every psychological state that could be experienced by self-observation. The conviction that gestures on stage were to be construed as the body's natural language continued to hold sway because, first, the gestural code of theater took the shape of a "perfection" or refinement of the gestural code commonly used by the bourgeoisie, and second, the audience was able to decipher and readily understand this code by virtue of the fact that the spectators were all members of the bourgeoisie.[93] During the Enlightenment, attempts were made to recreate this natural language on stage on the basis of observations and perfected imitation. By contrast, for Stanislavsky it was the authenticity and depth of feeling that was the most important guarantee that the most appropriate natural sign would be realized: the feeling to a certain degree necessarily led to that physical change which could then function as the natural expression of the feeling. Here, the conventionality of a particular theatrical gesture consequently counted as a gross violation of the principles of the bourgeois art of acting. The actor's gestural signs had rather to bow to Stanislavski's insistence that they be the natural expression of the emotion in question.

These three guiding principles, which determine the shape of bourgeois theater from its inception, were first abolished with the advent of the avant-garde. For, if art ceases to imitate life and/or puts itself in the latter's place, and instead professes its artificiality, then theater can no longer have the function of creating an illusion of real life or of expressing "real" feelings in a "natural" way. The gestural code that had been constituted during the Enlightenment was now useless and declared invalid. The moment the avant-garde views artistic means not as the result of organic growth, but rather as consciously chosen and applied aids, the actor's body can no longer be highlighted as the natural expression of the soul, but must rather be conceived of as material to be used. Using this material, Meyerhold, Brecht, and Artaud, for example, endeavored to generate gestures as extremely artificial, as emphatically conventional signs; they resorted to highly complex techniques—such as Meyerhold's biomechanics or Artaud's insistence on a specific technique for breathing and movement. It was not least due to the impact of an experience and knowledge of Asian forms of theater that they created new gestural codes which expressly constituted themselves as conventional codes, and proclaimed themselves to be such. The notion or postulate of natural gestural signs was completely undermined by the avant-garde movement's declaration that the three guiding principles were null and void[94]—and with that, the era of bourgeois illusionist theater came to an end.

III.

The Theatrical Code
as Speech

□ □ □ □ □ □

At the level of speech, the theatrical code includes all those elements that can be used functionally in the actual performance, i.e., that can be given a meaning in the context of a performance. As a system, the theatrical code contains all the general possibilities and conditions for the generation of meaning; as a norm, on the other hand, the theatrical code contains only those possibilities and conditions typical for and characteristic of a certain epoch or genre. At the level of speech, the theatrical code regulates the ongoing process of a unique generation of meaning: it refers only to one single production of meaning, namely to the respective individual performance. Thus, at the level of speech, the theatrical code constitutes the totality of all rules on which the production and reception of one particular performance rest. A study of the theatrical code at the level of speech can therefore only apply to one specific work, one particular performance: the performance in question has to be described and analyzed in order to understand the performance entailed.

This objective takes us into the domain of the analytical study of theater and thus into the least developed area of theater studies. Admittedly, there are descriptions of and documentation on magnificent courtly festivals and performances that were held during the Renaissance and baroque periods, and some of these accounts are very detailed. Numerous theater reviews also exist since the Enlightenment. Ever since then and, in particular, since Lessing's *Hamburgische Dramaturgie*, these reviews have tended to go much further than merely trying to recapitulate the plays in question. Rather, they provide carefully chosen descriptions intended as interpretations or critical evaluations of them. Nevertheless, none of these can be regarded as systematic analyses of performances.

This lack of analyses of individual works, which is so conspicuous and severe by comparison to other areas of art and literary studies, is attributable not least of all to the special ontological status of the performance, something we discussed at length in the first part of this study. For, since the artifact[1] of the performance cannot be preserved and handed down as something which is distinct from the process which produced it or independently of its producers, an analysis can, strictly speaking, only be carried out in the course of the performance and at the location of the performance. An analysis of past performances is thus out of the question. Yet, due to the inherently transitory nature of performance, even an analysis of contemporary performances is extremely difficult if not actually impossible. For if a performance, which is carried out as the realization of theatrical signs, can be separated neither temporally nor spatially from the reception of that performance—and the latter is the interpretation of those signs—then the receiver has no means of verifying his results by comparing them with the work itself. Nor can he correct these results wherever suitable—a possibility that forms an indispensable part of any analysis of an individual work. Consequently, it appears all too understandable that traditionally theater studies have exercised great restraint with regard to performance analysis. Whether it is justified or indeed necessary is something that still has to be ascertained.

The difficulties in analyzing a performance—and these stem from the special ontological status of performances—hinge for the most part on the impossibility of preserving it as an artifact. However, if it were possible to create a relatively appropriate correlate for the material artifact of the performance—since the latter cannot in principle be written down or passed down in history—then these difficulties would be reduced considerably, if not removed altogether. For this correlate would exist independently of the performance being carried out, and it would therefore always be possible to cross-check the preliminary results of the analysis against it and correct it accordingly. Extensive filmic or video documentation could serve as such a correlate, or even a graphic text into which the performance could be transcribed as completely as possible using a special system of notation. Of course, this correlate must under no circumstances be confused with the artifact of the performance, which exists as such only as that performance, i.e., in the course of a process in which the theatrical signs that have been devised and selected are actually realized. The correlate, by contrast, is only an aid, constructed in order to facilitate the analysis, which is so severely constrained by the transitory nature of theater.

If the possibility of analyzing a performance does indeed depend substantially on whether it is possible to create an unchanging correlate for the performance as artifact that retains its validity over time, then it would have to be able to rely on the development of corresponding procedures for documentation and notation. If, by contrast, the special ontological status of the performance were to give rise to a special epistemological status, then the creation of an adequate correlate would by no means yield the fundamental preconditions for conducting an analysis of the performance. In other words, the epistemological status of the performance must be clarified before any documentation and notation procedures are developed or methods of analysis devised. The question to be asked must therefore be how the performance can be defined and in what terminology we should couch the definition if we are to be able to treat the performance as an object of scholarly analysis.

7. Performance as Theatrical Text

❑ ❑ ❑ If, at the level of speech, the theatrical code regulates the choice and realization of those signs and combinations of signs which as a unit constitute the concrete individual performance, then the performance can in this respect be defined generally as a structured complex of signs. This description is well known and common in modern theories of textual analysis, which adopt it as the most general definition of the concept of text. In epistemological terms, the performance can thus be defined as a text and, since the signs it uses have been found to be theatrical signs, it can be defined as a theatrical text. Performance analysis can therefore be construed as a particular mode of textual analysis and conducted as such. In order to describe this particular mode more precisely, we must therefore establish which more specific, and by this I mean more sharply defined, concept of text can serve as the basis for the following remarks.

The Concept of the Theatrical Text

Since the most refined theories of the text are to be encountered in linguistics—as textual linguistics—we must examine the more specialized concept of text deployed there to assess whether or not it contains definitions which apply exclusively to linguistic texts or can rather be applied in the field of analytical theater studies. Only those concepts of text which claim to be valid for (a) all texts, (b) all forms of aesthetic texts and (c) all types of multimedial texts appear suitable for this purpose. It follows that in order to develop and use a concept of the theatrical text that goes further than the general definition of the performance as a structured complex of signs, we can only draw on those theories of the text which make use of a concept of text which comes under one of the above three headings.

In his *Textual Linguistics* Coseriu offers a definition of the concept of text that is applicable to all texts: "Every text has meaning."[1] He holds the basic problem of textual linguistics to be the following question: "How does 'meaning' arise and how do we understand it?"[2] Both the assertion and the question derived from it can be used without altering their wording to refer to performance, to the theatrical text. The general approach to be taken by performance analysis can thus be summarized in terms of the main question as to how the performance generates meaning, what procedures for creating meaning are involved, and finally what possible meaning is constituted by the performance.[3] These are the most important tasks to be fulfilled by performance analysis understood as analysis of the theatrical text, tasks formulated here as global goals. Such comprehensive objectives must be differentiated on the basis of other text theories and defined more closely.

Lotman initially takes a similarly general approach when defining the aesthetic text: "An artistic text is complexly constructed meaning. All of its elements are elements that bear meaning."[4] The aesthetic text is thus to be distinguished from the nonaesthetic text by the specific characteristic of not having any redundant elements. The meaning of a nonaesthetic text can be understood even if individual elements are absent, substituted for one another, or falsified, whereas an aesthetic text can only be understood if its structure is left unchanged. For its meaning can "neither exist outside the respective structure nor be conveyed by a separate entity."[5] Structural analysis would thus appear to be the only possible way to constitute meaning, to understand the artistic text.

In order to be able to describe such a structural analysis more precisely, Lotman defines the concept of text in more specific terms. A text is characterized by the following three features: 1. Explicitness, 2. Delimitation, and 3. Structuredness.

(1) "*Explicitness*. The text is determinately encoded in certain signs and in this sense is opposed to extratextual structures."[6] The signs preserve a meaning and give it a fixed form, a meaning that it would not have been possible to communicate without such objectification. The explicitness of a text is thus a precondition for its analysis: since the meanings conveyed receive a hard-and-fast form as signs, they can also be understood by those who perceive and interpret them. With regard to aesthetic texts, furthermore, the signs can only render the intended meanings explicit in the respective combination and position.

In the context of the theatrical text, it follows from the notion of explicitness that a list and description should be made of those signs factually realized as well as any combinations of them. Each individual theatrical text must accordingly be examined to assess (a) which of the generally available sign systems it uses, (b) which types of signs are realized within a system, and (c) which specific concrete signs are realized. In other words, the selection of the theatrical signs functions in three ways as an element bearing meaning. First, it serves as the selection of the sign systems to be used and this gives rise to the question: Which sign systems are involved in the text? Second, it functions as a selection within one system, and this prompts the question: Which stylized or realistic gestures are used, which historical or characterizing costumes, object-based or abstract decorations, etc. Third, it operates as a selection of particular concrete signs, which brings us to another question, namely: Does the performance use sobbing or sighing, are the actor's eyes closed in the process or not, what physical stance or hand position is adopted? How long are the robes, what color and cut are they? etc. Since the explicitness of the text is realized in the performance as a respectively particular selection of theatrical signs and combinations of signs, the selection of those elements that function in the text as theatrical signs must be considered to serve as an element of meaning at all three levels and must thus be interpreted accordingly.

(2) "*Delimitation*. The text is characterized by the fact that it is limited. In this respect, it is opposed, on the one hand, to all material signs that do not belong to it (in line with the principle of 'contains/does not contain'). On the other, it

is opposed to all structures which do not exhibit the characteristic of delimitation.''[7] The feature of delimitation thus refers to two things:

(a) *Delimitation in relation to elements that are not contained in the text.* In this sense, the delimitation of the text amounts to the inversion of the category of explicitness. For whereas in the latter case, the positive selection of certain signs functions as an element ·bearing meaning, in the former the same function is fulfilled by the exclusion of signs not selected from the text. A threefold exclusion is the equivalent here to the threefold positive selection outlined above. In this context, it is quite possible that exclusion is accorded greater importance than selection: consciously forgoing use of an otherwise common sign system, for example—such as that of lighting, decorations, costumes, props—can itself become a meaning essential to and constitutive of the performance. Therefore, under certain conditions delimitation as exclusion must be viewed as an element of meaning that is by no means unimportant.

(b) *Temporal and spatial delimitation.* This occurs in the theatrical text, on the one hand, as a certain segment of time, the duration of which may vary and which is demarcated by the beginning and end of the performance. On the other, it may take the form of the respectively defined delimitation of space, the space set aside for the actors and that for the spectators. Both temporal extension and spatial conception are to be considered as elements of meaning in the performance if they (a) deviate from the generally valid and accepted norm or (b) are conceived of as elements bearing meaning because there is no generally valid rule which can be applied to them.[8] For example, if there is a consensus that performances can only be held in special theater buildings, delimitation of a space for acting on the marketplace or in a factory must be conceived of as a sign. If, by contrast, there is no consensus as to the "correct" length of a performance, then the length of each play must be regarded as an element bearing meaning.

(3) *"Structuredness.* The text does not constitute a simple sequence of signs between two external limits. It is typified by an internal organization that transforms it at the syntagmatic level into a structured whole."[9] In order to be able to study the quality of a text as structure, all the combinations into which the signs enter with one another must be scrutinized. In part 1 of this book, three general rules of combination were outlined, each of which is realized in a specific way by the theatrical text:

(a) Each sign within a sign system can be combined with every other sign of the same and every other system. Performances must thus be examined with a view to establishing which signs are factually combined in them. Thus, for example, linguistic, paralinguistic, mimic, gestural, and proxemic signs as well as signs from the systems for mask, hair, and costume may be combined with one another—and all point to the same meaning, e.g., a particular emotion, and thus support and reinforce one another. Alternatively, the signs linked with one another may point to different meanings and thus weaken, neutralize, modify, or contradict each other.

(b) Each sign can be combined simultaneously or in succession with another sign. An assessment must therefore be made of whether the sign combinations occur simultaneously or successively. Whether two persons wearing the same costumes appear on stage simultaneously or in succession, and whether a figure sings while engaged in an activity, or sings after the activity, etc., are questions that may have a great bearing on the meaning of a sequence.

(c) The combination of signs taken from different sign systems may be treated as equals or in terms of their place in a hierarchy. Each theatrical text must therefore be investigated in order to assess whether a certain sign system is dominant in it. Should this transpire to be the case, then the meanings generated by that system will have a particular weighting compared with the meanings generated by signs from other systems.

On account of the special combinations that the signs of a theatrical text enter into with one another, the text amounts to a system of equivalencies and oppositions which, as a respectively unique totality, gives rise to the specific structuredness of the text and thus determines the shape it takes.

In other words, the three features Lotman lists—explicitness, delimitation, and structuredness—are realized above all by virtue of the particular selection and combination of those elements that function as theatrical signs. A specific meaning is thus generated in and/or by the theatrical text. The individual realization of the three constitutive features, i.e., the specific selection and combination of theatrical signs, appears in this light as a special mode of generating meaning in the theatrical (and more generally, in the aesthetic) text. The type of realization respectively employed must thus be taken into account as an element bearing meaning in the structural analysis.

Lotman attempts to establish equivalents for the general conditions under which meaning arises in an (aesthetic) text. He points in particular to all those cases in which

> at least two different chains of structure exist. . . . In the process of recoding, correspondences are created between pairs of elements that are different by nature, whereby one element in its system is grasped as the equivalent of another element in the other's system. It is, however, . . . only possible to distinguish between the two levels to a limited extent, . . . for relating elements of two different systems to each other as equivalents is admittedly the most frequent, but by no means the only, case in which meaning is generated. One need only think of the other semiotic systems that lay claim to universality and which in principle do not permit the substitution of meanings by structures from some other realm. In other words, we are concerned with relational meanings which arise from one element of a system being expressed by other elements of the same system. This can be defined as internal recoding.''[10]

Lotman accordingly makes a fundamental distinction between two different types of the generation of meaning, namely between external and internal recoding. Meaning in a concrete text is usually created by the alternating use of both procedures, whereby the text in many cases is characterized by the fact that one of the two clearly predominates.

In the case of *external* recoding, meaning arises by virtue of the fact that individual elements of the texts are related to extratextual structural chains: each textual element in question is to be allocated to at least one element of at least one other structure.

This mode of producing meaning is typical and characteristic of many theatrical texts. In part 1, we studied the systemic aspects of the procedures of producing meaning in theater in general. We discerned three types of such production that are also realized to differing degrees and in differing mixtures in contemporary theatrical texts—and it is only these that can be taken into account in our deliberations here. To adopt Lotman's terminology, we can now refer to these forms of generating meaning as representing different modes of external recoding:

(1) The signs and sign combinations realized in the performance can be referred to one specific underlying theatrical code which functions as a norm.

Performances of Far Eastern theater—such as the Peking Opera, Nô and Kabuki theater, etc.—comprise a particularly impressive example of this mode of producing meaning. In recent years, frequent guest performances have acquainted wider circles of people in the Western world with these forms of theater. Such performances can only be understood if one is able to refer their individual elements to the theatrical code underlying all the performances of this form, a code which foresees a certain meaning being attributed to each element used.

By contrast, contemporary Western theater performances cannot, of course, be related in like manner to such a code. Yet, even if we do not have fixed theatrical norms at our disposal today, this by no means implies that individual performances are not based on the presupposition that certain theatrical conventions are valid and generally accepted. Centuries-old conventions, such as asides, or certain types of costume (for example, the harlequin's patchwork costume) can be considered examples of such conventions, as can those which have only come into use over the last ten or fifteen years and yet have nevertheless become stable elements of the code. More recent conventions of this type include, for example, a specific usage of costumes, props, and decoration which may refer to all epochs and cultures without at the same time signifying that the person or space belongs to the respective epoch or culture. Such costumes are instead now used to characterize the persons and their specific situation.

A knowledge of this convention will, therefore, prevent a spectator of Peymann's production of *Iphigenia* from claiming that Iphigenia's typewriter is an anachronism and instead will enable him to perceive the typewriter in relation to Iphigenia and her particular situation and to interpret it as a sign in this sense. The element /typewriter/ can thus be accorded an adequate meaning in the context of the performance only via recourse to the corresponding convention. This convention admittedly does not assign one specific meaning to the element, but has at least given the universe of discourse to which the possible meanings may refer a clearly demarcated and unchanging form.

(2) The signs and sign combinations realized in the performance can be referred to extratheatrical cultural codes on which the primary cultural systems are based.

This mode of creating meaning determines all performances of realist theater as well as isolated realistic segments of otherwise nonrealist performances. It rests on the presupposition that actors and spectators are in like manner both acquainted with the primary cultural systems to which the performance refers. Thus, it will not be possible to constitute the meaning of the individual elements of a theatrical text unless they are referred to elements from the respective cultural systems. A certain collection of furniture on stage, for example, may be assigned the meaning "bourgeois living room" or "petit-bourgeois kitchenette"; costumes can be iden- tified as evening dress, smocks, or police uniforms; a nod of the head can be accorded the meaning of affirmation, and a hasty gait, a loud voice, or knitted brows all point to anger as an emotion. Different primary cultural systems such as language, facial expression, gestures and movement, clothing, makeup, etiquette, notions of interior design, etc., all function here as extratextual structural chains to which the individual elements of the theatrical text must be referred if meaning is to be created. A knowledge of them allows the spectator to assign an adequate meaning to the elements of the theatrical text in the context of this particular performance. However, the possibility of attributing meaning to elements of a theatrical text via recourse to the primary cultural systems of the culture in ques- tion is itself a convention of Western theater that has been valid, if at times to only a limited extent, for centuries now.

(3) The signs and sign combinations realized in a performance can be related to extratheatrical cultural codes upon which various different secondary cultural systems are based. Literature, painting, music, theater, film, myth, religion, and other social institutions are defined in this context as secondary systems.

This mode of creating meaning cannot be applied to the whole performance, but rather regulates the attribution of meaning solely in the case of the individual elements of a theatrical text. In this case, the assumption must again be that the spectators are acquainted with the respective secondary cultural systems to which reference is made. Thus, in Western culture we can assume that every adult member of the culture is able to identify a figure with horns and cleft hooves as the devil, a skeleton with a scythe and an hourglass as Death, a figure with wings and a halo as an angel, an old man with a long white beard, and a red hooded cape as Santa Claus, etc. In recent years, Westerns and crime films have acquainted us with numerous stereotyped appearances, movements, and locations which can now likewise be assumed to be general knowledge. Today, a certain manner of crossing the stage with a swaggering gait will be associated with the stereotype of a cowboy just as surely as the gesture of washing one's hands has, for centuries, been as- sociated with Pontius Pilate's famous words. Within the context of the perfor- mance, an appropriate meaning can be accorded such elements of the theatrical text only if they are related to elements of the extratextual structural chain of a secondary cultural system. In other words, each element of a theatrical text that alludes in one way or another to an element of another text receives its meaning only by being referred back to the text in which the element alluded to originates. This particular mode of external recoding is typical and characteristic of many contemporary performances.[11]

In the case of meaning constituted via *internal* recoding, each element of the text is determined by other elements of the same text. Theatrical texts contain particularly favorable conditions and numerous preconditions for this mode of generating meaning, a form that is usually encountered only in nonaesthetic texts in the case of definitions. For every theatrical text is composed of heterogeneous signs and the widest range of different systems of theatrical signs are involved in constituting it. It would thus appear obvious to generate meaning within the theatrical text by defining one element of a sign system by means of one or more elements of one or more other sign systems. This mode of generating meaning is so common that numerous dramatic texts make explicit reference to it. Thus, in *A Midsummer Night's Dream*, for example, Quince says: "Or else one must come in with a bush of thorns and a lantern, and say he comes to disfigure or to present the person of moonshine" (act 3, scene 1). The language here is intended to graft its meaning onto a nonlinguistic element. This type of internal recoding is, admittedly, to be found frequently in theatrical texts, but it is by no means the only approach that can be taken. Gestural actions can also more than adequately fulfill such a function: such actions can, for example, transform a simple stick into a rapier, a dirty rag into a flag to be honored, or a sparsely furnished room with a chair in it into a coronation room.

More complex forms are to be discerned alongside such simple forms of internal recoding, as in the case of Augusto Fernandes's staging of Pirandello's *Henry IV* in Frankfurt in 1978. In such instances, the internal recoding is based on its external counterpart. Thus, for example, a red carpet or a glove must be recognized as such on the basis of a knowledge of the primary cultural systems—i.e., in its current concrete function—before, in the further course of the performance and as a result of internal recoding, the carpet can be juxtaposed to the bare floor as the place where Henry is Emperor, the glove becomes a sign for clothing as a whole, etc. As a consequence, we can define and comprehend such a means of creating theatrical metaphors during the performance as a particular mode of internal recoding.

In keeping with his differentiation of the procedures of external and internal recoding, Lotman distinguishes between paradigmatic and syntagmatic meanings. Aesthetic texts are always based on both types of meaning; the constitution of meaning exclusively by one of the two forms is not possible, yet one of them may nevertheless be dominant. Both paradigmatic and syntagmatic meanings created within an aesthetic text seldom arise as the result of an unequivocal assignation. Usually, the element of the aesthetic text in question can be related to various elements of respectively different extratextual structural chains and/or differing textual elements. Almost every element can thus be construed as the point of intersection of various different syntagmatic and paradigmatic axes. The meaning of an element thus correspondingly arises on the basis of the relations that come into being in this manner.

What we have said with regard to the individual elements of a theatrical text, or for aesthetic texts in general, holds true, if modified in a specific way, for the whole text. To the extent that individual elements in it must be related to other texts if they are to be instilled with meaning, the text itself appears as the point at which those different texts that have entered into it via the individual elements cross and intersect. By referring to these other texts and at the same time marking itself off from them, the text constitutes itself as a special individual text in each case. Thus, the text's specific intertextuality appears to be the precondition for its constitution in the first place.[12]

Our efforts thus far have gone into attempting to define the concept of theatrical text more precisely by drawing on Coseriu's general concept of text and Lotman's concept of the artistic text. However, the theatrical text cannot be construed simply as an artistic text, but must also be considered a multimedial text. In this connection it can be compared with other multimedial texts of both an aesthetic and a non-aesthetic nature, such as comics, film, musicals, shows, happenings, performances, circus, etc.

The theory and the analysis of multimedial texts are both still in their infancy. Promising approaches have been developed and discussed with regard to specific fields (such as film, circus, happenings[13]), approaches that can be taken further, both qualitatively and quantitatively. Yet there can be no talk of a comprehensive theory of multimedial texts.[14]

At a quite general level, multimedial texts can be defined as those texts which are communicated by means of more than one medium,[15] such as film images and sound, the written word and pictures, actors, stage space, and sound, etc. Each medium involved may convey signs from one or more sign systems. No fixed allocation of sign system to medium occurs in this process. Signs from different systems may be conveyed by one and the same medium (by a film image or an actor), and conversely, the signs of one system may be communicated in different media: linguistic signs, for example, may be conveyed by a sound or by writing, gestural signs by the actor or by a film image, etc. The heterogeneous signs that go to make up a multimedial text must therefore not be equated with the different media that convey them. Mimic and gestural signs, or even signs of external appearance, can thus be used both in film and in a theater performance. Both types of multimedial texts can, in other words, be composed in part of the same signs. Whereas in the one case the sign is transported by the medium of the film image, it is conveyed in the other by the actor. Furthermore, the respective medium is directly involved in the process of generating meaning to the extent that it necessitates a particular choice, shaping, and combination of signs. Clearly, for example, the mimic sign presented in a close-up shot has a different quality from the same mimic sign realized by the actor on stage and necessarily in combination with other signs. Consequently, the same meaning cannot be attributed to the two signs. Here, the specific medium concerned has a substantial effect on the process of generating meaning and must therefore also be taken into consideration as a constitutive factor.

The theatrical text always requires at least two media: the actor, who conveys signs via optic and acoustic channels, and the surrounding space, which can be used to transport the widest variety of visual signs. In addition, other media can be used which are suited to transmitting heterogeneous acoustic signs. However, the actor and the stage space warrant closer attention, for they are both media which go to constitute the theatrical text.[16]

The theatrical text was defined above as a text composed in the language of theater. This language is characterized in particular by the fact that it cannot be reduced to one smallest homogeneous unit, but is instead comprised of heterogeneous sign systems. Moreover, the latter cannot all be divided up into their smallest elements of signification. In part 1 we attempt to construct, describe, and present the system underlying this language, which is to say, the *langue* in question. We must assume on the basis of the deliberations there that every theatrical text is composed of signs which originate in the widest variety of different sign systems which, as a whole, go to make up the language of theater.

This text is, as we have seen, always conveyed by the agency of at least two different media: the actor and the space surrounding him. Even if it would appear obvious to allocate certain sign systems to one of the two media, and even if this is usually de facto the case, this cannot be presupposed to constitute a general rule. Mimic, gestural, and proxemic signs can admittedly be conveyed only by the actor—unless, that is, films are used as part of the decor—but these signs must by no means serve exclusively as signs of a character embodied by the actor. Conversely, the signs constituted by the stage space cannot exclusively have the function of designating that space. The meaning of a theatrical sign is therefore by no means fixed once and for all by the choice of medium to convey it, although it may in part be defined by this choice. Rather, owing to the mobility of theatrical signs, the signs conveyed by the different media involved cannot be ascribed one clearly fixed function with regard to the one medium chosen. The medium of space can convey signs that point to the character embodied by the actor, just as, conversely, signs transmitted by the medium of the actor can help to give the stage space more tangible form. It is precisely this specificity of the theatrical text that reveals all the more clearly the part played by its specific use of different media in the process of producing meaning, for the unique way in which a certain theatrical sign can be conveyed via the medium of the actor, the space, or the loudspeakers can itself become an element bearing meaning.

Yet we must assume quite generally that both the use of numerous media and the specific form this may take each respectively influences the process of generating meaning in a specific way. To date, however, most of the investigations on the subject have not gone beyond the project level. Therefore, as yet no hard and fast rules have been developed to which one can refer when attempting to describe and understand the specific way in which multiple media can be used to achieve a certain effect—such as affective reactions prompted by multimedial stimulation. Given the present state of research, all we can assert is that multimedia-based texts are particularly well suited to creating tension and anxiety, sorrow and shock, joy and emotions, "pity and fear" (as the poetics of tragedy and *Trauerspiel* have postulated and claimed for centuries), and that they are particularly well suited to triggering processes of identification. However, this proposition cannot be falsified or verified scientifically.[17] Aristotle, at any rate, was of the opinion that the effect of tragedy "also manifested itself without performance or actors"[18]—in other words, did not require some multimedia realization in order to have the desired effect, i.e., the stimulation of pity and fear and the "cleansing of such affects."[19] Nevertheless, it will be assumed in what follows that the specific use of the actor and space as media has an essential underlying function for the process of creating meaning in the theatrical text.

On the Constitution of the Theatrical Text

The constitution of the text can, on the basis of the general definition of text put forward by Coseriu and Lotman, be described as a process of interpretation, that is, as a process of creating meaning. This process occurs on two complementary levels: as the production of the text and as the reception of the text. The following section will concentrate exclusively on the constitution of the text as a process in terms of an aesthetics of production; the act of reception will be focused on in the section on the hermeneutics of the theatrical text.

The theatrical text is, as a rule, produced by a collective; a director and various actors as well as the stage, costume, and mask designers are usually involved creatively in its production. The collectivity of production is thus one of the constitutive features of the theatrical text. The meanings generated with the aid of that text are thus created by different persons; and different subjects influence the process of overall interpretation arrived at on the basis of the text. The question as to the function and role of the Subjects* in the process of text constitution would therefore appear to be the most important one to be raised with regard to the constitution of the theatrical text. Indeed, the question is particularly complex and it is difficult to find an answer to it.

We shall in this regard take up the propositions put forward by Julia Kristeva, who treats this question as the key issue in her theory of the poetic text. Our observations here are intended to shed some light on the particular role of the Subject in the constitution of the theatrical text.

Kristeva defines the constitution of the poetic text as "one of the most daring explorations the Subject can allow itself, one that delves into its constitutive process."[20] She understands the text as being the location of an interpretative praxis (*Sinngebung*) which the producing Subject accomplishes as a process, and it is a process that demonstrates "the determining conditions of the Subject" per se. When applying this proposition to the theatrical text we would therefore first have to tackle the basic problem: In what way is it possible for the different Subjects participating in the production of the theatrical text to constitute themselves as Subjects in the process of that production? The question is, in other words, to

*Translators' Note: In what follows, "Subject" refers to the philosophical concept of "Subject" (as opposed to "Object") as elaborated in the German philosophy of consciousness and as questioned by French post-structuralism.

what extent the production of a theatrical text can be construed and defined as the interpretative praxis of all those Subjects creatively involved in it.

Kristeva bases her theory on a concept of Subject which defines the latter neither as a transcendental, phenomenological Ego, nor as a Cartesian Ego, but rather as "subject-in-process." She elaborates this concept of Subject by drawing on Freud's psychoanalytical theory of the Subject and Lacan's further development of it. To do so, she introduces the conceptual opposition of the "semiotic" and the "symbolic," which she then takes as the basis for her definition of the poetic text.

Kristeva does not explain the semiotic in the way it is predominantly understood. Thus, she precisely does not regard it as a form of sign usage that follows rules—which she characterizes as symbolic—but rather as a phase which both precedes that usage and substantively codetermines the process of interpretation.

> This modality is the one to which Freudian psychoanalysis refers in postulating not only the *facilitation* and the structuring *disposition* of instinctual drives, but also the so-called *primary processes* which displace and condense energies and their inscription. Discrete quantities of energy move through the body of the subject who is not yet constituted as such and, in the course of his development, they are arranged according to the various constraints imposed on this body—always already involved in a semiotic process—by family and social structures.[21]

By the same token, the semiotic also has a contradictory structure. For it is the "birthplace" of the Subject, on the one hand, and the location of its negation, the place "where his unity succumbs before the process of charges and stases that produce him," on the other.[22]

Kristeva distinguishes the symbolic from the semiotic, that is, the instinctual drives and their articulation. She defines the symbolic as a domain of meaning "which is always that of a proposition or judgment, in other words, a realm of positions."[23] In this sense, the symbolic is always based on something being posited; it arises as the consequence of a thesis. Each sign must therefore be conceived of as thetic, and each process of sign usage must accordingly be grasped as a sequence of positions. Without a thesis there would be no meaning, and yet without meaning there would be nothing symbolic. The thesis thus constitutes the most important precondition for the process of creating meaning. For "thetic signification . . . constitutes the subject without being reduced to his process precisely because it is the threshold of language."[24] The symbolic is, in other words, just as contradictory in structure as is the semiotic. As something thetic it is the conditio sine qua non for the Subject's being able to constitute itself, and as a system of intersubjectively valid meanings it amounts to the negation of that constitution.

According to Kristeva, the Subject is constituted at the interface of semiotic and symbolic, at the point where the two meet, for it is only from this interface that "meaning emerges."[25] It is, however, precisely the process of interpretative praxis that is exclusively able to constitute the Subject as Subject.

In the case of the constitution of a poetic text this process once again occurs in a manner that reveals the subjective condition underlying the creation of all meaning. For, whereas in most signifying systems the symbolic seeks to repulse and master the semiotic to as great an extent as possible, the poetic text can be defined as the "semiotization of the symbolic,"[26] i.e., as "this unceasing operation of the drives toward, in, and through language."[27] The semiotic thus breaks into the order of the signifiers of the intersubjectively valid denotative language and leads to that language's destructuration or restructuration. This is expressed not only in a particular musicality of language, in rhyme, rhythm, meter, and timbre, but also in the play of images, their specific agrammaticality, and much else besides. The intersubjectively valid sign system of the denotative language is more or less destroyed by the semiotic and transformed into a new system, namely that of poetic language. The text, the result of this process, thus signifies "the un-signifying: it assumes within a signifying practice this functioning (the semiotic), which ignores meaning and operates before meaning or despite it."[28] The Subject can, in other words, also find itself appropriately represented in the deformation of poetic language.

This last point will require careful examination when transposing Kristeva's theory from poetic onto theatrical texts. For the majority of theatrical signs belong to sign systems which do not have a system of denotative meanings at their disposal in the way that language does. The conjunction of semiotic and symbolic in positing mimic, gestural, and proxemic signs, for example, can therefore hardly be described appropriately as the deformation of a pregiven order of signifiers, as the semiotic bursts into the realm of the symbolic.

According to Kristeva, the constitution of the poetic text (and this constitutes the Subject) by no means constitutes an object in the process: the poetic text does not constitute some object or other. If we conceive of art as mimesis, it thus follows that mimesis as the realized form of poetic language can only participate in the symbolic order of denotative language to the extent that it "re-produce(s) some of its constitutive rules. . . . By the same token, it must posit an object, but this 'object' is merely a result of the drive economy of enunciation; its true position is inconsequential."[29] In other words, even if the subject imitates an object in the aesthetic text by reproducing a vocal, gestural, verbal, or other signifier, it does not by so doing match this object—even through the agency of the symbolic. Rather, it "crosses the border of the symbolic" and thus reaches the semiotic, which is located "on the other side of the social"[30] and beyond the object.

The poetic text, in which the semiotic deforms the symbolic in this manner and in so doing transforms itself into the symbolic, can accordingly be construed as that signifier which signifies "an *object* for an *ego*, thus constituting them both as thetic. Through its thetic, altering aspect, the signifier *represents* the subject— not the thetic ego, but the very process by which it is posited."[31] The process in which the Subject constitutes the poetic text can therefore be defined as that process in which the Subject itself is constituted as Subject. The poetic text functions in this manner as the signifier for that process of positing the Subject which constitutes the text.

Regardless of the individual criticisms that can be made of Kristeva's proposal—and we have only been able to provide a sketchy account of it here—this theory undoubtedly has the advantage of pointing firmly to the part the Subject plays in the process of text constitution. It thus reaffirms the link back from the text to the Subject constituting it without at the same time—and this has repeatedly occurred in that tradition of literary and art history which utilizes a concept of the expressive nature of art[32]—reducing it merely to the function of expressing the subjectivity of its creator. In Kristeva's theory, by contrast, the constitution of the text appears as the process of interpretative praxis in which the Subject producing the text constitutes itself as Subject in the first place. If we wish to deploy Kristeva's theory of the poetic text fruitfully as the point of departure for developing a corresponding theory of theatrical texts, then we must concentrate predominantly on the question how the praxis of individual interpretation is accomplished by the different Subjects involved in the process of constituting the theatrical text. Since it hardly appears meaningful in the present context to debate this problem in detail, discussion of it will be limited to that group of potential participants which was defined as being indispensable for a performance in the introduction to part 1. The discussion will, in other words, focus on one of the constituent factors of theater, namely the actors.

The work that the actor puts into constituting signs and text in dramatic theater—and we shall concentrate exclusively on this area in the following—is subject to three determining factors: the role given in the drama's literary text, the actor's physique, and the conventions of acting dominant at the time, i.e., the valid normative code of acting.

As Simmel noted quite unequivocally, the role cast in the literary text of a drama neither contains concrete instructions for the actor nor sets out conditions for his performance. For

> the stage character based on the script as a figure in the drama is not a complete person, as it were, not a human being in the tangible sense—but rather that composite of elements of a person which literature can grasp. Neither the voices nor the tone, neither the *ritardando* nor the *accelerando* of speech, neither the gestures nor the special ambience of the warm, living figure can be sketched out by the writer in advance; indeed, he cannot even give really clear premises for them. Rather, he has shifted the fate, appearance and soul of this figure into the but one-dimensional unfolding of the merely intellectual. Viewed as literature, drama is a self-sufficient whole; with regard to the totality of the action, it remains a symbol, from which the totality cannot be derived logically.[33]

It is not living figures that are present in drama, for all that exists is simply a literary text, with regard to which the actor or director must interpret certain elements or substructures with a view to character A, B, or C described in it. The character is, in other words, only predefined as that meaning which is attached respectively to the corresponding elements and substructures of the literary text, which, in turn, is made up of linguistic signs. The more ambiguous the drama is in this respect, the more different the appearance the characters will take. For this reason, Simmel lambasts the notion that

> the ideal way of playing a character is unequivocally and necessarily given with the description of that character. As if the pages of *Hamlet* could yield the complete sensuous theatrical form for him who is able to see sharply enough and construct things logically enough. The same notion suggests that there is only one "correct" depiction of each role by the actor, a depiction that the actor empirically approximates for better or worse. This is disproved by the simple fact that three great actors will play the part in three completely different ways, each having the same value as the other two, and none of which is more "correct" than the others. . . . It is, in other words, not possible to play Hamlet simply by relying on the lines the part has, for such an approach would legitimate the conception of a Moissi just as it would that of a Kainz or a Salviati.[34]

The different "conceptions" of one and the same character are thus the result of the ambiguousness of the aesthetic text of the drama and of its individual elements and substructures. All of the "possible" meanings of the corresponding elements and substructures of a literary text must therefore be conceived of as "legitimate" conceptions of a part and accepted as such. For the respective conception of a part constitutes nothing other than the result of that process of reception in which the elements and substructures of the drama that refer to the character in question are given a meaning in the context of the whole text. That is to say, they are the result of a process of constituting meaning that occurs on each occasion under different conditions.

When molding a character, the actor thus proceeds from a meaning which he has constructed, taking the literary text of the drama as the basis for his conception of the role—irrespective of the conditions or the way in which he does this. In this sense, the first factor determining his work arises at the very beginning: namely a hermeneutic process. It is of no consequence here how this process ensues or whether it is itself first completed at the end of the actor's work. For the character given in the literary text of the drama does not constitute a fixed quantity or figure toward which everyone can orient themselves in the same way, but rather must itself first be constituted as a respectively different meaning in each different process of reception.

In the present context it is of less importance how the actor progresses from the character constituted solely as a meaning to producing the character's concrete shape. It has been hotly and passionately debated in the various theories of acting over the last two hundred years, ever since Diderot advocated it, whether the actor should first create a "phantom" which he then tries to approximate in his presentation, or whether he should first try to induce emotions in himself that will then lead him to the "correct" shape, or indeed, and quite to the contrary, should best start with physical actions, etc.[35] This has no bearing on our topic, and as a consequence, we shall not go into the different phases of and possibilities afforded by the process of the actor's work. Rather, we shall focus on the general determining factors that, on the whole, govern the process of sign and text constitution by the actor in dramatic theater.

The actor, moreover, comes up against another factor determining acting, namely his own physique, the minute he tries to lend the meaning he wishes to constitute for the stage character an objective form by couching it in terms of signs of the art of acting, thus enabling him to communicate the role to an audience. And he comes up against this barrier irrespective of the methods and procedures he adopts. Whereas other artists process material that is detached from them and thus foreign—the poet processes language and the sculptor stone—the actor, as Plessner puts it, works "with the material of his own being."[36] Owing to this particular state of affairs, not all actors have the same material at their disposal; rather, each is allocated a set of unique, unmistakable material in the form of his or her own body. In the case of acting, the individuality of an artist's work does not first come to light in the way he or she processes the material or in the end result of this treatment—namely, the artwork. Instead, the actor's work itself proceeds from material that is already inscribed within his or her individuality. For the actor's body injects his own nature and his own particular history into the work process from the outset.

The human body amounts to material that can be clearly identified neither as nature—as the rock which the sculptor works on—nor as culture—the language the poet shapes. The body, by contrast, belongs to both nature and the symbolic order of a particular culture. The line separating the two runs right through the body; as an organism, it is undoubtedly part of nature, and, "as a respectively different organismic profile of a bodily need"[37] of a particular person. And that body is, furthermore, the respectively special individual inner nature of a person. This body has been shaped in a specific way by nature and yet the culture surrounding it has an effect on it from the very beginning—initially in the form of maternal care. Culture not only plays a considerable part in the development, restructuring, and regulation of bodily needs, the formation of strong psychological drives and the way these are expressed, but even influences the form of the adult body. The latter is largely subject to the conditions prevailing in the respective culture with regard to nutrition, hygiene, health care, etc., and depends on the ideals of the day. Every person's body thus constitutes the product of an interactive relation between his or her specific nature and the surrounding culture, a relation that commences with birth and ceases with death: this product, being specifically unique, is, in turn, completely individual.[38] The body, as nature, is not a signifier, yet as culture it can from time to time become one—the borderline between non-signifying and signifying runs right across the body. Both areas meet headlong in the body. Using this material, the actor must develop and realize the signs he has chosen; he must use it to shape the concrete character he is to portray. He must raise his physique, to the extent that the spectators can perceive it—e.g., his voice and the outer appearance of his body—to the level of signifier, must turn everything unsignifying into something signifying. His individual corporeality thus becomes thoroughly transformed into a symbolic order.

In this process of constituting such a "body-text,"[39] the actor comes up against the third factor determining his work, namely, the norm represented by the respectively valid code of acting. On the one hand, this code determines which ways of using or changing the body can or should be used as signs in the first place. On the other, it prescribes to differing degrees and with differing degrees of exactness the possible meanings that can be attached to these changes and appearances. The spectator will also refer to this code when interpreting the signs generated by the actor, that is, if he wishes to understand the body-text the actor constitutes. For example, great pathos both in recitation or in gestures and movements is no longer acceptable as an expression of "true" deep feelings in the case of the form of theater predominant in the Western world. Pathos may be used in order to demonstrate that the feelings shown are false, to denounce them as a pretense, or to reveal that they are exaggerated or inappropriate and therefore derisory, or, in a manner of speaking, to quote a historical way of expressing emotions, etc. However, compared with the code of acting in other forms of theater and in other periods, the code that is currently valid on German stages on the whole calls for and contains relatively few rules to which the actors are expected as a matter of principle to adhere. This fact arises from the loss of universally binding aesthetic norms, witnessed in all types of art and characteristic of post-avant-garde art in general. It considerably lessens the weighting of the third determining factor in the actor's work. Yet, the extent to which this is true can only be assessed on a case-by-case basis by taking into account the specific regional or genre-related traditions that may prescribe stronger adherence to a particular canon of rules. The code of acting can thus, as a whole, be conceived of as a set of stipulations. These may be more or less precisely formulated; indeed, in our case, they are left undefined. By taking them as a guideline, the actor is then meant to transform the unsignifying matter of his perceivable physique into something signifying.

To recapitulate: three factors fundamental to the process of creating meaning coincide during the constitution of the stage character as body-text. They are, first, the character inscribed in the literary text of the drama with the different possible interpretations it offers; second, the actor's individual physique with its respectively specific possibilities for shaping the role; and third, the given, generally valid code of acting. Thus, meaning—namely, the concrete character as the meaning of the specifically constituted body-text—arises at the point where they converge.

Now, can this constellation be conceived of as that conjunction of the "semiotic and the symbolic" which Kristeva put forward and described with regard to the process of signification which occurs in the constitution of the poetic text? In order to answer this question we must initially clarify the relation between semiotic and symbolic involved in each case when the actor brings the character encoded in language, his body, and the code of acting into contact with one another.

The linguistic text used to portray the character can be described as a symbolic order produced as part of a more comprehensive symbolic order, namely, the overall dramatic text. Now, to the extent to which the dramatic text has been constituted as a poetic text, the specific symbolic order of the dramatic text is produced when the semiotic infiltrates the domain of the symbolic order of denotative language. It accordingly represents a semiotized symbolic order.

When the actor "in-corporates" this text, as it were, a second semiotization occurs: his individual physique masters the text by making it an extension of itself. He thus creates the text a second time—under his body's own specific conditions—both as something foreign to him and as something integral to his body. In this respect, the actor produces the character as the meaning of the body-text constituted by him quite clearly on the basis of a "semiotization of the symbolic."

Conversely, however, the actor's body, which at this point in the process is only semiotized and thus not yet significant, is raised to the level of a signifier through the reference to the linguistically created role and to the actor's code. The nonsignifying physique is structured in such a way that a symbolic order can be established within it. It would thus be more appropriate to describe this process as a "symbolization of the semiotic."

The conjunction of the code for acting and the actor's individual physique thus occurs with regard to the body as a symbolization of the semiotic. By contrast, with regard to the code of acting, that convergence triggers a semiotization of the symbolic that may range from individual implementation of the rules to complete rejection of them. For the actor is clearly able to break the given, valid code in the process of molding a stage character and can establish a new code in its place. This new version rests on conditions and possibilities implied and first accessed, on the one hand, by the figure constituted as meaning in the literary text, and by the individual corporeality of the actor, on the other.

In other words, meaning is evidently also generated at the interface of semiotic and symbolic in the constitution of the actor's body-text, but not exclusively in the form of a semiotization of the symbolic. Rather, the stage character, as the meaning of a body-text, emerges from a process set in motion and determined by the interaction of semiotization of the symbolic, on the one hand, and symbolization of the semiotic, on the other. In this context, the actor as Subject makes use of the literary role, of his own individual physique, and of the generally valid code of acting. He press-gangs them into serving him with the intention of confronting the three elements with one another. It is this confrontation which he uses to create the stage character as the interpretation of the text constituted in this way. As the subject of precisely this process of interpretative praxis, he constitutes himself as that subject-in-process which Kristeva has in mind.

There are, of course, factors other than the three enumerated above that also play a role in the actor's constitution of a stage character as a body-text. However, the above three can be regarded as specific to and characteristic of the constitution of such a body-text, whereas the others also form the basis of the constitution of other types of texts. This is true in particular of intertextuality, which is to be encountered in all processes of text constitution, although to a different extent in each case.

The actor will accordingly refer to other texts when deciding on the signs which are intended as a whole to constitute the stage character. He may, for example, refer to previous portrayals of the same dramatis persona by another actor or his own portrayals of other characters, quoting himself, as it were. He can just as well resort to texts from other genres or nonartistic texts, whether filmic texts—such as the presentation of a person in an individual film or of a type of person in a particular film genre—or pictures that show people in a particular stance or pose, making funny faces or gesticulating strangely, or even literary descriptions that give a detailed account of a person's behavior, etc. It is, in fact, possible that all the elements refer to another text—regardless of how this is accomplished—and thus establish a relation to that text; they fulfill a quite essential, underpinning function in the process of constituting the stage character as body-text. Yet the simple fact that they are used cannot be taken to be a characteristic idiosyncrasy of this process, for corresponding forms of intertextuality are to be encountered in almost all processes of text constitution. The collision between a role shaped by literary means, the actor's individual physique, and the valid code of acting, by contrast, comprise a factor which is only specific to the process of constituting a stage character as a body-text.

The theatrical text, i.e., the performance, is not identical with one particular body-text, but is rather composed of a number of body and spatial texts, each of which points to one specific individual subject. The Subject in question has constituted that text in a series of positions which may have arisen as the result of working together with the director or other actors. The actors' body-texts are, in other words, not to be equated with other types of subtexts—such as the chapters of a novel or a segment of a picture—that stem from texts which have, as a unity, been constituted by one subject. Rather, they are subtexts created respectively by another individual subject. The performance is thus to be defined as a text characterized by the specific fact that it is constituted by numerous subjects simultaneously. Yet it is also characteristic that the respectively special individuality of each subject involved is not submerged by the collectively created structure to the point of being indiscernible. This feature so characteristic of the constitution of the theatrical text will be described using a term borrowed from music, namely "polyphony."[40] The theatrical text of the performance resembles the way the different voices in a choral passage or the different instruments in an instrumental work are differentiated from one another in terms of timbre, register, melody, etc., and can be distinguished from one another by the ear. For in the theatrical text the individual subjects creatively involved in its production—or at least the actors as subjects—can be recognized as individual subjects and distinguished from one another. The theatrical text would therefore appear to be fundamentally characterized by its polyphonic structure.

If a text is referred to as polyphonic in this sense, then one immediately comes up against the question as to the unity of its overall meaning. The analogy to music may be applicable in specific isolated respects, but evidently does not extend to the composition of overall meaning in a theatrical text as a whole. The meaning created by a subject as a stage character does not necessarily refer to the meaning created by other subjects as stage characters in such a way as to imply that the sum of such meanings will yield a uniform meaning in the same way as the composite of voices create the sound of a choral piece. We can most certainly presume that the director will take care to ensure that these different body-texts are related to one another. Yet, contrary to the popular view that a theatrical text is constituted and defined solely by the director, such texts are not objects that resemble set pieces in that the director can dispose over them at will. Rather a subject is behind each of them, a Subject who has constituted himself as a Subject in the process of constituting meaning. Consequently, it is entirely possible for the different body-texts to counteract such a process of unifying uniformity, and instead of producing a unity that is an overall meaning of the theatrical text, a multiplicity of meaning may be the result, albeit one that should not be confused with unequivocality. A multiplicity which can only be created by a polyphonic text cannot be equated with what Kristeva terms the polylogical specificity of poetic texts. For polylogy must be conceived of as the ability of a Subject-in-process to assume a variety of voices and bodies and thus create an awareness of and evoke a plurality of times and spaces via reference to other texts. Polylogy is thus to be understood as the consequence of an extreme form of intertextuality.[41] Polyphony, by contrast, designates the interaction of different texts which, since they are constituted by such a Subject-in-process, are themselves created polylogically.

The theatrical text can thus not be construed or defined as a signifier that represents a Subject as Subject-in-process—for example, the subject of the director. Rather, it represents as a signifier that process in which different subjects constitute themselves as such Subjects-in-process and accordingly relate to one another. We must therefore presuppose a multiplicity of overall meanings as a characteristic and fundamental feature of the theatrical text—a distinguishing feature which is especially suited to defining the constitution of the theatrical text.

The Transformation of the Drama's Literary Text into the Theatrical Text of the Performance

The different subjects involved in the process of constituting a performance as a polyphonic text have a common reference as their point of departure, namely the drama's literary text. Of all the texts that enter into the theatrical text in the form of individual elements or even as substructures and create its specific intertextual character, it is the drama's literary text which has a special significance, and it consequently occupies a privileged position. This is the case because the performance not only relies on individual elements or substructures of the drama's literary text, but rather rests on its totality: the theatrical text is a performance of the literary text. The relation between the two texts thus becomes a problem, for if the performance is conceived of as a scenic realization of a literary text,[42] then we must establish whether it solely transports the literary text into another medium—namely that of the stage and the actor. Alternatively, the transformation of the literary into a theatrical text may be a process of translation in which a switch is made from one sign system into another.

Books and typeface function as media which convey the drama's literary text and have no impact on the constitution of the meaning. And where the drama appears—whether in a magazine, as part of collected works, or in paperback form—has just as little effect. By contrast, actor and stage space comprise media which always introduce certain signifying qualities into the process of conveying meaning and thus cannot be used to convey meaning without altering the meaning.

As I tried to show in the last section, this is particularly true with regard to the actor. The actor's perceivable physical attributes all have to be conceived of as signifying elements. Due to their specific nature, in theater both the voice[43] and the body are completely unsuited when it comes to serving as media that can convey meaning without at the same time substantially influencing the process of constituting meaning. As a consequence, we did not define the actor's body above as a medium for conveying the stage character, but rather as material. In this sense, we established that it was one of the fundamental determining factors which, in colliding with others, forms the underlying basis for the constitution of the body-text. It follows that the actor himself cannot be conceived of as a medium that does not alter the text's meaning, but rather is the Subject of a process in which—via the development and realization of actorial signs—the stage character is created as the meaning of the body-text thus constituted.

The stage space, by contrast, may under certain conditions quite clearly function as a medium that does not alter meanings. If a theatrical norm prescribes that a specific stage form be adopted, then the conception of space on which the stage form is based can only be evaluated in relation to the norm which is a signifying element here. Yet it cannot be assessed with regard to the individual performance.[44]

As a consequence, in the nineteenth century the box set as a form did not affect the meaning of the individual performance, even though it can be understood and interpreted as a sign by reference to the theatrical norm on which it was based. In the individual performances it functions as a mere medium for the presentation of decorations, props, and actors. In the case of performances today, however, we must assume as a rule that the stage design adopted is itself intended as an element bearing meaning.

If the drama's literary text is transferred from the media of book and typeface, media that have no effect on its meaning, to the media of actor and stage, which are significant per se, then there must also be a change in the sign systems employed. Whereas the literary text consists exclusively of linguistic signs, the actor's body-text is necessarily a synthesis of gestural, proxemic, and paralinguistic signs as well as the signs contained in his external appearance. The transformation of the drama's literary text into the theatrical text of a performance can thus only be defined and described appropriately as the translation of signs from a linguistic sign system into those of a theatrical sign system. The drama's literary text is not, in other words, merely transferred into another medium.

In principle, a distinction must be made among three types of translation:[45]
(1) Intralingual translation—here, an expression in a language is translated into a different one in the same language, as occurs, for example, in a definition.

(2) Interlingual or translation in the usual sense—here, a text is transported from one natural language into another.

(3) Intersemiotic translation or transformation—here, a text in one sign system is translated into a completely different sign system.

Whereas the first two types of translation are effected within the same sign system or within the same type of sign system, in the third case the translation is made from one sign system into a different type of sign system: words are "translated" into gestures, letters into modes of lighting, sentences into mathematical formulae, etc. In this context, it can by no means simply be assumed that such an intersemiotic translation process can occur between texts from random sign systems. It will be just as difficult to translate Locke's *Essay Concerning Human Understanding* appropriately into the gestural signs of a pantomime as it will be to transform Wordsworth's "Daffodils" into mathematical signs. At any rate, an examination must be made of the conditions under which one set of signs can be translated into another.

A variety of questions arise with regard to the relation between drama and performance if we define the transformation of a drama into a performance as a process of translation:

(1) What are the special conditions that make possible the translation from linguistic into theatrical signs?

(2) How does the process of translation occur? Does it proceed from the individual words, from sentences, from complete passages, or from the whole dialogue? Are the signs which constitute individual, larger subtexts also translated, or is direct recourse had to these subtexts—such as stage character, scene, space? Is the dialogue translated in isolation from stage directions[46] or does the process take both sign groups concerned into account and then translate them individually?

(3) How can we define an "appropriate" translation of linguistic signs into theatrical signs, and of what does the resulting equivalence of source text—the drama as literature—and final text—the performance as theater—consist? In other words, are there theoretical justifications that can be cited in support of the criterion of "faithfulness to the work," which is applied so obdurately by theater criticism as a yardstick for judging the staging of a play?

The question as to the conditions which make the transformation of a dramatic text into a theatrical text possible was raised as early as the eighteenth century, albeit in the limited form of an inquiry into the translatability of linguistic into gestural signs. As described in chapter 6, the section entitled "The Genesis of a Gestural Code for Bourgeois Illusionist Theater," Diderot, particularly in his "Letter on deaf-mutes," and Lessing in his *Laocoon* dedicated much thought to the issue.[47] In his empirical comparison of linguistic and gestural signs in concrete communicative situations, Diderot comes to the conclusion that both types of sign are equally suited to indicate actions, concrete objects, and ideas that can be represented by metaphorical designation.[48] Gestural signs can hardly ever be used to depict abstract complexes, yet they surpass even linguistic signs when it comes to expressing extraordinary emotions and extreme emotional states. "Sublime gestures" are able to describe these in a manner "which cannot be matched by even the greatest linguistic virtuosity."[49] It follows from these investigations of the relation of drama and theater that drama should preferentially select actions and extraordinary emotions as objects for description if it is to prove possible to translate the linguistic signs it uses into the theatrical signs of mimicry, gestures, and movements.

Lessing's theoretical deliberations bring him to a similar conclusion.[50] He assumes that, because the signs of the art of acting not only extend into space, but also follow each other in a temporal sequence, they are capable of evoking a "true sensory impression" of two types of objects: those that exist alongside each other—such as in painting—and those that follow each other sequentially—as in poetry, and can imitate the body and actions alike. Because they are related to both types of objects simultaneously, these signs can imitate bodies which move and change position or actions carried out by certain bodies: they always imitate humans in action.

If actions are the object of drama as a work of literature, then it follows that the linguistic signs of drama can be translated into signs of the art of acting. Yet, since the signs of the art of acting signify not only the actions themselves, but also and invariably the persons in action, it is hardly possible to restrict their function to providing an appropriate translation of the actions depicted in the drama. Rather, they will always create additional meanings which the drama as literature is incapable of constituting: meanings that are attributed to the concrete corporeality with which the actors accomplish actions.

In attempting to assess whether drama's linguistic signs can be translated into another medium, especially into the gestural signs of the art of acting, Diderot and Lessing investigate the specificity of the linguistic signs, on the one hand, and of the gestural signs, on the other. Diderot proceeds empirically, Lessing theoretically. They then delineate the area of objects in which the two types converge with regard to what they are able to portray, or which gestural signs surpass their linguistic counterparts. Despite the difference between their respective approaches, the two come to the same conclusion: that drama's linguistic signs can be translated into the theatrical signs of the art of acting on the condition that the former refer to objects that can be equally well depicted by the signs of the art of acting. Both Diderot and Lessing take this conclusion as the premise and justification for a normative aesthetics of drama. For it necessarily limits drama to certain objects of portrayal.

We shall for the moment ignore the conclusions that lead both to adopt a normative poetics, or at least to legitimate such, and shall instead concentrate on the approach they respectively take. Both presume that there are objects that can be "appropriately" imitated by both linguistic and gestural signs. If these objects are first presented in linguistic signs and these are "translated" into the corresponding gestural signs, then it follows that the theatrical signs of the art of acting function as interpretants of the drama's linguistic signs. The latter must, in other words, always be transformed into the theatrical signs of the art of acting if the theatrical signs are to function as interpretants of them. According to Peirce, any "representamen" must be defined as an interpretant if "it is determined by another representamen."[51]

By drawing on the speech of the dramatis personae, Diderot and Lessing attempt to establish the group of those linguistic signs in the drama for which signs of the art of acting could serve as interpretants. Since linguistic and gestural signs can be used as interpretants for each other only with reference to certain types of objects, both conclude that the speech of the dramatis personae must focus on precisely such objects. Thus, both inevitably arrive at a normative restriction of the drama.[52]

If we wish to reformulate in descriptive terms the prescriptive condition under which a transformation is possible, then it would appear advisable to return to a level at which the question of the possible alternative "objects of imitation" cannot be raised. The same question can of course by no means be put at the level of the speech of the dramatis personae or at that of the definition of the characters suited to the dramatis personae.

The assertion made by Lessing and Diderot, namely that linguistic signs can be translated into theatrical signs only if both can be used as interpretants for one another, is accurate. If we wish to couch the conditions under which such a transformation is possible in descriptive terms, we must investigate the relevant signs at a level not accessible to normative restrictions and definitions. The speech of the dramatis personae and the respective idiosyncrasies and qualities of the dramatis personae are always open to normative-prescriptive deliberations and thus cannot be taken as the level for our investigation. Now, whereas it may be true that the dramatis personae and what they say may be continually defined or shaped differently, it is an equally incontrovertible fact that the existence of a dramatis personae is constitutive for every drama. To put it simply and banally: without a dramatis persona there can be no drama.

In the literary text this dramatis persona usually appears as a proper name (Oedipus, Hamlet), or as the designator of a species (human being, angel), or as the designation of sex (man, woman), of nationality (French, Scythian). Alternatively, it may don the guise of social estate (marquis, peasant), or profession (sailor, servant), of a type (the miser, the vain), as an ordinal (first, second), or simply as a letter (A, B). Whatever the case, designations of person are given in some form or another.

With regard to the theatrical text, by contrast, we defined the actor who represents a stage character as the irreducible, defining, and constitutive element. Here the dramatis persona appears in the shape of the concrete physicality of an actor. The dramatis persona can thus be defined as the object to which the designation of persons in the drama's literary text and the real corporeality of the actor in the theatrical text both refer, for they both function as signs for it. With regard to that person, the linguistic sign of the name/designation of person and the theatrical sign of the actor's physique can be used as interpretants for one another. The issue of which sequence is given priority is completely irrelevant here. It is completely unimportant, with reference to the two functioning respectively as interpretants of the other, whether the stage character is first given as the actor's embodiment of it and later denoted by the linguistic signs of the name/designation of person in a literary text. It is equally unimportant whether they are first mentioned in a literary text as a name/designation of person and then subsequently appear on stage as the embodiment of the character by an actor. For both the name and the actor's body are capable of representing the stage character.[53]

We have thus established the condition under which the drama can in principle be translated into a performance. Since the name in the drama's literary text can point to the stage character as can the actor's body in the theatrical text of the performance, it can always be translated by the actor into the language of theater. Here, the actor's body is used and understood as the interpretant for the linguistic signs of the name. The text assigned to the name can be realized as verbal speech by the actor who functions as the interpretant of this name, and in this manner the text is transformed into theatrical signs, such as paralinguistic and kinesic signs.

The process of translation proceeds from a constitution of meaning by the receiver: the literary dramatic text to be transformed is read and interpreted. All those premises and conditions which determine a hermeneutics of the literary text hold true for this process: the general problem of "prejudice," i.e., the location of the interpreter as determined by history and personal biography; the problem of historical distance, to the extent that a past drama is involved; the genre-specific problem of the form of the underlying genre and how this is to be realized; and the problem of its structure and intertextuality, a problem which refers solely to the text in question, etc. There can be numerous meanings to the individual elements and substructures as well as to the overall text, as is the case with any aesthetic text.[54] It follows that, even if all the individual subjects of a production team, indeed of different production teams, possess the dramatic text as artifact in the same way, the point of departure for the process of transformation, namely, the aesthetic object of the drama,[55] and its respectively constituted meaning may be different in each case. Just as a binding conception of the stage character as the "correct" meaning cannot be derived from the individual elements and substructures of the drama, so, too, it is impossible to constitute an exclusively valid meaning of the drama which is then given the form of a binding conception of the text.

The meanings encountered in the process of interpretation, meanings that may already be constituted with a view to application—in this case with regard to contemporary spectators and the current situation—thus comprise the real point of departure for the transformational process. In order to create these meanings, those signs must be chosen from among the repertoire of theatrical signs which— in the opinion of the producers of the theatrical text—are capable of functioning as appropriate and suitable interpretants for the meaning constituted in the literary text. The choice occurs, of course, with a view to a particular audience and the communicative situation at the time. This choice is in no manner prescribed, determined, or constrained by the literary text,[56] for it only yields those meanings for which theatrical signs are to be found as interpretants, not, however, the signs themselves. Rather, the choice of these meanings is influenced by the location in history and the personal biographies of the people involved in it—the actors, the director, the stage designer. This is the case because the choice depends substantially on how these people subjectively appraise the signifying possibilities and the capabilities of the theatrical signs available. It is constrained, on the other hand, by the repertoire of theatrical signs provided by the respective code. One must, however, consider here that every act of constituting signs or text can serve to expand and change this repertoire. We are at present not bound to one fixed theatrical norm—i.e., must not resort solely to one universally binding repertoire of theatrical signs. As a consequence, the only rule which must inform the actors' and the director's choice can be described as follows: the chosen sign or the sign to be chosen must, in their unanimous opinion, be capable of functioning for the audience in question and in the given situation as a suitable interpretant for the meaning the actors and director intend, i.e., the meaning which they have attributed to the element of the literary text in question. It follows that there is a virtually infinite number of theatrical signs that can be chosen as objectifications and agents of a meaning in contemporary Western theater.

The fact that the transformational process thus proceeds from the meanings constituted using the literary text[57] brings us to a second question. Should the meanings of individual linguistic signs, different sign groups or substructures, or the meaning of the overall text be expressed in theatrical signs? In other words, to which units does the process of transformation refer?[58]

We can from the outset exclude the structure of the drama as the structural principle underlying the transformational process. For the drama is always structured in terms of dialogue and stage directions, even though the stage directions may be reduced to a list of names, scenes, and beginnings and ends of individual acts. Whereas the signs of the dialogue always signify the direct speech of the dramatis personae, the dialogue and stage directions also contain signs that can point to different theatrical signs, such as paralinguistic or kinesic signs, masks, hair, costumes, props, decoration and lighting, music and sounds. This general bipartition of the literary text has no equivalent in the theatrical text of the performance. The transformation of the drama's linguistic signs into the theatrical signs of the performance must therefore be accomplished using principles other than this bipartition.

In general, three fundamental modes of transformation can be discerned. These are to be understood as ideal types, however, as one hardly ever encounters their perfect, exclusive usage:(a) linear, (b) structural, and (c) global transformation.[59] In concrete instances we are usually concerned with transformational processes in which all three, or at least two, of the modes are used.

With regard to the first type, the process takes a linear course in accordance with the choice made by the actors, who are meant to function as interpretants for the names of the literary text. This means that the process moves from sentence to sentence, from statement to reply, from dialogue to dialogue. The meaning of a sentence is first constituted in connection with the respectively different context involved—such as the characteristics of the stage character speaking, the theme and the line of argumentation adopted in the dialogue, the plot in the scene, the

semantic relations of the whole text, etc. Subsequently, theatrical signs are search-
ed for which are capable of functioning as interpretants for the meaning of this
sentence in line with the conception of the stage character that has been arrived
at relying on the literary text.

Because theatrical signs usually do not possess fixed, lexical meanings, as it
were, and their meanings can change depending on the context and communicative
situation, the main problem that has to be solved here is that of the linkage. It
must be guaranteed that the theatrical signs used as interpretants for a sentence
do not on account of their being linked to the course of the theatrical text—i.e.,
based on the previously, subsequently, and simultaneously realized signs—receive
a meaning which modifies in an unintended manner or no longer matches that
intended by the director/actor. The interpretants must therefore be chosen in such
a manner that they are clearly able to convey the meaning intended by the director
and actor during a performance, both along the paradigmatic axis of their relation
to the drama's linguistic signs and along the syntagmatic axis of their textual
linkage in the performance.

This mode of transformation for the most part follows the course taken by the
dramatic text. Sentence after sentence is transformed into words that the dramatis
personae are supposed to express in their speech in precisely this order. As a
consequence, the meanings of the dialogues dominate in the performance, for it
is they which are primarily addressed in the search for appropriate interpretants.

Naturally, if such an approach is taken, signs must be found which constitute
the external appearance of the stage character and the space, although their choice
cannot follow the sequential course of the text. This circumstance indicates expressly that linear transformation cannot be applied lock, stock, and barrel to the
dramatic text, but has to be linked with other modes. As the dominant mode,
however, it can largely determine the shape of the transformational process.

The mode of structural transformation proceeds from complex substructures
such as stage character, space, scene, plot. Initially, the meanings of such substructures are constituted on the basis of the dramatic text: for example, the psychological character of a role and its particular development during the course of
the drama are established, the specific architectonic and rhythmic structure of a
scene are traced and defined, or the spatial conception for individual scenes or for
the whole drama is brought to mind. Subsequently, possible theatrical interpretants
are sought for the meanings of such substructures constituted in this process. In
this manner, relatively independent subtexts arise, such as those illustrated in the
last section using the example of the body-text of a stage character.

These subtexts are characterized by the fact that they are different in an important way from the corresponding subtexts of the literary text. Whereas meanings
in drama are always only constituted in a temporal sequence, in the subtexts of
the performance they may to a certain extent be expressed simultaneously. To the
extent that the body-text of a stage character is involved, one must consider that
both the actor's external appearance and his stance, his way of moving and the
pitch of his voice may all evoke a wealth of meanings in the spectators the minute
he takes the stage, meanings that can only be established in the literary text in

the course of several scenes. The very first appearance thus provides the underlying structure of the body-text, as it were, on the basis of which all further information on the character is then given and processed.

The subtext may be that of a scene composed of and structured by a particular spatial conception; an impression created with the colors and forms of the decorations, costumes, and lighting; a specific choreographic arrangement of the figures and a fine musical harmonization of their voices, etc. In this case, an underlying structure is again initially created by theatrical signs used simultaneously, and it is on the basis of this structure that all changes are then introduced and understood.

By thus initially constituting subtexts, this mode of transformation comes up against the problem of linking the subtexts and referring them to one another. For the meaning of a performance does not emerge from a simple addition of these subtexts, but rather arises on the basis of the interaction of the meanings of the subtexts and the meanings of the relations between them, relations which result from the specific combinations involved. The meaning of the subtexts that is constituted with the theatrical signs must as a consequence be linked to each other in a way that renders the relations between them visible, relations that point to the structure of the whole text and thus to its meaning. These relations may entail simultaneity (for example, of numerous body-texts or of a body-text and a spatial text) or a temporal sequence (for example, several spatial or action texts).

Such relations can be created in the most different of ways. The sequence of dialogue offers one such possibility. These are able to engender relations between the different subtexts that they run through and are also suited to this task, for such dialogues exist throughout the theatrical text. In such a case, the interface becomes visible between the modes of linear and of structural transformation, for both are closely interlinked here in constituting the overall theatrical text.

Such a type of combination does not on the whole emerge if the dialogues fulfill a secondary, clearly subordinate function in the theatrical text. Specific forms of structuration can be implemented in the place of the combinations: for example, a repeated or characteristically varied use of individual elements, such as gestures or movements, costumes and colors, props and decorations, etc. Moreover, it is of course conceivable that supraordinated codes are introduced, on which the constitution of the subtexts are based. In this case, relations between the subtexts are guaranteed to occur, owing to the reference to such a hypercode on which all are based in the same way. The number of such opportunities for combination is at any rate considerable.

Linear transformation constitutes the theatrical text by translating the meanings of the individual sentences or passages in the dialogues successively into theatrical signs. These are carefully linked to one another sequentially with a view to the meaning intended by the director/actor. With the same purpose as its goal, structural transformation, by contrast, transfers, as it were, several such structural complexes en bloc which it relates to one another in a particular way. It may initially appear as if these two modes are respectively used preferentially in certain types of drama; thus, for example, linear transformation is used by productions of German classical drama, whereas structural transformation is used in performances of Romantic, naturalist and symbolist drama. Admittedly, the structure of these dramas would undeniably suggest that such a form of transformation is involved. Yet the recourse to one particular mode thereof can by no means be derived from the type of drama in question. Rather, it results from conditions outside the drama's literary text, conditions usually connected at the normative level with the theatrical code valid at the time.[60]

Unlike linear and structural transformation, the global variant proceeds from the meaning of the dramatic text and not from the meanings of individual elements or substructures. It wishes to constitute that meaning by selecting and realizing certain theatrical signs in the performance. A theatrical text is thus created which as a whole is supposed to be capable of functioning as an interpretant of the meaning of the dramatic text.

The viewpoint from which the global transformation is accomplished is more comprehensive than that governing the other two modes to the extent that it conceives of the latter two as possible subordinate forms of realization. For this transformational mode takes as its guiding principle the question as to the most appropriate way of constituting that meaning as a theatrical sign in a given communicative context which the subjects participating in the performance believe they have found to be the meaning of the literary text. The communicative context involves taking into account the current situation and above all the audience, which by no means always wishes to be enraptured, carried away from reality, moved, or even lectured to, but at times even shocked or hurt. It may thus prove to be expedient to transform the dialogues sentence by sentence or to synthesize subtexts as complex interpretants of substructures. Yet, one can equally plausibly imagine a case in which the subjects involved in the production are of the opinion that this meaning can be most accurately constituted in the performance if parts of the dialogue or even substructures are changed, shifted round, or even omitted completely, not to mention the addition of new substructures. Under such circumstances, the meaning of the literary text can be created anew in the theatrical text in such a manner that its individual elements or subtexts can be related to individual elements or substructures of the literary text only with great difficulty—indeed, in some cases it is not possible to establish such a relation.

We have used the label "global transformation" in order to define the mode in question clearly as the theatrical transformation of a literary-dramatic text. This approach must be carefully distinguished from other modes which at first sight seem similar but do not have the least bit in common with that transformation of the literary text which we have in mind.

Actors or directors can of course draw on different dramatic texts or on any other sort of text as material if they wish to produce in the course of a performance some notion or idea, series of actions or forms of behavior, conviction or thought. In short, they want to generate a meaning that does not arise from a concrete dramatic text but stems from some other textual complex or context of life. They may then extract certain individual elements as set pieces from different dramatic texts in order to mount these at some random point in the performance in the context of specific functions. In this case, however, what is involved is not a theatrical transformation of the respective dramatic text in the sense of the performance now being understandable as an interpretant of the drama. Rather, we are concerned solely with a quite normal case of intertextuality in which, in the process of textual constitution, different texts enter into the new text in different functions. Needless to say, global transformation may also make use in this way of dramatic texts other than those that are to be transformed. Yet this type of the intertextuality of different dramatic texts in a performance amounts only to a method of transforming another dramatic text: both processes must therefore be strictly distinguished from one another in theoretical terms.

The three transformational modes, the linear, the structural and the global—and we must emphasize this in conclusion—are all only to be thought of as ideal types that will hardly ever be used exclusively in the form described here. Rather, they represent certain dominant trends that may be stressed in respectively different ways in the transformational process.

In light of the above consideration of the transformational process, the issue as to the equivalence of source text and final text, a thorny question which can be posed in the case of any translation, appears to be highly complex when raised in connection with the relation between the drama's literary text and the performance's theatrical text. For the criteria on which an answer could be based can neither be formulated precisely nor called objective. There are numerous reasons for this state of affairs, and it can quite rightly be termed precarious. On the one hand, it is closely linked to the point of departure of the transformational process. Let us remind ourselves that the literary text that is to be transformed into a theatrical text can be understood in different ways with regard to both its meaning and the meanings of its individual elements and substructures. Accordingly, before judging the performance with reference to equivalence it must first be established that the meanings constituted by the producer of the performance using the literary text can be recognized and accepted as legitimate. If the spectator, on the contrary, should proceed from the meaning of the literary text that he has understood, and wishes exclusively to find this meaning constituted in the theatrical signs of the performance, then there is no basis for judging the equivalence of the two texts.

A second difficulty arises from the fact that neither wide-ranging concurrence on the interpretation of the literary text nor a similar understanding of the drama must necessarily result in a unanimous judgment on the suitability of the theatrical signs used, i.e., that they express this interpretation appropriately. If—as is the case in contemporary theater—no automatic reference to a common, underlying theatrical normative code exists from which the intersubjectively valid evaluative criteria can be derived, then the gap between that which is realized de facto on stage and that expected and postulated a priori by the spectator can become so great that the problem of equivalence can no longer be discussed meaningfully. Such a disparity can arise with regard both to the mode of transformation and the choice of individual theatrical signs or a group of such signs. If the spectator, for example, presumes that linear transformation is the valid norm, and is confronted with a global transformation which functions by means of shifts and changes, then he will usually not be capable of shedding his fore-understanding and becoming involved in the staging of the play. Alternatively, he may be of the opinion that decorations, props, and costumes should point clearly to the epoch and culture in which the drama takes place. The producers of the performance, however, may have adhered to the rule whereby these elements are elaborated and realized as signs of the characters of the dramatis personae. Here, there is practically no means of establishing a consensus on possible equivalence.

If we wish to describe and define equivalence without taking such subjective conditions into consideration, then we will have to be satisfied with a very general definition: equivalence exists if the performance can be understood as the interpretant of the possible meaning(s) of the drama on which it is based.

Even a definition that is kept so general does not relieve us of the obligation to inquire as to the extent to which such an equivalence between the drama's literary text and the performance's theatrical text can be created in the first place. For the specificity of theatrical signs is so different from that of linguistic signs that doubts are certainly in order whether the meanings constituted by linguistic signs can indeed be constituted in theatrical signs in an equivalent manner.

In their symbolic capacity, linguistic signs, even those that point to concrete objects, exhibit a high degree of abstraction and indeterminacy; even the most exact description of a costume, for example, will call to mind somewhat different notions of the object meant in different persons. Theatrical signs, however, as Lessing already noted and emphasized, are characterized by their iconic traits. Yet, this iconic quality introduces additional meanings into the performance, meanings that are not covered by the drama's linguistic signs, so that in the course of the transformational process a specific shift occurs.

This is already to be seen if one compares the name or designation of a person with the corporeality of the actor, which functions as interpretant for it in the theatrical text. Names such as Oedipus, Hamlet, or Faust immediately bring to mind many contexts in which they have been used—myths, tales, dramas, different receptions of these texts—as well as a wealth of meanings that result from these. Yet, as names they provide no information on the specific physique of those who bear the name, on the shape of their bodies, faces, and voices. The actor, by contrast, always takes the stage with a particular face, irrespective of whether he does so in his natural physical appearance or in one which has been specifically changed in shape or clad in costume. He fills out the indeterminacy of the name, which might refer to an infinite number of different bodies, with one single individual body. In its concreteness, e.g., shape, facial expression, or timbre, this body evokes meanings which the name alone would not be able to constitute. The actor's respectively specific corporeality thus amounts to a complex of meanings for the spectator, meanings which the reader is by no means able to attribute to the linguistic signs of the name in a comparable manner.[61]

This opposition between the relative indeterminacy of the linguistic signs and the substantially concrete nature of the theatrical signs is true of all objects and occurrences spoken about in the dialogue or stage directions in such a manner that they have to be conceived of as existing or taking place on stage.

If, in *Emilia Galotti*, Claudia's tone is described as "suspicious," or we learn of a valet in *Love and Intrigue* that he speaks the sentences that follow with a "frightful voice" or with an "awful laugh," then these sentences point to an impression that is supposed to be created for the spectator. Yet they do not convey even one concrete instruction as to which paralinguistic signs the actor should use to evoke this impression. The actor will speak the sentences in question in a quite specific manner to which as a rule far more meanings can then be attributed than can to the meaning: "suspicious," "frightful," or "awful."

The same is true of instructions with regard to mimicry, gestures, and movement. Sentences such as those that tell us that the Prince in Emilia Galotti "smiles" or that Appiani had a "downcast look," that Don Carlos "left slowly and silently" or that Karl Moor "ran up and down angrily" must be translated into theatrical signs. These are realized as a quite specific form of smiling, a quite specific expression of dejection, etc. Moreover, they are always realized in a specific face and individual body. In any case, a great many more additional signs will thus be attributed to the concrete theatrical signs than to the corresponding linguistic signs.

This indeterminacy is similarly characteristic of those linguistic signs that refer to costumes, props, decorations, or music. Thus, Luise simply brings in "the glass on a plate," without a statement being made on the concrete appearance of the glass and plate. Equally, Grillparzer's Sappho appears "exquisitely dressed" without there being a description of which articles of clothing she wears and what they look like. If, in *The Death of Danton*, all that is said of the decorations is that they are "a room," the "street in front of Danton's house," or "a dungeon," then innumerable specifically concrete spaces can correspond to these linguistic signs, even a completely bare stage. The objection will no doubt arise here that the reader will be able to fill in these "empty spaces"[62] effortlessly owing to his knowledge of the respectively valid theatrical norm, and that as a consequence this indeterminacy only holds true for readers who are not contemporaries of the time when the work is written. After all, if one is acquainted with the corresponding theatrical conceptions of costumes and space, then one will be able to complete the vague linguistic expressions with relatively concurrent notions. Furthermore, it should be noted that naturalist drama, for example, does indeed provide exact information on clothing, props, and decoration, so that detailed, for the most part concurrent, notions can be derived from the data.

These objections do not, of course, hold water with regard to theater productions today, because these can neither rely on a valid theatrical code, nor are they compelled to follow detailed information that refers to a theatrical code of a bygone age. Furthermore, they must be rebutted on principle. Notions will always differ and remain inexact in many respects. However, a specific costume, object, or decoration will be perceived in its concreteness—although not always in the same way—and can thus be clad in meaning that by no means need be attributed to the literary text. This is true to an even greater degree of the use of music. If, for example, the Duke in *Twelfth Night* commands the musician to play on, because "music is the food of love," then a quite specific type of music will sound out on stage—a type of music that can evoke meanings that go far beyond those of the meaning expressed by the duke. Music creates its own meanings to a far greater extent than do costumes, props, and the respective stage space.[63]

Since theatrical signs differ fundamentally from linguistic signs in terms of their iconic character, the meanings constituted in the transformational process will to some extent also deviate substantially from those constituted in the interpretation of the text. To the extent that meanings and not "designations" are translated in the transformational process,[64] indeterminacy—above all instructions that are kept unspecific—facilitates matters with regard to the transformation of past dramas into performances. For statements such as the following can be effortlessly transformed within every theatrical convention precisely because when we read of Sappho we are simply told that she is "dressed exquisitely" or of Karl Moor that he "runs up and down angrily," equally, the locations are merely designated a "street" or "room." The linguistic signs only reproduce an impression which can be conveyed in the performance by the use of respectively different theatrical signs.

However, there are linguistic signs the function of which is not restricted solely to reproducing an impression, but which rather provide detailed instructions—as, for example, in naturalist drama—on the theatrical signs that are to be used to create the impression required. Yet, the producers of the performance are by no means obliged to realize the concrete theatrical signs in line with these instructions. If they come to the conclusion that following these instructions would not lead to the desired impression, then they must themselves select the corresponding theatrical signs that are to be realized concretely, just as they would in every other case. After all, detailed data refers as a rule to the theatrical code valid at the time when the drama was written. For example, we read of Karl Moor that "he batters his head against a wall," or that "he rips all his clothes to shreds," because these sentences are aimed at theatrical signs which the "Storm and Stress" movement may have felt were appropriate signs of feelings of anger or despair. Should an actor today hit upon the idea of carrying out the actions that correspond to these sentences, then these acts would hardly be regarded as an appropriate expression for the feelings mentioned. By contrast, such an approach would create the impression of shammed feelings, and thus, in the final instance, would undermine the scene by making it appear derisory.[65] If actors and director believe that at this point the meaning of "anger" or "despair" should in fact be constituted, then they will most certainly choose other theatrical signs in order to accomplish the task.

Such a division of "designation" and "meaning" is often caused by historical distance, for the "designation" is rooted in the respective theatrical convention, whereas "meaning" by contrast has its basis in characteristics of the role in the drama or the logic of the sequence of action. The "designation," i.e., detailed instructions, is thus often to be understood as a set of historically determined proposals on the theatrical constitution of the respective "meaning." The transformational process should, as a consequence, not orient itself toward the "designations," but should rather proceed from the "meanings."

If we accept this assumption and adhere to it, then we can even transform those enunciations that cannot be translated if construed as direct instructions on the generation of certain theatrical signs. For example, in many dramas one encounters the reaction of a person described with the words "the color rushed out of her cheeks" (Lady Milford), "she paled" (Mrs. John), etc.[66] As Descartes already pointed out, blushing or paling are to be considered among those physiological processes which a person cannot bring about voluntarily. They are, as a result, not freely available theatrical signs. If the sentences that refer to them are understood as instructions that have to be strictly followed, then such sentences will inevitably appear not to be transformable. If, by contrast, they are understood as literary expressions of certain psychological processes—such as "fright," "fainting," or "horror"—then they can be translated smoothly into theatrical signs which are thoroughly suited to function as the interpretants of such meanings.

The theatrical signs chosen and realized in all such cases can by no means be completely reduced to one function, namely that of pointing to the meanings constituted using the literary text. Owing to their iconic nature, they introduce further, additional meanings into the theatrical text. As a result of this, a shift in meaning gradually occurs with regard to the literary text and the meanings originally constituted interpreting it. For even the additional meanings enter into certain relations, both among each other and with regard to the meanings gleaned from the literary text. As a consequence, in the course of the transformational process a completely new complex of meaning arises, one that is unique in terms of its structure and which can by no means be judged solely in terms of its relation to the underlying literary text of the drama. Rather, we encounter an independent artwork, and it is just as inappropriate to grasp this as a mere translation of the drama as it would be to understand the drama as a draft for a performance that functions in a manner similar to a score. Both the drama and the performance respectively comprise a work *sui generis*, a work that may have a multitude of referential connections linking it to the other, but which cannot be understood in terms of its respective specificity and specialty solely by focusing on these connections.[67] There are, therefore, indeed grounds for doubting whether this relation can be accurately grasped and described as equivalence.

However, if one is prepared to accept the quite general definition of the equivalence of theatrical and dramatic texts given above, then any further investigation of these reservations and objections becomes unnecessary. In terms of that definition, equivalence exists if the performance can be understood as an interpretant for the potential meaning(s) of a drama. This implies that it is possible to understand the performance as an independent text and at the same time as a transformation of a dramatic text. Since the interpretant is already defined as a sign prior to being defined by other signs for which he is an interpretant, he must be accorded a sign function irrespective of whether it actually refers to these other signs or not.

Under these conditions, equivalence between the drama's literary text and the theatrical text of the performance must therefore not be defined and construed as their complete equivalence in terms of sense and meaning. Rather the notion of equivalence, as used and understood here, means merely that both texts can be interpreted with regard to a common meaning.

The notion of faithfulness to the work, by contrast, appears to be of little use when viewed in this light. For it suggests that it is possible to refer to the literary work as if it were a fixed quantity. Here, the transformation would not be able to proceed from different aesthetic objects, but from one fixed meaning that is the same for all. There would, in other words, be one single "correct" transformation into a performance which would correspond to this "true" meaning of the literary work. Yet such an assumption would appear to be absurd in the light of the above deliberations.

It is theoretically possible to postulate equivalence in the above sense as being created in the process of transforming a dramatic text into a theatrical text. Nevertheless, this does not mean that intersubjectively valid, universally accepted, and thus objective criteria have to be drawn up to assess whether such an equivalence has been established. Since it is a value judgment, such an assessment will rather always be subject to subjective constraints and will thus hardly be able to expect or even demand universal acceptance. For equivalence in the way we have defined it can always only be presented as an equivalence for one subject and can only be realized, viewed, elaborated, and understood by precisely this subject: it constitutes a hermeneutic category par excellence.

The Hermeneutics of the Theatrical Text

Production and reception of the theatrical text behave, as it were, reciprocally towards each other.[68] Production occurs as a process of the constitution of meaning in which, under set conditions the subjects select, develop, and realize signs and sign combinations that serve to constitute the respectively specific individual theatrical text. Reception, by contrast, is a process of the constitution of meaning in the course of which, under set conditions the subjects accomplishing that constitution in turn attach a meaning to these signs and sign combinations and thus accord a specific overall meaning to the text.

If reception is described and construed in this manner, then it amounts to a complex process which can be examined as one of three things:

(1) As a reflection on the conditions of both the attribution of meaning—to the extent that individual elements or subtexts are involved—and of the ascription of overall meaning to the text, to the extent that the deliberations are aimed at the whole text. In the latter instance, it constitutes a reflection on the conditions under which it is possible to understand a theatrical text.

(2) As the development of a specific procedure of attributing meaning and ascribing overall meaning to the text, i.e., as the elaboration of methods that are intended to lead to an understanding of the theatrical text.

(3) As the analysis and interpretation of a concrete theatrical text made under the conditions given in (1) and using the methods elaborated in (2) with the

intention of attaching a meaning to the individual elements or substructures and an overall meaning to the whole text, i.e., with the intention of understanding this individual theatrical text.

The reception of a theatrical text as a process of constituting the overall meaning of a text (3) presumes the existence of both a theory of understanding (1) and a specific method of understanding (2). This takes us into the domain of hermeneutics which, in the course of its millennia-old tradition, has taken the shape of both the development of procedures for interpreting texts[69] and the reflection on the conditions under which understanding is possible.[70] It was predominantly construed and undertaken as the "artistic doctrine of interpretation" until well into the nineteenth century, i.e., as a system of rules to be applied to the text to be interpreted, a system that had to be created anew in each instance. In our century it has become one of the basic sciences, a discipline in the theory of science whose task is precisely not to "develop a procedure of understanding, but to clarify the conditions in which understanding takes place."[71]

Even if hermeneutics was, in other words, once "only" a canon of rules, whereas today it is a theory of understanding, this by no means implies that the application of rules in past times did not rest implicitly on a certain notion of understanding, nor that a hermeneutics today can simply ignore the arduous business of reformulating such rules.[72] It is Peter Szondi's great achievement to have stressed the necessity of tackling this, and he believed the basis for such an approach had already been laid out and preformed in Schleiermacher's hermeneutics.[73] Manfred Frank, among others, has taken this up and, by drawing on Schleiermacher's work, has tried to link the theory of understanding advanced by Heidegger and Gadamer with a theory of structural textual analysis.[74] A hermeneutics of the theatrical text today must not regress behind the state of hermeneutic theory as represented by the above works.

Since it is neither possible nor desirable to provide an exhaustive discussion of Gadamer's theory of understanding in the framework of the present study, it will have to suffice merely to point to my deliberations on the subject published elsewhere.[75] I will draw on them and render them more precise only in such instances where their application to the genre of the theatrical text would suggest such an approach being taken.

The point of departure in this connection is Gadamer's fundamental insight into the historical determinacy of all processes of understanding. The location of the interpreter, both in history and in his or her personal biography, determines the process of interpretation, and there is no nonhistorical standpoint which would predate or altogether eliminate this historical background. Rather, it determines that process with regard both to the specific approach taken and to the meanings constituted in that process. The category of "prejudice" which Gadamer introduced into hermeneutic theory has proven to be exceptionally fruitful in this context. Gadamer presumes that "the prejudices of the individual, far more than his judgments,[76] constitute "the historical reality of his being."[77] For, "long before we understand ourselves through the process of self-examination, we understand ourselves in a self-evident way in the family, society and state in which we live."[78]

These prejudices, which depend on and are determined both by the respective tradition to which the subject belongs[79] and by the particular experiences s/he has had, condition the process of understanding a text in such a manner that a respectively new and unique overall meaning is constituted in that process. The sum of these "prejudices" yields the respective fore-understanding with which the receiver approaches a text—a fore-understanding which cannot be ignored, yet upon which the receiver can reflect.

We are interested here only in those "prejudices" from among the set of universally possible prejudices relevant to any process of understanding that refers specifically to theatrical texts. Particular weighting must be attached in this connection to the understanding of the underlying drama. For the meanings that the receiver attaches to its elements and substructures, as well as the overall meaning he accords it, will substantially determine and preform the expectations which he has with regard to the corresponding performance. These expectations, developed interpreting the drama's literary text, may be of a relatively general nature, or, on the contrary, highly concrete. They may, on the one hand, concern the overall meaning of the drama or a general notion of space and roles, or, on the other, involve particular character traits of a person, a quite specific atmosphere in a room, or even concrete details such as elements of the decorations, props, costumes, indeed even face and physique of a dramatic figure. Irrespective of the actual shape these expectations take individually, as a whole they comprise or create a specific fore-understanding and thus a background or foundation for the process of understanding aimed at the performance.

The drama as an aesthetic text does not merely allow, but indeed positively promotes different possibilities for constituting individual meanings and the text's overall meaning as well as giving the audience access to such. Producers and receivers may thus quite easily have a respectively different understanding of the dramatic text in question. In this context a specific problem arises for the process of understanding intended by the performance, a problem already mentioned in connection with the question of equivalence: how is the understanding of a performance possible if the receiver has a fore-understanding of the dramatic text fundamentally different from that of the producers? After all, the receiver cannot ignore his own fore-understanding in such a way that he could pretend not to have one and thus approach the performance "free of prejudice." His prejudice may therefore not permit him to become engrossed in the performance in a manner which would enable him to accord it any overall meaning at all if the overall meaning differs from that which he has constituted interpreting or reading the corresponding literary text.

This objection can be countered at a fundamental level. For a person's respectively individual fore-understanding does indeed form the starting point for every process of understanding, but not in such a manner as to determine this one-sidedly. The meanings conditioned by the person's own fore-understanding are in fact only utilized on a test basis and have to be corrected and replaced by others if they prove in the further course of the process of understanding to be unsuitable.[80] The processes of constituting meaning carried out during the performance are, in other words, also clearly capable themselves of modifying the originally determinate fore-understanding and thus, for example, of contributing to a new understanding of the underlying drama.

This specific characteristic of every process of understanding must be stressed with regard to the reception of a performance, for this may affect any "prejudice" conditioning this process in such a way that the prejudice is itself subjected to change in the specific course of that process. Gadamer emphasizes that the individual's prejudices are the sum and result of his specific experiences, which are determined by his history and personal biography. This being the case, the performance—being quite a special opportunity to make new experiences—may have an effect on the "prejudices" and change them in some way or other.[81] The "prejudices," in other words, are a condition of understanding, but they do not determine it.

Meanings constituted during earlier performances of the same play, like the notions developed in the context of the drama's literary text, may preform a new process of understanding. This is true above all if such a performance is judged to be especially valid and convincing. This judgment may refer to the whole performance or merely to a given cast and the conceptions of the stage characters represented by those actors; whatever the case, it will substantially condition the reception of the new performance.

Conceptions, insights, and expectations devised or developed drawing on the drama's literary text or previous performances of the drama all have an impact on certain individual meanings or the overall meaning accorded to the new performance of the same drama. In addition to these expectations, factors which affect the normative theatrical code in the broadest sense must also be considered as conditioning the process of reception.

Such expectations include especially those that refer both to the principles and type of sign selection or sign combinations and to the transformational mode. Now, as mentioned above, the current situation with regard to theatrical or, more generally, aesthetic norms is unlike that in the past. In earlier periods, even in European theater, a performance was always received with regard to a specific norm; it was assumed that this norm was universal and that measuring up to it was a matter of course. Any substantial deviation from the norm was therefore to be interpreted as either the expression of a wish to create a special style or the sign of a new era.[82] Today, by contrast, we cannot have recourse to such universally accepted norms. It does not follow from this, however, that the place erstwhile occupied by the valid norm in the system of the "prejudices" conditioning the understanding of a performance must remain empty. Rather, it will be filled with expectations that have formed in each person on the basis of his or her specific experiences of theater. It is irrelevant whether these experiences are based on a knowledge of different types or styles of theater—ranging, for example, from naturalist theater to the diverse forms of avant-garde theater—or have been made on the basis of a fleeting acquaintanceship with a contemporary, regional form of theater. Here, the sum of individual experiences takes the place of a universally binding norm that can be both learned and passed down in time. With the aid of these experiences, "rudimentary" normative systems can be established for the different forms of theater that are then applicable to new performances and thus facilitate an understanding of them. For the choice of a certain theatrical form must itself always be construed as an element of meaning requiring interpretation, assuming that no theatrical form has been canonized and has therefore to be presumed to have the status of a norm.

Alongside these more general "prejudices," certain highly specific variants, such as the knowledge of locally conditioned preferences and idiosyncrasies, will influence expectations. The knowledge of other productions by the same director or other work by the same stage designer could be subsumed under this type of fore-understanding, as could a knowledge of an actor's abilities or limitations stemming from a familiarity with the various roles the actor has hitherto played.

Expectations with regard to the theatrical norm in the broadest sense can be geared to quite general aspects. A spectator may expect a certain realism of production, or some other style, the predominance of gestures rather than words, or an approach that either sticks to or disregards the chronology of the drama, etc. Alternatively, his expectations may be connected with quite specific details of the performance, such as the manner in which actor A doubles over when depicting despair, or director B's idiosyncratic manner of juxtaposing decorations and costumes from two different periods, or of deploying a special type of lighting, etc.

All these expectations are part of a system of "prejudices" determined by history and the receiver's personal biography. It is a system on which every process of understanding is based and which substantially shapes the course that process takes—in this case a process which focuses on a particular new performance. It is impossible to proceed as though these prejudices did not exist. Yet it is possible to reflect on them and thus change them, if necessary, within the process of understanding itself.

Gadamer's premise that understanding is historically conditioned causes him to assume that a person necessarily reflects not only on his own prejudices, but also on the historical distance between the period in which the receiver lives and the era which first gave rise to the text being interpreted. The second assumption is indispensable for and constitutive of hermeneutics today, yet it must clearly be modified in the case of the reception of theatrical texts. For the particular ontological status of the performance, the fact that it only exists as the performance the spectator watches, simply does not permit the existence of historical distance in Gadamer's sense between receiver and producer. Admittedly, in particular cases a cultural gap has to be taken into account—such as when Far Eastern theater troupes play in Western Europe or vice versa.[83] Such a gap or distance naturally disappears in the case of all performances of a particular type of theater put on in the culture in which they originate. With regard to understanding theatrical texts we must, in other words, invert the second hermeneutic premise, namely reflection on historical distance, into reflection on its absolute existence as performance.

This absolute contemporaneity between spectator and performance constitutes an essential factor in the process of understanding to the extent that it follows from it that during the performance the receiver can neither dart back and forth, nor immerse himself in some particular detail, nor acquire additional material on the context of the performance which he can then consult. For he cannot interrupt the course of the performance with a view to obtaining a better understanding of the latter.[84] Since realization of signs and sign combinations by the actor and their interpretation by the spectators are almost simultaneous occurrences, opportunities must also exist for spectators to accord these signs and sign combinations an ad hoc meaning.

The general presupposition that producers and receivers are members of the same culture and are contemporaries, even if they belong to different generations or social strata, is just such an opportunity. Consequently, they will still have a great deal in common based on the historically determined context even if their respective personal biographies may be far apart. This guarantees a minimum of common presuppositions. In addition to this minimum, theater has also endeavored in the course of its history to secure the understanding of its products by means of other specific procedures.

Two such procedures were presented in the chapter on theatrical communication in chapter 5 above: first, the creation of a theatrical code binding for directors and spectators alike, as can be found in baroque theater.[85] Second, restricting access to the theater to a homogeneous audience that is so harmonic in terms of views, notions, ways of life, knowledge, and valuations—in short, in terms of systems of meaning—that reference to a theatrical text on the basis of this system of meaning common to all the spectators enables it to be understood. This was the case in the bourgeois illusionistic theater and in Viennese popular theater.[86] What is involved is a respectively different procedure of external recoding. In the former the performance can be understood because its sign and sign combinations can be interpreted on the basis of a code normatively valid for all contemporaries. In the latter, by contrast, this is made possible by referring the signs and sign combinations to extratheatrical cultural codes to which all the spectators have comparable access, codes which may take as their basis either primary cultural systems or various secondary systems.[87]

In some cases, neither a binding theatrical code nor the homogeneity of the audience can be presumed to exist in sufficient measure to secure concurrent reference to the corresponding primary and secondary cultural systems. Here, the structure of the respective theatrical text and thus of its special internal recoding procedures assume a particular importance. In such instances, an understanding of the performance can only be forthcoming if we can presuppose two things: first, that the meanings of its elements and substructures are constituted on syntagmatic levels, and second, that the structure of the performance provides indicators as to those currently possible external structural chains to which an element can be related in order to be given a meaning. The structure may in fact also provide indications that the receiver can refer the element by association to any extratextual structural chains at random.[88]

The absolute temporal presence of the theatrical text as performance thus constitutes an essential factor determining its understanding in two ways. It may, on the one hand, restrict the opportunities for a differentiated, reflective constitution of meaning by inflexibly binding these to the course of the performance; indeed, it may severely restrict them. On the other hand, by so doing this may compel us to refer back to the potential for meaning that can either be activated by all the spectators or accessed by them ad hoc. In essential points producers and the different receivers will share the same potential for meaning as both groups participate in the same culture. This potential comprises a system of thought and behavioral patterns as well as other culturally specific idiosyncrasies, insights, and capabilities formed and passed down by the culture in question. It consequently appears particularly well suited to functioning as the common basis for the processes of constituting the overall meaning of the performance in production and reception alike. This holds true even if the results of these processes diverge as a result of socially and subjectively determined variances. Resorting to this system of meanings common to all the members of a culture thus secures in a quite general manner the possibility of understanding theatrical texts.

The fact that recourse can be had to such a system would seem to suggest that there are two fundamentally different modes of constituting meaning. First, an attempt can be made to search out and activate those elements in this system that have a meaning that we can assume is generally agreed on even in a pluralistic society. The receiver or producer can then operate on the basis of this artificially created homogeneity, i.e., the theatrical text's elements and substructures receive a meaning by being referred to the extratextual structural chains they have activated.[89] Secondly, the system as a whole is presumed to exist at the outset, and new meanings are then generated in the theatrical text on the basis of it, i.e., elements and substructures of the theatrical text are accorded a meaning owing to the specific system of relations that can be established between them.[90] Whereas in the first instance meanings are adopted from the underlying system, in the second, new meanings are created by reference to these meanings. Even if in each case a respectively different tack is taken, that recourse to an ad hoc activated potential of meaning necessitated by the absolute contemporaneity of the performance thus amounts to a substantial factor determining the understanding of theatrical texts.

With regard to understanding theatrical texts, we must reflect on a third factor constitutive of the understanding of such texts, namely, the circularity of such understanding. Analytical theories of science doubt its relevance or at least contest that it is relevant, although its importance would appear absolutely obvious from the viewpoint of hermeneutic theory owing to the hermeneutic premises of "prejudice" and "temporal distance" involved.[91] Analytical theories assert that the process of interpretation is solely a "mere heuristics of anticipations for which henceforth verification or falsification is forthcoming on confrontation with the discursive facts of the text."[92] They thus claim that there can be no talk of an unavoidable circle. This objection must be carefully examined, because it goes to the core of hermeneutic theory.[93]

If, as we have said, the receiver embarks on the reception of a (theatrical) text on the basis of his fore-understanding of it, which is, in turn, determined by history and his personal biography, then he will initially try to attach meanings to the signs presented to him, meanings that they have for him in terms of his own system of meanings. Should he ascertain that these meanings do not yield an overall meaning in the context of the performance, then he will attempt to replace them with others which, on the basis of his now greater knowledge of the performance, he thinks will result in an overall meaning. If, in the course of the performance, these meanings also appear unsuitable, then they, in turn, will also have to be modified or accordingly replaced by more suitable ones. In other words, new interpretative hypotheses are continually created on the basis of the respective fore-understanding, and this also changes constantly as the performance progresses. Analytical theory is correct in regarding these hypotheses as continually new ways of anticipating the overall meaning of the performance. Yet, these hypotheses cannot be substantiated or proved false once and for all at the end of the performance, as the analytical theory of science would have it.[94] Since in its capacity as an aesthetic text the performance allows for different possibilities of constituting meaning, we cannot assume the existence of one single "correct" interpretation against which the justification of the individual interpretative hypotheses can be tested in an intersubjectively valid manner. Every completed process of the constitution of the overall meaning of the performance is thus to be construed not as the end of the reception process, but only as a temporary end and thus as a point whence the process of constituting the overall meaning of the performance can always be started up anew. The final constitution of the overall meaning may very well accord the individual elements and substructures a meaning and thus, at least with regard to them, affirm or reject certain interpretative hypotheses. Yet it is nevertheless not the only possible or correct constitution of the performance's overall meaning, but is always itself merely temporary. It is thus a meaning that is to be integrated into the current fore-understanding—and this, in turn, can at any time be revised by a continuation of the process.

However, the fact that the interpretative process cannot in theory be completed with regard to the interpretation of theatrical texts must be considerably relativized owing to the ontological status of such texts. For the process cannot be restarted following the end of the last performance. The temporarily last overall meaning of the performance must thus remain the last meaning, and it can only be revised on the basis of memory and not by comparison with the text. The absolute simultaneous presence of performance and spectator thus also holds true for interpretations of the performance—they cannot be continued ad infinitum. The hermeneutic circle thus forfeits much of the relevance it has at a general, theoretical level.

The concept of the hermeneutic circle refers usually not just to the fact that, in principle, no process of understanding can ever be complete, but rather—and this is implied by the first assertion—also maintains that the specific relation of the parts to the whole on which that process is based can never be completely given. For the meanings of the individual elements and substructures of a text can be constituted only with a view to its overall meaning just as, conversely, the overall meaning can only be constituted on the basis of the meanings of the elements and substructures.[95] In other words, aside from the question of whether an interpretative process can ever be complete, there is a second important hermeneutic problem which arises. It is posed by the relation between the individual elements and the substructures they go to make up, between less complex substructures and more complex substructures, and, finally, between more complex substructures and the whole text which they go to make up. Each of these levels of semantic coherence also plays a part in constituting the meaning of the next highest level, even though it itself can only acquire a meaning by reference to the latter. As long as hermeneutics was oriented solely to linguistic texts, it was able to concern itself with this problem by reflecting on the hermeneutic circle. Thus, it did not have to address the question of the circle's underlying division into different levels of semantic coherence, nor did it have to regard this as a problem. For such coherence was given in the shape of the grammatical and stylistic organization: words, sentences, passages, and chapters, and, of course, the overall text.[96]

However, if the task is to develop a hermeneutics of nonverbal texts, then, with regard to an elaboration of the relation of parts to whole, we must first find a model for the structuration in terms of different levels of semantic coherence that can claim validity for such texts. In his *Structural Semantics: An Attempt at Method* A. J. Greimas has devised such a model, one which promises to meet all of these requirements. He distinguishes four levels of semantic coherence, levels that respectively potentiate the others: (1) the elementary level, which embraces the semes in the synthesis of lexeme/sememe; (2) the classematic level, constituted by the lexical units connected in meaning to a phrase; (3) the isotopic level, the elements of which are recurring classemes; and (4) the level of the totality of the overall text.[97] Greimas thus describes and defines four levels of semantic coherence in such a general way that it would appear possible to apply the classification to nonlinguistic texts.

These levels can be distinguished in the following manner in the case of theatrical texts:

(1) the elementary level: this includes all types of individual theatrical signs, such as individual gestures, movements, props, individual parts of the decorations, or costumes, etc. (in this context, we shall initially exclude the problem of how such elements can be treated in isolation).

(2) the classematic level: this includes all simple sign combinations such as behavioral sequences, a certain costume, spatial subdivisions, etc.

(3) the isotopic level: this is realized by the different body-texts and spatial texts.

(4) the level of totality: this is made up of the overall theatrical text.

Reciprocal reference of these different levels of semantic coherence to one another should allow us to constitute the meanings of the individual elements and substructures and the overall meaning of the theatrical text as a whole.

In this connection, it is important to bear in mind that the theatrical text was defined as a polyphonic text—in other words, as a text the subtexts of which in turn referred to a respectively different subject that had constituted them.

It would therefore be in order to assess whether it is legitimate to situate body-texts at the isotopic level or whether, in fact, it is not just as justifiable to regard the body-text as the totality of the text, something which is itself composed of the three levels of lesser semantic coherence. In this case, the first level would again be made up of individual signs, such as gestures, movements, parts of the costume, etc.; the second, of kinesic sequences, dialogical sequences, a complete costume; and the third, of the totality of all costumes of the dramatis persona in question. The level of totality would thus, in the final instance, be generated by the overall meaning of the whole body-text as the constitution of the stage character.

Such an approach may well be justified if the emphasis is placed on the role played by respective subjects in the constitution of the theatrical text. To my mind, however, one must lose sight neither of the fact that the overall meaning of the individual body-texts can in turn be substantively altered if they are linked into a theatrical text, nor that it is these altered meanings that subsequently constitute the overall meaning of the overall theatrical text. If one wishes to do justice to the feature of polyphony, then it would appear suitable to adopt a procedure for constituting meaning and the overall meaning of the text that is capable of highlighting the element of tension that may exist between the overall meaning of body-texts and the overall meaning of the total theatrical text. For this element of tension is a factor which itself generates meaning, and we need to make use of this tension in a manner that is fruitful for the interpretation. However, if such tension is not to be found or activated, then the insight that every body-text is constituted by a respective subject will, for the most part, play no part in the process of the receiver's constitution of meaning.

In the course of this chapter, reference has repeatedly been made to the aestheticity of the theatrical text. In conclusion, this feature will be discussed in terms of the extent to which it functions as a specific, conditioning factor in understanding.

The aesthetic text is to be distinguished from the nonaesthetic especially by its ambiguity.[98] In nonaesthetic texts, the possibility of attributing meanings to signs is substantially restricted by the following: (a) the position of the sign in the syntagma (the syntactic dimension); (b) its relation to its object, for which the element in question functions as a sign (the semantic dimension); and (c) by the respective users of the signs in the particular communicative situation (the pragmatic dimension). As a consequence, the greatest possible unequivocality arises, although this may differ in degree, depending on the kind of text concerned. By contrast, the three semiotic dimensions refer to one another in aesthetic texts in a manner which has precisely the opposite result, namely, a considerable enhancement of their ambiguity.

As Mukařovský has convincingly shown, an aesthetic text which takes certain objects or a specific reality as its topic does not point to these objects or precisely this reality in the way corresponding nonaesthetic texts would. Rather, it uses them as "agents" for the message it wishes to convey. He writes: "The factual reference is of a multifold nature here and points to realities that are known to the observer and yet are by no means themselves expressed or even hinted at in the work; nor can they be, for they form part of the observer's experience."[99]

The aesthetic text thus does not intend the objects and realities about which it provides a direct account to be its message. As a consequence, the relation between them and the signs denoting them cannot be considered to form the semantic dimension of the text: the aesthetic text does not exhibit an independent semantic dimension. This specific feature, which distinguishes it fundamentally from all types of nonaesthetic texts, is the root cause of its innate ambiguity. For, as a result of this characteristic, it is not possible to refer the text's individual statements to a reality that exists outside it, nor, for that matter, to pinpoint its meaning.

Since an independent semantic dimension cannot be presumed to exist in the aesthetic text, every receiver has to first create it in the process of reception indirectly via the syntactic and pragmatic dimensions. Its constitution would therefore appear to depend largely on the specific structure of the text (the syntactic dimension), on the one hand, and the individual receiver's experiences (the pragmatic dimension), on the other. The overall meaning attributed to an aesthetic text thus arises as a result of interaction between a respectively particular subject and the specific structure of this respectively special text. It is consequently to be considered the result of a subjective positioning that is probably motivated by the "sign stocks" of the artifact, without, however, necessarily arising from these. For the overall meaning of an aesthetic text cannot be derived solely from the order of its signs as if it were some objective meaning that came into existence with the text. Rather, that overall meaning must first be constituted by an interpretation, which itself amounts to a subjective, singular use of signs, because it involves constructing the absent semantic dimension that is dependent on a subject and the specific conditions governing the latter. Interpretation can thus quite definitely be conceived of as "steered creation"[100] which engenders new meanings that are both permitted and motivated by the text, yet are neither clearly demanded by it nor necessarily to be derived from it.

In its capacity as an aesthetic text, the theatrical text in other words opens up various possibilities for processes of attributing meaning and ascribing an overall meaning to the text. Yet the subject receiving these signs must interpret them, although neither the overall meaning of the text's signs nor the meanings of the order of those signs can be deduced unequivocally and in the same way by all receivers—indeed, they cannot view these as fixed meanings. In other words, the subject has to ascribe meaning to the signs in line with his personal experiences and taking the specific structure of the text into account. In so doing, he constitutes the overall meaning of the text for himself. A meaning valid for all cannot be attributed to a theatrical text, for its aesthetic character ensures precisely that it is innately ambiguous.

In view of the different general conditions under which the understanding of the theatrical text ensues, this act can be defined in summary as follows. To understand a theatrical text means to attach meanings to its signs and their order in a process that cannot in theory be completed, while bearing one's own system of meanings in mind, a system that is determined by history and one's own personal biography. It must, furthermore, be possible to construct from these meanings an overall meaning motivated by the text which is, for the receiving subject, logically consistent as well as valid. In other words, in the process of understanding neither those meanings are necessarily reconstructed which the producers of the theatrical text intended to constitute in it, nor are those meanings attributed to the signs which they may have had for the receiving subject outside their insertion into the symbolic order of the theatrical text. Rather, by virtue of the fact that the receiver constructs this order in line with a rule he has found or invented himself, he creates meanings that are not identical to the meanings that these signs have in the two systems of meaning mentioned. Viewed in this light, understanding a theatrical text involves a productive process in which the different systems of meaning—those of the producers and those of the receivers—mesh with one another via the symbolic order of the text, thus subjecting the receiver's system of meaning to a potentially substantial change.[101] The result of this process is the overall meaning of the theatrical text constituted in it, a meaning which is ineluctably subjective and inevitably individual.

It by no means follows from this that understanding a theatrical text is such a subjective matter that it is not possible to develop either procedures for ascribing meanings or an overall meaning to it that can be verified intersubjectively and understood by all persons, or for that matter methods of understanding.[102] The above simply implies that it is not possible to devise such procedures or methods with the aim of constituting a universally valid, overall meaning. The goal cannot be to constitute an objectively given "correct" meaning, nor can such a goal be arrived at by means of such procedures.

8. The Process of Constituting Meaning and Sense as a Method of Analyzing Theatrical Texts

Theory and Method

❏ ❏ ❏ It is only possible, logically speaking, to derive a method that will yield an understanding of theatrical texts from one of two kinds of theory—either from a theory of understanding (*Verstehen*) or from a theory of the theatrical text.[1]

In the first case, one would proceed from the concept of understanding and examine the individual definitions on which it rests in order to ascertain whether it can provide the basis for identifying and formulating methodological postulates that are applicable to all theatrical texts. One would also have to isolate and differentiate the individual methodological steps to be followed in the process of generating an interpretation of theatrical texts. In the second case, by contrast, one proceeds from the concept of the theatrical text and, based on its individual definitions, attempts to generalize aspects of textuality that can be reformulated as rules. The latter apply to the general principles of the process of creating an interpretation as well as to the individual operations that are to be performed as a part of this process. Both approaches are theoretically legitimate and equally valid with regard to developing a methodology.

If we adopt the first approach, however, we encounter certain difficulties. For the hermeneutic theory taken as the basis for it is intended to reflect on the conditions under which the process of understanding takes place. The first of these conditions, however—namely, that of a location that is determined by history and personal biography, is a condition that hinges on the subject of the receiver. The second condition, namely, that of absolute contemporaneity, is rooted in the ontological status of the performance. Consequently, it will hardly be possible to derive any methodological maxims or postulates from either of the two conditions that could then be applied to the interpretation of a theatrical text. It is only the third—the hermeneutic circle—which can ultimately be regarded as a condition related to the text itself, inasmuch as it involves the special relation of parts to whole which constitutes the text.

The nature of this relation implies the existence of a number of presuppositions, and these must be explicated if the process of creating an interpretation is to take place in a methodically reflected manner. For a meaning can only be ascribed to a textual element if the former is first incorporated into the next highest level of semantic coherence. Conversely, the meaning at this level can only be constituted through recourse to the meanings of the elements on the next lowest level. It follows from this that the text has to be divided into levels with varying degrees of semantic coherence if an overall meaning is to be attributed to it at all. In other words, first of all we can derive from the relation of the parts to the whole of a theatrical text the general methodological requirement that the text be segmented into various levels of semantic coherence that are, or so it would appear, relevant to the process of attributing overall meaning to the text.[2]

Such a segmentation is the prerequisite for all hermeneutic operations, no matter how minor they may be. For, even if it is only one's own meanings that are initially employed on a trial basis in the process of interpretation, such a procedure nevertheless implies that it is clear at which levels of semantic coherence the constitutive elements are to be understood as signs. After all, only if they can be recognized as signs can they then be assigned meanings on the basis of the respective system of meaning. In other words, recognizing an exclamation, a relatively long behavioral sequence, a single prop, or a complete stage set as a sign presupposes that a corresponding segmentation has already occurred.[3]

It should now be possible in the further course of the reception process to modify these meanings, which are initially ascribed only on a trial basis, and to replace them with others that appear better suited to indicating the overall meaning of the text. The latter is thus repeatedly anticipated, but each time in a new and different way. Again, this process implies a number of operations which, if explicitly identified as such, could lead to the enumeration of possible steps for an analysis. For if the attribution of a meaning can be corrected by subsequent elements of the text, then the relationship of these elements to the preceding elements itself gains particular relevance for the analysis. We must therefore clarify which subsequent elements or substructures would at least appear to urgently call for, if not necessitate, a modification or even a substitution of the initial overall meaning ascribed to the text, just as we must also ascertain under which corresponding conditions this is the case. It is accordingly necessary to examine the specific relations which exist between successive elements (a) at the same level of semantic coherence and (b) at different levels of semantic coherence.

We have, however, thus far put particularly this second methodological postulate derived from the concept of the hermeneutic circle in such general terms that it can hardly be taken as the basis for precise instructions how to conduct concrete analytical operations. Starting from the general postulate, such instructions must rather be pinpointed more precisely and developed further on the basis of other theoretical premises before that postulate can be applied to theatrical texts as a procedure that anyone can follow and verify.

In other words, a set of precisely formulated rules and instructions for action cannot be derived directly from the concept of understanding that we took as our basis. On the other hand, the concept of the theatrical text as we have defined and explained it contains a series of definitions that could be reformulated in a manner that would provide such rules.

This is true for the very first general definition which served as the point of departure for our considerations: we defined the theatrical text as the realization of the theatrical code at the level of speech. At the level of the system, the theatrical code contains all the general possibilities and conditions for theatrical processes of creating meaning; and at the level of the norm, it entails all the possibilities and conditions characteristic of a specific period or genre. At the level of speech, however, it regulates the process of a singular creation of meaning, the constitution of the overall meaning of an individual theatrical text. In this particular form, the text thus amounts to a selection and combination of the possibilities afforded at the systemic and normative levels, and one which occurs only once.

This first definition of the theatrical text yields a first rule of interpretation. Since the text is defined as the singular application of a general, intersubjectively valid semiotic system, it can be understood only through recourse to that underlying semiotic system. The theatrical text must, in other words, be situated in the context of the theatrical code as (a) a system and (b) a norm, and analyzed in relation to the contexts these respectively engender. In this respect, there is no question that the theatrical code as system—the *langue* of theatrical speech—represents the most comprehensive context for the theatrical text.

The first methodological postulate to be adopted follows from this. The theatrical text must be analyzed on the basis of the semiotic system of which it is intended to be a realization—in other words, on the basis of the theatrical code at the systemic and normative levels.

Our second definition concerned the theatrical text as an artistic text. Lotman defines it as an overall meaning with a complex structure: "All of its elements bear meaning."[4] This statement has two implications. First, no element of a theatrical text, to the extent that it is an aesthetic text, can be regarded as redundant; in other words, every element can, in principle, be interpreted.[5] Second, taken as a whole, these elements, which function as vehicles of meaning—and in this respect they must all be accorded an equal value—constitute a complex structure, i.e., must at the same time belong to different stages of semantic coherence. Complexity, in other words, refers to the same peculiarity of the text that is implied by the special relation of parts to whole contained in the notion of hermeneutic circle. By the same token, it also implies the necessity of dividing the theatrical text into different levels of semantic coherence. Since every element of the theatrical text is in principle open to interpretation and at the same time helps to constitute varying levels of semantic coherence, it is necessary to clarify in each case of ascribing an overall meaning to a text at which level of semantic coherence the meaning arrived at can be ascribed to the element in question. The totality of the levels of semantic coherence as well as their reciprocal relationships thus make up the complexity of the theatrical text. As a consequence, this complexity can be appropriately analyzed and thus newly synthesized only if the text is subdivided into segments that belong to different levels of semantic coherence.

In other words, this second definition of the theatrical text brings us to a second methodological postulate, namely, that the text be divided into different levels of semantic coherence. It also yields a general rule of interpretation, according to which a meaning can, in principle, be attributed to every element of a theatrical text.

Our third definition of the theatrical text consisted of enumerating and explicating the three features of explicitness, delimitation, and structuration. It is now possible to derive methodological postulates directly from them. For explicitness and delimitation refer to the selection of signs and sign combinations that are de facto realized from among the generally available possibilities as well as to the signs and combinations specifically not selected. They thus define (1) the choice of sign systems which are employed or, as the case may be, not employed; (2) the choice of the kind of signs within the sign system; and (3) the choice of individual concrete signs as signifying elements. Consequently, a theatrical text has to be investigated with a view to determining (1) which of the generally available sign systems are actually employed in it and which of them are dispensed with, (2) what kind of signs within the system are preferred and which kinds are excluded, and (3) which specific concrete signs are in fact realized.

Structuration, on the other hand, refers to the special relations which obtain among the elements which are selected and realized. An investigation must be made of the combinations effected among the signs in order to arrive at the relations involved. In other words, it is necessary in the case of each sign to determine with which sign of the same or a different sign system it is combined (a) simultaneously and (b) successively, and whether the ensuing combinations are subject to a specific hierarchy in which certain elements are dominant. Such an approach enables us to reconstruct the system of equivalencies and oppositions that determines and generates the special structure of the text to be analyzed.

It is now possible, by referring to explicitness, delimitation, and structuration, to give the methodological postulate, couched until now in general terms, greater precision: The theatrical text must be examined with regard to the specific selection and combination of theatrical signs that have been made within it.

The fourth definition referred to the specific mode by which meaning was generated in theatrical (aesthetic) texts. Lotman distinguishes in principle between two modes of generating meaning in texts, namely, external and internal recoding, the reciprocal relationship of which constitutes the overall meaning ascribed to the text. We can conclude from this that it is necessary to clarify which kind of recoding serves as a basis for the creation of a meaning attributed to an element. In other words, we must establish whether the meaning involved is paradigmatic or syntagmatic in nature. In the former case, it is necessary to examine first to which extratextual structural chains the relevant element can be related if it is to be given a meaning, and second, what meaning, in turn, may be given to the relation of the textual element to the extratextual structural chain thus pinpointed. In the second case, by contrast, it is a matter of determining to which other textual element the textual element in question can be related when assigning it a meaning. This question can be answered through recourse to the system of equivalencies and oppositions already reconstructed in the analysis. At the same time, however, the very answer to the question helps us reconstruct the system.[6]

The reciprocal relationship of paradigmatic and syntagmatic meanings in a theatrical text thus gives rise to our fourth methodological postulate. The respective mode by which meaning is generated and the specific reciprocal relationship that obtains between the two possible modes have to be ascertained and their specific function must be specified.

We have defined the theatrical text, moreover, as a multimedial text. However, since the theory of multimedial texts is still in its infancy, it would seem to make more sense—at least for the time being—to forgo any attempt to derive methodological postulates from it.

In other words, our various definitions of the concept of the theatrical text clearly proved to be a suitable basis for deducing and establishing methodological postulates, whereby we assume that the receiver constitutes the overall meaning of a theatrical text by adhering to them. In light of them, we accordingly drew up the following four requirements that have to be met by the receiver:

(1) The theatrical text has to be related to the underlying semiotic system.

(2) It has to be divided into different levels of semantic coherence.

(3) It has to be examined with regard to the specific selection and combination of theatrical signs undertaken in it in each case.

(4) The various kinds of generating meaning have to be ascertained and their respective function determined.

In order to comply with these requirements, the receiver has to apply appropriate procedures to the text; we must therefore establish what these are and explain them. First, however, brief mention should be made of a few general principles to be followed in the course of interpretation when applying these procedures.

Every statement has to be formulated in such a way as to guarantee that it is intersubjectively comprehensible (i.e., employs defined concepts).[7] It must not contain any contradictions.[8] It must be possible for anyone to link it back to the text and must thus lend itself to assessing whether it is legitimate.[9] This does not mean that it should be possible to verify or falsify every statement by means of reference to the text—this is not possible in any case according to the hermeneutic premises for interpretative sentences we adopted. Rather, it is only necessary to establish that a point of reference for this statement actually exists in the text.[10] Any further principles to be adhered to beyond those just listed are related to individual analytic procedures and thus cannot be considered general principles in the sense defined above, i.e., cannot be taken as the basis for the respective individual analytic procedures.

Individual Analytic Procedures

Recourse to the Theatrical Code as a System and a Norm

Recourse to the theatrical code as a system and as a norm is not comparable to the other three methodological postulates inasmuch as it is not actually a specific procedure to be carried out separately from the others, but is rather a prerequisite for applying the procedures to be derived from the other postulates. For segmentation can only be undertaken on the basis of the possibilities for forming units afforded by the theatrical code as a system. A selection must always be understood as a selection from the repertoire of theatrical signs made available by the system and/or the norm. Similarly, a combination is always a singular realization of the possible combinations that the system and the norm foresee and permit. External recoding creates a special relation to the theatrical code as a norm inasmuch as the norm establishes the extratextual structural chains to which elements of the text can be related in order to be given a meaning. And a relation can be established between internal recoding and the possible combinations offered by the system and the norm inasmuch as it is based on and builds on these possibilities.

In other words, we must have recourse to the theatrical code as a system and a norm in order to describe any of these procedures. However, reference should also be made to the specific relation that the theatrical code establishes between the levels of (a) system and norm, (b) system and speech, and (c) norm and speech. All three are initially arranged on a rising scale of generality and increased validity—or, if viewed the other way around, in terms of increasing individualization and decreasing validity. Whereas the theatrical code as speech forms the basis in each case of only one performance and is valid only for this performance, as a norm it regulates the production of a whole series of performances, and as a system, it claims final validity for all potential performances. At the level of respectively lesser validity the theatrical code thus represents a restricted selection from all of the possibilities offered at the more generally valid level. By the same token, however, the more specific level can, in turn, cause changes in the theatrical code at the more general level(s): every new norm can multiply those signs, possible combinations, and meanings provided for by the system. Equally, every performance is capable of changing the norm underlying it or even establishing a new norm and thus, for its part, modifying and expanding the repertoire of the system.[11] A theatrical text can therefore very well be understood, on the one hand, as a specific realization of the possibilities offered by the system and the norm, but if necessary, it can also be understood, on the other, as a specific alteration and/or suspension of the underlying norm and as a specific expansion of the underlying semiotic system.[12] Every performance thus has to be examined to determine (a) to which norm or norms it refers, (b) whether it fulfills, violates, or suspends these norms, and (c) whether it perhaps introduces a new norm, or (d) whether and to what extent this happens in the framework of the possibilities generally offered by the system, and (e) whether and to what extent it results in an expansion of the repertoire of the system. The interlinking analysis of the theatrical code as speech—from the performance—and the theatrical code as norm and system is, in other words, to be understood and undertaken in two directions: both as an analysis that identifies the text as a singular application of the general system underlying it and as an examination that, if necessary, highlights the alteration and expansion of precisely this system and is accordingly capable of describing it.[13]

Segmentation

Segmentation of the theatrical text is a fundamental operation in any analysis. If the text cannot be divided into units which have a lower degree of semantic coherence than does the text as a whole, then it is not possible to conduct an analysis in the first place, whereby analysis is understood as the very process of attributing a meaning to individual elements and substructures and an overall meaning to the text.

The segmentation of the text into different levels of semantic coherence has to be strictly distinguished from the linking of the underlying semiotic system back to its smallest signifying units. Although it presupposes this procedure in a certain sense, it is nevertheless not identical with it; theoretically speaking, it is a procedure sui generis. This division of the system into its smallest signifying units admittedly pinpoints that unit which constitutes the uniqueness of the system as a special semiotic system—for example, the word, being the smallest signifying unit, constitutes the special nature of the semiotic system of language. As a consequence, every statement in this system has to be broken down into its smallest signifying units which cannot, in turn, be broken down further into signifying units, but only into differentiating units. The case of segmentation is different; here the text is divided into the various levels of semantic coherence, to each of which the smallest signifying unit as its constitutive element at the same time belongs: the word, for example, constitutes the level of the word, as well as that of the sentence, the chapter, and the written work as a whole.

In the case of the theatrical code as a system, however, the situation is different, in that the code cannot be traced back to such homogeneous smallest signifying units. Since the code is constituted by a large number of different semiotic systems, it can only be reduced to their smallest signifying units—and thus, in its totality, to heterogeneous smallest signifying units. As a result, all attempts to break theater as a semiotic system in some way down into homogeneous units that could also be made the basis of a performance analysis have not borne fruit to date. This is true, for example, of Kowzan's proposal for a minimal simultaneous unit whose duration is identical to that of a temporally shortest sign, or Ruffini's division into *segni parziali* and *segni globali*, Hamon's introduction of the "personnage" as a theatrical unit, or Jansen's definition of the situation as the smallest constitutive unit.[14] Instead of continuing the search for a homogeneous unit, we should acknowledge the heterogeneity of the various smallest signifying units as a conditio sine qua non and taken as the starting point for further investigations.

The procedure of segmentation must be distinguished fundamentally from this approach. For it is not geared to the level of the system, but rather exclusively to that of speech, in other words, to concrete theatrical texts. For this reason, the kind of division it undertakes cannot, as it were, be transposed back onto the level of the system. Since both types of division involve operations which are qualitatively and, above all, functionally different from one another, any attempt to find a model that could be taken as a foundation for the system as well as for the concrete text is bound to fail. It can thus be assumed that the impermissible equation of both levels, or at least treating both as equals, is the reason why so many of the proposed approaches are inadequate.[15]

We summarized Greimas's proposed approach to the division of the text into four levels of semantic coherence in connection with the problematics of the hermeneutic circle and initially adopted it as a suitable model for the segmentation of theatrical texts. The intention must now be to provide justifications for that decision and to elaborate on the details.

Greimas's elementary level is realized in the theatrical text by the various individual theatrical signs, by word and gesture, parts of the costume and the decoration, a floodlight position or a prop, etc. Thus, the problematics which we encountered in the attempt to reduce every system involved in the constitution of the theatrical code as a system to its smallest signifying elements first becomes virulent at this level.[16] The elementary level of the text is, in other words, made up of those heterogeneous smallest signifying units to which the theatrical code in its totality as a system can be attributed; and the elementary level of the text is the location at which the two different operations of division—namely, the reduction of the system to its smallest signifying units and the segmentation of the text into different levels of semantic coherence—come into contact and intersect. After all, reduction serves to identify those smallest signifying units that are capable of forming the elementary level of semantic coherence of the text in the first place. In this respect, segmentation presupposes reduction but is not identical to it.

At the elementary level, needless to say, only those meanings can be attributed to the individual theatrical signs which do not rely on a specific context, i.e., the incorporation of the sign into higher levels of semantic coherence in order to be constituted. Therefore, only such meanings can be presupposed which are attributable to the corresponding signs on the basis of their occurrence in other contexts of application. A certain piece of furniture, for example, can be identified ad hoc as a clothes-rack—even if this meaning has to be corrected in the course of the production and replaced by the meaning "tree" (*Waiting for Godot*). Equally, it must be possible to recognize an article of clothing as a shirt or sweater—and more precisely, as the shirt of a nobleman from the period of Louis XIV and the sweater of a craftsman from the beginning of the nineteenth century. Or, for that, to identify a particular change in posture as leading to the act of sitting down and a twist at the corner of the mouth as a smile, to mention but a few examples. The elementary level indeed represents that level at which a meaning can be ascribed to the signs exclusively on the basis of the respective receiver's system of meaning; that is, unless the relevant sign is unknown, in which case no meaning can be attributed to it.[17]

Greimas defined the next highest level of semantic coherence as the classematic level. It is not easy to pinpoint this in the theatrical text. For theatrical classemes can be formed by sequences of widely varying duration and complexity. In this respect, they are entirely comparable to the sentence, although they are not yet subject to a delimiting criterion as is the case with the sentence. As combinations of signs, they are already higher than the elementary level of the individual signs, but still lower than the level of isotopes. This allows us to conclude that a simple combination of a few signs must come under the category of classemes just as much as do complex combinations of various behavioral sequences, costumes, and elements of decoration.

A second problem is posed by the fact that combinations of signs from a single sign system can be specified as classemes, and that this is also true of combinations of signs from different semiotic systems, just as can a combination of all those signs which are realized simultaneously or a combination of all signs of one or several sign systems that are realized successively. The choice of combinations one wishes to investigate at the classematic level is not, therefore, limited beforehand, but will depend both on the specific sign combinations that are defined as isotopes in each case and on the particular objective of the investigation.[18]

Based on their combination into classemes, the meanings of the individual signs which are constituted ad hoc can, if necessary, be confirmed to be legitimate and can supplement each other to form a supraordinated meaning of the overarching classeme involved. The individual components of a costume, for example, can constitute the meaning "clothing of a nobleman at Louis XIV's court" and thus identify the person wearing them in a particular way. Various sequences of dialogue or behavior, costumes, props, and elements of decoration may go to make up the meaning "Christmas dinner with the several generations present."

Alternatively, the combination of individual signs into classemes can also offer the first opportunity for a correction to be made in the sense of specifying, expanding, or replacing the meanings which have been constituted ad hoc. If, for example, the shirt from the Louis XIV period is worn together with otherwise contemporary clothing and the actor is in the process of taking off this shirt, one cannot—as in the above case—conclude from the meaning of the shirt that the person wearing it has to be a nobleman at Louis XIV's court. The incorporation of the individual sign "shirt" into a classeme thus substantially modifies the meaning originally attributed to it.

Finally, a third possibility arises if the meanings of individual signs which have been constituted ad hoc at the level of their combination into classemes are not then confirmed and yet cannot be replaced by more suitable meanings. If the shirt mentioned above, for example, is worn together with oriental breeches, modern rubber boots, and a Prussian three-cornered hat, it will not be possible either for the meanings of the individual signs to reciprocally modify one another, nor can an overall meaning of the classeme as a whole be constituted without the analysis abandoning this level and moving to the next higher level, namely that of isotopes.

The level of the isotopes is formed, in turn, by such recurrent classemes. This level is of particular relevance for the process of attributing meaning and an overall interpretation of the theatrical text inasmuch as an analysis can hardly proceed from the elementary level of individual theatrical signs or from that of the classemes, but rather will always consider the two lower levels of semantic coherence only in relation to the level of the isotopes. Consequently, it is especially important to delineate it more closely.

There are various ways of arriving at the level of isotopes. One can opt for a method which is geared to (a) individual sign systems involved, or (b) syntagma of varying sizes, or even (c) intertextual categories as constituents.

In the first case an attempt will be made to define all of the signs of either a single sign system or a group of related sign systems—such as that of the kinesic signs, the signs of external appearance, the spatial signs—or two or more opposing sign systems, such as the verbal and nonverbal signs of direct communication. Subsequently, they can be assigned a meaning, through recourse respectively to the classematic and elementary levels which form them. In this method, the relevant sign systems are in each case analyzed simultaneously throughout the entire course of the performance and are examined for the separate meaning each of them has, a meaning constituted only by them, without the others interfering.[19] Such a selection of isotopes is justified and advisable above all in the following three cases: first, if the individual systems or groups of systems are in themselves capable of constituting a meaning that essentially determines the overall interpretation of the text—such as a spatially constructed opposition in principle between inside and outside; second, if the individual systems or groups of systems are based on different principles of creating meaning—for example, a realistic design of the costumes is adopted although the space is designed symbolically; and third, if the opposing sign systems can constitute a specific meaning based on their partial or consistent opposition—such as the special relationship between verbal signs, on the one hand, and paralinguistic and kinesic signs, on the other. It is therefore judicious to select the sign system at the isotopic level whenever a sign system is capable of constituting a meaning based on its specific design or its particular relationship to another sign system as a whole, a sign system that is relevant for the overall interpretation of the theatrical text.[20]

In the procedure used to form syntagmas, the course of the performance is followed, and the situation, scene, or act is pinpointed at the level of isotopes. Here, in other words, segments are chosen which are already pregiven and marked as such in the literary text of the drama.[21] In the theatrical text, they are usually delineated by the entrance or exit of a character, a change of scenery, fading or brightening the lights, or lowering or raising the curtain. The totality of all signs and sign combinations realized between these two "boundaries" forms the relevant isotope. The classemes and individual signs contained in it will thus have to be investigated with regard to the way in which they construct the meaning of this situation, scene, or act and which meaning they constitute for the situation/scene/act in the process. The selection and combination of theatrical signs in this approach are thus always related to the unit of the situation/scene/act as a supraordinated dimension from which its/their function and meaning are determined and can therefore be ascertained.

The choice of situation/scene/act as an isotope would appear to be particularly suitable, especially in the case of two types of performance: (1) for those which proceed from the individual situation or scene and assemble the various individual scenes next to one another according to a supraordinated overriding principle—such as that of contrast, and (2) those in which precisely the logic of the sequence of the plot is emphasized by a sequence that highlights the coherence between the scenes. For, no matter how different the structural principles of the two performance types may be, even if diametrically opposed, they nevertheless converge in the particular status which they assign the situation or scene as a unit of action or presentation.[22]

Like the syntagma-forming method, the third method of constructing the level of isotopes is related to quantities which already exist in drama theory. In this instance segments are formed which are bound neither to the sequence of the performance nor to the realization of a specific sign system, but rather are constituted intratextually. Here, the character could be selected and defined as an isotope—a category, in other words, which has dominated discussion in the field of drama theory since the "Storm and Stress" period.[23] If it is to qualify and function as an isotope, all individual signs and classemes which contribute to its constitution have to be examined with regard to the meanings that can be ascribed to them in relation to the figure in question or, conversely, which meaning they receive sub specie dramatis personae X.

If the character is selected as an isotope, then the problem arises for the first time as to how the classemes/individual signs constituting it are to be ascertained. In the first method the classemes that are relevant with regard to the selected isotope can be conclusively determined via recourse to all the factually realized signs of the sign system or group of sign systems in question. In the case of the syntagma-forming method, via recourse to the markings that indicate the boundaries of the respectively chosen units, consideration must be taken of all of the classemes realized between these boundaries. In the third method, however, the prerequisites for conducting this procedure are not nearly as favorable. Although it can be assumed that all signs or classemes realized by or through the actor form the level of the selected isotope, we cannot rule out the possibility that signs of other systems—props, decoration, music, sounds—will also be assigned the same function. In this case, in other words, the complete body of signs and classemes to be potentially investigated is not automatically enumerated and given by defining the level of isotopes. Rather, the process of establishing that corpus has to take place, at least in part, at the same time as the process in which the unit "character" is assigned a meaning based on the investigation of the classemes which go to form it.

The character can be chosen as the level of the isotope in the case of any performance. Unlike the two other methods, it is not dependent on certain structural features.[24] Since theater always takes place where actor A represents a character X, while spectator S looks on, this selection is already a possibility in the case of the minimal definition of theatrical processes. In other words, every analysis can begin with the segment of the character and does not have to be based on a preliminary "unscientific" reception that has already taken place and thus made prior assumptions regarding the structure of the performance and its resulting suitability for a certain method of constructing isotopes. It is thus, in a certain sense, the fundamental level of the isotope.

The preceding discussions may have created the impression that we are developing models of unit formation that are quite similar to Jansen's unit of "situation" and Hamon's "personnage." Nevertheless, it should be emphasized once again that the dimensions of "situation/scene/act" and "character" are not defined here as homogeneous smallest signifying units of the theatrical code as a system, but rather as complex levels of semantic coherence of concrete theatrical texts. In other words, they are to be understood exclusively as segments of the text and thus as units of the theatrical code at the level of speech; their theoretical status thus substantially differs from that of the factors "situation" and "personnage."

The choice of the respective isotopic level is not determined. It will depend, on the one hand, on certain presumptions regarding the structure of the performance and, on the other, on the particular objective of the analysis. If, for example, one wishes to ascertain or verify the specific capacity or innovative power of individual sign systems involved,[25] one will surely choose the first approach. If, however, the structure or the category of the action is the focus of interest, one will opt for the second approach. Yet again, if the investigation is aimed at the characterization of types, at psychological processes or processes of interaction, the category of the dramatis persona will be preferable as the level of isotopes.[26]

Moreover, it should not be forgotten that there is no compelling reason to adhere to the same isotope level, once chosen, for the entire course of the analysis. There may very well be good reasons for switching from the character, for example, to the situation/scene/act or to individual sign systems, and vice versa. In such a case, however, it is imperative that the reasons for such a switch of isotope level and the objectives of such a procedure be made understandable and plausible.[27]

The fourth level of semantic coherence consists, finally, of the "totality of overall meaning" of the entire theatrical text. It is formed by the totality of the isotopes and is thus to be constituted above all through recourse to the level of the isotopes. In other words, the particular relationships that obtain between the segments chosen as isotopes have to be examined in each case—the relationships, in other words, between the various sign systems and the groups of signs involved, between the successive scenes or acts, between the individual dramatis personae of the performance. Based on this nexus of relations, the meaning of the corresponding units as constituted through recourse to the classemes can, on the one hand, be confirmed or corrected and, on the other, will constitute the overall meaning of the performance in the same process.

Understandably, the level of isotopes in a certain sense occupies a special place in the hierarchy of the different levels of semantic coherence. For the levels of lower semantic coherence which constitute it, as well as the level of higher semantic coherence which it constitutes, all hinge on it as a kind of axis or pivot. Thus, the classemes refer to one another depending on their relation to this pivot and are accordingly ascribed a meaning. The same is true of the individual theatrical signs of which the classemes are composed, whereas the overall meaning of the text is based on the foundation of the complex of relationships formed by their units.

Although the segments chosen at the level of the isotopes are—like the segments of the other levels—only given a meaning on the basis of the particular reciprocal effect between the levels of varying semantic coherence, this level nevertheless occupies a special place. This is the case because all analytical operations are related to that isotopic level as their central axis. The choice of the isotopic level is thus particularly relevant, not only with regard to the procedure of segmentation, but also with regard to the overall analytic process.[28]

Selection and Combination

The investigation of the singular selection and combination of theatrical signs that constitute a performance in its individuality and mark it off from all others has, above all, to consider two important premises. It must (1) take recourse to the possibilities offered by the theatrical code as a system and as a norm and (2) be conducted in each case in relation to one specific level of semantic coherence.

Whereas the first premise refers in particular to the investigation of selection—since a selection can only be made from the possibilities afforded by the system or the norm—the second tends to obtain rather more for the examination of combination. For the combinations are made on each level of semantic coherence as a combination of respectively different elements: as a combination of individual, heterogeneous signs at the classematic level; as a combination of classemes at the isotopic level; as a combination of isotopes at the level of the text as a whole. Consequently, every investigation should take this difference into account.

We have defined *selection* as an element bearing meaning in three respects: (1) as the choice of sign systems to be used, (2) as the choice of the sign type to be realized within the individual sign systems employed, and (3) as the choice of all those special signs factually realized. A threefold exclusive definition, which may itself also function as a signifier, corresponds to this threefold positive selection.

Thus, the analysis must first examine which of the fourteen generally possible sign systems have actually been employed as systems generating meaning. If one or several of the systems that can potentially be used have been left aside, then it is necessary to determine why this has occurred or the function it is intended to serve. If the norm prescribes that this system should not be used—such as the species norm of pantomime with respect to the linguistic signs—or if a system is assigned a low priority because of a particular performance situation—such as dispensing with lighting at an afternoon performance or a matinee in an outdoor theater—then the absence of the system in question naturally has no relevance to the overall meaning of the theatrical text.

In all other cases, on the other hand, the specific choice in each case is indeed an element bearing meaning. In this respect, essentially three possibilities come into question: (1) the norm calls for the use of a particular sign system, yet the latter is not used; (2) the norm demands that it not be used, but the norm is not observed; (3) the norm allows for the use of the sign system in question, and the system is indeed employed.[29] Thus, we can only assess whether the function of the respective selection is significant or insignificant by referring back to the underlying norm. If it cannot be assumed that a corresponding norm applies, every selection as well as every nonuse has, in principle, to be regarded as an element bearing meaning.

Second, the selection has to be examined as the selection of the sign type to be realized within the individual sign system employed. If this procedure is applied with regard to the kinesic signs, for example, it is necessary to examine whether they are realized on the basis of a code that regulates the generation of kinesic signs in the surrounding culture in a comparable manner and is therefore perceived for the most part as "natural." Alternatively, they may be attributable to a code which has to be regarded as artificial—in whatever respect. One must, for example, assess whether the costumes are in keeping with reality, i.e., accord with the standards of historical, cultural, social, occupational, etc., givens. They may, however, have been designed according to some other criteria—as in the case of characteristic or fantasy costumes. With regard to set decorations, it would be necessary to ascertain whether they are given two-dimensional or three-dimensional forms and have been, on the one hand, constructed in detail, or on the other, designed on the whole according to a realistic or abstract model, to mention but two. In this respect, every sign system has to be examined separately in order to determine whether the signs in the various systems are realized on the basis of the same or a similar principle or whether differences arise which, in turn, themselves must be understood as elements bearing meaning and thus interpreted accordingly.

Once the respective underlying type has been ascertained, we can proceed to investigate its relation to the applicable norm. For if the norm itself prescribes the choice of the type factually realized, then the actual realization has to be considered irrelevant in terms of meaning. In this case, in other words, the rule again applies that only a deviation from the norm—even the most minor one—can be understood to be significant.[30] If a norm cannot be supposed to be given or if the underlying norm does not contain any rules applying to the sign type to be realized, then every selection must in principle be regarded as an element bearing meaning. For then all of the sign types—which is to say, all possible sign types—contained in the system have to be regarded as the repertoire from which the selection is made.[31]

Third, and finally, the selection has to be examined as a selection of all signs realized de facto in the performance. In this procedure the respective specificity as well as the meaning of its selection has to be ascertained for each sign—at least in theoretical terms. In other words, in each case the question has to be raised as to which sign was chosen and for what reasons and/or for what purpose and in order to serve what function precisely this one sign was chosen. In all probability, even the most ambitious analysis will not be in a position to be so thorough and complete that it can answer this question with regard to every individual sign realized in a performance. Unlike the investigation of the selections made in the first and second stages, which can definitely be conducted in extenso, the examination of choices regarding the individual signs selected has itself to proceed selectively. It will always only be able to relate to a limited corpus of such individual signs.

We thus find ourselves confronted with the problem of which criteria should govern how we go about compiling such a corpus. According to what we have said thus far about the performance as an aesthetic text, it has to be assumed that all individual signs are relevant because none of them are redundant.

If we are unable to examine all of the signs relevant for the text as a whole, then logically we must limit our field of investigation to smaller areas. In such a case we only need to consider those signs which can be deemed relevant in relation to this area. Such a limitation could, for example, be undertaken with a view to differentiating in levels of various semantic coherence. Here, for example, the investigation would apply only to all of those signs which are relevant for segment A at the classematic level—such as for the costume of character X—or for segment A at the level of isotopes—as in the case of character X. There would be some justification in assuming that the analysis of an area limited in this way would be thorough, and in all likelihood it will in fact be so. If, on the other hand, the perspective has been delimited in terms of a level which is too broad in scope— for example, to all segments at the level of isotopes (e.g., all dramatis personae)—a second selection would have to be made within this limited area, regardless of which criteria are used to do so. In such a case, therefore, it would be necessary first to solve the problem of which selection and formulation criteria are justified.

If the area is sufficiently delimited to allow an overview, then the above question can again be taken up and examined in relation to every single sign realized with it. In so doing, however, one important prerequisite must not be overlooked: the choice of an element can always only be significant if an alternative is provided for this element.[32] If no other element can take its place, its choice is, by contrast, irrelevant in terms of meaning. In order to determine whether the selection of this sign can already be posited as an element bearing meaning, an examination must be made of whether the theatrical code as a system or as a norm holds available alternatives for the sign in question. This, in turn, can only be ascertained via a substitution which can of course itself only be effected mentally as far as the theatrical text is concerned. In other words, a different element that could come into consideration owing to its occurrence and position in the repertoire of the norm or the system can be put in the place of the element actually selected: one can then test whether the meaning of the classeme to which the sign involved belongs is changed by this operation.[33] If it transpires that the investigated sign can be replaced in this way, then its selection can be regarded as a signifier and treated accordingly in the further course of analysis.

The investigation of whether the selection is significant can thus clearly be conducted with regard to the selection of the first and second stages in the form of respectively separate procedures. Yet it would seem doubtful whether this can also be regarded as worthwhile with respect to the investigation of factually realized theatrical signs. Since such an investigation can only be conducted in each case for a limited area, it is embarked on as a consequence of a decision which has already been made with regard to preferred levels or objectives of the analysis. Consequently, it will be possible both to incorporate it into different analytic contexts to be derived in each case from these objectives and accordingly to carry out such an inquiry in changing contexts.

With regard to *sign combinations*, the general rule applies that in principle every sign of a sign system can be combined with every other sign in the same sign system or any other sign system, both simultaneously or successively. It is consequently necessary—if the respectively realized combinations are to be verified as possible signifiers—to examine the relations which obtain (a) on the classematic level between the individual theatrical signs, (b) on the level of the isotopes between the different classemes, and (c) on the level of the text as a whole between the segments chosen as isotopes.

In other words, the complex of possible relations must be constructed separately for each level of semantic coherence, yet the principles underlying the production of such relations on the individual levels can obviously be identical. In principle, only two kinds of relations can be distinguished: those of (1) equivalency and (2) opposition; all conceivable relations can thus be described either as an equivalence or as an opposition. At the same time, however, it should be noted here at the outset that substantial differences may exist between the respective features and aspects with reference to which equivalency or opposition is found to obtain.

We speak in terms of equivalency if two units ascertained on the same level of semantic coherence can be substituted for one another with regard to at least one feature. However, a further condition must also hold, namely that this common feature be given a specific function by the text, which at the same time neutralizes the divergent features.[34] Equivalency exists, for example, if two persons appear who have different hair colors and hairstyles, but their hair is in any case dyed, and the feature of tinted hair then has a function. The same is true if two completely different persons are wearing similar or identical costumes or commit the same action and the feature of similarity or identicalness of the costumes/actions appears significant. Alternatively, two different kinds of set decorations, e.g., interior and exterior decorations, both exhibit /door/ as an element and precisely this feature is given a particular function. Indeed, two different scenes may take place in the same setting and the text may point to this being significant, etc. In other words, identity cannot generally be equated with equivalency; rather, it is only a special or borderline case of equivalency.[35]

We shall refer to two equivalent units (i.e., elements that are situated on the same level of semantic coherence) as oppositive if they are mutually exclusive with regard to at least one feature. Again, the opposition only exists if the oppositive feature is assigned a function by the text and all correlating features are neutralized by it. In the case of equivalency we differentiate only quite generally between differing degrees of correspondence ranging all the way to the highest degree possible, namely two features that are identical. By contrast, oppositions can in principle be divided into three classes or types of opposition: in (a) privative, (b) gradual, and (c) equipollent oppositions.[36]

In the case of privative opposition, the two units in question are different from one another in that the one highlights the relevant feature and the other does not. We can speak in terms of such privative opposition, for example, if person A changes her external appearance by wearing a wig in situation X, and yet does not in situation Y, and wearing or not wearing it both appear significant. Alternatively, one and the same set decoration contains a particular element a in scene

X—a cabinet, for example—but does not in scene Y, and again the fact of including the cabinet as well as that of not including it in the set decoration both have functions. Yet again, if a person displays a feature—a crown, for example—which places him in opposition to all other persons because no other person is wearing it, and this contrast is in turn given meaning, etc.

We have to do with a gradual opposition if the feature justifying the opposition is differentiated by degrees. In linguistic semantics the series of descriptions for degrees of warmth—ice-cold, cold, cool, lukewarm, warm, hot—is a popular example cited to describe this type of opposition. In theater we are dealing with a gradual opposition if, for example, the degree of brightness of the lighting changes between situations v, w, x, y, z and these gradual differences as well as the fact of the changes from one to the other all have a specific function (perhaps because every degree of brightness corresponds to a particular time of day). The characters may, for example, differ on the basis of their social standing, and these differences lend themselves to the formation of a rising/falling series of social status signified by different complex classemes, such as beggar, farmer, burgher, nobleman, king, which in turn appear significant. Alternatively, the volume of the sounds in situations X and Y differs by degree and this difference is semanticized (because it may indicate the proximity or distance from the object signified by the sound). Numerous other examples could be cited.

In the case of equipollent opposition, the relevant feature is realized in a different way in each of the units compared, but all realizations have to be regarded as being of equal ranking or value and are mutually exclusive. Thus, for example, with regard to the reactions of different dramatis personae, we can speak in terms of an equipollent opposition if a message delivered to A provokes an outburst of rage, whereas B steps to the window with a sad expression on his face and looks out, which actions lead to an amused smirk by C, whereas D and E go on talking about a completely different subject, as if nothing had happened, and the fact of the differing reactions is, for its part, given meaning. Alternatively, and with regard to the sequence of set decorations, equipollence obtains if every scene plays in a different surrounding, which is why every individual scene stands in opposition to all others, and this peculiarity is highlighted as significant in the course of the performance. With regard to an individual sign, such as head covering, the same is true if in one scene A is wearing a straw hat, B a hunter's cap, C a felt hat, and E a beret, and this difference is given a function based on the context.

Thus, to the extent that a relation of equivalence or of opposition exists between two or more units, it always applies only with regard to one or more specific features. These features can, in turn, be grouped in classes, the most important being (1) type and/or appearance (similarity), (2) extension, (3) position, (4) distribution, and (5) frequency. Equivalence and opposition can thus exist (1) with regard to the type or appearance of the units investigated. This feature refers to possible correspondences and differences in the materiality of the segments which can be perceived by the observer and are created in a specific way. Thus, individual signs—such as a gesture, a prop, an element of costume or decoration, a sound, etc., not to mention different classemes (such as behavioral sequences, costumes, decorations, tone sequences, etc.) or the various isotopes (such as characters, scenes, sign systems) can be similar or dissimilar. They can correspond to one another in the specific form they take or they can mutually exclude one another. Now, similarity is a feature which quite obviously—above all when equivalence is involved—is especially easy for the observer to recognize. A one-time repetition or varied repetition of a tone of voice or of a gesture may escape even the most astute observer when it first occurs; props, costumes or parts of costumes, decorations or elements of decoration, or musical passages that are similar to one another are by contrast so noticeable to the eye and ear that they are noticed ad hoc, so to speak. Therefore, equivalencies and oppositions with regard to the feature of appearance (similarity/resemblance) are particularly relevant in the reception process.[37]

The units of the same level of semantic coherence can be equivalent or oppositive with reference to the feature of extension (2). Individual signs, classemes, or isotopes must therefore be studied in order to assess whether they are of the same or of different sizes, volumes, durations, dimensions, etc. Thus, for example, the fact that two parts of the set decoration—two chairs—are not the same size may be significant, as may be the fact that two elements of costume—two hats—are the same size. This holds true in a variety of contexts: the volume of a sound—the ringing of a trolley-car—may stay the same in the course of the performance, the speech of person A may be slow and quiet, whereas that of person B is loud and abrupt; a behavioral sequence a carried out by A lasts a shorter period of time than the presence of the costume a worn by A; A and B in scene X may be on stage for the same length of time, but A is there longer than B in scene Y. The individual scenes may be of the same or different durations, and minimal or even no decoration whatsoever is juxtaposed to richly designed costumes. There are numerous other examples of instances where extension may be significant.

Equivalence and opposition can exist with reference to the position of the units (3). With regard to the theatrical text, it can be concluded that the position of an element both in space and in time can function as significant. That is, the temporal sequence of the performance, in its relationship to the corresponding position of another element of the same level of semantic coherence, can have a specific meaning. Thus, we must scrutinize the relevant units with regard to (a) at which point in the temporal sequence of the performance they appear and (b) in which spatial point or segment they are placed in which manner. It goes without saying that in the first instance the places which stand out in any way such as beginning, end, climax, before or after the entrance of A, or before or after event X are particularly relevant, whereas in the second we have to do with whether they face or turn away from one another, have their back to the audience or face the audience, to mention but two possibilities. Both investigative procedures can naturally be linked with one another. For example, if at the beginning of scene X person A is standing front-stage right with his back turned to B, who is downstage left, and at the end of the scene is also standing downstage left, with his face turned to B, then this can clearly be interpreted as an element bearing meaning. Every change in position of every unit, no matter on what level of semantic coherence, in this sense has to be regarded as a signifier. At the same time, differing changes in position can be equivalent or oppositive to one another—change of person A from position α1 to position α2, change of person B from position β1 to position β2, etc.—or their remaining in one position—A in position α1, B in position α2. On the other hand, change in position and remaining in the same position can enter into opposition with one another: A remaining in α1 versus B changing from β1 to β2, or A remaining in α1 in situation X versus A changing from α1 into α2 in situation Y, etc. Oppositions and equivalences with regard to the feature of position can in this way be highly relevant, particularly in the theatrical text, and should therefore always be investigated with the greatest of care.

As mentioned, distribution is the fourth feature with regard to which units may be equivalent or oppositive to one another. Like that of position, this feature also applies to space and time. In other words, it applies on the one hand to the presence of an element at various points in the temporal course of the performance, and on the other, to the simultaneous spatial arrangement of several elements. In the first case, two or more units are examined to determine at which places in the course of the performance they are present on the stage—whether, for example, A and B always appear on stage simultaneously or whether B appears only when A does not, or whether A and B are both present in scenes 1, 7, and 9, but A is alone in scenes 2, 3, and 6 as is B in scenes 4, 5, and 8, etc. In the second case, by contrast, the focus must be on the spatial arrangement of the elements at different points in time during the performance. Every change in position of a single element places the entire arrangement in opposition to the arrangement which existed prior to the change in position. In this regard, however, not only should the constellations of the elements which immediately follow upon one another be examined in each case, but so should the relationships between the distribution of elements which lie far apart from one another, such as the arrangement of elements in space at the beginning and end of a sequence, of a scene, of an act, or even of the whole performance, to cite an extreme case. The temporal distribution of the various spatial distributions can, moreover, also be significant in that individual spatial distributions at specific places are repeated either completely or with a characteristic variant, whereas others do not occur at all or only at one point. As one can readily see from these brief explanations, position and distribution are closely related to one another, but for methodological reasons they should be strictly differentiated in the analysis.[38]

Equivalence and opposition can exist with regard to the frequency of the units (5). For the individual elements of all levels of semantic coherence can be employed either with the same or approximately the same frequency or with differing frequencies. In a study of a unit with regard to its distribution, attention is focused precisely on the specific places or points at which it is present in the temporal sequence or in space. However, we must limit that focus when examining its frequency to the statistical frequency with which it occurs in a temporal sequence or in space, and disregard the respective point in time or location at which it is realized completely. If the spatial frequency of a unit is at issue, the number of versions in which it appears on stage must be ascertained (e.g., two pictures, one chair, three persons, etc.). If, on the other hand, frequency in the temporal sequence of the performance is the subject of scrutiny, then one must determine how often it appears on the stage (e.g., one cry, seven walks across the stage, fifteen appearances on stage, etc.).

Of the different classes of features, the above five classes of features are the most important with reference to the existence of equivalency or opposition between two or more units. As explained above, although they have to be analyzed separately, the specific correlation between two or more of these sets of features can also be significant. Thus, for example, a difference can definitely be considered relevant if two units are equivalent or oppositive with regard to one, two, or even more features. This is also true if there are unequivocal correlations between two features such as frequency and extension, or similarity and position—in other words, if high frequency correlates with broad extension, low frequency with minimal extension, similarity with corresponding or, instead, contrary positions. Yet it may also be significant if it is not possible to verify a relationship of this type.

In order, for example, to assess whether a sign system is dominant, it is advisable to determine whether extension, distribution, and frequency correlate with one another. Should it transpire that this sign system is superior to all other sign systems in terms of its extension, the distribution in particularly highlighted places, and frequency of application, and thus stands in opposition to all of them, then it can be assumed that this system dominates the others. The meanings of its signs would in this case have a higher relevance than the signs of the other sign systems. As a general rule we can say that a clear-cut correlation between two or more of these features will always be significant.[39]

Equivalencies and oppositions among units are established in the text with the help of specific operations. If one wishes to examine the text for equivalencies and oppositions, it is thus logical to conduct the same operations, albeit in the opposite direction: addition, subtraction, permutation, and substitution.[40]

In the case of addition and subtraction, equivalency and opposition are produced by adding or taking away something from one of the elements in question. If, for example, one of the persons is given a crown, then she enters into opposition to all others by virtue of this attribute. If she is then deprived of it, a relationship of equivalency again arises between her and the others with regard to this attribute. Addition and subtraction are procedures that are used with particular frequency especially with regard to the features of extension, frequency, and—albeit in somewhat more restricted measure—appearance. The addition or omission of a gesture, a part of the costume or decoration, a prop, or a spotlight, can induce similarity or difference in a behavioral sequence, the costume, the external appearance, the room, the atmosphere. It can change the extension of a behavioral sequence, a costume, the decoration, or the brightness and, moreover, may reduce or increase the frequency of this gesture, of this part of the costume or of the decoration, of this prop. It would thus appear expedient with regard to pinpointing equivalencies and oppositions in terms of the features of appearance, extension, and frequency, to undertake the operation of addition or subtraction for the units concerned. This will then reveal whether the units examined are to be defined as equivalent or oppositive with regard to the feature in question.

Permutation and substitution, by contrast, are related to the features of distribution and position. If one wishes to clarify the question whether two or more units are equivalent or oppositive with regard to their position, a substitution has to be performed. If the units in question can be substituted for one another with regard to their position, then they are equivalent with regard to their position. However, should such a substitution prove to be impossible, an opposition with regard to position is clearly indicated.

Finally, with the help of permutation one can determine whether two or more units are equivalent or oppositive with regard to their distribution: a successful permutation indicates the presence of an equivalency, whereas unsuccessful permutation points to one of opposition.

The individual procedures are thus related in each case to one or more specific features. They can therefore only be used meaningfully in order to ascertain the presence of equivalencies or oppositions if they are deployed exclusively in connection with the feature(s) to which they must be assigned. An exception in this case is the feature of similarity. Even if equivalencies and oppositions in connection with similarity frequently, indeed perhaps in most cases, have to be determined through addition and subtraction, in some cases it is easier to reach this goal via substitution. It appears to be more suitable above all if similarity/dissimilarity does not arise from a plus or minus, but rather—as, for example, in all equipollent oppositions—from principally equivalent differences and homologies. This exceptional rule underscores the particular relevance of the feature of appearance (similarity), something which we have already stressed above.

The totality of elements selected, on the one hand, and of the equivalencies and oppositions between them, on the other, provides the basis for the specific structure of the theatrical text. It is on the basis of this alone that the meanings of its elements at the different levels of semantic coherence as well as its sense can be constituted.

Internal and External Recoding

If meaning in the text is created via internal or external recoding, then the receiver can assign a meaning to a textual element by relating it either to a different textual element or to an extratextual structural chain. However, this is possible only under one general precondition: the receiver must at least have a minimum competence with regard to the theatrical code as a system and as a norm. If he does not know the syntactical, semantic, and pragmatic rules that are followed in creating meaning at the systemic level or that of the relevant norm, he will not be able to constitute the meanings of individual elements of the text. Knowledge of the underlying semiotic system is thus the conditio sine qua non of every ascription of meaning, of every overall meaning assigned to the text.[41]

We have made various references to the fact that today we do not need to adhere to stable, generally valid theatrical norms. It is therefore not possible to rely on fixed, more or less lexical attributions of meaning in which the possible meanings of a textual element are delineated and set by the norm. Nevertheless, it is certainly possible to draw up a few general rules for a large number of performances which, in this sense, can be related to a common norm underlying all of them; these rules are followed in the creation of meaning in the individual performance.

One rule of this type has already been mentioned, namely, the specific use of costumes, props, and decorations that are not employed as signs showing that a dramatis persona belongs to a certain period, country, or social class, but in order to characterize them.[42] In this case, in other words, the norm calls for recourse to specific cultural knowledge and thus a particular form of external recoding.

The opposite rule applies to performances in boulevard theater. Here costumes, props, and decorations as well as mimicry and gestures are used and interpreted in accordance with the conventions of realistic theater. Thus, the audience knows that it can rely on its knowledge of the primary cultural system of its culture when attributing meanings.[43]

Contemporary avant-garde theater, by contrast, follows a general rule which prescribes the semanticization of previously insignificant elements, on the one hand, and the desemanticization of heavily conventionalized signs, on the other. This rule presupposes a specific reciprocal relationship between methods of internal and external recoding.[44]

If the receiver wants to assign a meaning to the individual elements of a performance, he can thus conduct the internal and external recodings only via recourse to the general rule for the generation of meaning adhered to by the performance. It goes without saying that this is a rather trivial maxim, but it should nevertheless be put in explicit terms to avoid possible misunderstandings.

Internal recoding is a method of attributing meaning that proceeds from the specific relations between the elements of the text at the various levels of semantic coherence. Owing to the particular equivalencies and oppositions into which an element enters with regard to certain features, a meaning can be assigned to it that goes further than that ascribable to it if the generally valid normative rule for generating meaning is obeyed. We shall demonstrate briefly how this ensues, taking the example of Augusto Fernandes's staging of Pirandello's *Henry IV* in Frankfurt in 1978.[45]

In the case of *Henry IV* the general rule says that costumes, props, and decorations denote those pieces of clothing and objects which they represent: a glove is thus initially to be understood as a glove, a crown as a crown, spectacles as spectacles, a candelabra as a candelabra, and so on. In act 2, following the words "Do you truly love your daughter?" Henry, on bended knee, takes off his glove in front of Donna Mathilda, who appears as Henry's stepmother Adelheid. Then, with his right hand bared, he takes Donna Mathilda's glove off the left hand, brings it to his lips and kisses it. Since at this point the glove has been introduced merely as a glove and the hand, accordingly, as a hand, Henry's action can be interpreted as a sign of courtly etiquette, of submissiveness. A few minutes later, however, the hand and glove are assigned a different meaning, and as of that point, Henry's action is to be understood in a different way as well.

At a distance from the other dramatis personae and on bended knee, Henry removes his second glove with the words "In bed . . . me out of my costume" and puts it on the floor. A relationship of equivalence is thus established between the words "my costume" and the glove. Henry continues: "she, out of hers . . . yes, my God, naked . . . a man and a woman . . . , it's only natural. We don't bother about who we are anymore, with our clothes abandoned on their hangers" (p. 46). With these words Henry places his two bare hands before him on the ground, looks at the right hand when speaking the words "a man" and at the left hand on saying the words "a woman," and bends forward over them. In this way an equivalence is created between "man and woman naked in bed" and the two bare hands next to each other on the ground, whereas an opposition is established between glove and hand that is equivalent to the opposition between clothing and naked person.[46]

This internal recoding lends hand and glove a specific meaning which recodes the previous action as well as the subsequent action with the glove: when Henry takes off his glove, he wants to imagine Donna Mathilda as a "naked" person, i.e., completely without costume or mask. This is how this action can be reinterpreted based on the now valid premises, and by removing her glove, he is demanding the same of her. At the same time, however, he maintains a certain distance from her; for he only kisses the glove, the costume that has been removed, which is dear to him, but not her hand, not the person herself, who has remained foreign to him. In this way, Henry's action is given additional meaning after the fact via the later recoding.

The meaning introduced in this way for the glove as the dress or costume of the relevant person functions in the subsequent course of the performance as the source meaning on which further recodings are based. Henry continues with the words "on their hangers like dreams!" (p. 46) and in so doing produces Donna Mathilda's glove, holds it up to his extended arm, touching it only with his thumb and index finger, far away, and allows it to dangle. The glove is now given the additional meaning of "dream" owing to the equivalence established in this way. Since in the following words dreams are defined as "little stirrings of the soul, fantasies which can't be kept within the realm of sleep" (pp. 149–50) and "they scare us," (pp. 149–50) this also holds true for the glove, and it would appear under these circumstances to be the image which Henry has made for himself of Donna Mathilda, his image of her which scares him. When he then bobs his arm up and down and resolutely lets it go limp, he consciously and deliberately gives this idea up and forgoes any further relationship with Donna Mathilda, since such a relationship could only exist between "dreams," and not between people. Henry ends his monologue by pulling a dagger out from under his haircloth shirt, spikes the glove on it and stabs it to the floor. He pierces the image that he has of Donna Mathilda, thus destroying his image of her, and in so doing, as far as he is concerned frees himself from his past.[47]

By means of a series of such internal recodings, the element "glove" acquires a complex of meanings with regard to the relationship between Henry and Donna Mathilda—meanings which go far beyond the meaning of glove as originally constituted on the basis of the applicable norm.

All of these meanings must now be constituted through recourse to the equivalent and oppositive relations in which the text puts the element "glove." It follows from this that the general rule that the receiver must apply when effecting internal recodings consists of first finding or constituting the different relations that the element in question is capable of entering into with other elements that are either simultaneously, previously, or subsequently present. For if the relevant element is to be ascribed a meaning, then it is only possible to deduce the other textual element(s) to which the relevant element can be related from the specific order of these relations. The syntagmatic meanings can thus be defined as those meanings which are to be constituted in the knowledge of the underlying semiotic system *only* on the basis of the particular relations that obtain between the textual elements of the different levels of semantic coherence. Thus, the identification and/or construction of equivalencies and oppositions in the theatrical text are an absolute prerequisite for internal recoding.

External recoding, by contrast, is based in each case on the premise of a specific cultural knowledge. For a textual element can clearly be related to one or more element(s) of an extratextual structural chain only if the relevant structural chain is known to the receiver, i.e., is part of the stock of his or her cultural knowledge. In the case of theatrical texts, as opposed to other texts, no historical distance can be established between the producers and the receivers because the theatrical text exists only in the audience's presence. To the extent that both producers and receivers are members of the same culture, they will, like all members of that culture, share the cultural background of this culture. Appropriate external recoding is guaranteed if the extratextual structural chain to which an element of text must first be related in order to acquire meaning is part of that knowledge of the culture. Every member of the culture will thus be able to relate the textual element to the relevant extratextual structural chain. Cultural knowledge, which can surely be presumed to exist on the part of all members of our culture, includes, for example, the knowledge that human beings have been on the moon, that Christ's birth is celebrated on Christmas, that the Nazis killed millions of Jews, that Goethe was the greatest German poet, that the majority of Africans are black, or for that matter that we live in a democracy. Aside from such special knowledge, of course, such stocks of knowledge include all forms of cultural stereotypes such as the image of a king wearing a crown; an Indian with a feather headdress; and the stereotypes of the stiff Englishman, the thrifty Scotsman, the proud Spaniard, etc. All textual elements which allude to such common cultural stocks can thus be assigned the appropriate meaning ad hoc by each of the observers who are members of this culture if the stocks to which they have to be related in order to take on a meaning can be taken for granted, are generally prevalent stereotypes, are generally accepted, and consist of shared ideas, opinions, and convictions.

The cultural knowledge necessary for external recoding to occur may, however, also exist only in the form of the special knowledge of a particular group of varying size. Whereas a knowledge of the Christian tradition, for example, could still be regarded as generally widespread cultural knowledge at the turn of the century, today it already has to be regarded as special knowledge shared by a relatively large group of members in our culture, but no longer something that by any means exists generally. If elements of a performance thus refer to portions of this knowledge, then we cannot assume that all members of the audience will be in a position to attribute a meaning to these parts, unless, that is, the audience is homogeneous in this particular respect. This is all the more true with regard to all those elements which have to be related to extratextual structural chains which, as part of a very special cultural knowledge, can only be known to a very small circle of spectators. Examples would be particular historical events, a knowledge of physics or little known literature, and images or pictures hardly available to the general public, etc. However, since a person in the audience cannot interrupt the performance in order to obtain the special knowledge that is necessary for an understanding of individual elements, the reception of the meanings and sense attributed in such a case is seriously jeopardized if appropriate syntagmatic elements cannot be constituted for the respective elements, that is, in addition to the necessary paradigmatic meanings. Falling back on special cultural knowledge, on the other hand, does not pose a problem if it can be assumed from the composition of the audience that the spectators for the most part have the requisite knowledge with which to attribute meanings to the elements in question.

If, however, the relation between the textual element and an element of an extratextual structural chain can only be created on the basis of the producer's special knowledge or entirely individual experience, then no member of the audience will be able to find the meaning that has to be constituted. Textual elements which stem from a producer's personal opinions, value judgements, problems and obsessions, or some form of personal mythology can thus only be employed as signifiers on the condition that their meaning does not have to be constituted by means of external recoding, but is instead introduced and developed via internal recodings.[48] External recodings can only be performed if at least one group is familiar with the respective reference to the extratextual structural chain in question. Naturally, the external recodings also presuppose that the audience has a competent knowledge of the underlying semiotic system. If, for example, the recourse to conventions of realist theater applies as the general rule for generating meaning, then historical costumes consequently function as signs for the period, social class, profession, etc. of the dramatis personae involved. Their interpretation thus rests on the spectator's having a knowledge of the class- and occupation-specific mode of dress in that period. If, on the other hand, it is assumed that the rule is for historical costumes—including those of various periods—to be used to characterize the dramatis personae, recourse must be had not only to knowledge of period dress in order to interpret them. Rather, there must be a more extensive knowledge of the period in question—for example, of the views prevalent in that period regarding the type of person, views actualized with regard to the dramatis personae. If, for example, in a production of *A Midsummer Night's Dream*,[49] Hermia, Helena, Lysander, and Demetrius appear in the button-up shoe style, which was popular among the youth at the turn of the century, then the audience has to have a certain amount of knowledge of the young people of this period and the social norms that applied to them. If the audience wishes to interpret the stocks as signs for the dramatis personae, in other words, it must be acquainted with the historical, social, and literary context evoked by these costumes. The general rule thus accordingly delimits the set of possible extratextual structural chains to which a textual element can generally be related.

A further restriction is imposed by the syntagmatic meanings. For the paradigmatic and syntagmatic meanings are not constituted independently of one another, as the processes involve close reciprocity. A modification of meaning can thus take place in two directions: the paradigmatic meanings can be changed through subsequent internal recodings and, conversely, the syntagmatic meanings can be changed through external recodings performed afterward.

Thus, in the above-described glove sequence, for example, the introduction of the dagger gives rise to further possible meanings that were not covered by previous internal recodings. As a weapon, the dagger can refer to a historical structural chain—military conflict—to which at other places in the text other textual elements—especially verbal sequences—can also refer.[50] With regard to this structural chain, Donna Mathilda's glove, which Henry allows to drop, can also be interpreted as a gauntlet which he throws down at Donna Mathilda's feet, and the spiking of the glove would then be the waging and victorious end of the duel.

Since the corresponding verbal sequences thematize love relationships,[51] the dagger and glove can, however, equally be related to a corresponding psychoanalytical structural chain: the dagger then has to be attributed the meaning of a phallic symbol and the glove that of a sexual fetish. The spiking of the glove could, under these presuppositions, be interpreted as the symbolic consummation of sexual intercourse between Henry and Donna Mathilda.

These two structural chains can naturally also, in turn, be related to one another, and/or the spiking of the glove can be related to both at the same time. Seen thus, Henry's action can then be interpreted as the expression of his ambivalent, aggressive as well as libidinous, relationship to Donna Mathilda, as the sign for his love-hate relationship with her.

These paradigmatic meanings are substantive aspects that supplement the syntagmatic meanings, yet do not contradict them. This brings us to an important general condition which functions as a determining factor in the relationship between syntagmatic and paradigmatic meanings: If textual element a has meaning y, this being constituted via external recoding, and this contradicts meaning x constituted via internal recoding, then y cannot be applied to a. If, on the other hand, y contains propositions which are either contained in x or go beyond x or stand in a recognizable relationship to the propositions contained in x without, however, contradicting them, then y, in addition to x, can also be assumed as a possible meaning for a. The initially constituted syntagmatic meanings thus delimit in a specific way the quantity of paradigmatic meanings which could possibly be constituted for the element of text in question.

If an external recoding is first undertaken, then a modification of the paradigmatic meanings of the textual element can be effected through subsequent internal recodings. If in Neuenfels's production of Goethe's *Iphigenie*[52] a glass case in which a human-like figure is reclining can be seen at the front of the stage at the very beginning of the performance, then this element can be related ad hoc to glass shrines containing relics, on the one hand, and to Snow White in a glass coffin, on the other.[53] Later in the course of the performance, this glass case is addressed as "Diana's image," thus clearly eliminating the second possibility. Now that the equivalence between the glass case and the image of Diana has been established, the apparent opposition between the two textual elements attributable to the two different cultural contexts from which they are respectively taken ceases to have a function: the shrine containing relics is a cult object in Christian religion, whereas Diana's image is a cult object in ancient Greek religion. The performance therefore creates an equivalent relationship between the two as cult objects. Thus, "cult object" is the only possible meaning that remains from among the originally possible paradigmatic meanings.

This meaning now undergoes additional modification via further internal recodings. I would like to cite only two examples: a bull skull buried in the sand next to the glass shrine is placed in opposition to this cult object, whereby the latter is revered by Iphigenia and officially by the Scythians as well. The half-naked Thoas digs the skull out of the sand with his hands, puts it on a waist-high pedestal and fervently worships it, murmuring unintelligibly. In contrast to the literary text of the drama, which calls for a cult object that is common to Greeks and Scythians, in the theatrical text of the performance, an opposition is introduced between this cult object and a second cult object also introduced into the scene. This opposition categorizes the bull's skull as a magical way of dealing with the gods and the glass shrine is allocated to a rational-argumentative dialogue with them. The bull's skull and glass case thus function as the sign and embodiment of two cultural life-forms which are different in specific ways.[54]

When Iphigenia later wraps the glass case in brown paper and ties it up like a parcel on which she writes the destination "Delphi," the meaning it has hitherto had is again modified in a decisive way. For Iphigenia's action now places it in opposition to cult objects of any kind, since these are commonly carried in ceremonial processions,[55] and thus equates it with a mundane object that can be handled by the post office. As a result of the internal recodings effected by Iphigenia's action, the glass case now functions as an indicator for internal processes in the dramatis personae: it signals the beginning of that process in which Iphigenia subjects the "images of the gods," her ideas about the gods (she has nurtured these unchanged since childhood) to critical examination. This sequence reaches a climax when she has the content of "the gods' image" (= the sand) run through her fingers.

The paradigmatic meanings of a textual element which were possible at the beginning of the performance are thus, on the one hand, limited by subsequent internal recodings and yet, on the other, subsequently expanded by these. The rule that applied to the relationship of syntagmatic and subsequent paradigmatic meanings also applies to the relationship between the paradigmatic and later syntagmatic meanings. Meaning y of textual element a, constituted via an external recoding, cannot be applied to a if it contradicts meaning x of the same element which has been constituted via internal recoding. The exception to the rule would be if this contradiction were itself to be suspended in a more comprehensive meaning z subsequently constituted and capable of containing x as well as y as its elements.

Every textual element, irrespective of the level of semantic coherence on which it is located, can thus be given differing syntagmatic and paradigmatic meanings in the course of the performance. In other words, more than one meaning can be attributed as a rule to one and the same element. Since these differing meanings cannot be randomly substituted for one another, but are constituted in each case on the basis of a specific combination of the textual element with other elements in a particular position in the course of the performance, the overall meaning of the relevant element can also not be described as the sum total of its different individual meanings. Rather, the overall meaning can only be elaborated in terms of an order of these individual meanings structured according to certain principles. Nor is this order complete, even after the analysis is concluded, for its elements never represent all the meanings that could in principle be constituted on the basis of all conceivable potential internal and external recodings. Rather, these meanings amount only to those which the receiver was able to attribute to the relevant element through recourse to both his personal cultural knowledge and the nexus of relations he creates on the basis of the special aspects pursued in his analysis. Every change in the nexus of relations (as a result of changed goals of the analysis) and any specific expansion in cultural knowledge can increase the number of individual meanings and make a restructuring of their order necessary. We can thus never regard the process of attributing meaning as having been exhausted or completed once and for all.[56]

On Applying the Method

Analyzing a performance means (re)constructing the order underlying it in order to assign a meaning to each of its elements and to find an overall meaning for it. The procedures we have enumerated thus far are all to be applied with this objective in mind.

However, in order for them actually to be applied as an exhaustive analytical method to a specific theatrical text, several questions still have to be clarified with regard to whether a hierarchy obtains between the individual steps and/or, if necessary, a sequence in which they should be followed. We have already seen that certain procedures presuppose one another. For example, the investigation of the combinations presumes prior segmentation, which, in turn, has to precede internal recoding, and all three have to have recourse to the underlying semiotic system. Does this interdependence compel us to proceed in a certain order?

There is no easy answer to this question. Although the investigation of the selection does indeed, for example, require recourse to the underlying semiotic system, recourse to this system can only be meaningfully had with regard to the respective elements investigated and not globally or in isolation from the question of specific elements. Furthermore, although internal recoding presupposes that a relation of equivalence or opposition has been ascertained between two or more elements concerned, it can, for its part, conversely represent the point of departure for a redefinition of the relations that obtain. By the same token, while the various levels of semantic coherence first have to be pinpointed and distinguished from one another before relations between elements of one level can be produced, these relations can, for their part, require a switch in isotopic levels and thus a revision of the original segmentation, etc. We can conclude from the particular nature of this situation that it is not possible to establish a certain sequence of individual procedures to be followed in the sense that each could only be carried out after completion of the preceding step. No step can be cited that must logically be taken first in the analysis. To summarize, every choice of a procedure has a prejudicial effect on the subsequent course of the analysis in that it necessarily influences the execution of certain others that follow it. Therefore, each of the procedures mentioned can, in principle, be chosen and carried out as the first step in an analysis. Yet, after taking this first step, a certain sequence has to be observed.

Since the first step of the analysis can thus not be prescribed, the final question to be clarified is whether the analysis has to take a specific element of the text as its point of departure.[57] On the one hand, we have accepted Lotman's principle that every element of the text has to be considered relevant. On the other, one feature of the performance is that it is structured, i.e., each of its elements bears a relation to other elements which, in turn, form a relationship with others, and so on. These two premises lead to the conclusion that it must in principle be possible to begin with any element of the text when reconstructing the order underlying that text. In other words, it is completely arbitrary which step is taken first and which element of the text is then chosen for examination.

This liberty to choose may, of course, be contingent upon the particular aspects and goals of the investigation. Since an analysis cannot per se be exhaustive in the case of a text that is as expansive as a performance, it must invariably be assumed from the outset that it will only be possible to conduct a partial analysis, which will differ in each case. It would thus seem useful to begin by outlining the objectives and aspects under which the investigation is to be conducted, and then to move on to an analysis of those textual elements which are particularly relevant in light of the objectives thus designated.[58]

This principle applies not only to the choice of the textual element with which the analysis is to begin, but also to the choice of which findings connected with the text have to be taken into account. After all, if the analysis cannot be complete, then the investigation will also never cover all the conceivable data which can in principle be gathered with regard to the text, but will only draw on a highly restricted set of data. Therefore, the date should be selected according to whether it can respectively be assumed to be relevant with a view to the investigative objectives formulated.

It is possible, of course, that two receivers will have such differing objectives in mind that the sets of data they take into account in their respective investigations hardly overlap at all. Since the (re)constructed order of the text is based in each case on diverging data, it may well be that two deviating orders have been created. The question then is whether these orders must be regarded as compatible and as necessarily complementing one another[59] because they have followed the same procedures—albeit with different sets of data—or whether it is possible in principle for them to mutually exclude one another—at least in a few points. If the latter is presumed to be true, then we must inquire further whether this is possible in the case of orders that are set up on the basis of divergent data, or whether in fact it also occurs with regard to orders that are supported by data which largely coincides. To put it succinctly, does the application of the same method and procedures, each step of which can be intersubjectively verified, also necessarily imply agreement of results?

At the end of our discussion of the hermeneutics of the theatrical text we preempted the answer to this question. There, we more or less concluded that intersubjectively verifiable and understandable procedures of assigning meaning and arriving at an overall interpretation cannot be carried out with the intention of generating a generally valid interpretation of the theatrical text. That is, finding some "correct" overall meaning which is objectively given with the order of the signs is neither possible, nor can such be the goal of an analysis. The correctness of this thesis can only be proven now that we have developed the appropriate procedures by going into the specifics of these individual analytical tools.

We assume that the (re)construction of the order underlying the theatrical text does not hinge on what the producer's intention is. Rather, we must only take relations into account which can be established between the textual elements— with or without the producer's knowledge, and in accordance with or against their will.[60] The receiver may thus, if he so wishes, relate a textual element via external recoding to an extratextual structural chain that the producer did not have in mind if the paradigmatic meaning constituted in this manner meets the above-formulated conditions. Indeed, that chain may be unknown to the producer so that we can even rule out the possibility of his having unconsciously referred to it. Since a reciprocal relationship exists between paradigmatic and syntagmatic meanings, this paradigmatic meaning can, to the extent that it opens up new possibilities of signification of the element concerned, engage with other textual elements and thus also prompt the constitution of new syntagmatic meanings. These may, in turn, permit reference to yet other extratextual structural chains, etc.

Another receiver may adopt a different paradigmatic meaning with regard to the relevant element. He may in fact choose the meaning that had been intended by the producer or by a third party, and which appeared plausible to him on the basis of his specific cultural knowledge. We cannot rule out here that the order he finally constructs may deviate so significantly from that of our first receiver that it will no longer be possible to harmonize the two.

Every single step completed by our fictitious receivers should be assumed to be verifiable and justifiable; both should have assessed the meanings constituted by them in accordance with the postulates formulated by us. Yet they nevertheless arrive at differing results, although neither of them can be shown to have made a mistake. There are in particular two reasons which account for this difference.

(1) In the further course of the analysis, in each case the relations between two or more textual elements cease to be established independently of the meanings that were previously assigned to these textual elements via internal or external recoding. Rather, each recoding may itself potentially render possible the formation of further relations that could not be produced on the basis of the meanings which existed hitherto. In its capacity as an aesthetic text, the theatrical text does not provide any clear-cut rules that prescribe to which other textual element (in the case of internal recoding) or to the element of which extratextual structural chains (in the case of recoding) the relevant element must then be related. The result is a large number of equally justifiable possibilities for such a choice. Each of two different internal or external recodings thus respectively forms the point of departure a receiver takes when constructing a specific nexus of relations.

(2) The identification of a possible relation between two or more elements of text does not at the same time predicate the potential meaning of this relation. The meaning to be accorded a relation between two elements cannot be derived from its mere existence according to some mathematical equation, as it were. The meaning that can or even should be assigned to the equivalence (or opposition) of elements A and B in relation to characteristic X by no means automatically follows from the fact that such an equivalence or opposition exists. For the meaning is not an automatic result of the functioning of a generative system; rather, an interpretative act on the part of a receiving subject is always necessary for its constitution.[61] Although attribution of meaning will be motivated by the context in which the relevant relation stands—such as other relations or meanings of elements A and B already constituted through internal or external recodings. Yet the context by no means compels selection of one particular meaning. There are always several options for selection. A constitution of meaning completed in this manner can therefore be neither right nor wrong, since it does not have to be derived compellingly from certain premises. Rather, it is only possible and thus permissible given adherence to the above-mentioned conditions or is not possible and thus inadmissible if they are violated.

In other words, we must assume that there is a wide variety of possible orders underlying the text that receivers can construe as underlying the text and furthermore that there is a wide variety of possibilities for interpreting the order once it is established. Both premises allow us to conclude that the application of a method that can be verified and understood intersubjectively—the necessity of which requires no further comment at this point—can neither guarantee nor bring about agreement on the results of the analysis.

Problems of Notation

We have made several references in passing to the fact that the analysis of performances can only be conducted as a scholarly discipline if it is possible to create a relatively adequate correlate for the material artifact of the theatrical text, for the latter is per se transitory. It must be possible both to lay this correlate down in an unchanging form and for it to stand the test of time. Theoretically, video recordings or film reproductions are suitable for this purpose, as are graphic notation systems.

The advantage of video recordings is that they are capable of reproducing the various theatrical signs in their respectively specific iconicity, albeit always only in visual extracts of the whole. For if the camera takes in the entire stage—and thus everything visible to the audience from its perspective—it is, in many cases, hard to recognize not only movements (a) carried out by a person in the shadow of another or (b) which only slightly change the position of the corresponding part of the body, but also the mimic signs. If, on the other hand, it focuses on individual persons or movements, for that matter, the simultaneous context in which the signs identified have to be placed if they are to be assigned a meaning is lost from view. Moreover, the drawback of video recordings is that the individual sections of it analyzed in the course of an investigation cannot be adduced in a written form as ad hoc, verifiable evidence as if they were written versions to which every reader could have recourse in the same manner. As a result, however, the comparability of the analysis, and consequently its verifiability, is considerably restricted. In the long term, it will prove impossible to forgo developing a procedure which allows the individual signs of the theatrical text to be transcribed into graphic signs. This is particularly true of the paralinguistic and kinesic signs, as they cannot otherwise be documented.

Such procedures have already been tried out for many centuries in dance theater—of course, only in relation to the body's movements, i.e., with regard to gestural and proxemic signs. Most attempts, however, have not gained much currency outside the innermost circles of their creators. The only method which became widespread and popular was that which Raoul Auger Feuillet advocated in the textbook he published in 1701 on dance notation,[62] but he did not develop it himself. This was the accomplishment of Pierre Beauchamps.[63] His dance notation contained an alphabet for the artistry of leg- and footwork as well as signs for the limited number of common arm and hand movements. The movements of the torso required no notation, since the body was always held exclusively upright and in line with the etiquette of grace which had been drilled into everyone who had received an aristocratic education. Beauchamps's notation system was thus completely sufficient and suitable for the rendition of dances in the courtly style of the time and in such a way that they could be reproduced by other dancers at any time.

The system commonly used for dance notation today was developed in the 1920s by Rudolf von Laban.[64] It therefore already takes into account the revolutionary innovations in dance theater, such as expressive dance or modern dance. This system is designed to cover the signs for (1) direction in space, (2) height, (3) duration of movement, and (4) part of the body executing the movement. Every written sign is designed in such a way that it can at the same time provide information about these four factors.[65] Labanotation, as it is called, is thus capable of recording all relevant aspects of movement in dance and of fixing a sequence of movement in such a way that it can be reproduced at any time on the basis of the notation.[66]

The question that concerns us at this point is whether it will be possible to devise a system of this type for dramatic theater. Labanotation—much like the system of notation developed by Bouissac for acrobats[67]—upholds the principle that a sign element must be foreseen only for those aspects of a movement which are considered relevant on the basis of consensus. In other words, not everything which can generally be observed about a movement is notated, but only that which has been determined to be relevant beforehand. Thus, such a method can also only be employed in cases where such a consensus already exists.

In the domain of contemporary dramatic theater, this condition is fulfilled only in the case of certain Far Eastern forms of theater, such as the Peking Opera or Nô theater. Since the respective norm in these cases provides only for a limited number of kinesic signs which can be applied, each of which can be precisely described and clearly distinguished from the others, it must therefore also be possible to select a graphic sign for each of these signs which is capable of representing them in written form—in other words, in a form that is legible and can be understood by anyone.

In theater in the Western world, on the other hand, we cannot assume either that there is a limited number of movements which can be performed or that certain aspects of a movement can be established as relevant. In principle, any possible movement can also be executed in theater and every conceivable aspect can thus be relevant. We therefore require a system of notation which is not, in turn, based on the premise of such a preselection.

We thus find ourselves confronted with the problem of data acquisition. For it is naïve to think that we could simply observe the movements executed by the actors on the stage without interpreting them and then subsequently invent signs for the movements thus observed. The segmentation of movement into units which could be notated as such always presumes an interpretation having occurred: it is only because a certain segment of the flow of movement appears significant to the observer that it can be perceived by him as a distinguishable unit (set off from any other).[68] The description of the flows of movement will thus initially always have to be based on the patterns of perception that are valid in the given culture. An unprejudiced, "objective" description of flows of movement is consequently not possible. If a descriptive procedure is to be applied on the basis of which a corresponding system of notation can subsequently be developed, then the premises and specific categories in line with which the description is to be carried out must first be clarified. The development of a system of notation is thus by no means a purely technical matter, but is also evidently a hermeneutic problem.

Be that as it may, attempts have been made in recent years to develop notation systems that are supposedly capable of representing all of movement behavior. The most well-known of these is that put forward by Birdwhistell,[69] whom we have discussed in relative detail with regard to gestural signs in part 1. Birdwhistell proceeds from the proposition that the linguistic principle of division into two levels can also be transposed onto behavioral movement. In analogy to the linguistic model, he thus attempts to break down the flow of movement into kinemorphs or acts (morphemes) which, in turn, are to be further subdivided into kinemes (phonemes). If this premise were valid, behavioral movement could be described as a series of combinations of kinemes from a limited repertoire which link to form acts which, in turn, are incorporated into contexts of action. If this is assumed to be the case, then it should also be possible to find a graphic sign to represent every kineme and, consequently, flows of movement could be described as a succession of the graphic signs employed for the kinemes.

Although Birdwhistell developed a notation system of this type, he himself has only tried it out on a few interaction sequences.[70] Other researchers have been disconcerted by the high degree of complexity and time-consuming effort involved in the use and verification of this system. It is therefore hardly possible to make any sound statements on the practicability and reliability of this method at the present time.

Nor, on the other hand, has it been proven to date that a behavioral movement can in fact be segmented into kinemorphs and kinemes. This presupposes that a repertoire of constantly recurring minimal discrete units can actually be identified. Yet such an assumption will be extremely difficult to prove. It should be borne in mind that, on the one hand, behavioral movement not only is culturally specific, but also exhibits great differences that depend on the individual case—and also the respective physical constitution. On the other, it is only coded arbitrarily in exceptional cases (nodding or shaking the head, in greetings, shaking one's fist as a threat, etc.), for it usually has the character of iconic reproduction of reality. Thus, owing to the variance in the signs a division into discrete units is not possible, a fact that has already been emphasized by various researchers.[71] Yet the notating method developed by Birdwhistell depends on such: if the flow of movement cannot be broken down into kinemorphs composed of kinemes, then a form of notation which presumes the existence of kinemes becomes superfluous.

Frey has recently attempted to develop a comprehensive notation system of this type.[72] He takes as his point of departure the idea that nonverbal behavior is registered by the observer in the form of discrete behavioral units of "movements" and "resting positions." From this he concludes that the measurement and resulting notation of behavioral movement is most feasible if a temporal succession of positions adopted is analyzed. In other words, one begins with the resting position, which is described, then the next position is described, and so on. The more the difference in time between two such resting positions is reduced, the greater the accuracy of measurement becomes. So far, Frey and his collaborators have succeeded in developing a relatively accurate system of description and notation for the resting positions. The degree to which positions recorded in this manner can be reproduced is remarkably high.[73] However, it remains to be seen whether movements can actually be appropriately notated by using series of such positional codes and then reproduced on the basis of these notations.

Scherer takes a different approach.[74] He dispenses with such an ambitious attempt from the very beginning, yet does not rule out the possibility that a system for the comprehensive description of human movement behavior may one day be developed. His intention is aimed rather at adapting the notation system for behavioral movement relevant to communication—and he limits the subject matter in this way—to the demands of the respective scientific inquiry. In other words, he does not want to describe behavioral movement exhaustively, but rather to analyze it with reference to specific aspects and issues. Since the functions of nonverbal modes of behavior in social interaction and their relationship to verbal interactive behavior is of particular interest to such an analysis, Scherer initially presumes that such functions exist and buttresses his assumption by drawing on the work of Ekman and Friesen, which we have presented in detail in part 1 in the chapter on gestural signs.[75] He accordingly distinguishes between five basic functions of nonverbal behavior which are performed by five classes: (1) illustrators: these supplement, clarify, and accentuate what is said; (2) adaptors, which portray even manipulative or autoerotic movements as well as nonfunctional object manipulations which, among other things, can serve the purpose of abreaction or gratification; (3) emblems: these have an unequivocally fixed meaning which can also be expressed with one word or sentence; (4) regulators, which regulate the course of communication, the alternation of the speaker-listener role, and similar phenomena; as well as (5) affect-presentations which serve to express a mood or an affect.[76]

Scherer initially made this functional division the basis for classifying hand movements, and later also for those of the head and body.[77] Every behavioral unit examined thus has to be assigned to one of the five functions. Every position and every movement is considered a unit of behavior. Consequently, the beginning and end of a unit of behavior first has to be ascertained, and a function is then assigned to this movement or this position. The degree of agreement between the allocations made by different coders has proved to be highly satisfactory.[78]

Needless to say, this method assumes that—as in a theater performance—the person who performs the movement investigated and the person judging the function to which it should be allocated belong to the same culture. The relatively high agreement in the assessment must therefore be attributed not least of all to the fact that all coders, as members of the same culture, can rely on similar patterns of perception and criteria of assessment. It is precisely the membership of all participants in one and the same culture which forms the condition for (a) the person observed carrying out precisely that movement which various coders agree is significant, and (b) a conspicuously high percentage of the coders assigning this movement to the same function. It is the prerequisite for being able to conduct such an analysis under the current circumstances in the first place.

To the extent that we proceed from similar premises in performance analysis, it would initially appear possible to adopt the procedure developed by Scherer lock, stock, and barrel. This would also seem to be suggested by the fact that it calls for a simultaneous description of (the) vocal behavior according to the criteria of (a) pause or language, (b) vocal intensity, and (c) intonation curves as well as a corresponding notation.[79] Unfortunately, however, this procedure has a serious drawback when it comes to the analysis of a performance, for it has, until now, only been used to analyze movements of the hands, head, and torso, but not body movements which lead to a significant change of position in the room, such as walking across the stage. Therefore, it can only be applied to a particular segment of behavioral movement which, however, may not necessarily always be important in a performance or also may not occur very frequently. For this reason, it cannot be assumed—at least for the time being—that this method is generally applicable.

In other words, there is at present no fully developed system of notation available that can be taken wholeheartedly as the basis for analyzing a performance. The systems which are currently being refined are either too complex or have not been sufficiently tested to be used for the analysis of a performance. Indeed, some are still in statu nascendi, or at best partially developed, i.e., have only limited applications.

The semiotics of theater itself is not capable of developing such a method. It will therefore have to wait until a method—such as that of Scherer or even that of Frey—has been developed to the point where it can be applied to all possible forms of significant behavioral movement. It will then perhaps be possible for specific points in it to be modified to meet the needs of a performance analysis. At that juncture, such a method will provide the basis for performance analysis. Since the discussion regarding methods of notating behavioral movement is currently still in progress, there is definitely reason to hope that a practicable system will be available in the not-too-distant future. Until then, we will have to continue to rely on video tapes and written accounts consisting of verbal descriptions that are as precise as possible.

Concluding Remarks on
the Kinesic Code of the German
Theater of the 1970s

❏ ❐ ❏   As shown in the analysis of *Henry IV* carried out with the procedures[1] outlined in chapter 2, the section "Internal and External Recoding," kinesic signs are preferentially used with a view to the problems of "role play." The same is true of costumes. Kinesic signs serve to generate self-presentation one intends when observed by others, they define the roles which the dramatis personae plan to play within the interaction and, finally, they specify more closely the relations that obtain among the dramatis personae. In this context, the relations between costume and kinesic signs—they run along the axis of principle opposition between the historical and the contemporary—fulfill the function of pointing to the understanding of a role adopted by the different persons and/or groups of persons. The colors chosen for the costumes provides the first, general assessment. The uniformly dark tones of contemporary costumes indicates that the contemporary repertoire of roles used is narrowly limited. By contrast, the colorful hues of historical costumes point to the manifold possibilities of different roles.

If the costume denotes an externally defined role (determined by "Henry" or society), then equivalence between costume and gestural behavior indicates completely external definition, i.e., a puppet-like status. An opposition between the two, by contrast, denotes the inability to make use of another proffered role. Should the costume be chosen freely from among various possibilities (such as those for the Emperor's mother, the abbot of Cluny, and a monk from the Cluny monastery), then equivalence between costume and kinesic signs points to the ability to change roles (as is in part the case with the figure of Mathilda), whereas if the two are juxtaposed to one another this indicates that one single role is being adhered to (such as that of Belcredi and the Doctor), namely a role determined long in advance. In this context, "Henry," who chooses the signs of his external appearance in such a way that they not only allow for highly varied gestural behavior and above all many levels of such behavior but in fact enable these to occur in the first place, would thus seem to be a paradigm of self-determined existence.

Irrespective of this quite specific task which kinesic signs can only accomplish in connection with signs of external appearance, the function they fulfill in the performance can in general be inferred from the manner in which they refer to the process of interaction among the dramatis personae. For it is the kinesic signs which first make possible the self-representation of the latter, and which initiate the specific relations between them and then define these more closely. In other words, such signs create meaning preferentially at the intersubjective level.

Can one infer the general function of kinesic signs in contemporary theater in Germany from this unique use of kinesic signs? We wish, in summary, both to pose this question and to discuss it, even if we cannot come up with a conclusive answer.

We have repeatedly stressed that a universally binding theatrical norm does not exist nowadays. Rather, different theatrical forms and, correspondingly, different theatrical codes exist alongside each other, each with a respectively limited validity. It will therefore not be possible to pinpoint a general function of kinesic signs, that is, one valid for all forms of theater or, to qualify this somewhat, valid for all forms of dramatic theater. Nevertheless, we cannot as a consequence refuse in principle to question whether the function of kinesic signs uncovered in the analysis of the performance is to a certain extent representative of a particular form of dramatic theater. It would certainly not be irrelevant to pose such a question.

A satisfactory answer can of course only be found on the basis of a comprehensive investigation which takes a sufficiently large number of productions into account and analyzes them all in terms of the above inquiry. We will, by contrast, have to restrict ourselves here merely to affirming the validity of such an inquiry on the basis of individual observations made in connection with various productions. And we would like to stress that such a mutually shared function may indeed exist; in fact, it most probably does.

Fernandes's production of Pirandello's *Henry IV* can be classified as part of a trend in dramatic theater which Günther Rühle has termed "the theater of new figurativeness."[2] This trend developed in the 1970s in West Germany in close connection with the genesis of a new form of stage set, such as the sets created by Herrmann, Wonder, Minks, and Freyer. The most prominent and most forceful directors who are representative of this movement are Stein, Grüber, Minks, Zadek, Fernandes, Neuenfels, and Peymann. There are admittedly great differences among their respective works, and these should not be overlooked. Nevertheless, one can discern a certain common approach in their treatment of different genera of kinesic signs. These include: (1) the way the actor uses his body in the sense of its constituting a fundamental gesture (*Grundgestus*) of the dramatis persona; (2) the grouping of several persons on stage, above all: (a) the way in which persons are, on the one hand, assigned to the stage space and, on the other, to one another; and (b) the horizontal and vertical distances between them; (3) the way they walk across the stage, and (4) the manner in which they use props. The aforementioned directors prefer to use precisely these types of kinesic signs in order to characterize the persons with regard to both their specific situation and the relationships that obtain among them.[3]

The kinesic signs used in the theater of new figurativeness thus predominantly fulfill a function fundamentally different from that of the kinesic signs used in bourgeois illusionist theater up until the turn of the century and in contemporary theater of the type produced by Rudolf Noelte. For whereas in the latter two forms of theater they serve to express the feelings, psychological processes, and the subtlest of emotions experienced by a dramatis persona, in the former they are intended to shed clearer light on the situation and the relationships involved. In other words, they refer especially to the interactive processes that ensue among the persons.

Theater has, at the very latest since the turn of the century, unflaggingly thematized the difficulties, indeed the impossibility, of linguistic communication. It has thus not tired of depicting the lack of success and the failure of the widest range of attempts to communicate using language and in a language. The theater of new figurativeness takes up this heritage and investigates the communicative processes that occur beyond all language, namely in terms of the stance, distance, gait, and gestures people adopt, i.e., communication via body language.

There is an interesting parallel here to Enlightenment theater. For in the latter a new kinesic code unfolded as an answer to questions that also prevailed in the scientific discussions of a "gestural language" at the time. And today there is undeniably some sort of corresponding relation between the development of a new theatrical body language and scientific research into gestural behavior. This is not to suggest that the one has a direct influence on the other, irrespective of the direction such an influence might take. However, it is surely indisputable that both the scientific study of gestural behavior and the development of a new theatrical body language both focus on those functions of kinesic signs involved in the course taken by interactive processes and geared toward bringing these processes about.

We must not overlook in this connection that, and here the parallel with Enlightenment theater ceases to obtain, the kinesic code of the theater of new figurativeness is to be regarded as only *one* possible kinesic code. On the contemporary (West) German stage, at least, it has been present as one code among equals, i.e., it has existed alongside other kinesic codes (e.g., those of realist bourgeois theater or of political theater). It thus represents but one segment of the spectrum of forms of dramatic theater possible today, even if it is a segment that carries particular weight and is aesthetically highly advanced.

Notes

Introduction

1. We do not understand the concept of theater to include merely the autonomous theater of Western and Far Eastern cultures, but also theatrical activities that are part of rituals. We shall always use the term "theater" when talking about cases where the following condition is met: A represents X while S looks on. This condition is, however, fulfilled not only by autonomous theater but also by the theatrical activities of primitive peoples, activities partly carried out as magic practices in connection with rituals. Cf., among others, R. Cornevin, *Le théâtre en Afrique noire et à Madacaskar* (Paris, 1970); B. Holas, *Les masques Kono: leur rôle dans la vie religieuse et politique* (Paris, 1952).

2. The following are examples of this: the Persian Ta'zieh passion play, the Turkish Karagöz shadow-puppets, the Katakali dance theater in India, Malayan shadow theater, Nô and Kabuki theater in Japan, and the Chinese Peking Opera.

3. Cf. Arnold Gehlen, *Anthropologische Forschung* (Hamburg, 1961); Johan Huizinga, *Homo ludens*, tr. R. F. C. Hull (London, 1949).

4. Cf. Helmuth Plessner, "Conditio Humana," in *Propyläen Weltgeschichte*, vol. 1 (Berlin, 1961); and his *Diesseits der Utopie* (Düsseldorf and Cologne, 1966) and *Philosophische Anthropologie* (Frankfurt, 1970); H. P. Dreitzel, *Die gesellschaftlichen Leiden und das Leiden an der Gesellschaft* (Stuttgart, 1968); F. Znaniecki, *Social Relations and Social Role* (San Francisco, 1964); U. Rapp, *Handeln und Zuschauen* (Darmstadt, 1973).

5. Cf. G. W. Allport, *Pattern and Growth in Personality* (New York, 1961); H. G. Auch, *Mimus und Logos* (Emsdetten, 1962); H. Kunz, "Zur Psychologie und Psychopathologie der mitmenschlichen Rollen," *Psyche*, II/4 (1949): 551–95; W. Lange-Eichbaum, *The Problem of Genius*, tr. C. Paul (London: Kegan Paul, 1931); H. Reich, *Der Mimus*, 2 vols. (Berlin, 1903); K. Schlüter, *Der Mensch als Schauspieler* (Bonn, 1966).

6. We shall ignore the distinction frequently encountered in German language publications between culture and civilization and rather give the concept of culture such a broad meaning as to include in it everything which human beings make, whether "intellectual" or "material" products. On the concept of culture see J. Ritter, ed., *Historisches Wörterbuch der Philosophie* (Stuttgart and Basle, 1971).

7. On this problem, see A. J. Greimas, *On Meaning* (London, 1987).

8. See S. L. Rubinstein, *Grundlagen der allgemeinen Psychologie* (Berlin, GDR, 1968; Moscow, 1946); K. Holzkamp, *Sinnliche Erkenntnis—Historischer Ursprung und gesellschaftliche Funktion der Wahrnehmung* (Frankfurt/Main, 1973).

9. For an elaboration see E. Fischer-Lichte, *Bedeutung—Probleme einer semiotischen Hermeneutik und Ästhetik* (Munich, 1979).

10. We speak of signs if the following conditions are met: "(1) It must be possible to perceive an example of a sign with the senses; in addition, certain invariances must obtain if the sign is frequently reproduced. (2) A sign or example of a sign must point to or represent something, and fulfill a certain function; . . . it points beyond . . . itself, it has a 'meaning'. (3) A sign must always be a sign for someone—for the producer of the sign and the receiver— i.e. in the case of natural languages, signs (words, morphemes) exist only if there are people or a group of persons who use them as signs and understand them. (4) A sign—this is in

particular true of signs as elements of natural languages—must be embedded in a sign system" (H. Brekle, *Semantik* [Munich, 1972], pp. 47–48).

11. On Morris's concept of the sign see C. W. Morris, "Foundations of a Theory of Signs," in *International Encyclopedia of Unified Science*, vol. 1, no. 2 (Chicago, 1938).

12. The concept of connotation originates in scholastic philosophy of language, was taken up by St. Mill in the nineteenth century, and was first used as a linguistic term by L. Bloomfield. On the history of the concept, cf. the article "Connotatio" in *Historisches Wörterbuch der Philosophie*, ed. J. Ritter; J. Molino, "La connotation," *La Linguistique*, 7 (1971): 5ff. For more recent work on connotation see M.-N. Gary-Prieur, "La notion de connotation(s)," *Litterature*, 4 (1971); Molino, "La connotation"; U. Eco, *Einführung in die Semiotik* (Munich, 1972); K. H. Stierle, "Versuch zu einer Semiotik der Konnotation," in his *Text als Handlung* (Munich, 1975), pp. 131–51; G. Rössler, "Konnotation, Untersuchungen zum Problem der Mit- und Nebenbedeutung," *ZDL*, Supplement, no. 29 (Wiesbaden, 1979).

13. We understand the process of denotation to be the unequivocal allocation of a signified to a signifier on the basis of a knowledge of the semantic system. Cf. U. Eco, *Einführung*, pp. 101–108.

14. Such meanings are investigated by historical semantics and a history of concepts. What is involved here is a description of an age in terms of its political attitudes on the basis of such fundamental concepts. Cf. R. Koselleck, "Begriffsgeschichte und Sozialgeschichte," in *Kölner Zeitschrift für Soziologie und Sozialpsychologie*, Special Issue, 16 (1972), Peter C. Ludz, ed., 116–31; H. Lübbe, "Sein und Heissen. Bedeutungsgeschichte als politisches Sprachhandlungsfeld," in his *Fortschritt als Orientierungsproblem* (Freiburg, 1975), pp. 134–53; H. G. Meier, "Begriffsgeschichte," in *Historisches Wörterbuch der Philosophie*, vol. 1, 788–808; *Geschichtliche Grundbegriffe. Historisches Lexikon zur politisch-sozialen Sprache in Deutschland*, O. Brunner, W. Conze, and R. Koselleck, eds., 6 vols. (vols. 1 and 2, Stuttgart, 1972–1975).

15. On the concept of rules see J. Searle, *Speech Acts. An Essay in the Philosophy of Language* (Cambridge: Cambridge University Press, 1969). Searle distinguished fundamentally between two types of rules, namely regulative and constitutive rules. "Regulative rules characteristically take the form of or can be paraphrased as imperatives, e.g., 'When cutting food, hold the knife in the right hand,' or 'Officers must wear ties at dinner.' Some constitutive rules take quite a different form, e.g. 'A checkmate is made when the king is attacked in such a way that no move will leave it unattacked,' 'A touchdown is scored when a player has possession of the ball in the opponents' end zone while a play is in progress' " (p. 34). The constitutive rules, in other words, first constitute the activity in question, the existence of which depends logically on the rules. Whenever the concept of rule is used in the present study it always refers to constitutive rules.

16. On the concept of code, cf. Eco, *Einführung*, especially pp. 57ff. and pp. 129ff.

17. On the philosophical foundations of art's claim to autonomy in German idealism, see Fischer-Lichte, "Literaturdidaktik als ästhetische Reflexion," in R. Schäfer, ed., *Germanistik und Deutschunterricht* (Munich, 1979), pp. 44–73.

18. See on this point C. Lévi-Strauss, *Structural Anthropology*, tr. C. Jacobson and B. G. Schoepf (New York and London, 1963).

19. See on this point Eco, *Einführung*, pp. 127–45. Eco attempts to prove that the arrival of new messages can change the underlying code. He introduces the following example to prove the validity of his thesis: in the winter of 1969 a scientific study discovered by chance that cyclamates, until then used as a sweetener for diet foods, were carcinogenic. As a consequence, all diet foods using cyclamates were withdrawn from the market and a new diet food with the label "with sugar added" was introduced, even if this sounded paradoxical. To explain this phenomenon, Eco provides the following hypothesis: a code has validity in a culture if it exhibits the semantic axes $\acute{A}$, β, $\acute{O}$ and $\check{S}$ in the following form:

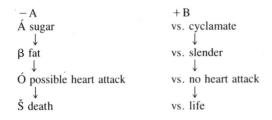

The new scientific knowledge led to a new equation: cyclamate = cancer. The following change in the code occurred as a result:

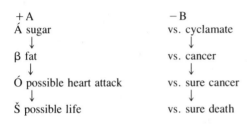

In this way, the arrival of a new message effected a change in the code.

20. See Eco, *Einführung*, pp. 293ff.

21. I attempt to prove that this assertion is correct in my *Bedeutung*; see also my "Zur Konstitution ästhetischer Zeichen," in A. Eschbach and H. Sturm, eds., *Semiotik und Ästhetik* (Tübingen, 1980), pp. 17–28.

22. On the concept of the artifact, see J. Mukařovský, *Kapitel aus der Ästhetik* (Frankfurt/Main, 1970).

23. Dietrich Steinbeck, *Einleitung in die Theorie und Systematik der Theaterwissenschaft* (Berlin, 1970), pp. 149ff.

24. Just because these processes may occur parallel to one another by no means implies that they occur analogously: there is no reason why actors and spectators must attribute the same meanings to the signs produced by the actors. Often, the meanings the actors have in mind when constituting a sign diverge from those that the spectators constitute in the process of reception. On this problem, cf. Fischer-Lichte, *Bedeutung*.

25. In the absence of an audience it is indeed possible to depict play, but not role play, etc. Yet, we wish on principle to speak of theater only if spectators are present during such play.

26. Cf. U. Rapp, *Handeln und Zuschauen*, especially chap. 3 entitled "Performance," pp. 171–243.

27. Ibid., pp. 91–111.

28. This definition is introduced by E. Bentley, *The Life of the Drama* (London, 1965).

29. In this context, depiction does not mean the reproduction of something similar, but the creation of signs which signify cultural reality.

30. Cf. U. Rapp, *Handeln und Zuschauen*.

31. These inventions are, however, always made in the context of the formation of a theater-specific code, and not in that of the invention of a fundamentally new type of sign. Thus, for example, gestural signs exist in Chinese culture—the Peking Opera forms its own specific gestural signs with special meanings: whereas the cut and color of clothing have a meaning in the same culture, the Peking Opera forms a specific repertoire of costume signs, etc.

32. In the following we shall use the concepts of system, norm, and speech in the manner defined by Coseriu in his study *Sistema, norma y habla* (Montevideo, 1952). The system is defined as the level of functional oppositions of a language; norm as that level which contains everything which is independent of the functional domain and determined by tradition; speech as the concrete layer of texts, i.e., as the realization of the techniques of speech. We shall use these concepts in this manner in the present study with reference to the theatrical code.

33. The extent to which the theatrical code as a system—if merely a theoretical construct—can clearly be highlighted by pointing to the way it parallels *langue*: no concrete texts correspond to the *langue*, which is, rather, the level which contains all the signs and rules with which concrete texts can be produced. Equally, the theatrical code as a system contains only those signs and rules with which concrete performances can be produced.

34. We shall go into the concept of norm in greater depth at the beginning of the section on the theatrical code as a norm.

35. We understand "text" as any interlinking of signs. The use of the concept must therefore not be restricted to literary texts alone, but can be applied in the same way to complexes of signs that are not made up of written signs. On the concept of text cf. P. Hartmann, "Texte als linguistisches Objekt," in W. D. Stempel, ed., *Beiträge zur Textlinguistik* (Munich, 1971), pp. 9–29; S. J. Schmidt, *Texttheorie* (Munich, 1973); H. Plett, *Textwissenschaft und Textanalyse* (Heidelberg, 1975).

I. The Theatrical Code as a System

1. The concept of mask does not, in other words, refer simply to that which we term a mask in colloquial speech, namely a fixed facial form that can be detached from the face. We understand theatrical mask to include all forms of mask created by makeup and paint, and, in addition, all artificial changes in physical form. It is obvious that the borderline between mask and our concept of costume is thus far from rigid.

2. Tadeuz Kowzan was the first to enumerate all the signs possible in theater (in his "Znak w teatrze," *Dialog* 3 (1969): 88–104; a French translation is available in his "Le signe au théâtre. Introduction à la sémiologie de l'art du spectacle," *Diogène* 61 (1968): 55–59, as well as in his *Littérature et spectacle dans leur rapports esthéthiques, thématiques et sémiologiques* (Warsaw, 1970), pp. 133–83). Kowzan lists the following signs: word, intonation, mimicry, gestures, the actor's movement in the space of the stage, characterization, hair style, costume, props, decoration, lighting, music, sound effects. The main difference between this and our own list is that Kowzan does not introduce the stage conception as an independent sign system. Clearly, he proceeds from a specific form of theater building that he assumes is fundamental to theater. We must, however, pay attention to the stage conception if we wish to consider all signs that could have a function in a theatrical code.

3. Charles S. Peirce first introduced the distinction between iconic, indexical, and symbolic signs. Cf. Charles S. Peirce, *Collected Papers*, 2 vols. (HUP, 1932). The concept of icon, which Peirce defined more precisely in terms of the similarity between sign and signified, is still the subject of dispute in contemporary discussions. Eco has attempted to reformulate the concept, in his *Einführung in die Semiotik*. On the application of this tripartite division to the theater cf. especially Patrice Pavis, *Problèmes de sémiologie théâtrale* (Montreal, 1976).

4. This definition initially ignores the case of artificially created faces, i.e., made-up faces. We shall go into this extensively in chapter 2, in the section on mask.

1. The Actor's Activities as a Sign

1. We shall therefore only refer to the theory of language to the extent that it explicitly takes the form of a theory of signs used in language. In this context, we shall ignore all

those theorists of language who devised a theory of signs used in language in antiquity, the Middle Ages and the age of the Enlightenment. We shall, in other words, base our study on modern linguistics as developed by Saussure, Sapir, Bloomfield, and Hjelmslev.

2. Ferdinand de Saussure, the founder of the linguistic strand of modern semiotic theories, defined language as a system of signs and wished to compare them in terms of this function with other sign systems, such as writing, the deaf-and-dumb alphabet, symbolic rites, forms of politeness, military signals, etc. In his lectures, "Foundations of a General Linguistics," held between 1906 and 1911, he calls for the foundation of a science that "examines the life of signs within the framework of social life; this would form a part of social psychology and thus a part of general psychology; we shall term it semeology" (*Course in General Linguistics*, tr. R. Harris (London: Duckworth, 1983). Cf. also Gerhard Vigener, *Die zeichentheoretischen Entwürfe von F. de Saussure und Ch. S. Peirce als Grundlagen einer linguistischen Pragmatik* (Tübingen, 1979).

3. The concept of convention can easily lead one to falsely infer that the assignation of certain "fixed" meanings to a certain sound sequence is the result of a one-time agreement. On the contrary, the assignation of meanings (which are never "fixed") occurs in the course of a historical process, the beginning and end of which cannot be specified with any precision. The meaning changes constantly as a result of this processuality.

4. The members of the community can make themselves understood because there are lexical meanings which apply for all members of the community. However, it becomes necessary for the parties to communication to reach an understanding with each other as to what meanings are meant, for the meaning actualized in communication is almost never identical to the lexical meaning, and an understanding can only be reached about something to the extent that the meanings used by the respective members are substantially similar. Cf. on this E. Fischer-Lichte, *Bedeutung*, part 1.

5. N. S. Trubetzkoi first pointed to these rules and the manner in which they are formed by opposition in his *Grundzüge der Phonologie* (Prague, 1939, reprinted Göttingen, 1967).

6. We refer here to the so-called organon model of language that Karl Bühler, the language psychologist, developed in his 1934 theory of language. Here, Bühler defines language as a tool (organon) of communication. Every linguistic sign fulfills three functions: it is the speaker's expression, represents some contents, and appeals to the listener, whose behavior it is supposed to effect. All three functions exist in every linguistic utterance. We can, however, differentiate between linguistic utterances in terms of the specific manner in which they form dominants. Thus, for example, the presentation function predominates in so-called scholarly texts, the appellative function is dominant in a cry for help or a sermon, and the expressive function is foregrounded in a confession. The other two respective functions are always present, if decisively weakened in impact.

7. In this context, Jindrich Honzl has pointed to the fact that, although the use of mimic signs was not possible when Greek tragedies were performed because the players wore masks, the Greek tragedians frequently referred to such mimic signs in their texts. Thus, in Euripides' *Heracles* we read: "Observe, how he already shakes his head, a runner, judging by the hurdles/ and turns the whites of his eyes, silently and with a wild gaze/ breathes in pants, already crazed, like a bull ducks to charge,/ terrifying, roars, summoning the caryatides from Tartarus." The audience cannot see what is treated in the text. They have to imagine its presence. (Jindrich Honzl, "Die Hierarchie der Theatermittel," in A. v. Kesteren and H. Schmid, eds., *Moderne Dramentheorie* [Kronberg, 1975], pp. 133–42.)

8. This is theoretically true but has the practical consequence that in specific normative systems only one or two sign systems are replaced by language. Even forms of theater in which language clearly dominates can hardly dispense with costume and masks.

9. We shall ignore radio plays in our remarks and refer exclusively to theater in the sense that an actor is physically present. This means that our concept of theater includes puppet theater, in which the function of actor is fulfilled by a puppet that factually exists.

10. The interconnection of all signs used simultaneously in direct communication cannot be sufficiently stressed. The meaning of a sequence of communication can first gel when all the signs are considered in relation to one another.

Notes to pages 22–25

11. See Quintilian, *De institutione oratoria*, tr. H. E. Butler (New York and London, 1820–22).

12. See Cicero, *De Oratore*, tr. E. W. Sutton and H. Rackham (London: Loeb, 1948).

13. Representative of many is Gilbert Austin's textbook on recitation, *Chiromania or a treatise on rhetorical delivery: comprehending many precepts, both ancient and modern, for the proper regulation of the Voice, the Countenance and Gesture. Together with an investigation of the elements of gesture and a new method for the notation thereof; illustrated by many figures, printed for T. Cadell and W. Davies in the Strand* (Cleveland Row, St. James's: W. Bulmer and Co., 1806). The book had an impact far beyond the shores of England. It was translated into German by Chr. Fr. Michaelis in 1818 and was used in various ways in rhetoric and acting classes.

14. On this classification see also George L. Trager, "Paralanguage: A First Approximation," in Dell Hymes, ed., *Language in Culture and Society* (New York, 1964), pp. 274–88.

15. One repeatedly comes across mention of these characteristics, e.g., in Trager, "Paralanguage." The major language-diagnostic protocol sheets presented in R. Fährmann, *Die Deutung des Sprechausdrucks* (Bonn, 1967), account in like manner for normal phonetic parameters, which are partly given verbal form and partly assessed in terms of opposing poles:

Pitch (high—low, etc.),
Intensity (loud—quiet, etc.),
Strength of voice (strong articulation, minor articulation, etc.),
Tone color (timbre, major—minor, etc.),
Speed (slow—fast, etc.),
Rhythmic sequence (regular—irregular, etc.),
Accentuation (melos, dynamics, agogics),
Articulation (unclear—clear, etc.).

For a discussion of the problems involved in the different forms of classification see P. Winkler, "Notationen des Sprechausdrucks," *Zeitschrift für Semiotik* 1, no. 2/3 (1979): 211–21.

16. Georg Heike, *Suprasegmentale Analyse* (Marburg, 1969), p. 122.

17. On the problematics of the relation between sound and meaning see Klaus R. Scherer, "Affektlaute und vokale Embleme," in R. Posner and H. P. Reinecke, eds., *Zeichenprozesse, Semiotische Forschung in den Einzelwissenschaften* (Wiesbaden, 1977), pp. 199–214.

18. On the problem of interpreting voices cf. especially W. Broeren, "Über die Zuverlässigkeit der Beschreibung von Sprechstimme und Handschrift" (doctoral thesis, Marburg, 1964); Karl Bühler, *Ausdruckstheorie* (Jena, 1933); K. Bühler and H. Herzon, "Stimme und Persönlichkeit," *Zeitschrift für Psychologie* 130 (1933); D. Görlitz, "Ergebnisse und Probleme der ausdruckspsychologischen Sprechstimmforschung. Eine historische, begriffliche und sachsystematische Untersuchung der empirischen Beiträge zum Ausdruck der Sprechhandlung als einem Teilbereich der Phonognomik" (doctoral thesis, Berlin, 1970); C. E. Osgood and T. E. Sebeok, eds., *Psycholinguistics—A Survey of Theory and Research Problems, Supplement of the Journal of Abnormal Social Psychology* 49, no. 4 (1954); P. F. Ostwald, *The Semiotics of Human Sound* (The Hague, 1973); C. V. Riper and J. K. Irvin, *Voice and Articulation* (Englewood Cliffs, N.Y., 1958); J. Rudert, "Vom Ausdruck der Sprechstimme," in R. Kirchhoff, ed., *Ausdruckspsychologie, Handbuch der Psychologie*, vol. 5 (Göttingen, 1965); F.-H. Sanford, "Speech and Personality," *Psychological Bulletin* 39 (1942): 811–45.

19. For a discussion of emphasis see, among others, A. Martinet, "Accents et tons," *Miscellanea Phonetica* 2 (1954): 13–24; K. L. Pike, *Phonemics* (Ann Arbor, 1947); his *Tone Languages* (Ann Arbor, 1948); and his *Phonetics* (Ann Arbor, 1962); H. Weinrich, "Phonologie der Sprechpause," *Phonetica* 7 (1961): 4–18.

· 20. Intonation is naturally alone not sufficient to pinpoint the speech act intended (such as a wish, a request, an order, a demand, etc.), but only allows a general distinction to be made between constative speech acts, interrogative speech acts, and demanding speech acts.

21. On the function of intonation see, among others, F. Danes, "Sentence Intonation from a Functional Point of View," *Word* 16 (1960): 34–54; Otto v. Essen, *Grundzüge der hochdeutschen Satzintonation* (Düsseldorf, 1964); G. Heike, *Suprasegmentale Analyse*; K. L. Pike, *The Intonation of American English* (Ann Arbor, 1958); H. J. Schädlich, "Über 'terminale' Intonation im Deutschen," *Beiträge zur Sprachwissenschaft, Volkskunde und Literaturforschung* (Steinitz-Festschrift) 5 (1965): 344–53.

22. On the expression of feelings via paralinguistic signs see K. Bühler, *Ausdruckstheorie* (Jena, 1933); J. R. Davitz and L. J. Davitz, "The Communication of Feelings by Content Free Speech," *Journal of Communication* 9 (1959): 6–13; A. T. Dittmann and L. C. Wynne, "Linguistic Techniques and the Analysis of Emotionality in Interviews," *Journal of Abnormal Social Psychology* 63 (1961): 201–204; J. Fonagy and K. Magdies, "Emotional Patterns in Intonation and Music," *Z PSK* 16 (1963): 293–326; G. Heike, *Suprasegmentale Analyse*; A. Musgrave Homer, *Movement, Voice and Speech* (London, 1970); K. Scherer, *Nonverbale Kommunikation: IPK-Forschungsbericht*, vol. 35 (Hamburg, 1970), and his "Acoustic Concomitants of Emotional Dimensions: Judging Affect from Synthesized Tone Sequences," in S. Weitz, ed., *Nonverbal Communication* (New York, 1974); H. Werner, ed., *On Expressive Language* (Worcester, 1955).

23. The interpretation of a supersign that consists of linguistic and paralinguistic signs is even more complicated if mimicry and gestures are taken into account. Cf. P. Ekman, W. Friesen, and K. Scherer, "Body Movement and Voice Pitch in Deceptive Interaction," *Semiotica* 16 (1976): 23–27; A. Hayes, "Paralinguistics and Kinesics. Pedagogical Perspectives," in Sebeok, Hayes, and Bateson, eds., *Approaches to Semiotics* (The Hague, 1964).

24. Cf. Goethe's "Rules for Actors." He writes, for example, in points 22–24 of the section on recitation and declamation:

Point 22. In order to ensure correct declamation one should take the following rules to heart: Once I have completely understood the meaning of the words and am thoroughly acquainted with them I must then attempt to accompany them with the requisite tone of voice and to speak them with force or feebly either swiftly or slowly, depending on what the meaning of each sentence demands. For example:

Peoples go into decline—must be spoken in a subdued manner, with a rush
Names die out—more clearly, tingling
And "Murky Past, Spreads its dark twilighting wings over whole races"—with a hollow, deep, foreboding voice.

Point 23. Thus a different, far quicker tempo must be chosen for the following passage compared with the sentence prior to it, for the actual words of the sentence require this:

"Swiftly throwing myself off my horse, I press after them . . . "

Point 24. In the case of passages that are interrupted by others, as if they were set off by dashes, then at the beginning and end one's voice must break off somewhat, and the tone of the speech interrupted by the interpolated part then continued. For example:

And nevertheless, 'tis the first child's quarrel which
Continued in an unfortunate chain of events
Has given rise to the injustice of this day.

must be declaimed as follows:

And nevertheless, 'tis the first child's quarrel which
—Continued in an unfortunate chain of events—
Has given rise to the injustice of this day. (J. W. Goethe, "Regeln für Schauspieler," in J. W. Goethe, *Sämtliche Werke in 18 Bänden*, vol. 14, "*Schriften zur Literatur* [Zurich, 1977], 77f.)

25. Cf. on the use of paralinguistic signs by Stanislavsky, K. S. Stanislavsky, *Building a Character* (Methuen, London, 1979), his *My Life in Art* (Methuen, London, 1980), and his *Creating a Role*, tr. E. R. Hapsgood (Methuen, London, 1980).

26. The mode of speech adopted in French classical tragic drama can only be assessed appropriately in the context of the social function and meaning of this theater as courtly theater. This mode of speech was retained in theater even well after the theater had undergone a functional change and as bourgeois theater had become a platform for the self-presentation and self-assertion of the bourgeoisie. It was impossible in this new context to attribute a meaning to this mode of speech. Lessing attacks its transfer onto German theater—which had adopted it along with French plays in the wake of Gottsched—with corresponding trenchancy; he called, instead, for declamation "appropriate to nature" (G. E. Lessing, "Hamburgische Dramaturgie," in *Sämtliche Werke* [Stuttgart, 1958], vol. 8, 34–48, esp. 36).

27. The differences in the "zero point" of meaning can already be made out taking old album recordings. The change can be clearly noticed if one contrasts recordings of Goethe's "Prometheus" read by Josef Kainz (1858–1910), Alexander Moissi (1880–1935), Ludwig Hülbner (1858–1938, recorded in 1928), and Rolf Henninger (born 1925).

28. Cf. on this G. L. Trager, "Paralanguage," and K. Scherer, "Affektlaute."

29. The distinctions in note 15 above must also be applied to laughter, weeping, and shouting, for in this instance the differences in meaning can also be considerable (e.g., ironic laughter, sobbing laughter, giggling, happy laughter, etc.).

30. We cannot be certain that we are witnessing a "pure" expression of emotions, as it were, if we encounter the expression of feelings in public life. The fact that this expression is shown in the face of others transforms it into an element in the communication process. We can only establish exactly what it communicates if we relate his expression to the rules valid in this culture for expressing emotions.

31. A good example of this is "Storm and Stress" theater, above all that practiced by Friedrich Ludwig Schröder. The expression of feelings was most certainly allowed in the bourgeois society of his time; in fact, it was encouraged as an expression of introversion, of sympathy within the close circle of the family. The eruption of strong passions was, however, not allowed either in the closed confines of the family nor in public. By contrast, playing out raging passions, wild tantrums was a constitutive element of Schröder's theater: it was intended to represent humankind in its natural state, in its creaturely vulnerability.

32. On the concept of proxemic signs and proxemics see Edward T. Hall, *The Hidden Dimension* (London, 1966). We deal extensively with proxemic signs in the respective section below.

33. P. Ekman, W. Friesen, and P. Ellsworth, *Gesichtssprache* (Vienna, Cologne, and Graz, 1974), p. 12.

34. If a partner to communication reacts to an assertion made by another by raising his eyebrows in order to express his doubt with regard to the correctness of the assertion, then facial expression in this instance cannot be interpreted as a sign for an affect. The same rules hold in such cases for the interpretation of mimic signs as obtain for that of gestural signs. For these mimic signs are culturally determined.

35. Charles Darwin, *Expression of the Emotions in Man and Animals* (London, 1972; reprint Chicago: Phoenix Books, 1965).

36. Universal validity should be understood to mean that mimic signs in every culture are to be interpreted as expressing the same emotion, but not to signify that the members of different cultures use the same mimic signs in comparable situations. If people cry during a funeral in one culture, and in another, by contrast, the people smile, then this should not lead to the conclusion that in the one sorrow is shown by crying and in the other by smiling. Rather, different rules of application are involved. See below for a further discussion.

The thesis of the cultural specificity of even mimic signs expressing emotions is advanced, among others, by R. L. Birdwhistell, "The Kinesic Level in the Investigation of the Emotions," in P. H. Knapp, ed., *Expressions of the Emotion in Man* (New York, 1963), p. ii.

37. The following scholars propose the following categorization:

Woodsworth: Love, cheerfulness, happiness, surprise, fear, suffering, annoyance, determination, revulsion, contempt (*Experimental Psychology* [New York, 1938]).

Plutchik: Shyness, happiness, joy, surprise, amazement, astonishment, worry, fear, fright, melancholia, troubled care, grief, vexation, annoyance, anger, tiredness, revulsion, loathing, attentiveness, expectation, anticipation, recognition, unification (*The Emotions: Facts, Theories, and a New Model* [New York, 1962]).

Tomkins and McCarter: Amusement, joy, surprise, sudden fright, fear, fright, pain, agony, annoyance, anger, revulsion, contempt, interest, enthusiasm, shame, humiliation ("What and where are the primary affects? Some evidence for a theory," *Perceptual and Motor Skills* 18 [1964]: 119–58).

Osgood: Relish, silent amusement, joy, joyfulness, tortured laughter, surprise, amazement, consternation, respect, fear, horror, despair, boredom, dreamy sadness, acute worry, despair, introverted annoyance, anger, stubbornness, determination, vexation, revulsion, scorn, disgust, anticipation, interest, pity, mistrust, anxiety ("Dimensionality of the semantic space for communication via facial expressions," *Scandinavian Journal of Psychology* 7 [1966]: 1–30).

Frijda: Happiness, surprise, fear, sadness, annoyance, revulsion, attentiveness, quietness, bitterness, pride, irony, uncertainty, skepticism ("Emotion and recognition of emotion," *Third Symposium on Feelings and Emotion* [Loyola Univ., Chicago] Oct. 10–12, 1968).

It is hard to apply these categorizations as they do not use clear lines of demarcation and thus often arrive at categories that overlap. For a discussion cf. Ekman et al, *Gesichtssprache*, pp. 47–76.

38. These categories are proposed in Ekman et al., *Gesichtssprache*.

39. The table lists the characteristic features which P. Ekman gives as the result of his study in *Unmasking the Face* (Englewood Cliffs, N.J., 1975).

40. Ekman/Friesen/Ellsworth, *Gesichtssprache*, p. 28.

41. The difference between a diagnosis based on the natural sciences or medicine and hermeneutics cannot be stressed sufficiently. Whereas such a diagnosis can only be applied in cases in which natural-biological findings can be interpreted as signs for natural-biological facts or processes, hermeneutics can be applied in all instances involving the interpretation of signs produced by humans as elements of a process of communication. We shall discuss the specific hermeneutic problems of interpreting signs especially at the beginning of part 3, which focuses on the analysis of a performance.

42. In general, etiological publications in the U.S. view obeying rules as normal, so that deviation from the rules is considered abnormal behavior. We shall, by contrast, emphasize most strongly that precisely breaking valid, generally accepted rules can be consciously practiced as a way of generating meaning.

43. Ekman, *Unmasking*, pp. 27f.

44. Obeying such rules is not a conscious process—as is breaking them—but occurs in a manner similar to that in which linguistic rules are adhered to. They are learned in the course of socialization and internalized, so that obeying them in no respect presupposes a prior, conscious structuring of rules. An adult can, of course, obey rules, just as he may break them, because he has reflected on them after completion of the phase of appropriative internalization and regards them as justified.

45. Subjectivity thus plays a major part in the production of signs that express emotions. This is one of the reasons for the difficulties in interpreting them adequately.

46. In other words, manifold factors have to be taken into account in order to understand a person's behavior in a sequence of communication. The danger of misinterpretation rises with each additional factor that is ignored.

47. A model of communication that is technical in this manner cannot as a matter of principle be applied to human communication. Many of the models of communication devised in the early days of communications research were flawed, for they conceived of communication via mechanical devices to be the basic model to which all communicative processes

could be referred back, instead of construing the relation the other way around, namely by taking technical communication itself as a derivative, special case.

48. Cf. here H. G. Gadamer, *Truth and Method* (London: Sheed and Ward, 1975). We shall go into this in greater detail in part 3.

49. For a description of this research and a review cf. Ekman et al, *Gesichtssprache*; Ekman, *Unmasking*; P. Ekman, "Cross-Cultural Studies of Facial Expression," in P. Ekman, ed., *Darwin and Facial Expression. A Century of Research in Review* (New York and London, 1973), pp. 169–220.

50. S. Birdwhistell, *The Kinesic Level in the Investigation of the Emotions.*

51. For a discussion of the problems posed by mimic signs see also F. H. Allport, *Social Psychology* (Boston, 1924); J. G. Borg, "Physiognomy, Facial Expression, and Abnormality," *Acta Universitatis Tamperensis*, ser. A, 52 (1973); J. C. Coleman, "Facial Expressions of Emotion," *Psychological Monograph* 63 (1949), 1, no. 296; R. C. Davis, "The Specificity of Facial Expressions," *Journal of General Psychology* 10 (1934): 42–58; J. Eibl-Eibesfeld, *Grundriss der vergleichenden Verhaltensforschung* (Munich, 1967), and her *Menschenforschung auf neuen Wegen* (Vienna, Munich, and Zürich, 1976); P. Ekman, "Body Position, Facial Expression and Verbal Behavior during Interviews," *Journal of Abnormal and Social Psychology* 68 (1964): 295–301, and his *Universals and Cultural Difference in Facial Expressions of Emotion* (Lincoln: Univ. of Nebraska Press, 1972); P. Ekman and W. Friesen, "Constants across Cultures in the Face and Emotion," *Journal of Personality and Social Psychology* 17 (1971): 124–29; P. Ekman, W. Friesen, and S. S. Tomkins, "Facial Affect Scoring Technique (FAST): A First Validity Study," *Semiotica* 3 (1971): 37–58; P. Ekman, E. R. Sorenson, and W. V. Friesen, "Pan-Cultural Elements in Facial Displays of Emotions," *Science*, 4 April 1969, 164 (3875), 86–88; N. H. Frijda, "The Understanding of Facial Expression of Emotion," *Acta Psychologica* 9 (1953): 294–362; with E. Philipszoon, "Dimensions of Recognition of Emotion," *Journal of Abnormal and Social Psychology* 66 (1963): 45–51; F. L. Goodenough, "Expressions of the Emotions in a Blind-Deaf Child," *Journal of Abnormal and Social Psychology* 27 (1932–33): 328–33; C. Laudis, "The Interpretation of Facial Expression in Emotion," *Journal of General Psychology* 2 (1929): 59–72; P. Lersch, *Gesicht und Seele. Grundlinien einer mimischen Diagnostik* (Munich, 1932); T. Nummenmaa, *The Language of the Face*, (Jyvaskyla, Finland: Jyvaskylan Studies in Education, Psychology and Social Research, 1964); L. Rubinstein, "Facial Expressions: An Objective Method in the Quantitative Evaluation of Emotional Change," *Behavior Research Methods and Instruments* 1 (1969): 305–306; H. Schlosberg, "The Description of Facial Expressions in Terms of Two Dimensions," *Journal of Experimental Psychology* 44 (1952): 229–37; W. Schüle, *Ausdruckswahrnehmung des Gesichts. Experimentelle Untersuchungen* (Frankfurt/Main, 1976).

52. The medium of film can, by using different shots, such as closeups and long shots, considerably facilitate the understanding of a sequence of communication compared with theater. The camera can focus exclusively on those signs or groups of signs which convey the meaning intended most clearly. Cf. Christian Metz, *Film Language. Semiotics of the Cinema*, tr. M. Taylor (New York: OUP, 1974), and Y. M. Lotman, *Semiotics of Cinema*, tr. M. E. Suino (Michigan Slavic Publications, 1981).

53. See chap. 2, the section titled "Mask," for a discussion of the mask as sign.

54. On makeup see also chap. 2, the section on mask.

55. Since naturalist theater considers itself a truthful mirror image of the reality of social life, it of course has to adhere to the rules of application that are valid for the expression of emotions within the society of which it is a part, when portraying emotions. Owing to this, in naturalist theater the mimic code to a great extent matches the code of the culture in question.

56. We have already pointed out that "Storm and Stress" theater follows different rules for the expression of emotions than does the bourgeois society of its day. Cf. note 31.

57. This is true of the special forms of comical-grotesque theater—the mimic code of which follows the rule of exaggerating certain features and characteristics, as do all its other

codes—of such forms of tragic theater as have a special code for expressing "major" emotions, and of forms of conventionalized theater which instill the sign used with a unique, specific theatrical meaning.

58. Ludwig Tieck's *Puss in Boots* parodies such an audience, i.e., those theater-goers who presuppose a code that is not that on which the play is based. The audience in *Puss in Boots* presupposes that theater "always represents only nature" (act 1, in the royal palace). They therefore attempt to apply the code that they know from social life to the theater and have great difficulties understanding what is happening, especially because the persons "do not remain true to character." The comicalness here is based precisely on the fact that "the poet" and "the audience" each presuppose a different theatrical code.

59. This distinguishing feature of theater has prompted Stefania Skwarcyńska to define the gesture as the smallest unit of signification in the theatrical sign system: "The 'material' of gestures is man himself with his own organic and spiritual life, man, in other words, understood as the fundamental and indispensable material from which to build the theatrical performance; it is thus only man's presence and appearance that are of importance in the sphere of fixed theatrical signs which the receiver perceives via the medium of sight. The gestures . . . cannot be separated from the human being, they do not have 'material' of their own, even if this is supposedly a secondary material" (Stefania Skwarczyńska, "Anmerkungen zur Semantik der theatralischen Gestik," in W. Kroll and A. Flaker, eds., Literaturtheoretische Modelle und kommunikatives System. Zur aktuellen Diskussion in der polnischen Literaturwissenschaft (Kronberg Taunus, 1974) p. 341.

60. It is very questionable whether such precise demarcating lines are even desirable. They are always justified in instances where they are made with a view to a certain approach to a study, and the particular purpose of the demarcation is thus always borne in mind. Such demarcations otherwise threaten to function as normative prescriptions that prevent any further theoretical development.

61. Cf. Aristotle, *Rhetoric*, tr. J. H. Freese (London: Loeb, 1926).

62. On the problem of gesture as a universal language cf., among others, James R. Knowlson, "The Idea of Gesture as a Universal Language in the 17th and 18th Century," *Journal of the History of Ideas* 16, no. 4 (1965): 495–508.

63. This conception has a considerable influence on gestures used in the theater in the second half of the eighteenth century, a time when especially "natural" gestures first began to be introduced. Cf., for France, the writings of Raymond de St. Albine, *Le Comédien* (Paris, 1747); Francesco Riccoboni, *L'art du théâtre* (Paris, 1750); and Denis Diderot, *Oeuvres complètes*, J. Assezat and M. Tourneux, eds. (Paris, 1875–1877). For Germany, see Gotthold Lessing's oeuvre, in particular his "Hamburgische Dramaturgie," in *Sämtliche Werke*; J. J. Engel, "Ideen zu einer Mimik," in his *Schriften* (Berlin, 1804), vols. 7 and 8; and Lichtenberg's *Vermischte Schriften* (Göttingen, 1800/1801). Cf. part 2 of the present study.

64. Wilhelm Wundt, "Gebärdensprache," in his *Language* (Mouton, The Hague, 1973) (originally vol. 1 of his *Völkerpsychologie*, 10 vols [Stuttgart, 1900]).

65. Marcel Mauss, *Sociology and Psychology*, tr. Ben Brewster (London: RKP, 1979). The lecture was presented to the Société de Psychologie on May 17, 1934, and first appeared in *Journal de psychologie normale et pathologique* 32, nos. 3–4 (1935): 271–93. It had a great impact on the French-speaking scholarly community, and the research efforts into gestures the lecture triggered have oriented themselves toward its methods and results.

66. David Efron, *Gesture, Race and Culture* (The Hague and Paris, 1972), vol. 9 in the *Approaches to Semiotics* series. This book had a substantial, lasting impact on U.S. research on the cultural specificity of gestures.

67. The cultural specificity of gestures can be considered the generally accepted point of departure in current scientific inquiry.

68. Cf. on this issue the publications by Ray L. Birdwhistell: *Introduction to Kinesics* (Washington, D.C., Dept. of State, Foreign Service Institute, 1952); "Kinesics and Communication," in E. Carpenter and M. McLuhan, eds., *Explorations in Communications*

(Boston, 1960), pp. 54–70; "Some Relations between American Kinesics and Spoken American English," in A. G. Smith, ed., *Communication and Culture: Reading in the Codes of Human Interaction* (New York, 1966), pp. 182–209; "Some Body Motion Elements Accompanying Spoken American English," in L. Thayer, ed., *Communication: Concepts and Perspectives* (London and Washington, 1967), pp. 53–75; *Kinesics and Context. Essays in Body Motion* (Philadelphia, 1970).

69. We shall return in greater detail to the problem of the notation of sequences of communication and interaction in part 3 and discuss the different notational procedures developed thus far more closely.

70. See Ray L. Birdwhistell, *Introduction to Kinesics*.

71. Any study of gesture as a system generating meaning must take this fact into account. A culture can most certainly accord a "fixed" meaning to certain gestures (such as nodding one's head means agreement and shaking it means negation, raising one's hand constitutes a greeting, etc.), yet these same gestures can be used with a different meaning in the same culture. This important difference between linguistic and gestural signs must not be ignored or trivialized.

72. Much of Birdwhistell's work has been devoted to establishing the American gestural code, above all the relation between American English and "American Movement." See Birdwhistell's "Some Relations"; "Some Body Motion Elements"; "Towards Analyzing American Movement," in *Kinesics and Context*, pp. 99–110; "Movement with Speech," in *Kinesics and Context*, pp. 110–27. Cf. also R. L. Saitz and E. C. Cervenka, *Handbook of Gestures: Colombia and the United States, Approaches to Semiotics*, no. 31 (The Hague, 1972).

73. Cf. Wundt, "Gebärdensprache."

74. A. J. Greimas makes this distinction. See his "Conditions d'une sémiotique du monde naturel," in his *On Meaning*. The distinction is important to the extent that it allows gestural signs to be examined in terms of whether they are used in processes of communication or of production, distribution, and consumption. In the first case they are intended to function as elements generating meaning and are therefore both produced as signs and at the same time interpreted; in the second, their primary function consists of producing, distributing, or consuming such objects as serve to satisfy needs—they can, however, also be generated and interpreted here as signs. Cf. the section of the present chapter on this point.

75. These signs are the preferential focus of research.

76. We thus classify gestural signs in line with Bühler's organon model, i.e., in terms of what the gesture can be a sign of, since this must be the point of inquiry in the context of our specific study. Other forms of classification are also possible: Cf. Birdwhistell's classification systems ("Some Relations," "Some Body Motion Elements," and "Movement with Speech"); P. Ekman and W. V. Friesen, "The Repertoire of Nonverbal Behavior: Categories, Origins, Usage and Coding," *Semiotica* 1 (1969): 49–98.

77. Ibid.; see also Albert E. Scheflen, *Body Language and Social Order* (New York: Prentice Hall, 1972), and his *How Behaviour Means* (New York, 1973).

78. See A. Scheflen, *Body Language*, and *How Behavior Means*; Ekman and Friesen, "The Repertoire."

79. See Birdwhistell, "Some Relations"; "Some Body Motion Elements"; "Movement with Speech"; R. Cresswell, "Le geste manuel associé au langage," *Langage* 10 (1968); A. Leroi-Gourhan, *Le geste et la parole*, 2 vols. (Paris, 1965).

80. Cf. here R. A. Barakat, *The Cistercian Sign Language: A Study in Non-Verbal Communication, Cistercian Studies Series II* (Kalamazoo, Mich., 1976), and his "On Ambiguity in the Cistercian Sign Language," *Sign Language Studies* 8(1975): 275–89; J. E. Cody, *Indian Talk* (London, 1972); Celia Hutt, "Dictionnaire du langage gestuel chez les trappistes," *Langages* 10 (1968); W. C. Stokoe, "Sign Language and the Monastic Use of Lexical Gestures," *Semiotica* 24, nos. 1/2 (1978): 181–94; W. Tomkins, *Indian Sign Lan-*

guage (New York, 1969); Maximilian, Prince of Wied, *Reise in das innere Nordamerika* (Munich, 1974); Wundt, "Gebärdensprache."

81. On the following form of classification cf. Wundt, "Gebärdensprache."

82. On this type of gestural sign see R. A. Barakat, "Arabic Gestures," *Journal of Popular Culture* (1973): 749–87; McDonald Critchley, *Silent Language* (London, 1975), esp. chap. 10, "Sign-Language and Symbolism"; P. Ekman, "Bewegungen mit codierter Bedeutung: Gestische Embleme," in R. Posner and H. P. Reinecke, *Zeichenprozesse*, pp. 180–98; R. Firth, *Symbols, Public and Private* (London, 1973); R. Jakobson, "Motor Signs for 'Yes' and 'No'," *Language Soc.* I (1972): 91–96; H. G. Johnson, P. Ekman, and W. V. Friesen, "Communicative Body Movements: American Emblems," *Semiotica* 15, no. 4 (1975): 335–53; R. Saitz and E. Cervenka, *Handbook of Gestures.*

83. In addition to Wundt, see the following on deaf language: C. F. Abbott, "Encodedness and Sign Language," *Sign Language Studies* 7 (1975): 109–120; V. Belluge, E. S. Klima, and P. Siple, "Remembering in Signs," in *Cognition. International Journal of Cognitive Psychology*, (The Hague, 1975); B. Hansen, "Varieties in Danish Sign Language and Grammatical Features of the Original Sign Language," *Sign Language Studies* 8 (1975); H. Lander, "Review of 'Sign Language Structure: An Outline of the Visual Communication Systems of the American Deaf,' by William Stokoe Jr.," *Language* 37, no. 2 (1961): 269–71; J. M. Schlesinger, "Problems of Investigating the Grammar of Sign Language," VRA-ISR Project Paper 32-67, U.S. Dept. of H.E.W., 1967; R. K. Sorensen, "Indications of Regular Syntax in Deaf Danish School Children's Sign Language," *Sign Language Studies* 8 (1975); W. C. Stokoe, Jr., *Semiotics and Human Sign Language* (The Hague, 1974). (Also published as *Approaches to Semiotics*, no. 21 and preprinted in *Semiotica* 9 [1973]: 347–82); W. C. Stokoe, "Die 'Sprache' der Taubstummen," in R. Posner and H.-P. Reinecke, *Zeichenprozesse*, pp. 167–79; W. C. Stokoe, Jr., *Sign Language Structure: An Outline of the Visual Communication Systems of the American Deaf, Studies in Linguistics, Occasional Papers* 8 (Buffalo, 1960); and his *A Dictionary of American Sign Language on Linguistic Principles* (Washington, D.C., 1965); B. T. Tervoort, "You Use Downtown Movie Fun 2," *Lingua* 21 (1968): 455–65, and his "Could There Be a Human Sign Language?" *Semiotica* 9, no. 1 (1973): 347–82.

84. Cf. Wundt, "Gebärdensprache."

85. Cf. Ekman/Friesen, "The Repertoire"; A. Scheflen, *Body Language*, and *How Behavior Means.*

86. On gestures of dominance cf. I. Eibl-Eibesfeld, *Grundriss*; R. Firth, *Symbols, Public and Private*; G. Maclay and H. Knipe, *The Dominant Man* (New York, 1972).

87. On greeting rituals see Eibl-Eibesfeld, *Grundriss*; Firth, *Symbols, Public and Private*, chap. 9; A. Kendon and A. Ferber, "A Description of Some Human Greetings," in *Comparative Ecology and Behaviour of Primates* (London, 1973), chap. 4; Desmond Morris, *Manwatching. Field Guide to Human Behaviour* (London: Cape, 1977); A. Scheflen, *Body Language.*

88. On the baroque gestural code see part 2 of the present study.

89. Cf. chap. 2, the section on costume.

90. Cf. A. Scheflen, *Body Language.*

91. In this context we must again point expressly to the importance of violations of the rules! Precisely the use of such gestures as are not foreseen in a society's valid gestural code for this situation become important signs, the appropriate interpretation of which allows us to understand the person concerned "correctly."

92. On the problems of such interpretations cf. the section on physiognomy in chap. 2, the section titled "Mask."

93. On the problem of expressing feelings see the sources listed in note 51.

94. On this point see especially Erving Goffmann, *Strategic Interaction* (Oxford: Blackwell, 1971); his *Presentation of Self in Everyday Life* (Harmondsworth: Penguin, 1971); his *Behaviour in Public Places. Notes on the Social Organization of Gatherings* (London: Green-

wood Press, 1980), and his *Forms of Talk* (Oxford: Blackwell 1981); and A. Scheflen, *Body Language*.

95. Scheflen, *Body Language*, especially chap. II, 5, provides examples of such "transcontextual" behavior.

96. The hermeneutics of direct communication addresses the problems and difficulties that arise from any attempt to understand "the other" in direct communication/interaction. For the hermeneutic problems involved here are in fact somewhat different from those entailed in a textual hermeneutics. Although the problem of prejudice has to be taken into account here as well (as does that of "cultural distance," when members of different cultures communicate with one another), that of historical distance does not and the question of the hermeneutic circle is posed differently. For here the whole to which each individual part must be referred is not only constituted by the sequentiality of the course of interaction but also by the concomitance of simultaneously presented signs. We shall go into this in greater depth in part 3 below. Cf., among others, B. Badura, "Kommunikative Kompetenz, Dialoghermeneutik und Interaktion. Eine theoretische Skizze," in B. Badura and K. Gloy, eds., *Soziologie der Kommunikation. Eine Textauswahl zur Einführung* (Stuttgart, 1972), pp. 246–64; E. Fischer-Lichte, "Bedeutung," pp. 130–34.

97. On behavior in greeting see note 87 above for secondary sources.

98. Cf. I. Eibl-Eibesfeld, *Grundriss*; G. Maclay and H. Knipe, *The Dominant Man*; A. Scheflen, *Body Language*.

99. Cf. A. Scheflen, *Body Language*, pp. 26–37.

100. Specifically proxemics studies this area. We shall discuss it thoroughly in the section on proxemic signs. On the function of distance in the process of interaction see E. T. Hall, *The Silent Language* (New York, 1969), and his *The Hidden Dimension*; C. Hutt and M. J. Vaisey, "Differential Effects of Group Size on Social Behavior," *Nature* 209 (1966): 1371–72; R. H. Knapp, "The Language of Postural Interpretation," *Journal of Social Psychology* (1965); N. Mackenzie, *Secret Societies* (London, 1967); R. Sommer, *Personal Space* (Prentice Hall, N.J., 1969); A. Scheflen, *Body Language*; "How Behaviour Means"; O. M. Watson and T. D. Graves, "Quantitative Research in Proxemic Behaviour," *American Anthropologist* 68 (1966): 971–85; O. M. Watson, *Proxemic Behaviour*, (The Hague, 1970).

101. Facial expression is frequently used in this way: the individual who expresses something with his face does not want to show that he really feels the emotion denoted by this expression, but rather to convey to the other person how he wishes to understand the relation between them. Ekman terms the mimic signs deployed in this context emblems. See Ekman, *Gesichtssprache*; and his *Unmasking*.

102. Quintilian, *De institutione oratoria*.

103. Cf. Scheflen, *Body Language*, chap II, 8 on kinesic monitors.

104. Ibid., II, 5 on kinesic behavior.

105. The contrary is the case: both groups form a unity which then generates what Birdwhistell, for example, terms "American movement" and "American gesture." Cf. on this point his "Some Relations"; his "Some Body Motion Elements"; and his "Movement with Speech."

106. Even naturalist theater, which pronounces as its program that it will put "reality" as it actually is on stage, cannot deploy nonsignificant gestures in a manner comparable to their frequent use in everyday communication. Significant gestures are involved when a character runs his fingers through his hair, scratches his ear, straightens his spectacles, because the audience interprets them with a view to the character in question. All gestures that are used in theater are expressly generated as signs; there can, in other words, be no insignificant gestures in theater. Even naturalist theater has to take this into account.

107. Such specifically theatrical gestural codes have been created above all in Far Eastern theater such as Indian Kathakali theater, Japanese Nô theater and the Peking Opera. Isolated examples are to be encountered in European theater traditions, such as in courtly baroque theater. See part 2 below.

108. On the gestures used by the Peking Opera see K. Brušak, "Signs in the Chinese Theatre," in L. Matejka and J. R. Titunic, eds., *Semiotics of Art. Prague School Contributions* (Cambridge, Mass., 1976), pp. 59–73; R. Howard, *Le théâtre chinois contemporain* (Paris, 1978); C. Macherras, *The Chinese Theater in Modern Times. From 1840 to the Present Day* (London, 1975); Sergei Obraszov, *Theater in China* (Berlin, 1963).

109. Since in Goethean theater the word functions as the most important system generating meaning, i.e., declamation was of particular significance, gesture had to take a back seat to linguistic meaning or was allowed merely a supporting role. The spectator was meant above all to grasp the meaning of the words the actor declaimed. As a consequence, the following is to be found in Art. 40/41 of the "Rules for Actors":

"40.: One should also take exceptional note not merely to talk into the theater hall, but always towards the audience. For the actor must always divide himself between two objects, namely the object with which he talks and the audience. Instead of turning one's head right round one should allow the eyes to do more of the work.

"41.: It is a most essential point that when two persons are acting together the speaker always move backwards and the person who has ceased to talk move slightly forwards. If one makes reasoned use of this advantageous setting, then the best effect is achieved both for the eye and with regard to the comprehensibility of the declamation. The actor who is a master of this art will be able to create beautiful effects with others who are as well versed as he, and will have a great advantage over those who do not observe this." (J. W. Goethe, "Regeln für Schauspieler," p. 82.)

110. On Ekhof, see among others, H. Kindermann, *Conrad Ekhofs Schauspieler-Akademie*, (*Sitzungsbericht der österr. Akademie der Wissenschaften*, no. 230, 2nd Treatise), (Vienna, 1956); J. Kürschner, *Conrad Ekhofs Leben und Wirken* (Vienna, 1872); C. Pietschmann, "C. Ekhof" (doctoral thesis, Berlin, 1954); H. Uhde, *Conrad Ekhof* (*Der neue Plutarch*, R. Gottschall, ed., part 4) (Leipzig, 1876). On F. L. Schröder, and on "Storm and Stress" theater see, among others, F. Hoffmann, *Friedrich Ludwig Schröder als Dramaturg und Regisseur* (*Schriften der Gesellschaft für Theatergeschichte*, no. 52), (Berlin, 1939); F. L. W. Meyer, *Friedrich Ludwig Schröder*, 2 vols., (Hamburg, 1819); B. Litzmann, *Schröder und Gotter. Briefe. F. L. Schröders an F. W. Gotter 1777 und 1778* (Hamburg and Leipzig, 1857), his *Friedrich Ludwig Schröder. Ein Beitrag zur deutschen Literatur- und Theatergeschichte*, 2 vols. (Hamburg and Leipzig, 1890/1894), and his *Der grosse Schröder* [*Das Theater*, vol. 1 (Berlin, n.d.)]; F. Riccoboni, *Die Schauspielkunst*, with an appendix by F. L. Schröder, "Auszüge aus Franz Riccobonis Vorschriften über die Kunst des Schauspielers mit hinzugefügten Bemerkungen," G. Piens, ed. (Berlin, 1954). On Stanislavsky's treatment of gestures see especially his writings, given in note 25 above, and *Stanislavski Produces Othello* (London and New York, 1948) and *The Seagull, Produced by K. S. Stanislavski*, S. D. Baluchaty, ed. (London, 1952).

111. The dominant use of gestural signs which create meaning at the level of intersubjectivity was to be seen in Peter Stein's production of Botho Strauss's *Trilogie des Wiedersehens* at the Schaubühne am Halleschen Tor in West Berlin. The problems of the possibility or impossibility of successful communication and interaction were elaborated here above all by using this specific group of gestural signs.

112. The gestures developed by commedia dell'arte were related specifically to a type who was immediately recognizable by the audience as such on his first appearance owing to his costume and mask, e.g., the dottore, brighella, arlecchino, capitano, etc. Here, masks, costume, and gestures constitute a stage character as a specific type. On the commedia dell'arte cf., among others, A. K. Yivegelov, *Commedia dell'arte. Die italienische Volkskomödie* (Berlin, 1958); P.-L. Ducharte, *La comédie italienne*, 2nd ed. (Paris, 1925), and his *La commedia dell'arte et ses enfants* (Paris, 1955); M. Kommerell, *Über die Commedia dell'arte* (Frankfurt, 1952); K. M. Lea, *The Italian Popular Comedy. A Study in the Commedia dell'arte 1560–1620, with Special Reference to the English Stage* (Reprint of the 1934 ed., vol. 1.2, Oxford, 1965); C. Mic, *La commedia dell'arte ou le théâtre des comédiens italiens*

des 16ᵉ, 17ᵉ et 18ᵉ siècles (Paris, 1977); V. Pandolfi, *La commedia dell'arte*, 6 vols. (Florence, 1957–1961); F. Taviani, *La commedia dell'arte e la Società barocca*, vol. 1, *La fascinazione del teatro* (Rome, 1971).

113. Since its beginnings, bourgeois theater has postulated the development of a set of gestures that enable the illusion to be created that that which happens on stage is happening in reality. Its main demand is therefore that the gestures be "natural"; only "natural" gestures permit the spectator to grasp the stage characters as his equals, as "human beings" with whom he can empathize and identify. The "naturalness" of the gestures thus functions as the most important factor determining the creation of an illusion of a reality in which the spectator is directly involved owing to his feeling of empathy.

114. The precondition for the development of a such a type of gesture was the elimination of the "naturalness" of the bourgeois, illusion-creating gestures and the transposal of the technique of alienation onto the gestures. "The precondition for the production of an alienation effect is that the actor ornaments what he has to show with the clear gesture of showing it. The notion of a fourth wall, which fictitiously closes the actors off from the spectators and as a result of which the illusion arises that occurrences on stage are actually happening in reality, without the audience, must of course be abandoned" (Bertolt Brecht, "Kurze Beschreibung einer neuen technik der Schauspielkunst, die einen Verfremdungseffekt hervorbringt," in *Gesammelte Werke*, vol. 15, *Schriften zum Theater 1* (Frankfurt/Main: Suhrkamp, 1973), 341–42. Cf., for English language texts, *Brecht on Theatre*, tr. J. Willett, (London: Methuen, 1964). This requires a particular gestural technique: "A simple method by means of which the actor can alienate his gestures is to sever them completely from all mimic elements. He only needs to don a mask and to follow his actions in a mirror. In this way he will easily be able to choose the gestures that are rich in themselves. Precisely the fact that the gestures are specially chosen generates the Alienation Effect" ("Hervorbringung des V-Effektes," *Gesammelte Werke*, vol. 15, 369–70). This prevents the spectator from empathizing with the stage character. Rather, the spectator adopts a critical, distanced stance toward the character. For, "it is the purpose of the A-Effect to render the social gesture that underlies all processes alien. I mean by social gesture the mimic and gestural expression of the social relations which obtain between people in a certain epoch" ("Kurze Beschreibung," p. 346).

115. On the gestural style of *tragédie classique* see, among others, G. Bapst, *Essai sur l'histoire de théâtre* (Paris, 1893); Chappuzeau, *Le théâtre français sous Louis XIV* (Paris, 1874); E. Mas, *La Champmeslé* (Paris, 1927); P. Mélèse, *Le théâtre et le public à Paris sous Louis XIV (1659–1714)* (Paris, 1934); Montgredien, *Les grands comédiens du XVIIe siècle* (Paris, 1927). On the gestural style used by Molière, and above all on the influence of the comédie italienne, cf., among others, R. Abirached, "Molière et la commedia dell'arte. Le detournement du jeu," Ds. RHT XXVI (1974), 223–28; K. Beck, "Le jeune Molière et la commedia dell'arte," Ds. RRO, 5 (1970), 1–16; C. Gundolf, "Molière and the Commedia dell'arte," Ds. AUMLA, 39 (May, 1973), 22–34; R. W. Herzel, "Molière's Actors and the Question of Types," *Theatre Survey* 16, 1 (May 1975): 1–24; S. Relyea, *Signs, Systems and Meanings. A Contemporary Semiotic Reading of Four Molière Plays* (Middletown, Conn., 1976); W. L. Schwartz, *Molière's Theatre in 1672/73* (Publication of the Modern Language Association of America, 1941); P. A. Wadsworth, *Molière and the Italian Theatrical Tradition* (Columbia, 1977).

116. O. Merlin in *Le bel canto* (Paris, 1969) writes on the gestures used by opera singers in the nineteenth century: "the dramatic art of the opera singers, could formerly be summarized as 4 or 5 gestures intended to express the whole gamut of human emotions and comparable with the visual signs made by sailors on the bridge of naval cruisers: (1) placing one's hand on one's heart: "I love you," "I suffer," "my sentiments are pure." (2) the fascist salute: "hallo," "wait a moment," "a guaranteed invoice." (3) putting a hand to one's ear: "What do I hear?" "Don't shout so loudly." (4) both arms outspread, one slightly further than the other: "the end of the verse, you may now applaud."

Although this is undoubtedly an exaggeration, one can nevertheless say that in general the gestures of opera singers at the end of the last century were strongly convention-bound. This first changed in the course of the present century. On the problematics of gestural signs in the opera, cf. N. Scotto di Carlo, "Analyse sémiologique des gestes et mimiques des chanteurs d'opéra," *Semiotica* 9 (1973): 289–318.

117. A. J. Greimas, "Conditions d'une sémiotique du monde naturel," and B. Koechlin, "Techniques corporelles et leur notation symbolique," in *Langages*, 10 (1968): 36–47.

118. Brecht accordingly often suggests the use of such gestures. In his opinion, these concrete activities convey a great deal especially about the stage character: "If Weigel depicts *bread-baking* in the *Gewehre der Frau Carrar*, then this is Mrs. Carrar *baking bread* the night before her son's execution, in other words something quite fixed, something absolutely untransposable. It unites numerous things: the baking of bread, the protest against another occupation, such as fighting, and at the same time *baking bread* as the clock timing the process: her change is accomplished in the time needed for *baking bread* ("Hervorbringung des V-Effektes," p. 370).

119. Brecht attached great importance to these possible ways of accomplishing gestures that fulfilled intentions. He wanted them to already be tried out by actors while still in acting school (e.g., as exercises for the actors: "For women: folding and stacking laundry. The same for men . . . exercises in temperament. Situation: two women calmly fold the laundry. They fake a wild argument based on jealousy for the benefit of their husbands. The husbands are next door—They get caught up in a real tussle while silently folding laundry" ("Übungen für Schauspielschulen, in *Gesammelte Werke*, pp. 423–24).

120. This specific feature makes clear the absolute preeminence of gestural signs over all other theatrical signs: the gestures which fulfill intensions can thus replace a mask, a hairstyle, costume, props, and decorations without one of these signs in turn being able to substitute for the former: theater without gestures is inconceivable.

121. A characteristic example of the validity of this syntactic rule in pantomime is re-corded in the fair scene at the beginning of the film *Les enfants du paradis*. Debureau, a young man played by Jean-Louis Barault, uses pantomime to depict a watch being pick-pocketed. He starts by introducing the persons involved in the scene, the person wearing the watch, and the thief, then points to the object in question—the watch—and subsequently presents the contested action, the robbery. If we can as a whole assume that these syntactic rules are generally adhered to in pantomime, then this still does not mean that they cannot be abandoned, so that the pantomime follows a different syntax. What is noticeable is that the above-mentioned rule is usually observed.

122. Naturally, in individual cases pantomime can get by without gestures that fulfill intensions, although this is not the typical case. Rather, such gestures comprise the type of gestural sign most frequently used in pantomime. Cf. on this point, among others, H. Bollmann, "Untersuchungen zur Kunstgattung Pantomime" (doctoral thesis, Hamburg, 1968); R. J. Broadbent, *A History of the Pantomime* (New York, 1964); E. Decroux, *Paroles sur le mime* (Paris, 1963); M. Frank, *Grundlagenprobleme der Informationsästhetik und erste Anwendung auf die Mime pure* (doctoral thesis, Stuttgart, 1959); M. Marceau, *Die Weltkunst der Pantomime. Bekenntnisse und Gespräche mit Herbert Ihering* (Zurich, 1961); K. G. Simon, *Pantomime. Ursprung, Wesen, Möglichkeiten* (Munich, 1960).

123. This is, for example, the case in the "nocturnal struggle," a famous scene in the Peking Opera. Here, blowing a candle out signifies that the stage is plunged into utter darkness: the spectator sees a punch-up in the room of a restaurant, all brightly lit, and the combatants stumble about in the supposed darkness and are thus unable to distinguish between friend and foe. It is solely the gestures of the actors which repeatedly remind the spectator that the punches are thrown in darkness.

124. Above all these signs have, to date, been exhaustively studied by investigations into proxemics. See E. T. Hall, *The Silent Language*, his *The Hidden Dimension*, and his "A System for the Notation of Proxemic Behavior," *American Anthropologist* 65 (1963): 1003–

27; C. Hutt and M. J. Vaisey, "Differential Effects of Group Size"; R. Sommer, *Personal Space*; O. M. Watson and T. D. Graves, "Quantitative Research"; O. M. Watson, *Proxemic Behaviour*.

125. Watson (1970) has researched this most thoroughly. He came to the conclusion that the differences between the individual cultures both with regard to their assessment of the suitable distance for a conversation and the meanings attached to individual elements of proxemic behavior (such as distance, eye contact, touch, voice volume) are considerable.

126. See Hall, *The Hidden Dimension*; A. Scheflen, *Body Language*.

127. That a breach of the respectively valid rules can function as an element bearing meaning must also be expressly stated in the context of proxemic signs. This element can create meaning both at the subjective and intersubjective levels.

128. This can be demonstrated most clearly by citing the example of the medieval simultaneous stage. Since here a change of scene cannot occur by means of a change of decorations, the change from one location to another is effected by moving from one part of the stage to another (e.g., from the ointment seller's stand to the grave). Since each part of the stage has a fixed meaning, only moving from one to another can depict a change of location. (For the medieval stage, cf. esp. W. F. Michael, *Frühformen der deutschen Bühne* [*Schriften der Gesellschaft für Theatergeschichte*, no. 62] [Berlin, 1963]).

129. Thus, for example, the binding convention existed in Greek comic theater from the fourth century onward that if an actor appeared from the right parados this signified that he "came from the market or harbor," whereas entry from the left constituted "arriving from the country." See H. D. Blume, *Einführung in das antike Theaterwesen*, (Darmstadt, 1978), chapter 3, "Die Theaterbauten"; A. W. Pickard-Cambridge, *The Theatre of Dionysus in Athens* (Oxford, 1946).

130. In this way, movement through space—whether circular, parallel or diagonal—can be instilled with symbolic meaning. Brecht made use of this in his model production of *Mother Courage*: he had Courage travel around and around the circular stage in her canvas wagon at the end of the play, thus creating the effect of her traveling for eternity. It became clear that this form of constituting meaning is only possible in theater when Brecht tried to film the production: in the film, the circular movement has the effect of making Courage appear to return continually. The requisite meaning was achieved here by the camera filming Courage moving ever further away in a straight line until she disappeared from sight. This type of proxemic sign becomes important especially for the choreography of dance, sword-fighting and mass scenes, above all, of course, in dance theater. See R. zur Lippe, *Natur-beherrschung am Menschen*, 2 vols. (Frankfurt/Main, 1974).

131. Dance can only be adequately grasped if the position and movement of the dancer in space are conceived of as the basic units of the investigation, i.e., if dance is interpreted as a text composed of proxemic signs. If existing theories of dance are studied in this light, then it becomes apparent that this assertion is nothing more than a commonplace, yet one that can only be stated in this manner in terms of a systematic study of theatrical sign. On theories of dance, cf. S. J. Cohen, *Dance as Dramatic Art. Source Readings in Dance History from 1581 to the Present* (New York, 1974); B. Kockno, *Diaghilev and the Ballet Russe* (London, 1971); B. Köllinger, "Der Tanz als Prozess—der Prozess im Tanz. Histor.-materialistische Untersuchung zur ästhetischen Spezifik der Tanzkunst unter besonderer Berücksichtigung des Widerspiegelungsaspektes" (doctoral thesis, Leipzig, 1972); R. zur Lippe, *Naturbeherrschung*, vols 1 and 2; J. Georges Noverre, *Letters on Dancing and Ballets*, tr. C. W. Beaumont (London: Beaumont, 1930); *Documents choreologica*; T. Shawn, *Dance We Must* (New York, 1974); A. Testa, *Discorso sulla danza e sul balletto* (Rome, 1970); A. J. Vaganova, *Die Grundlagen des klassischen Tanzes*, 4th ed. (Wilhelmshaven, 1977); G. B. L. Wilson, *A Dictionary of Ballet*, 3d ed. (New York, 1974).

132. On the realization of different norms in the history of ballet, see, among others, C. W. Beaumont, *Complete Book of Ballets. A Guide to the Principal Ballets of the 19th and 20th Centuries, Supplements 1–3* (London, 1951–1955); P. Brinson, *Background to European Ballet. A Note Book from Its Archives* (Leiden, 1966); J. Gregor, *Kulturgeschichte des*

Balletts. Seine Gestaltung und Wirksamkeit in der Geschichte und den Künsten (Vienna, 1944); U. Roslavleva, *Era of the Russian Ballet* (New York, 1966); C. Sachs, *World History of the Dance*, tr. B. Schönberg (London: Allen Unwin, 1938); H. Schmidt-Garre, *Ballett. Vom Sonnenkönig bis Balanchine* (Velber, 1966); R. Schrade, *Sowjetisches Ballett* (Berlin, 1977).

133. This state of affairs must be taken into account when undertaking the attempt to establish what the smallest units of dance are and the possible combinations and potential meanings thereof. Margot Laske accordingly assumes that "any theory of dance must begin with a description of the possible structures or patterns underlying its composition" (p. 107). In her study, she concludes that "the sequences of dance consist of alternative units of rest and motion, each sequence beginning and ending with a unit of rest" (p. 119). On the basis of this investigation she puts forward the following structural model for dance:

In this model, rest and motion function as the smallest distinctive units, from which a step can be created, for at present it is by no means legitimate to regard the step as the smallest unit. See M. D. Lasker, "The Pause in the Moving Structure of Dance," *Semiotica* 22 no. 1–2 (1978): 107–126.

134. We shall study this process with reference to norms in part 2, with regard to speech in part 3 of this book.

135. In the first case, the signs realized simultaneously thus express, for example, joy or anger: the statement "I am enjoying myself," or "I could burst with *anger*" are accompanied by paralinguistic, mimic, gestural, and proxemic signs that can be interpreted as expressions of the corresponding affect. In the second case, by contrast, the affects expressed by the different signs contradict one another: "I could burst with anger" is perhaps stated with a tone of subdued joy, a smile appears on the lips of the speaker, his arms outspread. Alternately, however, and this makes the interpretation difficult, linguistic, paralinguistic, and mimic signs occur parallel to one another, yet the gestural and proxemic signs express contradictory affects. Finally, in the third case, not all simultaneously realized signs refer to one another: the actress sews, weaves, spins yarn, or executes other gestures which fulfill an intension, whereby she sighs, laughs, or narrates something. Here, linguistic, paralinguistic, and mimic signs support each other; the gestural signs, however, are in no direct relation to the meaning they convey—that is, unless the way in which these movements are carried out can be related to the other signs.

136. In Goethe's Weimar theater, the spectator will doubtless have believed the linguistic and paralinguistic signs more than the kinesic signs—if the words and voice expressed sorrow, but the face and body did not, he would nevertheless have been convinced that stage character X was sad. In Stanislavsky's theater, however, the spectator would come to the conclusion in the same situation that the sorrow expressed by the words and voice were either not really true, or at least not the only feelings governing X at the time, indeed, that X in reality remains indifferent.

137. If Brecht, for example, forgoes the use of lighting as an element bearing meaning by having the whole performance take place on a brightly lit stage—whereby the lighting is, as it were, neutralized and loses its sign character—then this renunciation itself becomes a sign. Brecht uses it to convey his rejection of bourgeois atmospheric theater. The third

volume of the German edition of the present study provides an extensive analysis of a performance in which the notions developed here are put to concrete use.

2. The Actor's Appearance as a Sign

1. We cannot go into the problematics of identity in detail in the present framework, but must rather limit ourselves to a sociopsychological concept of identity. Since social psychology postulates identity as the product of communicative processes, this concept of identity would seem to be particularly suitable for our specific context. On the philosophical concept of identity, see above all D. Henrich, " 'Identität'—Begriffe, Probleme, Grenzen," in Odo Marquard and K. H. Stierle, eds., *Identität. Poetik und Hermeneutik VIII* (Munich, 1979), 133–86. On the problem of identity in drama see Fischer-Lichte, *Geschichte des Dramas. Epochen der Identität auf dem Theater*, 2 vols. (Tübingen: Francke, 1990).

2. G. H. Mead, *Mind, Self and Society, from the Standpoint of a Social Behaviorist* (Chicago, 1934).

3. Ibid.

4. G. Simmel, "Die Mode," in G. Simmel, *Philosophische Kultur. Gesammelte Essays*, 2nd expanded ed. (Leipzig, 1919), pp. 27–28.

5. In this context, we understand fashion solely as a canon of rules that describe what external appearance should look like, but not the canon which prescribes which cultural events are "in" and where "one" eats out at present, or even which "fashionable words" are preferred at present.

6. G. P. Stone, "Appearance and the Self, in A. M. Rose, ed., *Human Behaviour and Social Processes. An Interactionist Approach* (London, 1962), pp. 86–118. When devising a new definition for the concept of identity, Stone does not refer to Simmel, whose work he is clearly not acquainted with, but rather develops the concept on the basis of his own research.

7. Ibid, p. 90

8. Ibid, pp. 93 and 101.

9. Even in the case of a person wishing to present himself to other people in a way that differs from the way he sees and assesses himself, he will nevertheless have recourse to these mutual meanings. Because only by knowing which meanings are generally accorded this or that external appearance in society will he be able to modify his own external appearance in such a way as to permit the others to attribute the meaning he intends to it.

10. This is by no means only true of the case in which the actor's external appearance provides information on age, sex, social standing, epoch in question, race, nationality, profession, or stage character X's type. Rather, it also holds in general, in other words even if the actor's external appearance also provides an interpretation of the stage character. Thus, in Hans Neuenfels's 1978/79 Frankfurt production of *Oedipus*, Jocasta was made to look like a cow, with a black leather suit and a coat of hide with black and white patches. The costume thus functioned to convey a specific characterization of the particular stage role, one that the spectator is told the moment Jocasta takes the stage.

11. Aristotle, *De Anima*, tr. D. W. Hamlyn (Oxford: Oxford University Press, 1975).

12. The most important representatives of eighteenth-century physiognomics were Paracelsus (*Archidoxes of Magic: Of the Supreme Mysteries of Nature, and the Spirits, of Plants, of Occult Philosophy*, tr. R. Turner [Askin, 1975]) and G. B. della Porta (*De humana physiognomica* [1593]; *Della celesta fisonomia* [1616]). Physiognomic comparisons with animals are to be encountered from Aristotle to Lavater: a human with a sheep's head possesses the characteristics attributed to a sheep, someone with an "eagle's head" the properties of the eagle, etc.

13. This often asserted analogy only makes sense in the framework of a certain worldview, for example a theological conception which assumes that God created everything in such a

way as to ensure that each thing's external appearance is the visible signature of its essence. Paracelsus expressly promulgated this notion.

14. J. C. Lavater, *Physiognomic Sketches* (London, 1802).

15. G. C. Lichtenberg, "Bemerkungen vermischten Inhalts," in L. C. Lichtenberg and F. Kries, eds., *Georg Christoph Lichtenbergs vermischte Schriften*, vol. 1 (Göttingen, 1801), 181.

16. G. C. Lichtenberg, "Über Physiognomik, wider die Physiognomen. Zur Beförderung der Menschliebe und Menschenkenntnis," ibid., vol. 3, 448. See *The Lichtenberg Reader*, tr. F. Mautner and H. Hatfield (Boston: Beacon, 1959).

17. What Lichtenberg wished to investigate by means of pathognomics is today the subject studied by kinesics: mimicry, gestures, and spatial movement. Cf. chap. 1, the section on paralinguistic signs.

18. Kretschmar's typology is a particularly impressive example for such a renaissance in our century: he distinguishes between athletic, leptomose, and pyknic types of physique, each of which is supposed to correspond to a particular character structure. See his *Physique and Character*, tr. W. J. H. Sprott (London: Kegan Paul, 1936). By 1967 the German original had been through 25 editions.

19. Just how variable such stereotypes are within a culture can be seen by the attitude toward skin color in our culture. At the beginning of the century women with a very pale skin were greatly esteemed, because their skin showed that they did not need to work outside; today, by contrast, a brown skin is "fashionable." It attests to the fact that one can afford a long holiday in the sun—something which brings great prestige with it—and is a sign of health.

20. In cultures that accord a great value to advanced age, a wrinkled skin, which attests to great age, can indeed be understood as a sign for the high social status of the people in question.

21. Social psychology has discovered that this wish is the motivation for many forms of action and behavior. It is also at the root of the functioning of the sign system of "external appearance."

22. Lévi-Strauss has emphasized this function in chap. 8, "Split Representation in the Art of Asia and America," *Structural Anthropology*, pp. 245–68. He states (p. 259): "In native thought, as we saw, the design *is* the face, or rather it creates it. It is the design which confers upon the face its social existence, its human dignity, its spiritual significance. Split representation of the face, considered as a graphic device, thus expresses a deeper and more fundamental splitting, namely that between the 'dumb' biological individual and the social person whom he must embody."

23. Painting one's face is, in other words, not just something to be noted among so-called primitive peoples, but is common in almost all cultures. In our cultures, those periods in which almost all types of "makeup" were frowned on as "unnatural"—although makeup continued to be used—have alternated with periods in which it has been considered almost shameful nakedness to appear in public without makeup. Cf. M. Angeloglou, *A History of Make-Up* (London, 1970).

24. Scarring one's skin is not just something to be encountered among primitive peoples (such as the Sudanese). One needs only bear in mind the scars which twentieth-century German students inflicted on their cheeks in the fencing clubs. These functioned on the one hand as signs for a particular character trait: whoever had one or more such scars was considered courageous. On the other, they were a sign for membership of a social group: a fencing club, which, at the time, was highly prestigious.

25. More well-known forms of deformation are the practice of binding girls' feet in prerevolutionary China, "tying up wasp's waists" in Europe and America in the last century, and pressing heads. Desmond Morris, *Manwatching. A Field Guide*, (London: Cape, 1977).

26. In addition to the types of deformation mentioned, we must also consider other forms of changing one's shape, such as regulating body size by eating a great deal or only a little. Whereas, for example, women in Arabian countries often have to eat a lot in order to come

up to the ideal of beauty prevalent there, women in West Europe and North America often have to starve to the same end. Waist and body size is therefore also a question of the stereotype valid at the time.

27. This is important to the extent that otherwise certain methodological implications would arise. However, since the mask can be regarded as a sign of an already existing sign functioning in the respective culture, it can be examined with the same metholodogical tools as used for linguistic, paralinguistic, and kinesic signs. See chap. 5, the section entitled "The Specificity of the Theatrical Sign."

28. On the corresponding potential of stage makeup, cf. J. W. Baker, *Elements of Stagecraft* (Sherman Oaks, 1978); R. Balqué, *Die Maske des Schauspielers* (Leipzig, 1942); R. Corson, *Stage Make-up* (Englewood Cliffs, N.J., 1975); Motley, *Theater Props* (New York, 1979).

29. This is true of Peking Opera, of Kabuki theater, and of Katakali dance theater, in other words of theater forms in which the different ornamental masks have differing, precisely defined, and fixed meanings.

30. In the cases mentioned, there is often interaction between the theater mask and the notions predominant in the culture in question on what such a being should look like: on the one hand, a theater mask is part of the general mythological stocks, and, on the other, a quite specific mask arises on the basis of the general mythological stocks.

31. One of the few cultures that are not acquainted with masks is pygmy culture, although it has a rich theatrical tradition. The invention of masks and the development of theatrical forms must not, therefore, be deemed to always go hand in hand. On mask culture, cf. especially G. Burand, *Les masques*, (Paris, 1961).

32. For example, marriages, harvest festivals, and carnivals.

33. For example, initiation rites, exorcising a demon of sickness, etc. See G. Mehren, "Sinn und Gestalt der Maske," *Antaios* 11, No. 2 (1969): 136–53.

34. A hangman usually wears a mask when exercising his profession; this custom probably dates back to magical notions—the mask shields the hangman against the revenge of the dead, for his disguise prevents him from being recognized and therefore later persecuted. See Mehren, "Sinn und Gestalt."

35. This is true not only of secret societies, such as the leopard society in Africa, or the Ku Klux Klan, but also of every criminal who conceals his face behind a mask—frequently behind a balaclava helmet or a stocking. See I. Shallek, *Masks* (New York, 1973).

36. B. L. Ogibenin, "Mask in the Light of Semiotics—A Functional Approach," *Semiotica* 13, no. 1 (1975): 4–5.

37. For, "decoration is actually *created* for the face but in another sense, the face is predestined to be decorated, since it is only by means of decoration that the face receives its social dignity and mystical significance" (Lévi-Strauss, *Structural Anthropology*, p. 261).

38. On this point see Mehren, "Sinn und Gestalt." J. Jallat has the following to say on this problem: "The mask is initially an image of scission, of the person and the personality, of the body and the spirit, of me for myself and of me for others. A masked person is initially a divided person, someone who feels divided and is divided. Yet my division is merely the effect of reproducing the division of language. If, by virtue of an artefact (a grimace) 'the body ceases to be a thing and becomes a sign' (p. 206), then this occurs because 'the fracture is felt between 'nature' and the signs, between the sign and meaning, because the sign is solely a sign; it cannot experience us' (p. 195). The equivalence of 'me = me' (p. 197) is wrong and with it the reciprocity of the conscience' (p. 196). Donning a pseudonym or a mask is to redouble the two faces of signification, to turn the one back toward the exterior, although even there it remains "ineffable," mystery or absence. All attention is in effect focussed on the exterior, on the appearance, on the signified without a signifier which pretends to be the mask" ("Le masque ou l'art du déplacement," *Poétique* 5 [1971]: 482). The page numbers in parentheses are from J. Starobinski, "Stendhal pseudonyme," in *L'Oeil vivant* (Paris, 1951), from which Jallat quotes.

39. "Masks serve the purpose of and are used for the isolation (self-isolation) of the

wearer from the external social and cultural environment'' (Ogibenin, ''Mask in the Light,'' pp. 1–2).

40. ''It is not as a result of movement in itself that the mask has its effect, but of human life that is linked with the strange appearance—strange, even if the mask bears human traits. The observer therefore gets to know a more human strangeness, gets to know it sometimes at threateningly close quarters, and yet at the same time the strangeness is emphasized by the tension between mask and bearer'' (D. Frey, ''Zuschauer und Bühne,'' in *Kunstwissenschaftliche Grundfragen* [Vienna, 1946] p. 157).

41. An important function of the mask manifests itself here, namely, disguise as protection from spirits or humans bent on revenge and wishing to inflict injury. See Mehren, ''Sinn und Gestalt.''

42. This is to be seen above all when the person bearing the mask changes during the ritual. Ibid.

43. The members of the Ku Klux Klan are therefore not to be held responsible for their deeds as real subjects of society. For it is anonymous members of the Klan who perpetrate the deeds and not real, identifiable subjects.

44. Cf. Frey, ''Zuschauer und Bühne.''

45. This is also true if the mask bearer himself—e.g., in a trance—identifies subjectively with that which the mask signifies: for other persons, the mask always points to the difference.

46. To this extent, it is not surprising that in the language of theater the German expression ''Maske machen'' (''to make a mask'') means as much as ''to effect the transformation externally.''

47. The fact that masks can, of course, also be used outside theater—for example, at carnivals—remains untouched by this statement.

48. See on this point H. Luschey, ''Dionysosmasken,'' in *Ganymed* (Heidelberg, 1949), pp. 64–70; M.-P. Nilsson, *A History of Greek Religion*, tr. F. J. Fielden (Oxford: Clarendon Press, 1949); W. Wrede, ''Der Maskengott,'' *MDAI* (A) 53 (1928): 66–95.

49. See on this H. Bulle, ''Von griechischen Schauspielern und Vasenmalern,'' in *Festschrift J. Loev* (Munich, 1930), pp. 10ff.; P. Chiron-Bistagne, *Recherches sur les acteurs dans la Grèce antique* (Paris, 1976): A. W. Pickard-Cambridge, *The Dramatic Festivals of Athens*, 2nd ed., revised by J. Gould and D. M. Lewis (Oxford, 1968).

50. See on this H. D. Blume, *Einführung*, pp. 88ff.

51. On the history of the fixed theater mask cf. K. K. Kachler, ''Theater und Maske,'' in Hürlimann, ed., *Atlantisbuch des Theaters* (Zurich, 1966), and his ''Über Wesen und Wirken der Theatermaske,'' *Antaios* 10, no. 2 (1969): 192–208.

52. See Frey, ''Zuschauer und Bühne;'' K. W. Peukert, ''Verwandlung und Gegenwart der Maske,'' *Antaios* 11, no. 2 (1969): 121–35.

53. In this light, only those forms of theater can appear deficient that aim to create a complete illusion, such as, for example, bourgeois theater in the second half of the nineteenth century.

54. Such as, for example, comic theater in the Greco-Roman tradition. See on this G. Krien, ''Der Ausdruck der antiken Theatermasken,'' *JÖAI* 41 (1955): 84–117; H. Luschey, ''Komödien-Masken,'' in *Ganymed* (Heidelberg, 1949), pp. 71ff.; C. Robert, *Die Masken der neueren attischen Komödie (25th Winckelmann Programm in Halle*, 1911): T. B. L. Webster, *Griechische Bühnenaltertümer, Studienhefte zur Alterswissenschaft*, no. 9 (Göttingen, 1963).

55. Cf. on this especially D. Keene, *Nô. The Classical Theater of Japan* (Tokyo, 1975): Zeami, *On the Art of Nô Drama*, tr. J. T. Rimer and Y. Masakazu (Princeton: Princeton Univ. Press, 1984).

56. This is also attested to by the fact that the mask is often passed on from father to son. See Keene, *Nô*.

57. This demand was to be heard as early as the beginnings of bourgeois theater, for Lessing required that the actor should act in such a manner that the spectator could identify him with the stage character. He was of the opinion that only under this condition could the

spectator empathize with the character. He considered such empathy the precondition for catharsis, for the excitement of fear and pity. See G. E. Lessing, *Briefe, die neueste Literatur betreffend*, W. Bender, ed. (Stuttgart, 1972), especially Letter 17.

58. The mask is so well suited for nonillusionist forms of theater for precisely this reason, because they attempt to prevent the identification of actor and stage character and the spectator's resulting empathy with the character. Masks are therefore increasingly being used in experimental theater today.

59. See G. Mehren, ''Sinn und Gestalt'', pp. 138ff.

60. The interconnection of mask and dance is not only evidenced by all mask cultures— e.g., masked dances—but also in forms of theater that use masks: thus in the dances performed by the masked chorus members in Greek tragedy and comedy.

61. Almost all theories of the mask point expressly to this. See Frey, ''Zuschauer und Bühne''; Lévi-Strauss, *Structural Anthropology*; Mehren, ''Sinn und Gestalt''; Ogibenin, ''Mask in the Light''; Peukert, ''Verwandlung und Gegenwart''; and above all the excellent study by the Russian theater scholar A. D. Avdeev, *Proizchoždenie Teatra* (Leningrad and Moscow, 1959), in which Avdeev deals exclusively with the problem of the mask and then develops the genesis of theater from it. Cf. also his *Maska i ee rol' v prozesse vozniknoveniya teatra* (Moscow, 1969).

62. Kowzan already pointed to the fact that in principle the hair style can be used as a special sign distinct from that of the mask and that it is frequently used in this capacity in European theater in the twentieth century. See Kowzan, ''Znak w teatrze.''

63. In such a case we cannot speak of the signs ''mask'' and ''costume'' not being used, for the actor's face and his clothed or naked body are givens. In a certain historical context, however, the fact that makeup is not worn or that a black T-shirt is worn may indicate that the mask and costume are not being used in the usual way as signs here. In other words, that their meaning is exhausted in the statement that they have no further meaning. This can, of course, in turn be interpreted as a sign for the underlying conception of theater. Brecht used light in a corresponding way.

64. Literature and painting provide a wealth of material with regard to detecting such stereotypes for example in the history of our own culture.

65. See on this Wendy Cooper's summary of cultural history: *Hair, Sex, Society, Symbolism* (London, 1971).

66. This catalogue could be expanded to include the feature: type of hair style, e.g., tresses hang down/are tied in a bun; straight hair is braided/simply tied with a ribbon, etc. Since we have to do with a fact of artificial preparation, this feature must only be considered when discussing the social sign function of the hair style. It is irrelevant for the cultural interpretation of naturally given hair.

67. See Cooper, *Hair*, especially chapter 1.

68. Cf. on this issue, among others, A. Daraul, *Witches and Sorcerers* (London, 1962); W. Fischer, *Aberglaube in alten Zeiten* (Stuttgart, 1906); J. Michelet, *Satanism and Witchcraft*, tr. A. R. Allinson (London: Tandem, 1969); G. Tindall, *A Handbook on Witches* (London, 1965). A woman's red hair was held to be a sign of her bad character and so was a man's red beard. Thus Pagenstecher writes: ''Red beard always to be feared / Red beard, rascal neared.'' This has to do with the fact that Judas the ''arch-rascal'' was held to have had a red beard. Charlemagne thus declared it to be a punishable offense to call someone a redbeard. A blond beard, by contrast, counted as a sign of purity and courage: no wonder that many men dyed their beards in the Middle Ages. See R. Reynolds, *Beards—Their Social Standing, Religious Involvement, Decorative Possibilities and Value in Offence and Defence through the Ages* (New York, 1949).

69. On this notion see M. Bouisson, *Magic. Its History and Principal Rites* (New York, 1961); W. Cooper, *Hair*; E. R. Leach, ''Magical Hair,'' in *Journal of the Royal Anthropological Institute* 88 (1958): 147–64.

70. This stereotype has also found its place in trash literature: the good heroines of Courts-Mahler or Marlitt novels are of course blondes, their tricky antagonists are normally black-haired women.

71. This stereotype may clearly derive from a different strand of tradition, namely the same context as that of Loreley, the seductress with her blonde hair.

72. Cf. Leach, "Magical Hair," and Reynolds, *Beards*.

73. The cultural interpretation of natural phenomena rests—this much is apparent—on the same principles with regard to both physiognomy and hair. What is strived for is always a transformation of nature into culture, of being into signs.

74. A wealth of material proving this is to be found in ethnographical studies in which the social significance of hair style is repeatedly emphasized. On this function of hair see, among others, R. F. Fortune, *Sorcerers of Dobu* (London, 1932); J. H. Hutton, *The Anganue Nagas* (London, 1921); L. K. Iyer, *The Mysore Tribes and Castes*, 4 vols. (1928–35); E. R. Leach, "A Trobiand Medusa," *Man* (1954): 115f; and his "Magical Hair"; B. Malinowski, *The Sexual Life of Savages* (London, 1932); J. P. Mills, *The Rengma Nagas* (London, 1937); K. W. Morgan, *The Religion of Hindus* (New York, 1953); A. R. Radcliffe-Brown, *The Andaman Islanders* (Cambridge, 1933); M. N. Srinivas, *Religion and Society among the Coorgs of South India* (Oxford, 1952).

75. Cf. on this M. von Boehn, *Mode and Manners of the 19th Century*, tr. J. Joshua (vols. 1–4) and M. Edwardes (vol. 5) (London, 1909).

76. See Reynolds, *Beards*, chapter 2; "Of Antick Beards," pp. 17–42.

77. On this function see Cooper, *Hair*; Hutton, *The Anganue Indians*; R. König, *The Restless Image. A Sociology of Fashion*, tr. F. Bradley (London: Allen Unwin, 1979).

78. U.S. Army soldiers are still obliged to have their hair cut in a certain way. The profession-related haircut is by no means restricted to priests, monks, and soldiers: in ancient Rome the prostitutes, for example, wore yellow wigs as a sign of their profession. Wigs have often proved how suitable they are for fulfilling this function. One need think only of English judges who still wear them as a sign of their office.

79. P. Bogatyrev has stressed this function of hairdressing for certain regions of Slovakia. See his *The Functions of Folk Costume in Moravian Slovakia*, *Approaches to Semiotics*, no. 5 (The Hague and Paris, 1971).

80. This has to do with religious valuations. See above.

81. Cf. Reynolds, *Beards*, pp. 272ff. Kathrin Perutz has traced the political function of the afro look when it was first adopted in her *Beyond the Looking Glass: America's Beauty Culture* (New York, 1970), especially the chapter on hair, pp. 69–90.

82. Quoted from Reynolds, *Beards*, p. 271.

83. Ibid, pp. 41ff. B. Malinowski, *The Sexual Life*, concerns himself with this function of hair, as does G. A. Wilken, *Über das Haaropfer*, Special Issue of *Revue Coloniale Internationale* (Amsterdam, 1886). Wilken's comparative studies help him to uncover two types of hairstyles as signs of sorrow: (1) a totally shaven head and face, and (2) forgoing any type of hairdressing or treatment of facial hair. These examples make clear just how well suited hair is to function as a sign for special social situations.

84. In so-called primitive societies we can in principle assume that the rules are generally obeyed. The individual, as a special value, is accorded no special status in these cultures, just as is the case in numerous highly developed cultures.

85. For example, with the aid of feathers, ribbons, etc.

86. The type of hairdressing always constitutes a distinguishing feature in theater, because it is not based on a reference to natural phenomena, as is the case with stereotypes, but rather on a reference to cultural phenomena.

87. With regard to the function of the hair style, it is quite irrelevant whether the hair in question is the natural hair of the actress or a wig. Both function in theater as a sign of a sign.

88. The historical function can, needless to say, become important for the theatrical codes of such ages or cultures only if these exhibit an awareness of history. See R. Corson, *Fashions in Hair. The First Five Thousand Years* (London, 1971).

89. For example, in Greek theater, the hero had a blond wig, the "baddy" a black wig, and the comic figure a red wig.

90. It may well be that this color symbolism applies to the whole performance, i.e., also

determines the decorations and lighting. Attempts which foreground the painterly element are typical of the wide variety of forms taken by *Stilbühne*. See G. Fuchs, *Die Schaubühne der Zukunft* (Berlin, 1904) and his *Die Revolution des Theaters* (Munich, 1909).

91. J. Laver, *Costume in the Theatre* (London, 1964), p. 15.

92. This may be particularly true of our culture, yet it is to be encountered in different forms in almost all known cultures. See J. C. Flugel, *The Psychology of Clothes* (1930; London, 1952).

93. D. J. de Levita, *The Concept of Identity* (The Hague and Paris: Mouton, 1965).

94. Ibid.

95. On the concept of role-set, cf. R. Merton, "The Role Set," *British Journal of Sociology* 8 (1957): 106–120.

96. E. Gross and G. P. Stone, "Verlegenheit und Analyse der Voraussetzungen des Rollenhandelns," in M. Auwärter, E. Kirsch, and K. Schröter, eds., *Seminar: Kommunikation, Interaktion, Identität* (Frankfurt/Main, 1976), pp. 275–306, here p. 272.

97. I believe it apposite to forgo a more detailed discussion of the concept of role here. What is important for our purposes is above all the relation between role and identity.

98. See E. Goffmann, *Stigma, Notes on the Management of Spoiled Identity* (Harmondsworth: Penguin, 1968).

99. Cf. on this point the introduction to the chapter on actors' "external appearance."

100. Naturally, specific clothing is not foreseen for all conceivable social roles in the social life of the different cultures. Rather, as with primitive peoples, such clothing is in part envisaged for role distinctions that are important for the social structure, such as man/woman, chieftain/simple member of the tribe, shaman/noninitiate, etc. We take the "normal case" of our culture as the point of departure.

101. Clearly in connection with the respective mask; for precisely mask and costume belong very closely together in the aforementioned forms of theater.

102. This example clearly shows that the concept of social role and that of theatrical role can by no means be used synonymously. On the history of the transposal of the theatrical concept of role into society as a whole and on the differences between the two types of concept, see U. Rapp, *Handeln und Zuschauen*, above all chap. 2, "Rollenspiel," pp. 91–170.

103. Form is understood here to mean not only the cut of the clothes, but also the principles of internal arrangement used, such as repetition, symmetry, etc.

104. Cf. on this point Flugel, *The Psychology of Clothes*, chap. 1, "The Fundamental Motives: Decoration, Modesty, Protection."

105. Here, we follow the principle of division—one founded in a general semiotics of culture—suggested by Eco. Cf. Eco, *Einführung*, especially section C, "Funktion und Zeichen (Semiotik der Architektur)," pp. 293–360.

106. P. Bogatyrev has demonstrated the function of clothes as a sign of membership of a religion with regard to folk costumes in Slovakia—the costumes foresee different features for members of the Catholic and Protestant churches respectively. See his *The Functions*. As far as I know this study is the only comprehensive investigation using semiotic means of a regional form of clothing and can therefore be considered both to be pioneering and to set the methodological example for research efforts to follow. By contrast, the work preferentially mentioned in bibliographies, namely R. Barthes's *Fashion System* (London: Cape, 1985) cannot count as a semiotic study of western fashion, but rather as a structural analysis of the language which refers to fashion. Accordingly, the primary object of study is not fashionable clothing actually worn, but rather fashion magazines.

107. Cf. René König, *The Restless Image*.

108. Cf. P. Bogatyrev, *The Functions*.

109. Even if this type of clothing is donned owing to a practical function it has—such as a swimming costume—it nevertheless realizes a symbolic function: it points to a situation without having actually to be used appropriately in line with the situation. The swimming costume indicates that the wearer wishes to swim, even if s/he does not actually do this.

110. See on this S. Koessler, "Postal, Body-Image and Identity: A Comparison of Kwiakutl and Hopi," *American Anthropologist* 67 (1965): 455–61.

111. See Flugel, *The Psychology of Clothes*, chap. 6, "Individual Differences," pp. 85–102. Such investigations of individual differences can of course only be valid for one particular culture. Thus, Flugel's types can only be applied to members of western culture.

112. Cf. S. D. Messing, "The Nonverbal Language of Ethiopian Toga," *Anthropus* 55 no. 3/4 (1960): 558–61.

113. Cf. Flugel, *The Psychology of Clothes*, chap. 5, "Protection," pp. 68–84.

114. R. Broby-Johansen, *Body and Clothes* (London, 1968).

115. The third level which we were able to discern in the case of signs which are generated as activity by the actor, namely the object level, is missing here. We could say that a practical function has taken its place: clothing does not denote a particular object, but rather a use function. Cf. Eco, *Einführung*.

116. By contrast, Bogatyrev claims that the theater costume must also realize a practical function: "A theatrical paper Chinese costume, for example, has as its function to show that the wearer is playing the role of a Chinese, however, it serves as an object as well, insofar as it covers the actor's body" (*The Functions*, p. 82). It does indeed cover the actor's body, but it does not have the function of covering him, but rather of pointing to the stage character as Chinese. This must, to my mind, be kept separate. On this problem, see also P. Bogatyrev, "Costume as a Sign," in L. Matejka and J. R. Titunic, eds., *Semiotics of Art. Prague School Contributions*, pp. 15–19, as well as his "Semiotics in the Folk Theatre," in *Semiotics*, pp. 33–50, and "Forms and Functions of Folk Theatre," in *Semiotics*, pp. 51–56.

117. The function of general characterization of stage roles is indeed the predominant function of costume on German stages today. Examples of this are to be found above all in productions by Zadek, Peymann, and Neuenfels. Interestingly enough, recourse is frequently had there to cultural codes such as are at the root of comic or such as are formed and popularized by comics. Clearly, many directors assume that the mythology of comics is ground common to most and on which one can therefore rely in any case if one wishes to be understood.

118. Cf. D. A. Russell, *Stage Costume Design, Theory, Technique and Style* (New York, 1973).

119. This possibility is exploited above all by a form of theater which makes use of presentational settings. Particularly the writings of Appia and Craig make clear how the composition is based on a certain overall impression which harmonizes in terms of color. Thus, Craig writes of the director: " . . . but he first of all chooses certain colours which seem to him to be in harmony with the spirit of the play, rejecting other colours as out of tune. He then weaves into a pattern certain objects—an arch, a fountain, a balcony, a bed— using the chosen object as the centre of his design. Then he adds to this all the objects which are mentioned in the play, and which are necessary to be be seen. To these he adds, one by one, each character which appears in the play, and gradually each movement of each character, and each costume" E. G. Craig, *On the Art of Theatre* (Heinemann, London, 1911).

120. On the history of stage costume see, among others, M. von Boehn, *Das Bühnenkostüm in Altertum, Mittelalter und Neuzeit* (Berlin, 1921); I. Brooke, *Western-European Costume. Its Relation to the Theatre*, vol. 1.2 (London, 1939–40); J. Gregor, *Das Bühnenkostüm in historischer, ästhetischer und psychologischer Analyse, Wiener szenischer Kunst*, no. 2 (Zurich, 1925); J. Laver, *Costume in the Theatre*; R. Zitta, "Bühnenkostüm und Mode vom Naturalismus bis zum Expressionismus", (doctoral thesis, Vienna, 1961).

121. See on this P. Bogatyrev, "Semiotics in the Folk Theatre."

122. The aforementioned catalogues of costumes of contemporary German theater provide ample proof of this. They are usually based on general cultural codes, a knowledge of which can be assumed to exist owing to their wide dissemination by film and comics. In general, we can presume with regard to the costume codes of West European theater that they refer

to general cultural codes and specific codes for clothing that can be considered valid among the social stratum that supports the respective form of theater.

123. See the analysis on the German version of part 3.

124. In order to clarify this, I shall cite two completely different examples. Shaw's Eliza Doolittle wears a dress to the Ascot races which suggests the expectation of "ladylike" behavior by the character. Her linguistic and gestural behavior, however, only corresponds with this to a certain degree, because Eliza does not succeed completely in substituting elements in keeping with her clothing for the elements of her behavior which stem from the social context of a flower girl. At the beginning and end of the play, clothing and behavior are concurrent, yet the course of the play is characterized by their divergence. Quite the opposite is the case in Calderon's *Constant Prince*. At the beginning, clothing and behavior accord with one another. At the end, however, the clothing highlights the prince as a slave, a beggar, and an impoverished person, although his behavior has remained the same. This device reveals that the external appearance is a mere semblance which the enduring being of the character, something to be decided solely before God, confronts.

125. The body functions in this sense as a factor for identifying the individual identity. Cf. Levita, *The Concept of Identity*.

126. On this problem cf. especially G. Simmel, "Zur Philosophie des Schauspielers," in his *Das individuelle Gesetz, Philosophische Exkurse* (Frankfurt/Main, 1968), pp. 75–94. After completing the manuscript for this book I found the truth of this proposition impressively confirmed by an experiment launched by the Deutsche Schauspielhaus, Hamburg, on the occasion of the fourth Colloquium of the German Society for Semiotics. A short scene from Beckett's *Endgame* was performed twice, each time with the same costumes, props, paths taken, gestures, and emphases. All that was changed was that the actors depicting Hamm and Clov were switched around. The difference between the two versions was nevertheless substantial, indeed precisely in the sense of the analysis I have just given.

3. Spatial Signs

1. This is a precondition which can be regarded as generally acceptable and on which a consensus is possible in all the studies on the semiotics of architecture. Cf. Eco, *Einführung*, section C, "Funktion und Zeichen," pp. 293–360, on which I base my argumentation to a great extent.

2. I essentially follow Eco in this division into practical and symbolic functions. However, whereas Eco describes them as primary and secondary functions, I wish to avoid such a hierarchization in order to avoid suggesting that the practical is the prior function. See below.

3. Cf. on this W. Widdowson, "Semiotic Theory and Environmental Design," *Kodikas* 2 (1979): 150–64. ·

4. Eco cites the example of Brasilia to illustrate this signifying possibility. The city was built according to drafts that were supposed to refer to the idea of democracy and social justice. The factual settling and expansion of Brasilia, however, makes the city appear as a sign that designates the society inhabiting it as a class society. See Eco, *Einführung*, pp. 353ff.

5. Bogatyrev has pointed on various occasions to the different functions of residential buildings in rural regions, buildings that are to be defined aesthetically, magically, regionally, and status-specifically. See his *The Functions*, especially chap. 21, "The Structural-Functional Method in the Study of Village-Buildings, Farm Implements and Other Items of Material Culture, as Well as Folklore (Magic, Folk Tales, Songs, Incantations, etc.)," pp. 102–105.

6. Cf. on this problem Eco, *Einführung*, pp. 310ff.; E. Gross and G. P. Stone, "Verlegenheit und Analyse," in particular pp. 280–91.

7. Cf. here, and in general on the problem of the symbolic meaning of the medieval

church, especially J. Sauer, *Symbolik des Kirchengebäudes und seiner Ausstattung in der Auffassung des Mittelalters: Mit Berücksichtigung von Honorius Augustodunesis, Sicardus und Durandus* (Freiburg, 1902); L. Kitschelt, *Die frühchristliche Basilika als Darstellung des himmlischen Jerusalem* (Munich, 1938); H. Sedlmayr, "Vermutungen und Fragen zur Bestimmung der altfranzösischen Kunst," in *Festschrift Wilhelm Pinder zum 60. Geburtstag* (Leipzig, 1938); his 'Die dichterische Wurzel der Kathedrale," in *Mitteilungen des österreichischen Instituts für Geschichtsforschung* 14 (1939): 257–87; his "Architektur als abbildende Kunst, *Österreichische Akademie der Wissenschaften, Philos.-hist. Klasse, Protocol no. 225:3* (Vienna, 1948); his *Die Enstehung der Kathedrale* (Zurich, 1950); R. Krautheimer, "Introduction to an 'Iconography of Mediaeval Architecture,' " *Journal of the Warburg Institute* 5 (1942); R. Witthower, *Architectural Principles in the Age of Humanism, Studies of the Warburg Institute,* no. 19 (London, 1949); A. Stange, *Das frühchristliche Kirchengebäude als Bild des Himmels* (Cologne, 1950); E. Baldwin Smith, *The Dome: A Study in the History of Ideas* (Princeton, 1950); his *Architectural Symbolism of Imperial Rome and the Middle Ages* (Princeton, 1965); G. Bandmann, *Mittelalterliche Architektur als Bedeutungsträger* (Berlin, 1951); L. Hautecoeur, *Mystique et architecture: Le symbolism de cercle et de la coupole* (Paris, 1954); O. von Simson, *The Gothic Cathedral* (New York, 1956). These art-historical studies are of great importance in our context, for they point emphatically to architecture's ability to fulfill symbolic and not merely practical functions.

8. Cf. M. Wallis, "Semantic and Symbolic Elements in Architecture. Iconology as a First Step towards an Architectural Semiotic," *Semiotica* 8, no. 3 (1973): 220–38.

9. Above all Eco has pointed to the possibility of a change in function. See Eco, *Einführung,* pp. 315–24.

10. On the different suggestions made in this context cf., among others, D. Agrest and M. Gandelsonas, "Critical Remarks on Semiology and Architecture," *Semiotica* 9 (1973): 252–71; G. Dorfles, *Simbolo, Communicazione, Consume* (Turin, 1962); Eco, *Einführung,* pp. 329–31; G. K. Koenig, *Analisi del linguaggio architettonico* (Florence, 1970), and his *Architettura de communicazione* (Florence, 1970).

11. R. Schneider, "Zur Tätigkeit des Entwerfens in der Architektur," in R. Posner and H. P. Reinecke, *Zeichenprozesse,* pp. 49–57, specifically p. 53.

12. Cf. the bibliographical data in 83.

13. Cf. Eco "A Componential Analysis of the Architectural Sign /Column/," *Semiotica* 5 (1972): 97–117; G. Ghioca, "A Comparative Analysis of Architectural Signs (Applied to Columns)," *Semiotica* 5 (1972): 40–60; Sedlmayr, "Architektur als abbildende Kunst"; Wallis, "Semantic and Symbolic Elements."

14. Thus, we are hardly in a position to interpret the pyramids or even the monuments left by the megalithic cultures on the basis of the codes according to which they were built. We nevertheless attach meanings to them, meanings generated in the context of our culture.

15. Cf. on this problem, Eco, *Einführung,* pp. 315–24.

16. The term "global function" is meant here to refer to those over-arching functions such as space for living, learning, praying, sport, etc., as opposed to special functions such as entrance, seating, stairs, etc.

17. In particular the auditorium is always to be interpreted in terms of the form of state in question: democratic Athens, imperial Rome, courtly baroque states, and twentieth-century democracies have all developed specific auditoriums on the basis of an underlying constitutional idea. Cf. H. Kindermann, *Bühne und Zuschauerraum, ihre Zueinanderordnung seit der griechischen Antike* (Graz, Vienna, and Cologne, 1963); and H. Kindermann, ed., *Das Theater und sein Publikum, Referate der Internationalen theaterwissenschaftlichen Dozentenkonferenz in Venedig 1975 und Wien 1976* (Vienna, 1977).

18. On Athenian Dionysus theater cf., among others, W. Dörpfeld and E. Reisch, *Das griechische Theater* (Athens, 1898; rep. Aachen, 1966), pp. 1–96; H. Bulle, *Untersuchungen an griechischen Theatern, Abhandlungen Bayr. Akad. Wiss, no. 33* (Munich, 1928), pp. 15–80; E. Fiechter and R. Herbig, "Das Dionysos-Theater in Athen I–IV," in *Antike griechische*

Theaterbauten, vols. 5, 7, and 9 (Stuttgart, 1935–50); H. Schlief, "Die Baugeschichte des Dionysos-Theaters in Athen," *AA* 52 (1937): 26–51; A. W. Pickard-Cambridge, "The Athenian Theater of the Fifth Century, in *Studies Presented to D. H. Robinson* (St. Louis, 1951), vol. 1, 309–330; J. Travlos, *Bildlexikon zur Topographie des antiken Athen* (Tübingen, 1971).

19. On the Easter festivals, cf. above all H. de Boor, *Die Textgeschichte der lateinischen Osterfeiern* (Tübingen, 1967); O. B. Hardinson, *Christian Rite and Christian Drama in the Middle Ages. Essays on the Origin and Early History of Modern Drama* (Baltimore, 1965); B. Thoron, *Studien zu den österlichen Spielen des deutschen Mittelalters* (doctoral thesis, Bochum, 1909); K. Young, *The Drama of the Medieval Church*, 2 vols. (Oxford, 1933; rep. 1967).

20. On the medieval stage on the market place, cf., among others, H. H. Borchardt, *Das europäische Theater im Mittelalter und in der Renaissance* (Leipzig, 1935); E. K. Chambers, *The Medieval Stage*, 2 vols. (London, 1903); H. Kindermann, *Theatergeschichte Europas*, vol. 1 (Salzburg, 1966); A. M. Naglker, "Der Villinger Bühnenplan," *YEGP* 1–4 (1955): 318ff.; G. Wickham, *Early English Stages 1300 to 1660* (London, 1959).

21. While hunting for new locations to play, Reinhardt later had the Circus Schumann finally transformed into a theater building: in 1919 Hans Poelzig expanded it into the *Grosses Schauspiel*, whereby the character of an arena, of an amphitheater, was retained.

22. See on this P. von Becker, "In den kalten Tropen der Erinnerung begann, doch endete nicht Michael Grübers 'Winterreise' nach Hölderlin," *Theater heute* 2 (1978): 29–38; here, express reference is made to the political function of the location. See also R. Michaelis, "Bilder deutschen Wahns," ibid., p. 35.

23. New forms of theater building have been experimented with since the beginning of the twentieth century, yet these new forms have not been able to establish themselves as municipal theaters. On such experiments cf. D. Bablet and J. Jacquot, *Le lieu théâtrale dans la société moderne* (Paris, 1962); C. Dupavillon, *Les lieux du spectacle* (Boulogne sur Seine, 1970); W. Gropius, ed., *The Theatre of the Bauhaus* (Middleton, Conn., 1961); S. Joseph, *New Theatre Forms* (London, 1968); J. Polieri, *Scénographie moderne, Aujourd'hui* 42/43 (1963): 182ff.; H. Schubert, *Moderner Theaterbau. Internationale Situation, Dokumentation, Bühnentechnik* (Stuttgart, 1971); R. Southern, *The Open Stage and the Modern Theater in Research and Practice* (London, 1953); G. Storck, *Probleme des modernen Bauens und die Theaterarchitektur des 20. Jahrhunderts* (doctoral thesis, Bonn, 1971); *Theater Space. 8th World Congress* (Munich, 18–25 September 1977/*Der Raum des Theaters*), J. F. Arnold, general ed. (Munich, 1977). On the problem of the tension between old theater buildings and contemporary productions see in particular *Theater von heute—Räume von gestern. Schriften der Dramaturgischen Gesellschaft*, vol. 11 (Berlin, 1979); in our context, the following contributions are of especial importance: K. Völker, "Theater von heute—Räume von gestern," pp. 9–18; and G. Erken, "Der Auszug aus den Häusern," pp. 33–39.

24. Cf. U. Rapp, *Handeln und Zuschauen*.

25. Theater performance is accordingly to be conceived of as an affair concerning the whole polis; large sections of the population were involved in preparing it, carrying it out, and evaluating it. Cf. A. W. Pickard-Cambridge, *The Dramatic Festivals of Athens*.

26. The situation was different in France, where the confrontation of actors and spectators had already set in by the Middle Ages. Cf. on this G. Cohen, *Histoire de la mise en scène dans le théâtre religieux français moyen-âge*, 3rd ed. (Paris, 1951); G. Frank, *The Medieval French Drama* (Oxford, 1954); H. Mérimée, *Spectacles or comédiens à Valenciennes 1580–1630* (Paris, 1913); L. Petit de Julleville, *Les mystères*, 2 vols., *Histoire du théâtre en France*, vol. 1 (Paris, 1880); D. C. Stuart, *Stage Decoration in France in the Middle Ages* (Columbia, 1910).

27. Cf. on this D. Frey, "Zuschauer und Bühne," pp. 151–223.

28. In this context it is worth stressing that there were no professional actors in the Middle Ages; rather, the plays were enacted by citizens of the town; the spectators one year were the actors the next.

29. This confrontation had by and large already occurred in Roman theater; in other words, it is not to be considered exclusively a consequence of the picture frame set and may thus correspond with different social functions of theater. On the spatial conception of Roman theater cf., among others, W. Beare, *The Roman Stage*, 2nd ed. (London, 1955); M. Bieber, *The History of the Greek and Roman Theatre*, 2nd ed. (Princeton, 1961); G. Calza, *Il teatro Romano di Ostia* (Rome, 1927); E. Paratore, *Storia del Teatri Latino* (Milan, 1957).

30. It must not go unmentioned that at the same time the genesis of professional actors commenced. Cf. on this M. Herrmann, *Die Entstehung der berufsmässigen Schauspielkunst im Altertum und in der Neuzeit*, R. Mövius, ed. (Berlin, 1962).

31. On the spatial conception of baroque theater cf. part 2 of the German version of the present study as well as the bibliographical information given there.

32. It is clear that there is a close link between spatial conception on the one hand and acting style on the other: the absence of the famous fourth wall goes hand in hand with the development of a style based extremely on empathy. The development of the Stanislavsky system, for example, is completely inconceivable on a Shakespearean stage, on a market place theater, or in Gropius's total theater—it refers directly to the picture frame set with a darkened auditorium. To this extent, the spatial conception constitutes a substantial element of every theatrical code at the normative level.

33. Cf. on this problem the collection of essays *Autonomie der Kunst. Zur Genese und Kritik einer bürgerlichen Kategorie* (Frankfurt/Main: Suhrkamp, 1972); H. Marcuse, "The Affirmative Character of Culture," in *Negations: Essays in Critical Theory* (Beacon, Boston, 1968); B. J. Warneken, "Autonomie und Indienstnahme. Zu ihrer Beziehung in der Literatur der bürgerlichen gesellschaft," in *Rhetorik, Ästhetik, Ideologie. Aspekte einer kritischen Kulturwissenschaft* (Stuttgart, 1973), pp. 79–115.

34. This was precisely one of the predominant postulates put forward by *Theatre October*. The intention was to overcome the separation of stage and auditorium, of actors and spectators, to make theater a mass theater that had a political mission, indeed an important social function to fulfill, namely the development of a "new" socialist human being. See the writings of V. Meyerhold, above all his essays "Das Revolutionstheater," "Rekonstruktion des Theaters," and "Ideologie und Technologie im Theater," in *Theater-Oktober. Beiträge zur Entwicklung des sowjetischen Theaters* (Frankfurt/Main, 1972), pp. 121–83 (English ed. edited by Edward Braun).

35. There are various ways of attempting to overcome this division. Two extreme examples would be Brecht's *Lehrstücke* experiments and Julian Beck's *Living Theater*. On the different attempts see C. J. Woodbury, *Mosaic Theatre* (Provo, Utah, 1976), in particular chap. 8, "Stage-Auditorium-Audience Relationships," pp. 131–40.

36. Furthermore, in *Oedipus* Neuenfels had the chorus always appear from the audience entrances at the sides. It was in this manner intimated to the audience that the occurrences on stage were their affair and not merely some bygone problem: Neuenfels, in other words, used this means to restore the *tua res agitur* to its rightful position in theater.

37. Stage space is thus closely connected with the proxemic signs A realizes: the proxemic signs are always related to the space in which they are created, and can only be adequately interpreted in light of this relationship.

38. Cf. part 2 of the German version of the present study.

39. On the different ways of realizing decorations, cf. the pertinent histories of stage design, among others, D. Bablet, *Esthétique général du décor de théâtre de 1870 à 1914* (Paris 1965–1976); his *Les révolutions scéniques du XXe siècle* (Paris, 1975); R. Badenhausen and H. Zielske, eds., *Bühnenformen-Bühnenräume-Bühnendekorationen. Beiträge zur Entwicklung des Spielortes. Herbert A. Frenzel zum 65. Geburtstag* (Berlin, 1974); E. Berckenhagen and G. Wagner, *Bretter, die die Welt bedeuten. Entwürfe zum Theaterdekor und zum Bühnenkostüm in 5 Jahrhunderten* (Berlin, 1978); G. Ferrari, *La Scenografia* (Milan, 1902); O. Fischel, *Das moderne Bühnenbild* (Berlin, 1923); W. R. Fuerst and S. J. Hume, *20th Century Stage Decoration* (New York, 1967); M. Hampe, *Die Entwicklung der Bühnendekoration von der Kulissenbühne zum Rundhorizont-System* (doctoral thesis, Vienna, 1961);

C. Niessen, *Das Bühnenbild. Ein kulturgeschichtlicher Atlas* (Bonn and Leipzig, 1924–47); D. Oenslager, *Stage Design. 4 Centuries of Scenic Invention* (London, 1975); O. Schuberth, *Das Bühnenbild. Geschichte, Gestalt, Technik* (Munich, 1955); G. Schöne, *Die Entwicklung der Perspektivbühne von Serlio bis Galli-Bibiena nach den Perspektivbüchern* (Leipzig, 1944, repr. Nendeln, 1977 as *Theatergeschichtliche Forschung, no. 43*); P. Sonrel, *Traité de scénographie* (Paris, 1951); H. Tintelnot, *Barocktheater und barocke Kunst. Die Entwicklungsgeschichte der Fest- und Theaterdekoration in ihrem Verhältnis zur barocken Kunst* (Berlin, 1939); P. Zucker, *Die Theaterdekoration des Klassizismus. Eine Kulturgeschichte des Bühnenbildes* (Berlin, 1925).

40. Naturally, theater decoration is always closely linked to the respective applied arts, to the iconographic codes to which it clearly refers. Nevertheless, a strict distinction must be made between, for example, romantic landscape painting and a correspondingly painted backdrop. For the one as a picture and the other as theater decoration have completely different functions to fulfill, even if they both achieve this on the basis of the same iconographic code.

41. On decoration as the surroundings for the stage character, see also S. Selden and H. D. Sellmann, *Stage Scenery and Lighting* (Prentice Hall, 1964). This function of decorations is analogous to that of social spaces in relation to social role play. See on this E. Gross and G. P. Stone, ''Verlegenheit und Analyse.''

42. This is often the case with Jessner's neutral stair decorations, which can signify a different place depending on the scene. See L. Jessner, ''Das Theater. Ein Vortrag,'' *Die Scene* 28 (1928): 66ff; H. Müllenmeister, *Leopold Jessner. Geschichte eines Regiestils* (doctoral thesis, Cologne, 1956).

43. Decorations, such as those used by Piscator for his productions of *The Good Soldier Schweyk* and *Hoppla—wir leben*. In particular the conveyor belt is not meant to signify different concrete locations, but is related to a certain underlying idea of the production. See E. Piscator, *Political Theatre*, tr. H. Rorison (London: Methuen, 1980).

44. On this function of decoration cf. also J. Polieri, *Scénographie—Sémiographie* (Paris, 1971).

45. For these elements of decoration become props owing to the intentional gestures manipulating them. See below.

46. On this function see D. A. Russel, *Stage Costume Design*, pp. 3–30.

47. On Serlio's stage see Serlio, *The Booke of Architecture* (London, 1611); and on Serlio, G. C. Argau, ''S. Serlio,'' *L'Arte* 35 (1932): 183ff.; H. Leclerc, *Les origines italiens de l'architecture moderne* (Paris, 1946); G. Schöne, *Die Entwicklung der Perspektivbühne*.

48. Cf. on this H. Kindermann, *Theatergeschichte Europas*, vols. 8–10, ''Naturalismus und Impressionismus (1968–74).

49. See part 2.

50. See above all M. Grube, *Geschichte der Meininger* (Berlin, 1926).

51. See on this M. A. Carlson, *The German Stage in the Nineteenth Century* (Metuchen, N.Y., 1972); D. O. Evans, *Le théâtre pendant la période romantique (1827–1848)* (Geneva, 1974); G. Schöne, *Das Bühnenbild im 19. Jahrhundert* (exhibition catalogue) (Munich, 1959).

52. See V. Meyerhold, ''Das bedingte Theater,'' in *Theater-Oktober*, pp. 56–63; Balagan, in *Theater-Oktober*, pp. 64–100; ''Der Schauspieler der Zukunft,'' *Theater-Oktober*, pp. 101–105; A. Tairov, *Das entfesselte Theater* (Cologne and Berlin, 1964). Gordon Craig had put forward a similar choice of dominants a few years earlier. See his *On the Art of Theatre*.

53. This definition may not accord perfectly with the common use of the word ''props,'' but to my mind it is the most suitable for systematic reasons. For it clearly outlines that every object functions as a prop if A's intentional gestures are directed at it, even if it is otherwise an element of external appearance or decoration. Cf. J. Veltrusky, ''Man and Object in the Theater,'' in P. Garvin, ed., *Prague School Reader in Esthetics, Literary Structure and Style* (Washington, D.C., 1955), pp. 97–107; T. Kowzan, *Littérature et spectacle* (La Haye and Paris, 1975), pp. 196–98.

54. On the creation of props in the history of theater see the bibliographical data on stage

design given in note 39. It is interesting that theatrical codes which do not involve exact architectonic replicas as stage design, but rather decorational painting—such as during the baroque or romantic period—nevertheless called for as great a degree of accuracy as possible with regard to props. In the case of the Meininger theater group, by contrast, the attempt was even made to use "real" objects, or at least replicas that were absolutely true to detail. Cf. M. Grube, *Geschichte der Meininger.*

55. It becomes evident, then, that the spatial signs in theater thus also function as signs of signs.

56. Props function therefore on one occasion as signs of generally possible activities, and, on another, as signs of activities already carried out. If, in a given situation, X rushes off-stage brandishing a sword, the prop can be interpreted as a sign of a possible future action by X (e.g., that he will kill someone else); if he comes back on stage with a blood-red sword, then the prop serves as a sign of X's accomplished action. See Veltrusky, "Man and Object."

57. E. Gross and G. P. Stone have proved the existence of a corresponding function of props in social life. See their "Verlegenheit und Analyse."

58. This is at least suggested by the description of the costumes of allegorical figures that Franz Lang gave in his treatise on the art of acting (*Dissertatio de actione scenica* [Munich, 1727]). Cf. part 2 of the German version of the present study.

59. It can be concluded from this that props play an important role above all in forms of theater which make preferential use of dramatic action: a lost letter, a glove left lying, etc., can become the factor that forms the basis of an intrigue. The action here functions only because the props also play an active part.

60. On such symbolic actions in the baroque cf. A. Schöne, *Emblematik unf Drama im Zeitalter des Barock* (Munich, 1964). See also part 2.

61. A basin of water and Creon's use of it to wash his hands are, for example, used for such a meaning in Christof Nel's Frankfurt production of *Antigone* in the 1978–79 season.

62. For his Frankfurt *Oedipus* production in the 1978–79 season, Hans Neuenfels clearly relied on the audience's acquaintance with this symbolic meaning, for he has the old citizens of Thebes surround Oedipus with alarm clocks.

63. Thus, by the context it set, Augusto Fernandes's production of Pirandello's *Henry IV* in Frankfurt in the 1977–78 season constituted the meaning of the glove as an equivalent for "clothing" in general, and that of the naked hand as the equivalent of the body in general. This shows that theatrical symbols can also be formed with the aid of classical rhetorical tropes. (In this instance synecdoche, and, more closely, as *pars pro toto*; see part 2 of the German version of the present study.)

64. In this context, allow me to draw the reader's attention to the props for misfortune used in Romantic drama of fate.

65. On the use of props in Greek antiquity cf. above all J. Dingel, "Requisit und szenisches Bild in der griechischen tragödie," in W. Jens, ed., *Bauformen der Tragödie* (Munich, 1971), pp. 347–67; O. Zwierlein, "Aristophanes' Euripides Parodien," *Göttinger Gelehrten Anzeiger* 222 (1970): 218ff.

66. Cf. on this Goethe's *Rules for Actors.* Goethe demands (44) that the actor's hands neither carry a stick nor manipulate other props, "in order to allow the free movement of hands and arms."

67. The contrast between light and dark plays an important role in mythology, religions, and the literature of most peoples. Cf. on this problem, among others, F. J. Dölger, *Die Sonne der Gerechtigkeit und der Schwarze. Eine religionsgeschichtliche Studie zum Taufgelöbnis*, 2nd ed., supplemented by posthumous additions by the author (Munich, 1971); G. Dumézil, *Le troisième souverain. Essai sur le dieu indo-iranien Aryman et sur la formation de l'histoire mythique de l'Irlande* (Paris, 1949); G. P. Wetter, *PHOS, Eine Untersuchung über hellinistische Frömminigkeit, zugleich ein Beitrag zum Verständnis des Manichäismus* (Uppsala and Leipzig, 1915).

68. The practical function was fulfilled by natural light until the use of artificial lighting:

daylight made the stage visible. If light is used on stage as a sign for its practical function, e.g., a candle is lit in order to show that the room is illuminated, then this always functions simultaneously as the sign for its symbolic functions. Here, these would be, for example, the onset of dusk, character X's fear of the dark, X's intention of giving a signal, or showing the way by means of the light of the candle, which she has set on the window sill, etc. Light is thus used in theater either in its practical function or as a sign for its possible symbolic meanings.

69. If, for example, the stage servant in Kabuki theater approaches the actor and holds his candle up to the latter's face, then the candle exclusively fulfills a practical function: it is intended to make the actor's mimic gestures all the more visible. The issue whether light is used in a practical function or as a sign for its symbolic functions is something that can only be decided on the basis of the respective theatrical code.

70. On units of light, cf. W. O. Parker and H. K. Smith, *Scene Design and Stage Lighting* (New York, 1974), pp. 351f.; S. Selden and H. D. Sellmann, *Stage Scenery and Lighting*.

71. In such cases, the use and factual realization of light is usually closely linked to the poetic code realized in the respective play.

72. To my mind, Tairov was the first to use light in this function in individual scenes in various productions: the magic of the objects which moved through space without any visible cause was thus lent immediate expression. This type of use of light was later expanded further and perfected by the Black Theater in Prague and, in its train, numerous puppet and pantomime stages (such as the corresponding stage in Bratislava, and Velvets in Mainz). The world of objects is presented here in a completely new way for theater at least, although not for film.

73. On his use of light see A. Appia, *Die Musik und die Inszenierung* (Munich, 1898), and his *The Work of Living Art* (Florida, 1960). Appia was the first person who thought of giving light absolute dominance in the stage space, of shaping the stage space almost entirely by the use of light, solely supported by a special, heterogeneous use of stage flooring—and tried to put this into practice at a time when the technical aids he called for and assumed were necesssary by no means existed. He first developed his notions on lighting production with reference to Wagner operas, and later elaborated them with reference to Greek tragedy (Aeschylus's *Prometheus*, performed at the Basle Municipal Theater in 1925) and Goethe's *Faust*. (Carl Niessen has published the script of the latter production.) The stage becomes increasingly abstract in character, and props are not used. The stage consists only of stair, podia, and curtains. The production hinges completely on lighting effects.

74. Cf. J. Mukařovský, "Zum heutigen Stand der Theorie des Theaters," in A. v. Kesteren and H. Schmid, *Moderne Dramentheorie* (Kronberg, 1975), pp. 76–95.

75. On this function of lighting cf. H. Bay, *Stage Design* (New York, 1974), pp. 132–47; W. O. Parker and H. K. Smith, *Scene Design and Stage Lighting*, p. 352ff.; S. Selden and H. D. Sellmann, *Stage Scenery and Lighting*, pp. 220ff.

76. These meanings of light are of course formed and pregiven in the light codes of myth, religion, and art. Cf. the bibliographical data in note 67.

77. Appia contrasts this type of lighting, which he terms the use of "distributed" light, (it was the type of lighting exclusively used in his day on European stages—in the bourgeois theater of illusion) with the use of "shaping" light, which is supposed predominantly to transform stage space into a signifying space.

78. On Appia's notions on lighting production cf. especially the excellent study by D. Kreidt, "Kunsttheorie der Inszenierung. Zur Kritik der ästhetischen Konzeptionen Adolphe Appias und Edward Gordon Craigs" (doctoral thesis, Berlin, 1968).

79. It may perhaps appear astonishing that we have not dealt specifically with the use of film in theater in the context of the discussion of the sign systems of stage space. However, to my mind, film does not constitute a separate theatrical sign system, but rather an element of decoration, which, just like projector-based elements, only arises in this form on the basis of a developed technology. Film can, as can other elements of the decoration, point to a place or a time, or an action occurring at that time in that place, to situations, stage characters

(e.g., as a dream sequence, or as the character's memories), and ideas. It thus requires special treatment in connection with a study of the special theatrical code in which the film is used, such as, for example, an examination of the theatrical code Piscator developed. At the level of the theatrical code as system, any special attention is therefore unnecessary.

4. Nonverbal Acoustic Signs

1. Signs which refer to spatial conception can be ignored in this context.

2. On the problem of units of music, cf. C. Dahlhaus, "Fragments zur musikalischen Hermeneutik," in C. Dahlhaus, ed., *Beiträge zur musikalischen Hermeneutik* (Regensburg, 1975), pp. 159–72; M. Levy, "Sur le problème de la définition des unités musicales," *Semiotica* 15, no. 1 (1976): 8–27; J. J. Nattiez, *Fondements d'une sémiologie de la musique* (Paris, 1976), particularly section 2, chap. 2, "La spécificité sémiologique de la musique. Les unités musicales du point de vue étique et du point de vue émique," pp. 194–236; D. Osmond-Smith, "Problems of Terminology and Method in the Semiotics of Music," *Semiotica* 11 (1974): 269–94; his "L'iconisme formel: pour une typologie des transformations musicales," *Semiotica* 15, no. 1 (1976): 33–42; N. Ruwet, *Langage, musique, poesie* (Paris, 1972); R. Schneider, *Semiotik der Musik* (Munich, 1980), in particular pp. 113ff.

3. To this extent, the problem of units with regard to sounds is the same as that encountered with paralinguistic signs. For the complex of sounds is composed of both auditive—perceptible by the human ear—and characteristics of the substance in question which can only be ascertained and proved to exist by means of procedures for physical measurement.

4. Thus sounds can clearly be interpreted as sounds, not, however, as theatrical signs, for these are always signs of signs, i.e., always generated purposively.

5. Such differences can be regarded as specific features of certain theatrical codes.

6. In this way sounds can at the same time fulfill various functions as signs. In this case, they point not only to a sequence of actions but also to the epoch in which the latter occurs.

7. See the section on lighting in chapter 3.

8. Sound can also point to this meaning to the extent that this intensity receives a special meaning.

9. Cf. H. D. Blume, *Einführung*.

10. Cf. the section on the specificity of the theatrical sign in chapter 5. J. Honzl also polemicizes against the use of the notion of *gesamtkunstwerk* with regard to theater, because he views it as a negation of the rule he establishes according to which every element of theater—such as words, decorations, costumes, and actors—can substitute for another. See Honzl, "Dynamics of the Sign in the Theater," in L. Metjka and J. R. Titunic, eds., *Semiotics of Art*, pp. 74–93, in particular pp. 87ff. (first published as "Pohyb divadelniho znaku, *Slovo i Slovesnost* 6 (1940): 177–88).

11. It is also interesting in this context that the semiotics of music hardly concerns itself with vocal, operatic, or functional music, but develops its theories with reference to absolute music.

12. P. Faltin and H. P. Reinecke, eds., *Musik und Verstehen: Aufsätze zur semiotischen Theorie, Ästhetik und Soziologie der musikalischen Rezeption* (Cologne, 1973), is dedicated exclusively to this problem. The following articles in the above-mentioned work expressly take a stance on the issue: I. Bengton, " 'Verstehen'—Prolegomena zu einem semiotisch-hermeneutischen Ansatz," pp. 11–36; H. H. Eggebrecht, "Über begriffliches und begriffloses Verstehen von Musik," pp. 48–57; H. Goldschmidt, "Musikverstehen als Postulat," pp. 67–86; Z. Lissa, "Ebenen der musikalischen Verstehens"; A. Schaff, "Das Verstehen der verbalen Sprache und das 'Verstehen'der Musik," pp. 276–88. On this problem see further C. Dahlhaus, "Fragmente"; his "Thesen über Programmusik," pp. 187–204 in the same volume; P. Faltin, "Musikalische Bedeutung," *International Review of the Aesthetics and Sociology of Music* (1978): 5–32; P. Francès, *La perception de la musique* (Paris, 1958);

C. Hubig, "Musikalische Hermeneutik und musikalische Pragmatik. Überlegungen zu einer Wissenschaftstheorie der Musik," in Dahlhaus, ed., *Beiträge zur musikalische Hermeneutik*, pp. 121–58; T. Kneif, "Musik and Zeichen. Aspekte einer nichtvorhandenen musikalischen Semiotik," *Musica* 1 (1973): 9–12; his "Musikalische Hermeneutik, musikalische Semiotik," in Dahlhaus, ed., *Musikalische Hermeneutik*, pp. 63–72; Z. Lissa, *Czy muzyka jest sztuka asemantyczna, Kwartalnik muzyczny* 25 (1949): 120–38; L. B. Meyer, *Emotion and Meaning in Music* (Chicago, 1956); J. J. Nattiez, *La signification musicale*, pp. 129–93; R. Schneider, *Semiotik der Musik*, chap. 12, "Symbol," pp. 143–77; I. Supicic, "Expression and Meaning in Music," *International Review of the Aesthetics and Sociology of Music* 2.2: 193–212.

13. Cf. on this C. L. Boilès, "Sémiotique de l'ethnomusicologie," *Musique en Jeu* 10 (1973): 34–41; G. Kubik, "Verstehen in afrikanischen Musikkulturen," in P. Faltin and H. P. Reinecke, eds., *Musik und Verstehen*; Z. Lissa, "Über das Wesen des Musikwerkes," in his *Neue Aufsätze zur Musikästhetik* (Wilhelmshaven, 1975), pp. 1–54.

14. On this problem cf., among others, J. Chailley, *La musique et le signe* (Lausanne, 1967); H. H. Eggebrecht, "Symbol," in *Riemann Musiklexikon Sachteil*, 12th ed. (Mainz, 1967), pp. 921–23; T. Kneif, "Musik und Zeichen"; J. J. Nattiez, *Fondements*, particularly section 1, chap. 1, "La sémiologie musicale comme étude des signes de la musique," pp. 19–28; R. Schneider, *Semiotik der Musik*.

15. The concept of practical function can, in my opinion, be applied to music to the extent that specific musical genres are created for special social situations. They are, in this sense, destined for "use" in such situations, just as an apartment is destined for living in or a church for praying in. This type of music, which predominates in most cultures, must be regarded as functional and not as autonomous. On functional music, cf. H. H. Eggebrecht, "Funktionale Musik," *Archiv für Musikwissenschaft* (1973): 1–25.

16. It is thus completely erroneous to attempt to pinpoint a dichotomy of functional and autonomous (absolute) music in such a manner as to suggest that only autonomous music is art. The dichotomy of functional-autonomous does not touch the question as to whether music is art in any manner. One need only think of Bach's church music, which was intended expressly to fulfill the function of serving *ad maiorem Dei gloriam*. Such approaches only use a definition of art gleaned with the aid of the category of autonomy.

17. On the functionlessness of art as a characteristic of its autonomy, cf. the bibliographical information in note 33. On this development specifically in music cf. T. Kneif, "Über funktionale und ästhetische Musikkultur," in *Jahrbuch des Staatlichen Instituts für Musikforschung, Preussischer Kulturbesitz 1969*, D. Dreysen, ed. (Berlin, 1970), pp. 108–122.

18. As a consequence, with reference to music there is hardly any means of solving the problem as to whether the practical or rather the symbolic function is to be regarded as the primary function. Both so obviously codetermine one another, even if the practical function can then be disregarded.

19. Cf. T. Georgiades, *Musik und Rhythmus bei den Griechen* (Reinbek b. Hamburg: Rowohlt, 1958).

20. Such preferences are historically determined. Only to the extent that their particular orientation has survived is there a certain cause to speak of a "rotten aesthetics of the sentiments" (E. Hanslick, *The Beautiful in Music*, tr. G. Cohen [London: Novello and Ewer, 1891]). However, this is not the case as long as a developed emotional language of music does indeed exist within a society and fulfills special functions in it. On this issue cf. C. Dahlhaus, "Thesen über Programmatik."

21. I undertake this division owing to the lists of the possible meanings of music given predominantly in the collections of essays edited by Dahlhaus and by Faltin and Reinecke, and in the monographs by Francès, Meyer, Nattiez, etc.

22. R. Francès, *La perception de la musique*, p. 299.

23. On the problem of the cultural specificity of musical meanings cf. C. Hubig, "Musikalische Hermeneutik"; V. Karbusicky, "Das 'Verstehen der Musik' in der soziologisch-ästhetischen Empirie," in R. Faltin and H. P. Reinecke, *Musik und Verstehen*, pp. 121–47;

Z. Lissa, "Zur Geschichte der musikalischen Rezeption," in his *Neue Aufsätze zur Musikästhetik*, pp. 11–132; his "Prolegomena zur Theorie der Tradition in der Musik," in his *Neue Aufsätze zur Musikästhetik*, pp. 208–43, and his "Musik und Revolution," in *Neue Aufsätze zur Musikästhetik*, pp. 244–61; J. Molino, "Fait musicale et sémiologie de la musique," in *Musique en Jeu* 17 (1975): 37–62; J. J. Nattiez, *Fondements*, specifically chap. 6, "L'oeuvre musicale comme fait sémologique," pp. 107–127.

24. Cf. Nattiez, *Fondements*, section 2, chap. 1, "La signification musicale," pp. 129–93.

25. See the list Nattiez, (*Fondements*, p. 156) compiles of connotations used by Charpentie, Rameau, Hoffmann, and Lavignac.

26. Cf. J. Combarieu, "L'expression objective en musique d'après de la langage instinctif," *Revue philosophique* 35 (1893): 124–44.

27. Since the human voice is involved in singing, it must also count as an element bearing meaning. Cf. the chapter on paralinguistic signs.

28. This specific characteristic itself indicates that opera cannot be an illusionist form of theater. See below. On the problem of the relation of musical to linguistic signs, cf., among others, R. Husson, *Le chant* (Paris, 1962); M. Imberty, "Introduction à une sémantique musicale de la musique vocale," *International Review of the Aesthetics and Sociology of Music* 4 (1973): 175–95; G. Loiseau, *Notes sur le chant* (Paris, 1947); R. Mancini, *L'art du chant* (Paris, 1969).

29. On this problem see, among others, R. Husson, *La voix chantée* (Paris, 1960).

30. Quoted from "Peking Oper," in *Theater der Nationen* (Hamburg, 26 April–13 May 1979; Hamburg, 1979), pp. 10–17, p. 15.

31. This is of great importance to the extent that it follows that all those forms of theater in which music is a dominant component are hardly in a position to depict problems of interaction and communication, unless they develop a special gestural code, that is.

32. Music's function of pointing in its capacity as a specific genre to a specific social situation is clearly more important in dramatic theater than in musical theater. It plays a more subordinate role in opera, whereas in dramatic theater it is often the most important of the musical signs.

33. On the general problem of space in music cf. A. Wellek, "Der Raum in der Musik," in his *Musikpsychologie und Musikästhetik. Grundriss einer systematischen Musikwissenschaft*, 2nd ed. (Bonn, 1979).

34. On Wagner's use of leitmotifs cf., among others, H. Kolland, "Zur Semantik der Leitmotive in Richard Wagners Ring der Nibelungen," *International Review of the Aesthetics and Sociology of Music* 4 (1973): 197–210.

35. Karbusicky, "Das 'Verstehen der Musik'," has proved by means of experiment that electronic music is often ascribed the connotation of "space."

36. The musical signs take on these functions in dramatic theater far more clearly than they do in opera, because music is not "necessary" in dramatic theater; in other words, its use there must always be interpreted as an element bearing meaning.

37. See on this P. Faltin, "Die 'Freischütz-Ouvertüre', eine semiotische Interpretation der bedeutungsgebenden Prozesse," in R. Posner and H. P. Reinecke, *Zeichenprozesse*, pp. 250–61.

38. It should be remembered in this context that opera arose as a result of the attempt to bring Greek tragedy back to life.

39. On the special structuration of the theatrical code for opera cf. especially I. Osolsobě, *Divadlo které mluvi, zpívá a tančí. Teorie jedne komunikační formy* (Prague, 1974).

40. On the problem of gestures in opera, cf. N. Scotto di Carlo, "Analyse sémiologique des gestes et mimiques des chanteurs d'opera," *Semiotica* 9 (1973): 289–317.

41. The level of intersubjectivity is only touched on by musical signs indirectly, via the agency of the level of the subject. However, to the extent that in opera the level of intersubjectivity is involved, a "new" set of gestures must be introduced here, as has in fact happened in opera productions in recent years. For, as we shall see in the chapter on baroque

theater, the gestures developed there are hardly able to constitute meanings that refer to complicated processes of interaction. Given, however, that in opera precisely this level must be created by the gestural signs, it follows that a corresponding, new set of gestures becomes necessary. Only as long as opera is viewed as an expression of the introvertedness of human feelings is it possible to retain the old gestural code. Cf. on this T. Georgiades, *Das musikalische Theater. Eine Festrede* (Munich, 1965).

42. See on this A. Appia, *Die Musik und die Inszenierung*; E. G. Craig, *On the Art of Theatre*; V. S. Meyerhold, *Theaterarbeit 1917–1930*, R. Tietze, ed. (Munich, 1974); A. Tairov, *Das entfesselte Theater; Theater-Oktober*, the articles by Meyerhold, Tairov, Vachtangov.

5. Theater as a Semiotic System

1. P. Bogatyrev, *Znaky divadelni, Slovo a slovesnost* 4 (1938): 138–49; it has appeared in English as "Semiotics in the Folk Theater," in L. Matejka and J. R. Titunic, eds., *Semiotics of Art. Prague School Contributions*, pp. 33–50, and in French as "Les signes du théâtre," *Poétique* 3, no. 8 (1971): 17–30.

2. A short glance at the history of the semiotics of theater is relevant in this connection. It first developed as a scholarly discipline among the circle of Prague Structuralists in the 1930s and was first drawn up and the fundamental problems it involves first addressed by Peter Bogatyrev, Karel Brusak, Jindrich Honzl, Jan Mukařovský, and Jiri Veltrusky. All of them in one way or another took up the work of Otokar Zich, the Czech theater scholar, who had published his *Estetika dramaticeskeho umeni*, which contained his main thoughts, in 1931. The writings in Czech of the above group were mainly published in the journal *Slovo a slovesnost*, but remained almost unknown outside Czechoslovakia and thus had little influence on the second phase in the development of a semiotics of theater, which set in slowly in the 1960s and first started to unfold more fruitfully in the 1970s. This second phase was substantially initiated by French and Polish scholars. Poland saw a vigorous, semiotically oriented debate on theater in the 1960s that followed in the wake of Roman Ingarden's aesthetics and his work on the functions of language in theater plays. The discussion was led mainly by Jolanta Brach, Tadeusz Kowzan, Zbigniew Osiński, Stefania Skwarczyńska, and Irene Sławinska. Yet only Kowzan, who started at an early date to publish in French, was able to have an impact on work outside Poland.

In France, the semiotics of theater developed above all as a response to the structuralist linguistics of Ferdinand de Saussure, and it was not until a comparatively late date that the semiotics which took Peirce's work as its starting point found its way into French thinking. Roland Barthes and Georges Mounin can be considered early representatives of the French approach. The debate they sparked has been continued in the French discussions especially by Michel Corvin, Regis Durand, André Helbo, and Patrice Pavis. Furthermore, various works on theater semiotics appeared in Italy in the 1970s, of which those by Marco De Marini, Marcello Pagnini, and Franco Ruffini warrant special attention.

It was not until their translation into French, English, Italian, and German in the course of the 1970s that the thought of the Czech structuralists started to be incorporated into discussions. In Germany, specifically theater-oriented semiotic research first came into existence in the late 1970s.

3. The aesthetic signs function as signs of signs to the extent that during the process of constituting their meaning no recourse can be had to an independent semantic dimension. Their semantic dimension can first be derived from the relation between syntactic and pragmatic dimensions. See on this issue E. Fischer-Lichte, *Bedeutung—Probleme einer semiotischen Hermeneutik und Ästhetik*, and "Zur Konstitution ästhetischer Zeichen."

4. Cf. T. Kowzan, *Litterature et spectacle* pp. 208ff.

5. See especially P. Bogatyrev, "Semiotics in the Folk Theatre"; J. Honzl, "Dynamics

of the Sign in the Theater,'' in L. Matejka and J. R. Titunic, eds., *Semiotics of Art*, pp. 74–93; J. Mukarovsky, "Zum heutigen Stand der Theorie des Theaters."

6. For poetry would not be poetry without linguistic signs, just as music would not be music without sounds. Cf. on this problem J. Honzl, "Dynamics of the Sign in the Theater."

7. Cf. ibid.; J. Veltrusky, "Man and Object in the Theater."

8. Cf. on this point Bogatyrev, "Semiotics in the Folk Theater."

9. M. Corvin, "Approches sémiologiques d'un texte dramatique. La Parodie d'Arthur Adamov," *Littérature* 9 (1973): 86–110.

10. R. Barthes, "Literatur und Bedeutung," in his *Literatur oder Geschichte* (Frankfurt: Suhrkamp, 1969), p. 103.

11. See on this M. Corvin, "Approches sémiologiques."

12. See on this point R. Durand, "Problèmes de l'analyse structurale et sémiotique de la forme théâtrale," in A. Helbo, ed., *Sémiologie de la représentation, théâtre, television, bande dessinée* (Brussels, 1975), pp. 112–18.

13. See on this point J. Brach, "O znakach literackich i znakach teatralnych," *Studia Estetyczne* 2 (Warsaw, 1965): 241–59; Z. Osiński, "Przekład tekstu literackiego na język teatru (zarys problematyki)," in J. Trzynadlovsky, *Dramat i Teatr* (Wrocłav, 1967), pp. 119–56; Z. Osiński and E. Balcerzan, "Die theatralische Schaustellung im Lichte der Informationstheorie," in W. Kroll and A. Flaker, eds., *Literaturtheoretische Modelle und kommunikatives System. Zur aktuellen Diskussion in der polnischen Literaturwissenschaft*, pp. 371–411.

14. T. Kowzan, *Littérature et spectacle*, p. 215.

15. See note 13 above.

16. See on this point J. M. Diez Borque, "Aproximacion semiologica a la 'escena' del teatro del Siglo de Oro espanol," in J. M. Diez Borque and L. G. Lorenzo, eds., *Semiologia del teatro* (Barcelona, 1975), pp. 49–92, especially p. 58.

17. Cf. on this A. Helbo, "Pour un proprium de la représentation théâtrale," in *Sémiologie de la réprésentation*, pp. 62–72; P. Pavis, *Language of the Stage: Essays in the Semiology of Theatre* (P.A.J. Publications, 1982); I. Sławinska, *Współczesna refleksja o teatrze* (Krakow, 1979), pp. 226ff.

18. See on this issue F. Ruffini, "Semiotica del teatro: la stabilizzazione del senso. Un approccioi informazionale," *Biblioteca teatrale* 12 (1975): 205–239.

19. P. Hamon, "Pour un statut sémiologique du personnage," *Littérature* 6 (1972): 86–110.

20. Steen Jansen, "Entwurf einer Theorie der dramatischen Form," in J. Ihwe, ed., *Literaturwissenschaft und Linguistik*, vol. 2 (Frankfurt/Main, 1972), 223.

21. G. Polti, *The Thirty-Six Dramatic Siutations*, tr. L. Ray (Boston, 1944).

22. In E. Souriau, *Les deux cent milles situations dramatiques* (Paris, 1950).

23. "Person" and "situation" essentially represent a continuation of the categories of "stage figure" and "action" developed in dramatic theory.

24. P. Pavis, "Problèmes de sémiologie théâtrale."

25. See on this issue S. Skwarczyńska, "Anmerkungen zur Semantik der theatralischen Gestik."

26. R. Barthes, "Literatur und Bedeutung," p. 103.

27. See A. Artaud, *Das Theater und sein Double* (Frankfurt/Main, 1969); and J. Derrida, "Le théâtre de lka cruauté et le clôture de la représentation," in Derrida, *Writing and Difference*, tr. A. Bass (Chicago: Univ. of Chicago Press, 1978).

28. Honzl, "Dynamics of the Sign in the Theater," p. 93.

29. See Honzl, "Die Hierarchie der Theatermittel."

30. See Mukařovský, "Zum heutigen Stand der Theorie des Theaters."

31. G. Mounin, "La communication théâtrale," in Mounin, *Introductions à la sémiologie* (Paris, 1970), pp. 87–94.

32. E. Buyssens, *La communication et l'articulation linguistique* (Paris, 1967), quoted in Helbo, "Le code théâtrale," in Helbo, ed., *Sémiologie de la représentation*, pp. 12–27.

Mounin interestingly enough quotes this passage only as far as "ils ne communiquent pas avec le public," clearly in order to strengthen his position from the outset.

33. Mounin, "La communication théâtrale," p. 91.

34. Ibid, p. 92.

35. Helbo, "Le code théâtrale," p. 14.

36. Ibid, p. 17.

37. For a confutation of Mounin's proposition see also F. Ruffini, "Semiotica del teatro: Ricognizioni degli studi," *Biblioteca theatrale* 9 (1974).

38. On the problem of theatrical communication, compare especially E. Balcerzan and Z. Osiński, "Die theatralische Schaustellung;" P. Campeanu, "Un rôle secondaire: le spectateur," in Helbo, ed., *Sémiologie de la représentation*, pp. 96–111.

39. Cf. on the underlying concept of meaning E. Fischer-Lichte, *Bedeutung*, section 1, "Bedeutung als semiotische Kategorie," pp. 27–129.

40. This ambiguity results from the fact that the aesthetic sign does not have an independent semantic dimension of its own. Ibid; E. Fischer-Lichte, "Zur Konstitution ästhetischer Zeichen."

41. See on this point A. Tairov, *Das entfesselte Theater*.

42. See on this point Meyerhold's essays published in *Theater-Oktober*.

43. The theater critic Georg Hensel points expressly to this procedure. He regards it as the preferential procedure of a number of directors, such as Neuenfels, Wendt, and Heising. Cf. G. Hensel, "Ein Klassiker, nackt und ausgezogen. Schillers Maria Stuart und Elisabeth als Doppelrolle in Düsseldorf—Vorschläge für Theater-Semiotik," *Frankfurter Allgemeine Zeitung* 48 (26 February 1980): 23.

44. G. Rühle, for example, also shows that a language of theater has developed in theaters in the Federal Republic of Germany which is quite prepared to forgo making such borrowings from comics, film and advertising without as a consequence becoming incomprehensible. See G. Rühle, "Die Erfindung der Bildersprache für das Theater. Die Herstellung neuer Sinnlichkeit," in his *Theater in unserer Zeit* (Frankfurt/Main, 1976), pp. 224–32.

45. Cf. on this problem chapter 7, the section on the hermeneutics of the theatrical text.

46. See R. Durand, "Problèmes de l'analyse structurale at sémiotique de la forme théâtrale"; and Pavis, "Problèmes de sémiologie théâtrale."

47. See A. Schaeffner, "Le pré-théâtre," *Polyphonie* I (Paris, 1947–48), 7–14.

48. Cf. M. Leiris, *La Possession et ses aspects théâtraux chez les Ethiopiens de Gondar* (Paris, 1958).

49. Cf. on this point E. Fischer-Lichte, *Bedeutung*.

6. The Gesture in Eighteenth-Century German Theater

1. Cf. on the concept of norm in this sense E. Coseriu, *Sistema, norma y habla*.

2. On the problem of aesthetic norms see especially Jan Mukařovský, *Aesthetic Function: Norm and Value as Social Facts*, tr. M. C. Swine (Ann Arbor, Mich., 1970).

3. Ibid.

4. The second volume of the German edition of the present study, entitled *Vom 'künstlichen' zum 'natürlichen' Zeichen—Theater des Barock und der Aufklärung*, provided an extensive semiotic reconstruction of the internal code of baroque theater and the dissolution and reformation of a kinesic code in the Enlightenment. Readers interested in the history should therefore consult it.

5. G. Ballhausen, "Der Wandel der Gebärde auf dem deutschen Theater im 18. Jahrhundert, dargestellt an den Gebärdenbüchern" (doctoral thesis, Göttingen, 1957).

6. Ibid., p. 19.

7. Ibid., p. 185.

8. F. Lang, *Abhandlung über die Schauspielkunst. Dissertatio de actione scenica* (1727),

tr. and ed. A. Rudin (reprint, Bern and Munich, 1975), p. 163; Ronald G. Emgle, "Franz Lang and the Jesuit Stage" (doctoral thesis, University of Illinois, 1968).

9. Ballhausen, *Der Wandel*, p. 168

10. D. Barnett, "The Performance Practice of Acting: The Eighteenth Century," in: *Theatre Research International*. New Series 2, no. 3 (1977): 157–86; 3, no. 1 (1977): 1–18; 3, no. 2 (1977): 79–92; 5, no. 1 (1979/80): 1–36; 6, no. 1 (1980/1): 1–32. Since the studies by Ballhausen and Barnett concern themselves closely on the one hand with theatrical gestures in both the early and late eighteenth centuries and, on the other, exclusively with such gestures during this period, I shall limit myself here to drawing the reader's attention to their work. To my mind, they represent two important trends in theater history. Furthermore, I know of no works which go into the questions left open by Ballhausen's dissertation, or which have introduced new aspects into the discussion of the complex of problems addressed by Ballhausen and Barnett, or indeed which go further than they do.

11. On the principles of sign constitution in the seventeenth and eighteenth centuries see M. Foucault, *Order of Things: Archaeology of the Human Sciences* (London: Tavistock, 1974).

12. Cf. on this G. Leibniz, *Sämtliche Schriften und Briefe*, von Preuss, ed., vol. 6 (Darmstadt, Berlin, and Leipzig: Akad. d. Wiss, 1923), 500.

13. For Leibniz only considers as signs in this sense "the words, the letters, the chemical and astronomical figures, Chinese and hieroglyphic figures, musical notes, secret codes, arithmetic and algebraic signs, and all other signs which we employ to point to things (intercoitandum pro rebus)" (Leibniz, *Die Philosophische Schriften*, C. J. Gerhardt, ed., 7 vols. [Berlin, 1875–90], vol. 7, 204).

14. A. Arnauld, *Die Logik oder die Kunst zu denken*, (Paris, 1683; reprint, Darmstadt, 1972), p. 41.

15. See on this point Leibniz, "Quid sit idea," in *Die philosophische Schriften*, vol. 7.

16. Ballhausen, *Der Wandel*, p. 193.

17. E. Bodemann, *Die Leibniz-Handschriften der königlich öffentlichen Bibliothek zu Hannover*, (Hanover, 1895), pp. 80f.

18. J. Bidermann, *Ludi theatrales*, originally 1666, R. Tarot, ed., 2 vols. (1666; reprint, Tübingen, 1967), Sheet (+) 3f(+ +r). Cf. especially H.-J. Schings, "Consolatio Tragoediae. Zur Theorie des barocken Trauerspiels," in R. Grimm, ed., *Deutsche Dramentheorien*, vol. 1 (Frankfurt/Main, 1973), pp. 1–44.

19. G. E. Lessing, Letter to Nicolai of November, 1756 in the correspondence on the tragedy, *Werke*, vol. 4 (Munich, 1973), 160.

20. Ibid., 163. See on this point, among others, M. Kommerell, *Lessing und Aristoteles. Untersuchungen über die Theorie der Tragödie* (Frankfurt/Main, 1959); H.-J. Schings, *Der mitleidigste Mensch ist der beste Mensch: Poetik des Mitleids von Lessing bis Büchner*, (Munich, 1980); J. Schulte-Sasse, "Der Stellenwert des Briefwechsels in der Geschichte der deutschen Ästhetik," in Schulte-Sasse, ed., *G. E. Lessing, Moses Mendelssohn, Friedrich Nicolai, Briefwechsel über das Trauerspiel* (Munich, 1972), pp. 168–237.

21. On this theme see P. Rusterholz, *Theatrum Vitae Humanae. Funktion und Bedeutungswandel eines poetischen Bildes* (Berlin, 1970).

22. On the shape taken by the different sign systems in baroque theater cf. especially W. Flemming, *Geschichte des Jesuitentheaters in den Landen deutscher Zunge* (Berlin, 1923), *Schriften der Gesellschaft für Theatergeschichte*, vol. 32.

23. F. Lang, *Abhandlung*, p. 181.

24. Ibid., pp. 170f.

25. Ibid., p. 172.

26. This interpretation is also suggested by baroque painting. The portrait paintings of the leading figures of the day also indicate that this principle applied to every detail of the way in which the body was held. They clearly considered the posture an appropriate form of self-representation.

27. Cf. on this point Rudin's postscript to Lang's *Dissertatio de actione scenica*, especially pp. 324f.

28. Lang, *Abhandlung*, pp. 186f.

29. See on this point W. Benjamin, *The Origin of the German Tragic Drama*, tr. J. Osborne (London: NLB, 1977).

30. Lang, *Abhandlung*, pp. 200f.

31. See on this point in particular, R. Alewyn, "Der Geist des Barocktheaters," in R. Alewyn and K. Sätzle, *Das große Welttheater. Die Epoche der höfischen Feste in Dokument und Deutung* (Hamburg: Rowohlt, 1959), pp. 48–70.

32. See on this development, among others, W. Bahner, *Renaissance, Barock, Aufklärung* (Kronberg, 1976); E. Cassirer, *Philosophie der Aufklärung* (Tübingen: Mohr, 1932); P. Hazard, *Die Krise des europäischen Geistes* (Hamburg, 1939).

33. C. Wolff, *Vernünftige Gedancken von Gott, der Welt und der Seele des Menschen* (Halle, 1747), p. 236.

34. On the concept of *imitatio naturae* in the period in question see, among others, H. Dieckmann, "Die Wandlung des Nachahmungsbegriffs in der französischen Ästhetik des 18. Jahrhunderts," in H. R. Jauss, ed., *Nachahmung und Illusion* (Munich, 1974), pp. 28–59; H. P. Herrmann, *Naturnachahmung und Einbildungskraft* (Bad Homburg, 1970); U. Hohner, *Zur Problematik der Naturnachahmung in der Ästhetik des 18. Jahrhunderts* (Erlangen, 1976); S. D. Martinson, *On Imitation, Imagination and Beauty* (Bonn, 1977).

35. J. C. Gottsched, *Auszug aus des Herrn Batteux Schönen Künsten* (1754), p. 27.

36. J. C. Gottsched, *Critische Dichtkunst*, 4th ed., originally 1751, photomechanical reproduction (Darmstadt, 1962), p. 95.

37. Mylius accordingly terms nature "everything which is in the world and usually occurs within it in due manner." C. Mylius, "Critische Untersuchung, ob, und in wo fern die Gleichnisse in den Trauerspielen statt finden?" in *Beyträge zur Critischen Historie der Deutschen Sprache, Poesie und Beredsamkeit*, vol. 8 (Hildesheim and New York, 1970), 396.

38. Gottsched, *Critische Dichtkunst*, p. 161.

39. C. Battreux, *Einschränkung der schönen Kunste auf einen einzigen Grundsatz*, tr. J. A. Schlegel, 3rd ed. (Leipzig, 1770), p. 170.

40. K. W. Ramler, *Einleitung in die Schönen Wissenschaften nach Batteux*, 5th ed. (Leipzig, 1802), p. 20.

41. On the concept of good taste, which became one of the central categories of eighteenth-century aesthetics, see among others, A. Bäumler, *Das Irrationalitätsproblem in der Ästhetik und Logik des 18. Jahrhunderts bis zur Kritik der Urteilskraft*, 1st edn., (Halle, 1923), 2nd ed. (Tübingen and Darmstadt, 1967); L. Balet and E. Gerhard, *Die Verbürgerlichung der deutschen Kunst. Literatur und Musik im 18. Jahrhundert* (Strasbourg, 1936; republished, ed. G. Mattenklott, Frankfurt/Main, 1973); R. Peacock, *Criticism and Personal Taste* (Oxford, 1972); L. L. Schücking, *Soziologie der literarischen Geschmacksbildung* (Leipzig, 1931; 3rd ed. Bern, 1961).

42. Gottsched, *Critische Dichtkunst*, p. 125.

43. On the aims of early Enlightenment theater see, among others, K. Wölfel, "Moralische Anstalt," in R. Grimm, ed., *Deutschen Dramentheorien*, vol. 1, 45–122.

44. Both Locke and Hume upheld this principle.

45. See on this point Caroli Linnaei, *Systema naturae sistens in regna tria naturae, in classes et ordines, genera et species redacta, tabublisque aeneis illustrata* (Leyden, 1756), pp. 220f.

46. Through Lessing's endeavors, the German public was acquainted with most important French works in the form of translations or extensive reviews. Thus, they knew Remond de Sainte Albine's *Le Comédien*, which had been published in Paris in 1747 as *Auszug aus dem 'Schauspieler' des Herrn Remond von Sainte Albine*, Francois Riccoboni's *L'Art du Théâtre*, which came out in Paris in 1750 in a complete translation published the same year, Diderot's 1751 *Lettre sur les sourds et les muets* from a review printed the same year, and his *Entretiens*

sur Le Fils Naturel and *Discours sur la poesie dramatique*, which both came out in 1758, from their translation two years later entitled *Das Theater des Herrn Diderot*.

47. This issue referred above all to the fiery debate in the eighteenth century on whether the thesis of "ut pictura poiesis" was correct or not, a proposition Lessing had attempted to refute in his *Laokoon*. See on this debate, among others, N. R. Schweizer, *The ut pictura poiesis Controversy in Eighteenth-Century England and Germany*, (Bern and Frankfurt/Main, 1972).

48. D. Diderot, "Letter on Deaf-mutes," in D. Diderot, *Ästhetische Schriften*, F. Bassenge, ed., 2 vols. (Frankfurt/Main, 1968), 27–69, in particular here 34.

49. Ibid., 33.

50. The notion that the gestural language of deaf-mutes was a natural language was later to be taken up both by Sicard in his work on deaf-mutes and by Degérando in the context of his ethnological research; here, the language of deaf-mutes is investigated in terms of its being a universal language. See on this point R.-A. de Sicard, *Théorie des signes pour l'instruction des sourds-muets*, 2 vols. (Paris, 1808); and J. M. Degérando, *Des signes et de l'art de penser*, 4 vols. (Paris, 1800).

51. See on this point C. Hardenberg, "G. E. Lessings Semiotik als Propädeutik einer Kunsttheorie," *Zeitschrift für Semiotik* 1 (1979): 361–76.

52. G. E. Lessing, *Hamburgische Dramaturgie*, O. Mann, ed., (Stuttgart, 1958), *Passage 4*, p. 249.

53. G. E. Lessing, *Laokoon*, in his *Werke*, vol. 6, *Kunsttheoretische und kunsthistorische Schriften*, p. 110.

54. Cf. *Laokoon*, particularly pp. 100–105.

55. For if art imitates bodies, then, or so Lessing would have it, "beauty (is) its highest law;" if, however, it takes actions as the object of its imitations, then it is "truth and expression (which are) its first law" (*Laokoon*, p. 25).

56. *Hamburgische Dramaturgie, Passage 5*, p. 256.

57. J. J. Engel, *Ideen zu einer Mimik*, reprinted in J. J. Engel, *Schriften*, vols. 7/8 (Berlin, 1804; reprint, Athenäum, Frankfurt/Main, 1971), vol. 7, 83.

58. See on this point G. Chr. Lichtenberg, *Briefe aus England*, in his *Schriften und Briefe*, W. Promies, ed., vol. 3, *Aufsätze, Entwürfe, Gedichte, Erklärung der Hogarthischen Kupferstiche* (Munich, 1972), 326–67, here 352.

59. Lessing, *Hamburgische Dramaturgie, Passage 4*, p. 250.

60. Ibid.

61. Lichtenberg, *Briefe*, p. 355.

62. Lessing, *Hamburgische Dramaturgie, Passage 5*, p. 256.

63. Lichtenberg, "Vorschlag zu einem Orbis Pictus für deutsche dramatische Schriftsteller, Romanen-Dichter und Schauspieler, *Schriften und Briefe*, pp. 377–405, here p. 383.

64. Ibid., p. 388.

65. Diderot commented on this question, in particular on the issue of the relation between an intended action and an involuntary reaction, in his *Eléments de physiologie*. The answer he came up with was that "celle qu'on appelle volontaire ne l'est pas plus que l'autre, la cause en est seulement reculée d'un cran" (*Eléments de physiologie*, J. Mayer, ed. [Paris, 1964], p. 262). Leading doctors of the time, such as Louis Lacaze (*L'idée de l'homme physique et moral*, 1755), Claude-Nicolas Le Cat (*Traité des sensations et des passions en général, et de des sens en particulier*, 3 vols. [Paris, 1767], Le Camus (*Médecine de l'esprit*, 1769), Albrecht von Haller (*Kleine Physiologie, Biblioteca Anatomica*, 2 vols. [Zurich, 1774]), and others devoted much attention to this question, and for all the divergencies in the theories they produced, nevertheless they unanimously asserted that psychological processes had a direct effect on physical states; and their findings backed this up.

66. See on this point J. C. Lavater's *Physiognomik. Zur Beförderung der Menschenkenntniss und Menschenliebe. Vervollständigte neue Auflage der verkürzt herausgegebenen physiognomische Fragmente*, 4 vols. (Vienna, 1829), especially the essay written to provide the foundations for his position, "Die Physiognomik, eine Wissenschaft," vol. 1, 46–50.

67. C. Lichtenberg, "Über Physiognomik; wider die Physiognomen. Zur Beförderung der Menschenliebe und Menschenkenntnis," in his *Schriften und Briefe*, pp. 256–95.

68. Lessing, *Werke*, vol. 4, 727.

69. Engel, *Schriften*, vol. 7, 127.

70. The countless travelogues, whether by de Bougainville, Lafitau, James Cook or Hawkesworth, Carteret or Georg Forster, had already made it common knowledge that this was the case with "savages." It was concluded that it must be possible to communicate with "savages" using this sign language, as Degérando expressly advises travelers in his memorandum "Considérations sur les diverses méthodes à suivre dans l'observation des peuples sauvages." To his mind it "was obvious that one must resort to the signs closest to nature in initial communication; with the savages, as with children, one must start out with the language of action" ("Erwägungen über die verschiedenen Methoden der Beobachtung wilder Völker," in S. Moravia, *Beobachtende Vernunft. Philosophie und Anthropologie in der Aufklärung* (Frankfurt/Main, Berlin, and Vienna, 1977), pp. 219–51, here p. 226.

71. Lichtenberg, "Über Physiognomik," p. 278.

72. Ibid., p. 264.

73. Lessing, "Auszug aus dem 'Schauspieler' des Herrn Remond von Sainte Albine," in G. E. Lessing, *Theatralische Bibliothek*, part 1, play 1, 1754, in *Lessings Werke*, R. Boxberger, ed. (Berlin and Stuttgart, 1883–1890), part 5, *Theatralische Bibliothek*, pp. 128–59, here pp. 158f.

74. Ibid., p. 136.

75. Ibid., p. 159.

76. Ibid.

77. Engel, *Schriften*, vol. 7, 285.

78. Ibid., 236f.

79. Ibid., 238f.

80. Engel, *Schriften*, vol. 8, 283. Long before Watzlawick came up with the axiom that one cannot *not* communicate, because not only language but also all behavior conveyed something to the other person, Engel had observed that gestures—i.e., nonverbal behavior—are generated in uninterrupted sequence, in other words, that it is not possible to not make "gestures."

81. Engel, *Schriften*, vol. 7, 27.

82. Here, theater clearly dons a function that belongs in the domain of psychology. Interestingly enough, a special psychological science developed from the middle of the century onward in Germany—i.e., parallel to the new gestural code for theater. Johann Gottlieb Krüger, professor of medicine and philosophy, published one of the first books on "experiential psychology of the soul" or on the "experimental doctrine of the soul," namely *Versuch einer Experimental-Seelenlehre*. Psychology did not, however, become truly popular until the 1780s, when Carl Philipp Moritz started editing a psychological journal, the *Magazin zur Erfahrungsseelenkunde*—in other words, at a time when the basic traits of the new gestural code for theater had already been completely developed. This may to a certain degree appear paradoxical, since the constitution of the new gestural code required a knowledge precisely of the human emotions, a knowledge that the psychological sciences first had to gain. One must, however, bear in mind that the respective developments in the arts and sciences during the second half of the eighteenth century reveal parallels, interconnections, and mutual influences, even if a direct dependence of the one on the other cannot be proven.

83. R. Alewyn, "Der Geist," p. 48.

84. See on this point P. Rusterholz, "Theatrum Vitae Humanae," p. 9: "Courtly life, and in Vienna it was also modelled after the strict, indeed bizarre form of Spanish protocol, diplomacy's play of intrigues, the courtly theater festivals, during which members of the court took the stage as actors, indeed during which not only the Emperor himself played his own role, but the other members of the court were also addressed off-stage not in terms of their real rank, but according to their role: all of this contributed to making the members

of society themselves and the populace watching from behind the stands aware of the theatrical character of the courtly form of life.''

85. In this sense we can agree with Ballhausen's suggestion that ''theatrical gestures also played a role shaping manners,'' and that ''the 'aesthetic reality' of theatrical gestures . . . was carried into the 'concrete reality' of courtly life'' (Ballhausen, *Der Wandel*, p. 94). Yet, ''theatrical gestures'' and ''social gestures'' must not be thought of in this context as two isolated factors that are related to one another monocausally. Rather, they can only be related indirectly to one another via the context mentioned.

86. On the history of anthropology and ethnology in the eighteenth century, cf., among others, W. Krauss, *Zur Anthropologie des 18. Jahrhunderts*, (Munich, 1979); S. Moravia, *Beobachtende Vernunft*.

87. J. M. Degérando, ''Erwägungen,'' p. 220.

88. This was what was addressed by the prize question announced by Frederick the Great's Academy in 1771: ''Assuming human beings were left to their natural abilities, would they then be able to invent language, and, if so, with what means?'' Many of the entries (the first prize was won by Herder's *Abhandlung über den Ursprung der menschlichen Sprache*) made use of the relation or difference between sound and gesture in answering the question. On the discussion of an ur-language see W. Krauss, *Zur Anthropologie*. Interestingly enough, the attempt to develop a universal language of theater is to be observed in various forms of contemporary theater. Cf. on this Fischer-Lichte, ''Theatre in Search of a Universal Language,'' in Roger Bauer and Douwe Fokkema, eds., *Space and Boundaries. Proceedings of the XIIth Congress of the International Comparative Literature Association*, 5 vols. (Munich: Indicium, 1990), vol. 5, 131–38.

89. Cf. the short sketch of the development of an ''experiential psychology of the soul'' given in note 82. It first starts to develop fully at a time when the constitution of the underlying traits of the gestural code has already been accomplished.

90. Mutual influences can be assumed to occur in this process, particularly if one considers that developments in aesthetics and science often—as is the case with Diderot—occurred in one and the same person. It would nevertheless prove highly difficult to find arguments for, let alone prove, such an influence with regard to one specific case.

91. Cf. the writings of Stanislavsky, above all: C. S. Stanislavsky, *Das Geheimnis des schauspielerischen Erfolges* (Zurich and Vienna, n.d.); *My Life in Art* (Methuen, London, 1980); *Theater, Regie und Schauspieler* (Rowohlt, Hamburg, 1958) ; *Stanislavski Produces Othello*, ed. S. O. Baluchaty (London and New York, 1948); *The Seagull, Produced by K. S. Stanislavski* (London, 1952).

92. Cf. on this point Stanislavsky's theory of physical actions, in particular his ''On Physical Actions,'' in *Creating a Role*, tr. E. R. Hapgood (Methuen, London, 1980), and *Building a Character* (Methuen, London, 1979).

93. Cf. on this point, E. Fischer-Lichte, ''Theatrical Communication,'' in André Helbo, ed., *Actes du colloque Sémiologie du Spectacle, premier congrès Degrés 29, Modèles Théorique* (1982); 1–9.

94. See on this Fischer-Lichte, ''Theatre and the Civilizing Process: An Approach to the History of Acting,'' in Thomas Postlewait and Bruce A. McConachrie, eds., *Interpreting the Theatrical Past. Essays in the Historiography of Performance* (Iowa City: University of Iowa Press, 1989), pp. 19–36; and ''In Search of a New Theatre. Retheatricalization as Productive Reception of Far Eastern Theatre,'' in Günter Ahrends and Hans Jürgen Diller, eds., *Non-literary Tradition in Modern Theatre* (Tübingen: Narr, 1991).

Part III. The Theatrical Code as Speech

1. On the concept of artifact in the sense in which it is used here see Jan Mukařovský, *Aesthetic Function, Norm and Value as Social Facts*, tr. Martin Swino (Ann Arbor: Univ. of Michigan Press, 1979).

7. Performance as Theatrical Text

1. Eugenio Coseriu, *Textlinguistik. Eine Einführung*, J. Albrecht, ed. (Tübingen, 1980), p. 51.

2. Ibid.

3. Hitherto we have avoided using the term *Sinn* ("overall meaning") in the context of "interpretative praxis" (Sinngebung). "Meaning" can refer to individual elements, substructures, or the whole text, which is why we can speak of the *meaning* of the text and the *meaning* of individual elements; "overall meaning" always refers to the text as a whole.

4. Y. M. Lotman, *The Structure of Aesthetic Texts*, tr. Gail Lenhoff and Ronald Vroon (Ann Arbor: University of Michigan Press, 1977).

5. Ibid.

6. Ibid.

7. Ibid.

8. This can in general be presumed to be the case with contemporary performances.

9. Lotman, *Die Struktur literarischer Texte* (Munich, 1972), p. 85.

10. Ibid., p. 60.

11. On these three modes of external recoding see E. Fischer-Lichte, "Theatrical Communication," in A. Helbo, ed., *Actes du colloque Sémiologie du Spectacle, Degrés 29, Modèles théoriques* (1982), pp. 1–9.

12. Michail Bakhtin first addressed this phenomenon of intertextuality in his study of Dostoevsky's novels (*Problems of Dostoevsky's Poetics*, tr. C. Emerson, [Minneapolis: Univ. of Minnesota Press, 1984]), and he termed it "polyphony" there. We shall use the term differently in what follows, whereas what Bakhtin means is what Kristeva later termed "polylogy." Cf. Kristeva, *Polylogue* (Paris, 1977) and note 40 below.

13. Cf. the incisive works on film by Metz and Pasolini, Bouissac on circus, and Nöth on happenings.

14. See on this point E. W. B. Hess-Lüttich, *Soziale Interaktion und literarischer Dialog. I. Grundlagen der Dialoglinguistik* (Berlin, 1981), in particular chapter 3.3, "Medialität und Multimedialität. Zum Verhältnis von Kanal, Code, Sinn und Modus in Zeichensystemen," pp. 289–318.

15. On the concept of medium cf. especially G. Maletzke, *Grundbegriffe der Massenkommunikation* (Munich, 1964); H. Richter, "Zum kommunikationssoziologischen Inhalt des Medienbegriffs," in Hess-Lüttich et al, eds., *Stilforschung und Rhetorik-Patholinguistik-Sprecherziehung* (Stuttgart, 1978), pp. 37–43; F. Knilli, "Medium," in W. Faulstich, ed., *Kritische Stichwörter zur Medienwissenschaft* (Munich, 1979), pp. 230–51.

16. On the specific mediality of theater, see Hess-Lüttich, "Multimediale Kommunikation als Realität des Theaters," in K. Oehler, ed., *Zeichen und Realität* (Wiesbaden, 1984); M. Pfister, *The Drama* (London, 1990), in particular chap. 1.3, "Drama as a plurimedial Form of Representation." The objection must be made that the form of differentiation Pfister adopts (p. 27) does not distinguish sufficiently between medium and sign system. The different media, actors, space, and perhaps loudspeakers can indeed be allocated to certain channels, but cannot be assigned to sign systems in the same way. See the arguments I present in the course of the next few pages.

17. On the state of research, see E. W. B. Hess-Lüttich, *Soziale Interaktion*.

18. Aristotle, Horace, Longinus, *Classical Literary Criticism*, tr. T. S. Dorsch (Harmondsworth: Penguin, 1965/1986), p. 39.

19. Ibid., p. 41.

20. Julia Kristeva, *Revolution in Poetic Language*, tr. Margaret Waller (New York: Columbia University Press, 1984), p. 67.

21. Ibid., p. 25.

22. Ibid., p. 28.

23. Ibid., p. 43.

24. Ibid., p. 44–45.
25. Ibid., p. 215.
26. Ibid., p. 79.
27. Ibid., p. 17.
28. Ibid., p. 65.
29. Ibid., p. 57.
30. Ibid., p. 79.
31. Ibid., p. 67.
32. Cf. on this issue, E. Fischer-Lichte, "The Quest for Meaning," in *Stanford Literature Review* (Spring 1986): 137–55.
33. Georg Simmel, "Zur Philosophie des Schauspielers," in his *Das individuelle Gesetz. Philosophische Exkurse* (Frankfurt/Main: Suhrkamp, 1968), p. 75.
34. Ibid., p. 78.
35. See part 2 on this discussion, which dates back to the Enlightenment.
36. Helmuth Plessner, "Zur Anthropologie des Schauspielers," in his *Zwischen Philosophie und Gesellschaft* (Frankfurt/Main, 1979), pp. 205–19. The essay dates from 1948.
37. Alfred Lorenzer, *Über den Gegenstand der Psychoanalyse oder: Sprache und Interaktion* (Frankfurt/Main, 1973), p. 102.
38. On this issue see D. Kamper and V. Rittner, eds., *Zur Geschichte des Körpers* (Munich, 1977).
39. The concept of body-text most suitable for use in the present study was coined by Günther Lohr in his 1979 doctoral thesis, presented to the University of Frankfurt, "Körpertext: Historische Semiotik der komischen Praxis—vom Cinquecento bis zur Mitte des 18. Jahrhunderts."
40. As pointed out in note 12 above, Bakhtin introduced the concept into literary criticism. He meant the term to designate the polyphony of a text produced by a subject in the sense of the dialogical relations which constitute a text, and thus a particular form of intertextuality. Kristeva has taken this up in her concept of polylogy and made it known to a wider audience. I therefore believe it is apposite to use the expression polyphony in what follows to designate the matter in question.
41. Cf. on this Kristeva, *Polylogue*.
42. Cf. Pfister, *The Drama*.
43. In recent years, Helga Finter has done much to draw our attention to the voice as a sign. Cf. her "Soufflierte Stimme," *Theater heute* 1 (1982): 45–51, and her "Die Theatralisierung der Stimme im Experimentaltheater," a lecture she held at the 4th Colloquium on Semiotics in Hamburg and which has appeared in K. Oehler, ed., *Zeichen und Realität*.
44. Cf. my discussion of the spatial conception of baroque theater in section 2 of the German version.
45. On theories of translation see Wolfram Wills, ed., *Semiotik und Übersetzen* (Tübingen, 1980).
46. On the division of literary dramatic texts into dialogue and subtexts see Roman Ingarden, "Von den Funktionen der Sprache im Theaterschauspiel, in *Das literarische Kunstwerk* (Tübingen, 1960), pp. 403–25.
47. On the following summary cf. the discussion of Diderot and Lessing in part 2.
48. Diderot describes this using the example of a game of chess which the deaf-mute believes he has lost. See Denis Diderot, "Brief über die Taubstummen," in *Ästhetische Schriften*, F. Bassenge, ed., vol. 1 (Frankfurt/Main, 1968), 36f.
49. Ibid., 34.
50. Cf. Gotthold Ephraim Lessing, *Laokoon*, in *Werke*, vol. 6, *Kunsttheoretische Schriften* (Munich, 1974); and his "Hamburgische Dramaturgie," in *Werke*, vol. 4, *Dramaturgische Schriften* (Munich, 1973), esp. section 5.
51. Charles Sander Peirce, *Writings of Charles S. Peirce. A Chronological Edition* (Chicago, 1967). To Peirce's mind, the interpretant of a sign thus comprises everything which is explicit in the sign itself, irrespective of the context and conditions under which it is

spoken. On the concept of the interpretant, see also Umberto Eco, *Einführung in die Semiotik*, pp. 76–81.

52. Undoubtedly, both decisively change the dramatic norm valid up until that point, without, however, also renouncing their claim to formulating a new "correct" norm that is to be valid from now on.

53. In this connection, the function both of the name and the body as understandable documents of identity as developed by new theories of identity is of especial interest, particularly that put forward by symbolic interactionism. Both name and body thus refer to the identity of the stage character and are mutually exchangeable in this regard. On the function of name and body see Jean Marie Benoist, ed., *Identität. Ein interdisziplinäres Seminar unter Leitung von Claude Lévi-Strauss* (Stuttgart, 1980); David J. D. Levita, *The Concept of Identity* (The Hague, 1965); George H. Mead, *Geist, Identität und Gesellschaft* (Frankfurt/ Main, 1973); Gregory P. Stone, "Appearance and the Self," in A. M. Rose, ed., *Human Behaviour and Social Processes. An Interactional Approach* (London, 1962), pp. 86–118; Anselm Strauss, *Spiegel und Masken* (Frankfurt/Main, 1974). Cf. further Fischer-Lichte, "Signs of Identity—The Dramatic Character as 'Name' and 'Body'," in André Helbo, ed., *Approches de l'opéra* (Paris: Didier, 1986), pp. 79–88, and Fischer-Lichte, *Geschichte des Dramas. Epochen der Identität auf dem Theater*, 2 vols. (Tübingen: Francke, 1990).

54. On the problem of textual hermeneutics, cf. in this connection E. Fischer-Lichte, *Bedeutung*.

55. On the concept of the aesthetic object as with that of the artifact, cf. Mukařovský, *Ästhetische Funktion*.

56. Cf. on this Ansgar Hillach, "Sprache und Theater," *Sprachkunst* 1 (1970): 256–59 and 2 (1971): 299–328.

57. Jolanta Brach also emphasizes in her study, published at a much earlier date, that it is supposed to be possible to transfer meanings when transforming a dramatic text into a performance. She believes that this is above all possible because theatrical signs have no lexically encoded meanings. Cf. her "O znakach literackich i znakach teatralnych," *Studia Estetyczne* 2 (1965): 241–59.

58. In other words, the problem of transformation involves the question of smallest significant unit again, if in a modified manner, because the process of transformation initially proceeds from the units of the literary text of the drama. See the section of chap. 5 titled "Structure and Hierarchy."

59. Osiński also undertakes a tripartite division, although he relies on different criteria. He distinguishes between (a) the realist model, i.e., substantive translation with an orientation toward the substance of the literary work; (b) an antirealist model, i.e., a substantialist translation oriented toward the substance of the performance; and (c) a creative model, i.e., functional translation geared toward structural analogy (structural homology). Cf. Zbigniew Osiński, "Przekład tekstu literackiego na język teatru. (Zarys problematyki)," in Jan Trzynadlovsky, *Dramat i Teatr* (Wrocław, 1967), pp. 119–56. To my mind, it is unfortunate that the division is oriented toward certain styles, such as realist/antirealist. For both of the variants Osiński describes, that is, models (a) and (b) are both clearly possible in realist and antirealist performances. For this reason I have chosen to use the distinction between linear, structural, and global models. Such an approach does not tie the different modes to particular stylistic principles from the outset.

60. Cf. on this point E. Fischer-Lichte, "The Dramatic Dialogue—Oral or Literary Communication?" in A. van Kesteren and H. Schmid, eds., *Drama, Theatre and Semiotics* (Amsterdam, 1984).

61. Veltrusky came to a similar conclusion. Cf. Yiri Veltrusky, "Dramatic Text as a Component of Theater," in L. Matejka and J. R. Titunic, eds., *Semiotics of Art. Prague School Contribution* (Cambridge, Mass., 1976), pp. 94–117.

62. On the theory of blanks especially in narrative texts, see Wolfgang Iser, *The Implied Reader* (Baltimore and London: Johns Hopkins Univ. Press, 1978); and his *The Act of Reading* (Baltimore and London: Johns Hopkins Univ. Press, 1978).

63. Cf. on this Tadeusz Kowzan, "Le texte et le spectacle. Rapports entre la mise en scène et la parole," *Cahiers de l'association internationale des études françaises* 1 (1969): 63–72.

64. Coseriu stresses with regard to interlingual translation that it is not the meanings of the text but "by means of the meanings of another language" "the same meanings and the same overall meaning" that is reproduced. By contrast, in the case of the process of intersemiotic translation of a drama into a performance, the translation hinges on the historical determinacy of the designations (in the sense of exact data). Cf. E. Coseriu, "Falsche und richtige Fragestellungen in der Übersetzungstheorie," in *Nobel Symposium 39. Theory and Practice of Translation*, L. Grahs, G. Korlen, and B. Malmberg, eds. (Bern, Frankfurt/Main, and Las Vegas, 1978), p. 21.

65. If, however, one wishes to create an awareness of the historical distance involved and is thus prepared to expose the feelings mentioned to ridicule, then one way of accomplishing this is undoubtedly to abide closely by such instructions for the scene correctly.

66. On such linguistic signs in the literary text, cf., among others, E. W. B. Hess-Lüttich, "Drama, Silence and Semiotics," *Kodikas/Code* 1, no. 2 (1979): 105–120.

67. In other words, unlike Raszewski, Skwarczyńska, and Pfister, I do not assume that the drama is only to be considered the "score" for the performance and in this sense is on the other hand itself to be considered a multimedial text. Rather, I would like to emphasize the aesthetic specificity and autonomy of both. See Zbigniew Raszewski, "Partytura Teatralna," *Pamiętnik Teatralny* 7, no. 3/4 (1958): 380–412; Stefania Skwarczyńska, *Wokoł teatru i literatury* (Warsaw, 1970); Pfister, *The Drama*.

68. This is true not only of theatrical texts, but of all the different kinds of texts. Schleiermacher already mentions that "every act of understanding is the inversion of an act of speech;" he as a consequence saw this as the justification for referring hermeneutics to rhetoric (F. D. E. Schleiermacher, *Hermeneutik*, new. ed. by Heinz Kimmerle [Heidelberg, 1959], p. 80).

69. On the history of hermeneutics as a doctrine of interpretation, see, among others, E. Betti, *Allgemeine Auslegungslehre als Methodik der Geisteswissenschaften* (Tübingen, 1967); G. Ebeling, "Hermeneutik," in *Die Religion in Geschichte und Gegenwart. Handwörterbuch für Theologie und Religionswissenschaft*, ed. K. Galing, vol. 3, 3rd, completely revised ed. (Tübingen, 1959), columns 242–62; W.-H. Friedrich, "Allegorische Interpretation," in *Fischer Lexikon Literatur*, 2, part 1, W.-H. Friedrich and W. Killy, eds. (Frankfurt/Main, 1965), 18–23; H. Kimmerle, "Die Hermeneutik Schleiermachers im Zusammenhang seines spekulativen Denkens," (doctoral thesis, Heidelberg, 1957); F. Ohly, "Vom geistigen Sinn des Wortes im Mittelalter," in *Zeitschrift für deutsches Altertum und deutsche Literatur* 89 (1958/9): 1–23 (issued as special edition by the Wissenschaftliche Buchgesellschaft Darmstadt in 1966 as *Libelli*, vol. 218); P. Szondi, *Einführung in die literarische Hermeneutik* (Frankfurt/Main: Suhrkamp, 1975); J. Wach, *Das Verstehen. Grundzüge einer Geschichte der hermeneutischen Theorie im 19. Jahrhundert*, vols. 1–3 (Tübingen, 1926–33; reprint, Hildesheim, 1966).

70. This tradition of hermeneutics was founded by Wilhelm Dilthey and developed further especially by Martin Heidegger and Hans-Georg Gadamer. Cf. W. Dilthey, "Die Entstehung der Hermeneutik," in *Gesammelte Schriften*, vol. 5 (Stuttgart and Göttingen, 1961), 317–38; M. Heidegger, *Being and Time*, tr. John Macquarrie and Edward Robinson (Oxford: Blackwell, 1962); H.-G. Gadamer, *Truth and Method* (London: Sheed and Ward, 1975).

71. Gadamer, *Truth and Method*, p. 263.

72. Cf. on this E. Fischer-Lichte, "Zum Problem der Bedeutung ästhetischer Zeichen," *Kodikas/Code* 3 (1980): 269–83.

73. P. Szondi, "Schleiermacher's Hermeneutics Today," in *On Textual Understanding and Other Essays*, tr. Harvey Mendelsohn (Minneapolis: Univ. of Minnesota Press, 1986), pp. 95–114.

74. Cf. on this M. Frank, *Das individuelle Allgemeine* (Frankfurt/Main: Suhrkamp, 1977).

75. Cf. E. Fischer-Lichte, *Bedeutung*, and "What Is Understanding?" in Jonathan Evans

and John Deely, eds., *Semiotics 1983* (Lanham, New York and London: Univ. Press of America, 1987), pp. 361–71.

76. Gadamer, *Truth and Method*, p. 245.

77. The objections Stegmüller raises against the concept of "prejudice" do not appear to be quite watertight. He claims that the concept (a) cannot be derived from colloquial speech, (b) is not defined specially as a technical term, and (c) that it cannot be conceived of as a theoretical concept because no corresponding theory has yet been formulated. For Gadamer's theory of understanding develops the concept in a way that permits it to be defined as the sum of those internalized patterns of thought and behavior which guide action without being reflected on in this capacity. By contrast, full support must be forthcoming for Stegmüller's demand that a scholar must of course "speak . . . using clear concepts and must be able to take up a clear stance" (*Rationale Rekonstruktion von Wissenschaft und ihrem Wandel*, [Stuttgart, 1979], p. 31). The concept of prejudice can, however, evidently be defined and used in such a way that it can be regarded as "clear." See Stegmüller's essay "Walther von der Vogelweides Lied von der Traumliebe und Quasar³ C273. Betrachtungen zum sogenannten Zirkel des Verstehens und zur sogenannten Theoriebeladenheit der Beobachtungen," ibid., pp. 27–86. The essay is a substantially expanded and revised version of a lecture given at the German Congress of Philosophy in Kiel in 1972.

78. Gadamer, *Truth and Method*, p. 245.

79. Allow me to reiterate the validity of the critique of Gadamer's concept of tradition which I have made elsewhere. For Gadamer hypostatizes tradition in a manner that causes it to appear as a type of self-regulated system which occurs behind the backs of the subjects or even over their heads. This is the only possible interpretation of his definition of understanding "not . . . so much as an action of one's subjectivity, but as the placing of oneself within a process of tradition" (*Truth and Method*, p. 258), a statement that has repeatedly been criticized. Cf. on this M. Frank, *Das individuelle Allgemeine*, pp. 20–34; J. Habermas, "The Hermeneutic Approach," in his *Logic of the Social Sciences*, tr. Shierry Weber Nicholsen and Jerry Stark (Cambridge, Mass.: MIT Press, 1988), pp. 143–70; and E. Fischer-Lichte, *Bedeutung*, pp. 146–53.

80. I will go into the specificity of this process in greater depth in my discussion of the hermeneutic circle below.

81. On this problem see my *Bedeutung*, and "Literaturdidaktik als ästhetische Reflexion," in R. Schäfer, ed., *Germanistik und Deutschunterricht* (Munich, 1979), pp. 44–73.

82. We have shown this to be the case in part 2 with reference to the theatrical code during the transition from the baroque to the Enlightenment.

83. Naturally, a performance by the Peking Opera can be received using aesthetic criteria different from those pregiven and prescribed by the theatrical code. Indeed, such a performance can undoubtedly give rise to the highest aesthetic enjoyment. The concept of understanding can, however, not be used for such an reception. For its use would require that the code on which the performance relied, a code developed in a foreign culture under specific conditions, would have to be learned in this form and analyzed in terms of the specific conditions of its genesis. A cultural divide cannot be bridged simply by being ignored and the corresponding performance then being received in terms of the standards we have developed for theater in our culture. Rather, it can only be overcome by reflection on and intellectual engagement with the foreignness of this culture. Cf. Fischer-Lichte, "Intercultural Misunderstanding as Aesthetic Pleasure. The Reception of the Peking Opera in Western Germany," in Werner Enninger, ed., *Interdisciplinary Perspectives in Cross-Cultural Communication* (Aachen: Rader, 1985), pp. 79–93.

84. Without such a possibility, by contrast, the reception of the literary texts of past epochs would be almost inconceivable.

85. Cf. the construction of this theatrical code in part 2 of the German version.

86. This homogeneity was guaranteed in bourgeois illusionistic theater from the Enlightenment to the commencement of the avant-garde movements in this century by the clear reference to a social class, namely the bourgeoisie.

87. Cf. on this E. Fischer-Lichte, "Theatrical Communication."

88. This is the case, for example, if a performance is based on the principle of aleatorics, such as in Kagel's modern music-based theater. Cf. Christine Finkbeiner, "Aspekte des Allegorischen in der Neuen Musik" (doctoral thesis, Frankfurt, 1961).

89. We can assume that those structural chains are used which are known in the same way by all the members of the otherwise nonhomogeneous audiences of our cultures. Examples often used would be comics, crime films, Westerns, etc. Certain conceptions of character, behavior, and space are borrowed from these, as it were, as stereotypes. By topicalizing these stereotypes, a general basis is created on which the special meanings can then be constituted.

90. Such a procedure of the constitution of meaning can be shown to exist in the avant-garde theater of a Richard Foreman or a Robert Wilson.

91. Cf. the philosophical studies by Theodor Abel, "The Option Called 'Verstehen'," in Fergl and Brodbeck, eds., *Reading in the Philosophy of Science* (New York, 1953), pp. 677ff; W. Stegmüller, "Walther von der Vogelweide"; and Heide Göttner's work on literary criticism: *Die Logik der Interpretation. Analyse einer literaturwissenschaftlichen Methode unter kritischen Betrachtung der Hermeneutik* (Munich, 1979), pp. 62ff, especially, pp. 131ff; and Siegfried J. Schmidt, *Literaturwissenschaft als argumentierende Wissenschaft* (Munich, 1975), in particular pp. 196ff.

92. M. Frank, *Das individuelle Allgemeine*, p. 308.

93. It is above all M. Frank who takes up this objection. Cf. ibid., pp. 305–13.

94. Cf. the works by Göttner, Schmidt, and Stegmüller cited in note 91.

95. In the history of hermeneutics, especially in the eighteenth and early nineteenth centuries, it was considered possible to break out of the hermeneutic circle to the extent that it was only construed as a specific relation of parts to whole. Cf. P. Szondi, *Einführung*.

96. Schleiermacher accordingly discerns as many applications for the circle as he distinguishes levels, each of which exceeds the prior level in terms of the generality of reciprocal relations. He differentiates here between:
(1) The unique occurrence of a word and the context of the sentence;
(2) Sentence and speech;
(3) (a) Speech and the individual text of an author;
    (b) The main thought and the subordinate thoughts in the text;
(4) (a) The individual work of an author and the "total literature" of an age;
    (b) The individual work and the totality of the author's life;
(5) The totality of life and work of an author and the "common spirit" of an age. (*Hermeneutik*, pp. 147ff.)
As can be seen from this, different levels of ever greater generality can be constructed that go far beyond the levels constituted in the text itself.

97. Cf. A. J. Greimas, *Strukturale Semantik* (Brunswick, 1971).

98. The deliberations that follow are merely sketched cursorily. For an extensive argumentation see E. Fischer-Lichte, *Bedeutung*; and E. Fischer-Lichte "Zur Konstitution ästhetischer Zeichen," in H. Sturm and A. Eschbach, eds., *Ästhetik und Semiotik* (Tübingen, 1980), pp. 17–28.

99. Jan Mukařovský, *Ästhetische Funktion*, p. 97. On this definition of the specificity of the aesthetic sign, cf. my discussion in *Bedeutung*, "Literaturdidaktik," "Zur Konstitution ästhetiker Zeichen;" "Zum Problem der ästhetischen (Re)Konstruktion von Wirklichkeit," in K. Oehler, ed., *Zeichen und Realität*; "Kunst und Wirklichkeit."

100. Jean-Paul Sartre, *What Is Literature?*, tr. B. Frechtman (London: Methuen, 1978), p. 13.

101. On the recipient changing the system of meaning during the process of reception cf. my extensive remarks in *Bedeutung* and "Literaturdidaktik."

102. Some subjectivity or other of the method for constituting this overall meaning can hardly be derived logically from the subjectivity of the overall meaning constituted. In other words, all those who believe interpretation can only occur as an uncontrolled act of subjective

empathy must be challenged energetically. Equally, those who call for an intersubjectively verifiable method and therefore attempt to exclude all subjective elements from the processes of constituting meaning and a text's overall meaning must also be opposed. For they deduce the necessarily subjective and therefore unscientific nature of the method from the subjectivity of the overall meaning.

8. The Process of Constituting Meaning and Sense as a Method of Analyzing Theatrical Texts

1. On the corresponding issue in the philosophy of science cf., among others, H. Albert, *Plädoyer für einen kritischen Rationalismus* (Munich, 1971); W. K. Essler, *Wissenschaftstheorie* (Freiburg and Munich, 1970–1); D. Freundlieb, "Hermeneutics versus Philosophy of Science," *Poetics* 13: 47–105; H. Kuhn, "Methodenlehre," in D. Krywalski, ed., *Handlexikon zur Literaturwissenschaft* (Munich, 1974), pp. 306–10; F. v. Kutschera, *Wissenschaftstheorie*, 2 vols. (Munich, 1972); W. Leinfellner, *Einführung in die Erkenntnis- und Wissenschaftstheorie*, 2nd ed. (Mannheim, 1967); W. Stegmüller, *Probleme und Resultate der Wissenschaftstheorie und Analytischen Philosophie* (Berlin, Heidelberg, and New York, 1969).

2. Cf. on this point, M. Frank, *Das individuelle Allgemeine*, pp. 305ff.

3. The concept of sign does not, therefore, refer here only to signs at the elementary level, but also to the unity of the higher levels of semantic coherence, such as a costume, a song, a dialogue, a stage set, or a person. These signs are defined elsewhere as supersigns; however, such a definition does not delineate adequately among the different degrees of complexity. I shall thus differentiate among signs according to the level of semantic coherence involved.

4. Lotman, *Die Struktur*, p. 27.

5. Cf. on this point M. Titzmann, *Strukturale Textanalyse. Theorie und Praxis der Interpretation*, (Munich, 1977).

6. This reciprocal relationship is not, however, to be considered circular, but rather as complementary if placed in the context of certain aims and aspects of the present study.

7. Cf. M. Titzmann, *Strukturale Textanalyse*, in particular on the elementary rules of interpretation, pp. 20ff.

8. The logic in question leads us to postulate freedom from contradiction, for any random statement can be derived from mutually contradictory statements that nevertheless claim to be true. This postulate does not exclude the possibility that the text analyzed contains contradictions. Rather, it would be the task of the analysis to clarify what function such contradictions play. Yet, the analysis must not allow itself to become entangled in contradictions in the process.

9. In other words, the element to which the statement refers must be factually present in the text and not just present in the imagination of the interpreter. If it is accordingly a finding made in the text, then any receiver at random can confirm that it factually exists.

10. We can by no means derive the "correctness" of the interpretation from recourse to the findings made in the text. We cannot therefore make use of Titzmann's Rule 1c of interpretation, which states that: "It must be possible directly or indirectly to verify and/or falsify interpretatory statements" (*Strukturale Textanalyse*, p. 22). The only things that can be verified in this sense are descriptive sentences, not interpretative sentences derived from them. For the interpretative sentences are not "correct" or "false" if the respective descriptive sentence is true; rather, they are merely "justified" or "unjustified," "plausible" or "implausible."

11. The Russian formalists already recognized this, and gave it a theoretical underpinning by drawing on the binary of automation/de-automation.

12. It is in particular Kristeva who emphasizes this point when she terms poetic language

"the semiotization of the symbolic." Cf. also M. Frank, *Das Sagbare und das Unsagbare* (Frankfurt/Main, 1980).

13. To my mind Eco also implies this extension when he speaks of the "dialectic between codes and messages. . . . Whereby the codes admittedly steer the production of messages but new messages may change the structure of the code" (*Einführung*, p. 143).

14. Cf. the section "Structure and Hierarchy" in chap. 5 of the present study; on the issues involved see T. Kowzan, *Littérature et spectacle*; F. Ruffini, "Semiotica del teatro: la stabilizzazione del senso," *Biblioteca teatrale* 12 (1975): 205–39; P. Hamon, "Pour un statut sémiologique du personnage," in *Poetique du récit* (Paris, 1977), pp. 115–80; S. Jansen, "Entwurf einer Theorie der dramatischen From, in J. Ihwe, ed., *Literaturwissenschaft und Linguistik*, vol. 2 (Frankfurt/Main, 1973), 215–45.

15. This confusion considerably impairs the otherwise highly thoughtful approach taken by Marco de Marini. See his "Problemi e aspetti di un approccio semiotico al teatro, *Lingua e style* 10, no. 2 (1975): 343–47; and his "Lo spettacolo come testo," *Versus* 21 (1978): 66–104 (I) and *Versus* 22 (1979): 3–31 (II).

16. Cf. on this point part 1, where an attempt was made—with regard to the individual sign systems involved in the theatrical process—to establish the smallest significative units and the smallest distinguishing features. The problems faced there will of course make themselves felt in establishing the elementary level in question.

17. This is often the case with avant-garde performances, in which insignificant elements—for which there is generally no place in the systems of meaning used by the receivers—are introduced and receive a meaning in the course of the performance on the basis of internal recodings.

18. Cf. also the section "On Applying the Method," in this chapter.

19. The procedure of generating isotopes as parallels is of course closely linked with the systematics of theatrical signs, as elaborated by Kowzan. It consequently draws on the analyses carried out by students at the University of Lyon, analyses he encouraged and supervised. See *Analyse sémiologique du spectacle théâtral. Etudes dirigées et présentées par T. Kowzan* (University of Lyon II, Centre d'Etudes et de Recherches Théâtrales, 1976). This procedure is also used by A. Eschbach. See A. Eschbach, *Pragmasemiotik und Theater. Ein Beitrag zur Theorie und Praxis einer pragmatisch orientierten Zeichenanalyse* (Tübingen, 1979).

20. This is, of course, predominantly true of performances in which an innovative use of a sign system or a group of sign systems—such as, for example, of kinesic or architectonic signs—occurs. A particularly well suited example of this would be Robert Wilson's productions.

21. The debate in drama theory from Aristotle to Brecht on the concepts of "plot" and "occurrence" makes use, above all, of this division. Cf. M. Pfister, *The Drama*, chapter 6, "History and Plot," pp. 265–326, for a summary of this discussion and a discussion of it in light of new findings in research on narrativity (for example, C. Brémond, *Logique du récit* [Paris, 1973]; A. J. Greimas, *Eléments d'une grammaire narrative* [Paris, 1970]; T. Todorov, "La grammaire du récit," *Langages* 12 [1968]: 94–102).

22. Of course, we can draw in this sense in the case of this type of performance segmentation on the findings of the corresponding studies in drama theory which foreground the category of situation or scene. See on this among others R. Grimm and D. Kimpel, "Situationen," in Grimm and Wiedemann, eds., *Literatur- und Geistesgeschichte. Festgabe für O. Burger* (Berlin, 1968), pp. 325–60; A. Hübler, *Drama in er Vermittlung von Handlung, Sprache und Szene* (Bonn, 1973); S. Jansen, "Qu'est-ce qu'une situation dramatique?" *Orbis Litterarum* 28 (1973): 235–92; H. C. Lancaster, "Situation as a Term in Literary Criticism," in *Modern Language Notes* 59 (1944): 392–95; G. Polti, *Les 36 situations dramatiques* (Paris, 1895); D. Schnetz, *Der moderne Einakter. Eine poetologische Untersuchung* (Bern, 1967); R Scholes, "The Dramatic Situations of Etienne Souriau," in *Structuralism in Literature. An Introduction* (New Haven, 1974), pp. 50–58; E. Souriau, *Les deux cent mille situations dramatiques* (Paris, 1950); L. Spitzer, "Situation as a Term in Literary

Criticism Again,'' *Modern Language Notes* 72 (1957): 124–28; K. Weigand, ''Situation und Situationsgestaltung in der Tragödie'' (doctoral thesis, Frankfurt/Main, 1941).

23. Received opinion from Aristotle to Lessing was that plot was the primary content of drama, so that characters existed only in order to serve the plot. Lenz proposed the opposite, namely that the plot only served to help outline the characters. Nevertheless, the category of the character was at an earlier date—for example in Aristotle's thought and to a very emphatic degree in the writings of Diderot and Lessing—already an essential concept in drama theory.

24. Needless to say, parallel segmentation is always possible, because a performance will always use different sign systems. However, if this occurs in line with an existing valid convention (such as in popular theater today), then such a form of segmentation is not particularly fruitful. Segmentation which forms syntagma is, by contrast, impossible or at least highly unproductive in all those cases in which there is no plot, or no story is told—such as is frequently to be encountered in avant-garde theater today (e.g., in that of Robert Wilson), where the actors no longer represent characters.

25. Parallel segmentation would therefore appear to always be expedient in cases where individual sign systems and/or groups of sign systems are being used either in a completely new way or in such a manner as to contrast with one another.

26. Whereas in general principles can be followed in the analysis of the plot of a performance which are similar to those employed in analyzing the plot of a drama, when analyzing the persons, the premises are completely different. Here, external appearance and kinesic signs take a place by no means always foreseen in drama.

27. Thus, for example, the development of a person can only be described on the basis of his or her changing temporal and spatial location. Segmentation according to persons must accordingly be accompanied by segmentation according to sequence of actions and sequence of scenes.

28. Cf. below ''On Applying the Method.''

29. The first case is no doubt to be encountered most in recent theater history. For example, in Brecht's rejection of light as a system generating meaning, in the first use of black T-shirts in modern ballet, which thus initially denies that costume can be a signified, in Handke's renunciation of the spoken word in *Das Mündel will Vormund sein*, which, in opposition to Beckett's *Actes sans parole*, expressly declares itself to be a drama, thus excluding its being classified as pantomime.

30. In theater history, such a deviation often constituted the beginning of a general change of code. Nowadays, however, it is as a rule only to be considered a signified with regard to the corresponding performance.

31. Thus, Western theater can today use as material all the theatrical norms ever valid anywhere. If, for example, the productions put on by the international ''Parapluie'' troupe use costumes from medieval processions, costumes and gestures from commedia dell'arte, plot schemas and dramatic, pathetic gestures culled from melodrama, etc., then they are actualizing a potential already latent in the repertoire of the theatrical code as a system. Today, intertextuality can become a constitutive factor to a much greater degree than used to be the case, owing to the possibility of using elements of theatrical forms of past ages and foreign cultures today, and by so doing as it were to quote the respective theatrical forms, epochs, and/or cultures. However, it evidently requires an enormous breadth of cultural knowledge in order to be actualized.

32. Cf. M. Titzmann, *Strukturale Textanalyse,* pp. 86ff.

33. On substitution, see Titzmann, *Strukturale Textanalyse*, pp. 104ff. Titzmann gives a summarizing description of the constitutive operation involved in each structural procedure by referring to a variety of other researchers.

34. On the concept of equivalence, cf. Y. Lotman, *Die Struktur*, p. 143ff.

35. Lotman puts it accordingly: ''Equivalence is not the same as identity. The fact that text segments which, put in common language, have different semantics, may appear as equivalence forces us, on the one hand, to develop commonal (neutralizing) archisemes for

them, and, on the other, transforms their differences into a system of relevant oppositions.'' *Die Struktur*, p. 177.

36. Trubetzkoj first introduced the notion of opposition (in his *Grundzüge der Phonologie* [Prague, 1939]), and distinguished among privative, gradual, and equipollent oppositions. Since then, both the concept and the distinction have become part of the basic stocks of any structuralist methodology, irrespective of the area addressed.

37. This will also prove to be the case in our analysis of Augusto Fernandes's staging of Pirandello's *Henry IV*, where similarity in costume plays a key role. See my analyses of various performances: ''All the World's A Stage: The Theatrical Metaphor in the Baroque and Postmodernism,'' in Willmar Sauter, ed., *New Directions in Theatre Research* (Nordic Theatre Studies, Special International Issue, Copenhagen: Munksgaard, 1990), p. 80–92; ''Passage to the Realm of Shadows. Robert Wilson's 'King Lear' in Frankfurt,'' in Willmar Sauter and Jacqueline Martin, eds., *Handbook of Performance Analysis* (London: Routledge, 1991).

38. The investigation of the features ''position'' and ''distribution'' show that the categories of time and space function as a system of coordinates, as it were, a system into which the individual elements of the performance have then to be entered. Every analysis will correspondingly have to take time and space into consideration.

39. Such correlations enable us to show possible dominance with the aid of objectively given textual findings. This enables us to avoid such vague and useless categories as ''impression.''

40. This procedure is today part of the stock of methodological possibilities open to semiotic textual analysis. Cf. on this especially the pertinent studies by H. F. Plett, *Text-wissenschaft und Textanalyse* (Heidelberg, 1975), and Titzmann, *Strukturale Textanalyse*.

41. The recourse to the underlying semiotic system is, in other words, just as obvious a precondition for the procedures of internal and external recoding as it is for carrying out the other procedures.

42. In the 1970s, Zadek, Neuenfels, and Peymann in particular put on numerous productions which followed this rule. One need think only of their staging of various classics, especially Zadek's Shakespeare productions.

43. In this case, the norm not only prescribes that external recoding must be undertaken, but also the respective extratextual structural chains—the primary cultural systems—to which the individual elements of the performance must be related if they are to receive meaning.

44. Works by Wilson and Foreman, as well as by Kagel and Ligeti provide numerous examples of this.

45. Luigi Pirandello, *Henry IV*, tr. J. Mitchell (London: Methuen, 1979), pp. 44–45, and p. 46.

46. This is clearly an example of synecdoche composed of theatrical signs. It would appear to be a rewarding task with a view to the rhetorics or poetics of theatrical texts to study in what manner the classical rhetorical tropes are developed here and especially for which tropes there is a theatrical pendant. The terrain of a theatrological study of metaphors is as yet hardly staked out.

47. Cf. the analysis of the relations between ''Henry'' and Donna Mathilda carried out in part 3, chapter 3 of the German edition of the present study.

48. A director can therefore to my mind not be accused of resorting to such private elements if he introduces them via internal recoding, for they can either expand the experience of the receivers or be attributed to a general domain of experience. What s/he can be admonished for is only for assuming that they are known and pointing to external recoding in order to constitute their meaning, that is unless every receiver is meant to fill out this blank on the basis of his or her own personal experience.

49. The production by Wilfried Minks at the Municipal Theater, Frankfurt, during the 1977–1978 season.

50. Thus ''Henry'' speaks in act 1 of a possible sortie against the pope, a ''temptation''

which he only "resists" because he is "wise" (*Henry IV*, p. 65). However, "Henry's" breastplate, greaves, and jousting gloves evoke the context of a medieval battle.

51. Thus, in this and the previous act "Henry" repeatedly speaks to Donna Mathilda, the supposed mother of his historical wife Berta, of his relationship with Berta, of his feelings for her, of the possibility of loving her. As the detailed analysis in the German edition shows, the use of the theatrical sign systems of emphasis, mimicry, gestures, movement, and music enables "Henry's" statements about Berta to be interpeted as statements about his relationship to Donna Mathilda.

52. Frankfurt Municipal Theater, 1980–1981 season.

53. Intertextuality is accordingly a consequence of external recoding. If elements of the text can only be instilled with meaning under the condition that they are referred to the text from which they originate, then it follows that intertextuality as a complex of such references can only be constituted and realized as paradigmatic meanings, and solely on the basis of external recoding. The higher the degree of paradigmatic meanings, the more intertextuality comes to bear.

54. Such a difference between the literary text of the drama and the theatrical text of the performance naturally brings us to the question of equivalence. Evidently, on the basis of other literary textual elements, Neuenfels constituted the dichotomy of two cultures as an important meaning—quite in keeping with Adorno's famous interpretation, which was reprinted in the program. Neuenfels sought for specific theatrical signs for this dichotomy, such as, in addition to the ox's skull, the opposition of Thoas in a street coat and with spectacles, sitting on the chair reading a book, and Thoas, half-naked, with a tatooed skin, crouching on the earth. The introduction of elements that are not foreseen in the literary text thus comprises no argument against possible equivalence.

55. Iphigenia accordingly says to Arkas in act 4, scene 2: "Now I hasten with my virgins to the sea, to net the Goddess' image from the fresh wave, to mystery shrouded consecration. Let no one disturb our silent procession!" (V. 1436–1440).

56. This shows particularly impressively that hermeneutic premises and semiotic structuralist methods by no means exclude one another, but, as M. Frank intended, can be interwoven. Cf. on this M. Frank, *Das individuelle Allgemeine*, pp. 247ff. as well as the following section.

57. R. Barthes would seem to have been the first to raise this question, namely in his essay "L'analyse structurale du récit. A propos d'Actes X–XI," *Recherches de science religieuse* 58: 17–37. Titzmann also studies this, and comes up with an answer similar to the one I have given, without, however, giving any justifications for this: "IR 42: The TA can select any 'text' data or class of 'text' data at random as the point of departure to the extent that the respective data are only 'observable' " (*Strukturale Textanalyse*, p. 368).

58. The receiver can, of course, only judge which of the elements of the text has particular relevance vis-à-vis the aims formulated on the basis of a certain experience of using theatrical texts. For there is no "objective" criterion for such relevance, for nothing is relevant in itself. The rule obtains here that x is relevant for domain y with regard to criterion z. On the question of relevance see Titzmann, *Strukturale Textanalyse*, pp. 343ff. Assessing the respective relevance depends, in other words, largely on the person who is the receiver.

59. Titzmann expressly answers this question in the affirmative. I would like to take this opportunity to refer explicitly again to his study, which I have cited frequently, even if I do not subscribe to all of his proposals. To my mind, he has set the standards for all future textual analysis. *Strukturale Textanalyse* should therefore form the basis of all future textual analysis that claims to be scholarly. Nevertheless, I have fundamental objections to some of the individual premises and conclusions. Titzmann asserts, for example, that "there is but one optimal textual analysis at that particular point in time" (p. 381); I do not believe sufficient grounds can be given for such a proposition, as I shall attempt to show below. To my mind, Titzmann is too unwilling to engage himself with hermeneutic premises and incorporate them seriously into his deliberations, something that is quite conceivable, as M. Frank has shown.

60. Cf. Frank's remarks on Schleiermacher's fundamental proposition "To understand an author better than he understood himself," in *Das individuelle Allgemeine*, pp. 358ff.

61. Dan Sperber puts things similarly on the occasion of a critique of structuralist descriptions of myth: "No grammar therefore generates by itself the set of myths, any more than the mechanism of visual perception generates by itself the set of possible perceptions. The device that would generate myths depends on an external stimulus; it is thus similar to cognitive devices and opposed to semiological devices: it is an interpretative, and not a generative, system" (*Rethinking Symbolism*, tr. A. L. Morton, pp. 82–83). Sperber's theory of symbolism in myths can largely be transposed onto the symbolism of art and can in this sense serve as the foundation for an interpretation of aesthetic texts.

62. See on this point R. A. Feuillet, *Choréographie* (Paris, 1701).

63. Beauchamps's copyright as the originator of the method of notation for dance steps was expressly recognized by the French government in 1666. Nevertheless, after Feuillet's book appeared in 1701, a court action ensued on the copyright involved, which was duly accorded Beauchamps.

64. See on this point R. von Laban, *Methodik, Orthographie, Erläuterungen*, 1st pamphlet in the *Schrifttanz* series (Vienna, 1928); and his *Principles of Dance and Movement Notation* (London, 1956).

65. See on this *Die fünf Grundsätze der Kinetographie Laban* (and diagram on p. 314):

"1. Spatial direction is represented by the form and shading of the signs (see 2.). The signs are stylized pointer arrows (Fig. 1).
2. Height and thus the third dimension is expressed by the shading of the signs.
Fig. 3a: Height is shaded.
Fig. 3b: Medium height is expressed by a dot in an otherwise empty sign.
Fig. 3c: Depth is expressed by black blocking.
3. Duration of movement is visualized by the length of the sign (Figs. 5 & 6)
4. The position of the signs in and on the system of lines shows which part of the body is to be moved.
5. The signs are read from bottom to top continuously (Fig. 7). The sequence of the signs thus shows when a movement is to be carried out. Each notational sign thus answers the following fundamental questions at one and the same time: Which part of the body is to be moved, for how long and in what direction? Example 9 gives four relatively rapid steps forwards, whereby the right arm is slowly moved rightwards and the left arm moved at a medium speed forwards and upwards.
The principles are used in the case of the body being rotated. The form of the sign shows whether the body is rotated left (Fig. 2a) or right (Fig. 2b); the length of the sign indicates the duration of the movement. The position of the sign in the system of lines shows whether the whole body is to rotate (first column) or only a single part of the body (see the other columns in Fig. 7)."

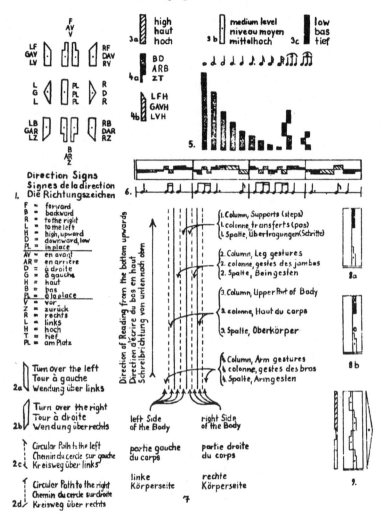

66. On Labanotation cf. also A. Hutchinson. *Labanotation* (New York, 1954), and his *Labanotation or Kinetography* (New York, 1970); A. Kunst, *Abriss der Kinetographie Laban* (Munich, 1952), and the same author's *A Dictionary of Kinetography Laban (Labanotation)* (Plymouth, 1980); V. Preston-Dunlop, *An Introduction to Kinetography Laban* (London, 1963), and the same author's *Practical Kinetography Laban* (London, 1969).

67. S. P. Bouissac, *La mesure des gestes* (The Hague, 1973).

68. Cf. on this problem, among others, E. W. B. Hess-Lüttich, "Medial Transformation and Semiotic Structure: Problems of Notation in Corpus Analysis," in E. W. B. Hess-Lüttich, ed., *Multimedial Communication*, vol. 1, *Semiotic Problems of its Notation*, vol. 2, *Theatre Semiotics* (Tübingen, 1982), vol. 1, 263–86; B. Switalla, "Die Identifikation kommunikativer 'Daten'," *Zeitschrift für Semiotik*, 1, nos. 2–3 (1973): 161–75.

69. Birdwhistell's findings were already presented in *Introduction to Kinesics*.

70. I give one such example (taken from Birdwhistell, *Introduction to Kinesics*, p. 29):

DATA: Conversation B: Hostess-guest event.
Observed April 17, 1952; analyzed (with G. L. Trager) on April 18.
Introductory note: Guest of honor forty-five minutes late. Three couples waiting, plus host and hostess. Host had arranged guest list for function.

Description:
1. As the hostess opened the door to admit her guest, she smiled a closed-toothed smile. As she began speaking she drew her hands, drawn into loose fists, up between her breasts. Opening her eyes very wide, she then closed them slowly and held them closed for several words. As she began to speak she dropped her head to one side and then moved it toward the guest in a slow sweep. She then pursed her lips momentarily before continuing to speak, nodded, shut her eyes again, and spread her arms, indicating that he should enter.
2. He looked at her fixedly, shook his head, and spread his arms with his hands held open. He then began to shuffle his feet and raised one hand, turning it slightly outward. He nodded, raised his other hand, and turned it palm-side up as he continued his vocalization. Then he dropped both hands and held them, palms forward, to the side and away from his thighs. He continued his shuffling.
3. She smiled at him, lips pulled back from clenched teeth. Then, as she indicated where he should put his coat, she dropped her face momentarily into an expressionless pose. She smiled toothily again, clucked and slowly shut, opened, and shut her eyes again as she pointed to the guest with her lips. She then swept her head from one side to the other. As she said the word "all" she moved her head in a sweep up and down from one side to the other, shut her eyes slowly again, pursed her lips, and grasped the guest's lapel.
4. The guest hunched his shoulders, which pulled his lapel out of the hostess's grasp. He held his coat with both hands, frowned, and then blinked rapidly as he slipped the coat off. He continued to hold tightly to his coat.

71. Cf. on this point P. Ekman and W. Friesen, "The Repertoire of Nonverbal Behavior: Categories, Origins, Usage, and Coding," *Semiotica* 1 (1969): 49–98; K. R. Scherer, "Die Funktionen des nonverbalen Verhaltens im Gespräch," in D. Wegner, ed., *Gesprächsanalyse: Bericht zum fünften IPK-Kolloquium* (Hamburg, 1977), pp. 273–95.

72. See on this S. Frey and J. Pool, "A New Approach to the Analysis of Visible Behavior," in *Forschungsberichte aus dem Psychologischen Institut* (Bern, 1976); S. Frey, H.-P. Hirsbrunner, and A. Bieri-Florin, "Vom Bildschirm zum Datenprotokoll: Das Problem der Rohdatengewinnung bei der Untersuchung nichtverbaler Interaktion," *Zeitschrift für Semiotik* 1 (1969), 1979: 193–209; S. Frey, H.-P. Hirsbrunner, and U. Jorns, "Time-Series Notation. A Unified Method for the Assessment of Speech and Movement in Communication Research, in E. W. B. Hess-Lüttich, ed., *Multimedial Communication*.

73. Cf. the table on p. 317—from *Zeitschrift für Semiotik* 1 (1979): 202.

74. Cf. on this K. R. Scherer and H. G. Wallbott, eds., *Nonverbale Kommunikation: Empirische Untersuchungen zum Interaktionsverhalten* (Weinheim, 1978); K. R. Scherer et al, "Psychoakustische und kinesische Verhaltensanalyse zur Bestimmung distaler Indikatoren affektiver Erregungszustände," in W. H. Tack, ed., *Bericht über den 30. Kongress der Deutschen Gesellschaft für Psychologie in Regensburg* (Göttingen, 1977), pp. 324–25; K. R. Scherer, H. G. Wallbott, and U. Scherer, "Methoden zur Klassifikation von bewegungsverhalten: Ein funktionaler Ansatz," *Zeitschrift für Semiotik* 1 (1979): 177–92.

75. Cf. P. Ekman and W. Friesen, "The Repertoire."

76. Scherer has attempted to categorize some of these functions in terms of Morris's schema of syntactic, semantic, and pragmatic dimensions of signs. See Scherer, "Die Funktionen."

77. In this context, Scherer bases his work on the procedure developed by Krout et al. Cf. Ekman and Friesen, "The Repertoire"; M. Freedman and S. Hoffman, "Kinetic Behavior in Altered Clinical States: Approach to Objective Analysis of Motor Behavior during Clinical Interviews," *Perceptual and Motor Skills* 24 (1967): 527–39; M. H. Krout, "Autistic Gestures: An Experimental Study in Symbolic Movement," *Psychological Monographs* 46 (1935): 119–20; G. F. Mahl, "Gestures and Body Movements in Interviews," in J. Shlien, ed., *Research in Psychotherapy* (Washington, D.C., American Psychological Association) 3 (1968): 295–346; H. M. Rosenfeld, "Instrumental Affiliative Functions of Facial and Gestural Expressions," *Journal of Personality and Social Psychology* 4 (1966): 65–72.

78. See, for an example of such a procedure, the table on p. 318.

79. We have thus far ignored the problems of notation of paralinguistic signs. However, to date there are no standardized generally applicable procedures that can be used in this area. Cf., among others, J. Bortz, *Physikalisch-akustische Korrelate der vokalen Kommunikation* (Arbeiten des Psychologischen Instituts der Universität Hamburg 9 [1966]); I. Fonagy and E. Bérard, "'Il est huit heures': contribution a l'analyse sémantique de la vive voix," *Phonetica* 26 (1972): 157–92; W. Geiseler, "Zur Semiotik graphischer Notation," *Melos—Neue Zeitschrift für Musik* 4, no. 1 (1978): 27–33; J. Laver, "Labels for voices," *Journal of the International Phonetic Association* 4, no. 2 (1974): 62–75; P. Winkler, "Notationen des Sprechausdrucks," *Zeitschrift für Semiotik* 1 (1979): 211–24.

Concluding Remarks

1. See the German version of part 3 of the present study for a far more exhaustive analysis of this performance.

2. See G. Rühle, "Die Erfindung der Bildersprache für das Theater," in his *Theater in unserer Zeit* (Frankfurt/Main, 1976), pp. 224–32.

3. Cf. on this the lively debate in the 1970s in the journal *Theater heute* on the different productions put on by the directors discussed here. The journal also offered a thorough description and a careful assessment of each production.

Part of Body	Number of Coded Dimensions	Dimension	Level on Scale/ Number Position	Describable Variation of Movement
(1) Head	3	Sagittal	Ordinal / 5	Lifting/lowering the head
		Rotational	Ordinal / 5	Left/right turn of the head
		Lateral	Ordinal / 5	Left/slant of the head
(2) Torso	3	Sagittal	Ordinal / 5	Bending torso forward/backward
		Rotational	Ordinal / 5	Left/right turn of the torso
		Lateral	Ordinal / 5	Left/right slant of the torso
(3) Shoulders*	2	Vertical	Ordinal / 3	Lifting/lowering shoulders
		Depth	Ordinal / 3	Hunching shoulders forwards/backwards
(4) Upper arms*	3	Vertical	Ordinal / 9	Lifting/lowering upper arms
		Depth	Ordinal / 9	Bending upper arms forwards/backwards
		Touching	Nominal / 7	Upper arm contact with chair/table/body
(5) Hands*	9	Vertical	Ordinal / 14	Hand shifted upward/downward
		Horizontal	Ordinal / 9	Hand shifted left/right
		Depth	Ordinal / 8	Hand tilted forwards/backwards
		x/y orientation	Ordinal / 9	Hand direction changed in the vertical
		z orientation	Ordinal / 5	Hand bent forwards/backwards
		Rotational	Ordinal / 9	Palm moved upwards/downwards
		Opening	Ordinal / 4	Hand clenched/opened
		Folding	Nominal / 2	Fingers interwoven/not interwoven
		Touching	Nominal / 52	Hand contact with chair/table/body
(6) Thighs*	3	Vertical	Ordinal / 5	Lifting/lowering thighs
		Horizontal	Ordinal / 5	Left/right turn of the thighs
		Touching	Ordinal / 3	Thigh contact at knee level
(7) Feet*	7	Vertical	Ordinal / 9	Foot moved upwards/downwards
		Horizontal	Ordinal / 7	Foot moved left/right
		Depth	Ordinal / 5	Foot moved forwards/backwards
		Sagittal	Ordinal / 5	Foot tilted forwards/backwards
		Rotational	Ordinal / 5	Foot turned inwards/outwards
		Lateral	Ordinal / 5	Foot tilted inwards/outwards
		Touching	Nominal / 10	Foot contact with chair/table/body
(8) Seated Position	2	Horizontal	Ordinal / 3	Left/right shift in seated position
		Depth	Ordinal / 3	Forward/backward change of seated position

*Separate coding for left and right body half.

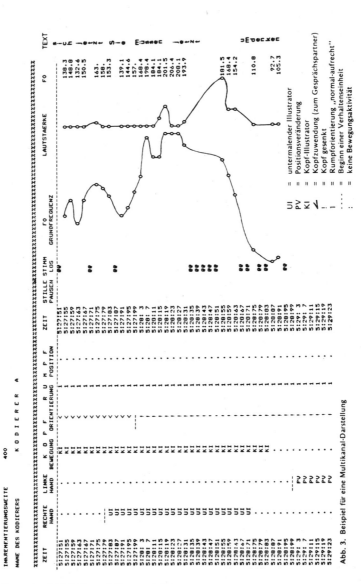

Abb. 3. Beispiel für eine Multikanal-Darstellung

Example of Multichannel Representation

Bibliography

Abercrombie, D. "Paralanguage." *British Journal of Disorders of Communication* 3 (1968): 55–59.

Agrest, D., and M. Gandelsonas. "Critical Remarks on Semiology and Architecture." *Semiotica* 9 (1973): 252–71.

Alewyn, R., and K. Sälzle. *Das große Welttheater: Die Epoche der höfischen Feste in Dokument und Deutung.* Hamburg: Rowohlt, 1959.

Angeloglou, M. *A History of Make-up.* London: Macmillan, 1970.

Aristotle. *De Anima.* D. W. Hamlyn, trans. Oxford: Oxford University Press, 1975.

———. *Rhetoric.* J. H. Frees, trans. London: Loeb, 1926.

Arnauld, A., and P. Nicole. *La logique ou l'art de penser (la logique de Port Royal).* P. Clair and F. Girbal, eds. Paris: Presses Universitaires, 1965.

Arndt, H. W. "Die Semiotik Christian Wolffs als Propädeutik der ars characteristica combinatoria und der ars inveniendi." *Zeitschrift für Semiotik* 1 (1980): 325–31.

Austin, G. *Chironomia or a treatise on rhetorical delivery: comprehending many precepts, both ancient and modern, for the proper regulation of the Voice, the Countenance and Gesture. Together with an investigation of the elements of gesture and a new method for the notation thereof; illustrated by many figures.* Printed for T. Cadell and W. Davies in the Strand, by W. Bulmer and Co., Cleveland Row, St. James's, 1806.

Avdeev, A. D. *Maska i ee rol' v prozesse vosniknoveniya teatra.* Moscow, 1969.

Baader, H. "Diderots Theorie der Schauspielkunst und ihre Parallelen in Deutschland." *Révue de littérature comparée* 33, no. 2 (1959): 200–223.

Bahner, W. *Renaissance, Barock, Aufklärung.* Kronberg: Scriptor-Verlag, 1976.

Bakhtin, M. *Problems of Dostoevsky's Poetics.* C. Emerson, trans. Minneapolis: University of Minnesota Press, 1984.

Balcerzan, E., and Z. Osiński. "Die theatralische Schaustellung im Lichte der Informationstheorie." H. Orłowski, trans. *Zagadnienia Rodzajów Literackich.* 8, no. 2 (1966): 65–68; 10, no. 1 (1967): 122–31.

Balet, L., and E. Gerhard. *Die Verbürgerlichung der deutschen Kunst, Literatur und Musik im 18. Jahrhundert.* Strasbourg, 1936. New ed. by Gert Mattenklott. Frankfurt am Main: Ullstein, 1973.

Ballhausen, G. "Der Wandel der Gebärde auf dem deutschen Theater im 18. Jahrhundert, dargestellt an den Gebärdenbüchern." Dissertation. Göttingen, 1957.

Bandmann, G. *Mittelalterliche Architektur als Bedeutungsträger.* Berlin: Mann, 1951.

Barker, D. "A Structural Theory of Theatre." *Yale/Theatre* 8, no. 1 (1976): 55–61.

Barnett, D. "The Performance Practice of Acting: The Eighteenth Century." *Theatre Research International, New Series* 2, no. 3 (1977): 157–86; 3, no. 1 (1977): 1–18; 3, no. 2 (1977): 79–92; 5, no. 1 (1979/80): 1–36.

Barthes, R. *Fashion System.* London: Jonathan Cape, 1985.

———. *Literatur oder Geschichte.* Frankfurt am Main: Suhrkamp, 1969.

———. *Writing Degree Zero & Elements of Semiology.* London, 1984.

Bassenge, F. "Einführung in die Ästhetik Diderots." In *Ästhetische Schriften* by D. Diderot; F. Bassenge, ed. Frankfurt am Main: Europäische Verlagsanstalt, 1968, vol. 1, v–lxxxix.

Batteux, Charles. *Einschränkung der Schönen Künste auf einen einzigen Grundsatz.* 3rd ed. J. A. Schlegel, trans. Leipzig: Weidmann, 1770.

Bäumler, A. *Das Irrationalitätsproblem in der Ästhetik und Logik des 18. Jahrhunderts bis zur Kritik der Urteilskraft.* 1st ed., Halle, 1923. 2nd ed. Tübingen and Darmstadt: Wissenschaftliche Buchgesellschaft, 1967.

Bayer, U. "Lessings Zeichenbegriffe und Zeichenprozesse im 'Laokoon' und ihre Analyse nach der modernen Semiotik." Doctoral thesis. Stuttgart, 1975.

Benjamin, W. *The Origin of German Tragic Drama.* London: New Left Books, 1977.

Bense, M. *Aesthetica* (I–IV). Stuttgart: Deutsche Verlags-Anstalt, 1954–60.

———. *Zusammenfassende Grundlegung moderner Ästhetik und Dichtung.* Munich, 1965.

Bentley, E. *The Life of the Drama.* London: Methuen, 1965.

Bettetini, G., and M. De Marinis. *Teatro e comunicazione.* Florence: Guaraldi, 1977.

Betti, E. *Allgemeine Auslegungslehre als Methodik der Geisteswissenschaften.* 1955. Reprint. Tübingen: Mohr ⟨Sieback⟩, 1967.

———. *Teoria generale della interpretazione.* Milan, 1955.

Biblioteca teatrale 20 (1978): *Dramma/spettacolo: studi sulla semiologia del teatro,* Rome.

Bidermann, J. *Ludi theatrales.* 2 vols. R. Tarot, ed. Tübingen: Niemeyer, 1967.

Birdwhistell, R. L. *Introduction to Kinesics.* Washington, D.C.: Department of State, Foreign Service Institute, 1952.

———. "Some Body Motion Elements Accompanying Spoken American English." In *Communication: Concepts and Perspectives,* L. Thayer, ed. London and Washington: Spartan Books, 1967, 53–75.

———. "Some Relations between American Kinesics and Spoken American English." In *Communication and Culture: Reading in the Codes of Human Interaction,* A. G. Smith, ed. New York: Holt, Rinehart and Winston, 1966, 182–209.

———. *Kinesics and Context: Essays in Body Motion.* Philadelphia: University of Pennsylvania Press, 1970.

Bodemann, E. *Die Leibniz-Handschriften der königlich öffentlichen Bibliothek zu Hannover.* Hanover: Hahn, 1895.

Boehn, M. von. *Das Bühnenkostüm in Altertum, Mittelalter und Neuzeit.* Berlin: Bruno Cassirer, 1921.

———. *Mode and Manners of the 19th Century.* J. Joshua and M. Edwardes, trans. London, 1909.

Bogatyrev, P. "Costume as a Sign." In *Semiotics of Art. Prague School Contributions,* L. Matejka and J. R. Titunic, eds. Cambridge: MIT Press, 1976, 15–19.

———. "Forms and Functions of Folk Theatre." In *Semiotics of Art. Prague School Contributions,* L. Matejka and J. R. Titunic, eds. Cambridge: MIT Press, 1976, 51–56.

———. *The Functions of Folk Costume in Moravian Slovakia, Approaches to Semiotics,* no. 5 The Hague and Paris: Mouton, 1971.

———. "Semiotics in the Folk Theatre." In *Semiotics of Art. Prague School Contributions,* L. Matejka and J. R. Titunic, eds. Cambridge: MIT Press, 1976, 33–50.

Boilès, C. L. "Sémiotique de l'ethnomusicologie." *Musique en Jeu* 10 (1973): 34–41.

Borg, J. G. "Physiognomy, Facial Expression, and Abnormality." *Acta Universitatis Tamperensis,* ser. A., vol. 52, Tampere, 1973.

Bouissac, S. P. *Circus and Culture: A Semiotic Approach.* Bloomington: Indiana University Press, 1976.

———. "Circus Performances as Texts: A Matter of Poetic Competence." *Poetics* 5 (1976): 101–118.

———. *La mesure des gestes: Prolégomènes à la sémiotique gestuelle.* The Hague: Mouton, 1973.

———. "Volumes sonores et volumes gestuels dans un numéro d'acrobatique." *Langages* 10 (1968): 128–31.

Brach, J. "Dramat—spektakl—widownia (współczesne teorie dzieła teatralnego)." *Studia Estetyczne* 7 (1970): 105–129.

———. "O znakach literackich i znakach teatralnych." *Studia Estetyczne* 2 (Warsaw, 1965): 241–59.
Broby-Johansen, R. *Body and Clothes*. London: Faber, 1968.
Brooke, I. *Western-European Costume: Its Relation to the Theatre*. Vol. 1.2. London: Macmillan, 1939–40.
Brušak, K. "Signs in the Chinese Theatre." In *Semiotics of Art. Prague School Contributions*, L. Matejka and J. R. Titunic, eds. Cambridge: MIT Press, 1976.
Bühler, K. *Ausdruckstheorie*. Jena: Fischer, 1933.
———. *Sprachtheorie*. 2nd ed. Stuttgart: Gustav Fischer, 1965.
Burand, G. *Les masques*. Paris: Club des Editeurs, 1961.
Burns, E. *Theatricality: A Study of Convention in the Theatre and in Social Life*. London: Longman, 1972.
Cassirer, E. *Philosophie der Aufklärung*. Tübingen: Mohr, 1932.
———. *Philosophy of Symbolic Forms*. 3 vols. R. Manheim, trans. New Haven: Yale University Press, 1965.
Chailley, J. *La musique et le signe*. Lausanne: Editions Rencontre, 1967.
Cicero. *De Oratore*. E. W. Sutton and H. Rackham, trans. London: Loeb, 1948.
Cooper, W. *Hair, Sex, Society, Symbolism*. London: Stein and Day, 1971.
Corson, R. *Fashions in Hair: The First Five Thousand Years*. London: Hilary House, 1971.
———. *Stage Make-up*. Englewood Cliffs, N.J.: Prentice-Hall, 1975.
Corvin, M. "A propos des spectacles de R. Wilson: Essai de lecture sémiologique." *Cahiers Renaud-Barrault* 77 (1971): 90–111.
———. "Approches sémiologiques d'un texte dramatique. La parodie d'Arthur Adamov." *Litteratur* 9 (1973): 86–110.
Coseriu, E. *Sistema, norma y habla*. Montevideo, 1952.
———. *Textlinguistik. Eine Einführung*. Jörn Albrecht, ed. Tübingen: Gunter Narr, 1980.
Cresswell, R. "Le geste manuel associé au langage." *Langages* 10 (1968): 119–27.
Critchley, M. D. *Silent Language*. London: Butterworths, 1975.
Dahlhaus, C., ed. *Beiträge zur musikalischen Hermeneutik*. Regensburg: Bosse, 1975.
Danes, F. "Sentence Intonation from a Functional Point of View." *Word* 16 (1960): 34–54.
Davitz, J. L. *The Communication of Emotional Meaning*. New York: McGraw-Hill, 1964.
De Marinis, M. "Problemi e aspetti di un approccio semiotico al teatro." *Lingua e stile* 10, no. 2 (1975): 343–57.
———. "Lo spettacolo come testo." I: *Versus* 19/20 (1978): *Semiotica testuale: mondi possibili e narratività*, 66–104. II: *Versus* 22 (1979): *Teatro e comunicazione gestuale*, 3–31.
———. *Semiotica del teatro. L'analisi testuale dello spettacolo*. Milan: Bompiani, 1982.
Deák, F. "Structuralism in Theatre: The Prague School Contribution." *The Drama Review* 20 (1976): 83–94.
Degérando, J. M. "Erwägungen über die verschiedenen Methoden der Beobachtung wilder Völker." In *Beobachtende Vernunft, Philosophie und Anthropologie in der Aufklärung* by Sergio Moravia. Frankfurt am Main, Berlin, and Vienna: Ullstein, 1977, 219–51.
———. *Des signes et de l'art de penser*. 4 vols. Paris: Goujon fils; Henrichs, 1800.
Degrés 13 (1978): *Théâtre et sémiologie*, Brussels.
Degrés 29–32 (1982): *Actes du colloque sémiologie du spectacle Bruxelles 23.–25. avril 1981*.
29: *Modèles théoriques*
30: *Performance/representation*
31: *Reception*
32: *Sens/culture*
Derrida, J. *Writing and Difference*. A. Bass, trans. London: Routledge, 1979.

322   *Bibliography*

Descartes, R. *Ausgewählte Schriften*. A. Buchenau and F. Baumgart, trans. Gerd Irrlitz, ed. Leipzig: Reclam, 1980.
———. *Oeuvres de Descartes*. 11 vols. Reprint of the 1896–1908 ed. Paris: Editions du C.N.R.S., 1964–74.
Diderot, D. *Ästhetische Schriften*. 2 vols. Friedrich Bassenge, ed. Frankfurt am Main: Europäische Verlagsanstellt, 1968.
———. *Eléments de physiologie*. Jean Mayer, ed. Paris: Didier, 1964.
———. *Oeuvres complètes*. 20 vols. J. Assezat and M. Tourneux, eds. Paris: Garnier frères, 1875–77.
Dieckmann, H. *Cinq leçons sur Diderot*. Paris: Minard, 1959.
———. "Diderot's Conception of Genius." *Journal of the History of Ideas* 2, no. 2 (1941): 151–82.
———. "Die Wandlung des Nachahmungsbegriffs in der französischen Ästhetik des 18 Jahrhunderts." In *Nachahmung und Illusion*, H. R. Jauss, ed. Munich: Eidos Verlag, 1974, 28–59.
Diez Borque, J. M., and L. G. Lorenzo, eds. *Semiologia del teatro*. Barcelona: Planeta, 1975.
Dinu, M. "L'interdépendence syntagmatique des scènes dans une pièce de théâtre." *Cahiers de linguistique théorique et appliquée* 9 (1972): 55–69.
———. "La stratégie des personnages dramatiques à la lumière du calcul propositionnel bivalent." *Poetics* 10 (1974): 147–59.
———. "Structures linguistiques probabilistes issues de l'étude du théâtre." *Cahiers de linguistique théorique et appliquée* 5 (1968): 29–46.
Dressler, W. *Einführung in die Textlinguistik*. Tübingen: Niemeyer, 1971.
Dressler, W., ed. *Textlinguistik*. Darmstadt: Wissenschaftliche Buchgesellschaft, 1978.
Durand, R. "Problèmes de l'analyse structurale et sémiotique de la forme théâtrale." In *Sémiologie de la réprésentation*, André Helbo, ed. Brussels: Editions complexes, 1975, 112–21.
Duvignaud, J. *L'Acteur: Esquisse d'une sociologie du comédien*. Paris: Gallimard, 1965.
———. *Sociologie du théâtre: Essai sur les ombres collectives*. Paris: Presses Universitaires de France, 1963.
Eco, U. "A Componential Analysis of the Architectural Sign /Column/." *Semiotica* 5, no. 2 (1972): 97–117.
———. *Einführung in die Semiotik*. Munich: Fink, 1972.
———. "Semiotics of Theatrical Performance." *The Drama Review* 21 (1977): 107–112.
———. *A Theory of Semiotics*. Bloomington: Indiana University Press, 1976.
Efron, D. *Gesture, Race and Culture*. The Hague and Paris: Mouton, 1972.
Eggebrecht, H. H. "Funktionale Musik." *Archiv für Musikwiss* (1973): 1–25.
Ekman, P. *Cross-Cultural Studies of Facial Expression: A Century of Research in Review*. New York and London: Academic Press, 1973, 169–220.
———. *Universals and Cultural Difference in Facial Expressions of Emotion: Nebraska Symposium on Motivation*. Lincoln: University of Nebraska Press, 1972.
Ekman, P., and W. Friesen. "The Repertoire of Nonverbal Behavior: Categories, Origins, Usage and Coding." *Semiotica* 1 (1969): 49–98.
Ekman, P., W. Friesen, and P. Ellsworth. *Emotion in the Face*. Cambridge: Cambridge University Press, 1983.
Ekman, P., W. Friesen, and E. R. Sorenson. "Pan-Cultural Elements in Facial Displays of Emotions." *Science* 164 (April 1969): 86–88.
Ekman, P., W. Friesen, and S. S. Tomkins. "Facial Affect Scoring Technique (FAST): A First Validity Study." *Semiotica* 3 (1971): 37–58.
Elam, K. *The Semiotics of Theatre and Drama*. London and New York: Methuen, 1980.
Engel, J. J. "Ideen zu einer Mimik." 1785–86. Reprinted in his *Schriften*. Vols. 7/8. Berlin, 1804. Reprint. Frankfurt am Main: Athenäum, 1971.

Eschbach, A. *Pragmasemiotik und Theater. Ein Betrag zur Theorie und Praxis einer pragmatisch orientierten Zeichenanalyse.* Tübingen: Gunter Narr, 1979.

Essen, O. von. *Grundzüge der hochdeutschen Satzintonation.* Düsseldorf: Henn, Ratingen, 1964.

Etudes littéraires 13, no. 3 (December 1980). *Théâtre et théâtralité. Essais d'études sémiotiques.*

Fährmann, R. *Die Deutung des Sprechausdrucks.* Bonn: H. Bouvier, 1967.

Faltin, P. "Musikalische Bedeutung." *International Review of the Aesthetics and Sociology of Music* (1978): 5–32.

Faltin, P., and H. P. Reinecke, eds. *Musik und Verstehen: Aufsätze zur semiotischen Theorie, Ästhetik und Soziologie der musikalischen Rezeption.* Cologne: Volk, 1973.

Finter, H. "Die soufflierte Stimme." *Theater heute* 1 (1982): 45–51.

————. *Die Theatralisierung der Stimme im Experimentaltheater.* Lecture held at the 4th Semiotic Colloquium in Hamburg. In *Zeichen und Realität*, Klaus Oehler, ed. Tübingen: Stauffenburg-Verlag, 1984.

Fischer-Lichte, E. *Bedeutung—Probleme einer semiotischen Hermeneutik und Ästhetik.* Munich: Beck, 1979.

————. "Der Bedeutungsaufbau des theatralischen Textes." *Kodikas/Code* 3, no. 3/4 (1981): 309–319.

————. "The Dramatic Dialogue—Oral or Literary Communication?" In *Drama, Theatre and Semiotics*, A. van Kesteren and H. Schmid, eds. Amsterdam: Benjamins, 1984, 127–73.

————. "Kunst und Wirklichkeit." *Zeitschrift für Semiotik* 5 (1983): 1.

————. "The Theatrical Code." In *Multimedial Communication*, 2 vols. E. W. B. Hess-Lüttich, ed. Tübingen: Gunter Narr, 1982, vol. 2: 46–62.

————. "Theatrical Communication." In *Actes du colloque Sémiologie du spectacle, Degrés 29, Modèles théoriques*, André Helbo, ed. Brussels, 1982, 1–9.

————. "Zum Problem der Bedeutung ästhetischer Zeichen." *Kodikas/Code* 3 (1980): 269–83.

————. "Zur Konstitution ästhetischer Zeichen." In *Ästhetik und Semiotik*, H. Sturm and A. Eschbach, eds. Tübingen: Gunter Narr, 1981, 17–28.

Flemming, W. *Geschichte des Jesuitentheaters in den Landen deutscher Zunge.* Berlin, 1923.

Flugel, J. C. *The Psychology of Clothes.* London: Anglobooks, 1952.

Fonagy, J., and K. Magdies. "Emotional Patterns in Intonation and Music." *Z PSK* 16 (1963): 293–326.

Fontenelle. "Digression sur les anciens et les modernes." In *Oeuvres.* Vol. 6. Paris: Bastien, 1790.

Foreman, R. *Plays and Manifestos.* Kate Davy, ed. New York: New York University Press, 1976.

Foucault, M. *The Order of Things.* London: Tavistock, 1974.

Frank, M. "Grundlagenprobleme der Informationsästhetik und erste Anwendung auf die Mime pure." Dissertation. Stuttgart, 1959.

————. *Das individuelle Allgemeine.* Frankfurt am Main: Suhrkamp, 1977.

Frey, D. "Zuschauer und Bühne: Eine Untersuchung über das Realitätsproblem des Schauspiels." In his *Kunstwissenschaftliche Grundfragen.* Vienna: R. M. Rohrer, 1946, 151–223.

Frey, S., and J. Pool. "A New Approach to the Analysis of Visible Behaviour." In *Forschungsberichte aus dem Psychologischen Institut.* Bern, 1976.

Gadamer, H.-G. *Truth and Method.* London: Sheed and Ward, 1975.

Garvin, P., ed. *A Prague School Reader on Esthetics, Literary Structure and Style.* Washington, D.C.: American University Language Center, 1958.

Gebauer, G., ed. *Lessings "Laokoon" in semiotischer Sicht.* Frankfurt am Main, 1983.

Genot, G. "Caractères du lieu théâtral chez Pirandello." *Revue des études italiennes* 14 (1968): 8–25.

Gerhards, F. "Sprache des Lichts. Ihr Wandel von der Antike bis zur Gegenwart." Dissertation. Vienna, 1960.

Gleijeses, V. Il teatro e le maschere. Naples: Guida, 1972.

Goethe, J. W. von. "Regeln für Schauspieler." In Sämtliche Werke in 18 Bänden. Vol. 14. Schriften zur Literatur. Zurich: Artemis-Verlag, 1977.

Goffman, E. Behaviour in Public Places: Notes on the Social Origin of Gatherings. London: Greenwood, 1980.

————. Strategic Interaction. Oxford: Blackwell, 1971.

————. Where the Action Is. London, 1969.

Gottsched, J. C. Versuch einer kritischen Dichtkunst. 4th ed. 1751. Reproduction. Darmstadt: Wissenschaftliche Buchgesellschaft, 1962.

Greimas, A. J. On Meaning. London, 1987.

————. Sémantique structurale. Paris: Larousse, 1966.

Hall, E. T. The Hidden Dimension. London: Doubleday, 1966.

————. The Silent Language. New York: Doubleday, 1959.

————. "A System for the Notation of Proxemic Behaviour." American Anthropologist 65 (1963): 1003–27.

Hamon, P. "Pour un statut sémiologique du personnage." Litteratur 6 (1972): 86–110.

Hardenberg, C. "G. E. Lessings Semiotik als Propädeutik einer Kunsttheorie." Zeitschrift für Semiotik 1 (1979): 361–76.

Harris, J. Three Treatises. London, 1744.

Hayes, A. "Paralinguistics and Kinesics: Pedagogical Perspectives." In Approaches to Semiotics, Sebeok, Hayes, and Bateson, eds. The Hague: Mouton, 1964, 145–72.

Heike, G. Suprasegmentale Analyse. Marburg: Elwert, 1969.

Helbo, A., ed. Sémiologie de la répresentation. Théâtre, télévision, bande dessiné. Brussels: Editions complexes, 1975.

Herrmann, H. P. Naturnachahmung und Einbildungskraft. Bad Homburg: Gehlen, 1970.

Hess-Lüttich, E. W. B. "Drama, Silence and Semiotics." Kodikas/Code 1, no. 2 (1979): 105–120.

————. "Multimediale Kommunikation als Realität des Theaters." In Zeichen und Realität, Klaus Oehler, ed. Tübingen: Stauffenburg-Verlag, 1984.

————. Soziale Interaktion und litarischer Dialog, I. Grundlagen der Dialoglinguistik. Berlin: Erich Schmidt, 1981.

Hess-Lüttich, E. W. B., ed. Multimedial Communication. Vol. 1: Semiotic Problems of Its Notation. Vol. 2: Theatre Semiotics. Tübingen: Gunter Narr, 1982.

Hillach, A. "Sprache und Theater." Sprachkunst 1 (1970): 256–59; 2 (1971): 299–328.

Hobson, M. "Le paradoxe sur le comédien est un paradoxe." Poétique (1973): 320–39.

————. "Sensibilité et spectacle: le contexte médical du 'Paradoxe sur le comédien' de Diderot." Revue de metaphysique et de morale 82, no. 2 (1977): 145–64.

Hohner, U. Zur Problematik der Naturnachahmung in der Ästhetik des 18. Jahrhunderts. Erlangen: Palm and Enke, 1976.

Honzl, J. "Die Hierarchie der Theatermittel." In Moderne Dramentheorie, A. van Kesteren and H. Schmid, eds. Kronberg: Scriptor-Verlag, 1975, 133–42.

————. "Dynamics of the Sign in the Theater." In Semiotics of Art, L. Matejka and J. R. Titunic, eds. Cambridge: MIT Press, 1976, 74–93.

Huizinga, J. Homo ludens. R. F. C. Hull, trans. London, 1949.

Husson, R. La voix chantée. Paris: Gauthier-Villars, 1960.

Ihwe, J., ed. Literaturwissenschaft und Linguistik. Frankfurt am Main: Athenäum-Verlag, 1972.

Imberty, M. "Introduction à une sémantique musicale de la musique vocale." International Review of the Aesthetics and Sociology of Music 4 (1973): 175–95.

Ingarden, R, The Literary Work of Art. Evanston, Illinois: Northwestern University Press, 1973.

Jakobson, R. "Linguistics and Poetics." In *Style in Language*, Thomas A. Sebeok, ed. Cambridge: MIT Press, 1960, 355–77.

―――. *Selected Writings.* 2 vols. The Hague: Mouton, 1971.

Jakobson, R., and M. Halle. *Fundamentals of Language.* The Hague: Mouton, 1956.

Jallat, J. "Le masque ou l'art du déplacement." *Poétique* 5 (1971).

Jansen, S. "Esquisse d'une théorie de la forme dramatique." *Langages* 12 (1968): 71–93.

―――. "L'unité d'action dans 'Andromaque' et dans 'Lorenzaccio'." *Revue Romane* 3, no. 1 (1968): 16–29.

―――. "Qu'est-ce qu'une situation dramatique?" *Orbis Litterarum* 27, no. 4 (1973): 235–92.

Jauss, H. R. "Diderots Paradox über das Schauspiel." *GRM* NF. 11, no. 4 (1961): 380–413.

Kamper, D., and V. Rittner, eds. *Zur Geschichte des Körpers.* Munich: Hanser, 1977.

Kasperski, E. "Aktor—gest—widownia. Prototypy form." *Nowy Wyraz* 3 (1973): 54–60.

Kesteren, A. van, and H. Schmid, eds. *Drama, Theatre and Semiotics.* Amsterdam: Benjamins, 1983.

―――. *Moderne Dramentheorie.* Kronberg: Scriptor-Verlag, 1975.

Key, M. R. *Paralanguage and Kinesics.* Metuchen, N.J.: Scarecrow, 1975.

Kindermann, H. *Bühne und Zuschauerraum.* Graz, Vienna, Cologne: Böhlau, 1963.

―――. *Conrad Ekhofs Schauspieler-Akademie.* Vienna: Rohrer in Komm., 1956.

―――. *Theatergeschichte Europas.* Salzburg: Müller, 1966–74.

Knapp, R. H. "The Language of Postural Interpretation." *The Journal of Social Psychology* (1965): 371–77.

Kneif, T. "Musik und Zeichen: Aspekte einer nichtvorhandenen musikalischen Semiotik." *Musica* 1 (1973): 9–12.

Knilli, F. "Medium." In *Kritische Stichwörter zur Medienwissenschaft*, W. Faulstich, ed. Munich: Fink, 1979, 230–51.

Knowlson, R. "The Idea of Gesture as a Universal Language in the 17th and 18th Century." *Journal of the History of Ideas* 16, no. 4 (1965): 495–508.

Knust, A. *A Dictionary of Kinetography Laban (Labanotation).* Plymouth: Macdonald and Evans, 1979.

Koch, W. "Le texte normal, le théâtre et le film." *Linguistics* 48 (1969): 40–67.

Koechlin, B. "Techniques corporelles et leur notation symbolique." *Langages* 10 (1968): 36–47.

Koenig, G. K. *Analisi del linguaggio architettonico.* Florence: Libreria editrice fiorentina, 1970.

―――. *Architettura e comunicazione.* Florence: Libreria editrice fiorentina, 1970.

Kommerell, M. *Lessing und Aristoteles: Untersuchung über die Theorie der Tragödie.* Frankfurt am Main: Klostermann, 1957.

König, R. *The Restless Image: A Sociology of Fashion.* F. Bradley, trans. London: Unwin, 1979.

Kowzan, T. *Analyse sémiologique du spectacle théâtral.* Lyon: Centre d'études et de recherches théâtrales, Université de Lyon II, 1976.

―――. "Le texte et le spectacle. Rapports entre la mise en scène et la parole." *Cahiers de l'association internationale des études françaises* 1 (1969): 63–72.

―――. "Le texte et son interpretation théâtrale." *Semiotica* 33, no. 3/4 (1981): 201–210.

―――. "Znak w teatrze." *Dialog* 3 (1969): 88–104. Reprinted in his "Le signe au théâtre. Introduction à la sémiologie de l'art du spectacle." *Diogène* 61 (1968): 55–59, and in his *Littérature et spectacle dans leurs rapports esthétiques, thématiques et sémiologiques.* Warsaw: Editions scientifiques de Pologne, 1970, 133–83.

Krauss, W. *Zur Anthropologie des 18. Jahrhunderts: Die Frühgeschichte der Menschheit im Blickpunkt der Aufklärung.* H. Kortum and C. Gohrisch, eds. Munich: Hanser, 1979.

Kristeva, J. "Le geste, pratique ou communication?" *Langages* 10 (1968): *Pratiques et langages gestuels*, 64–84.

————. *Polylogue*. Paris: Editions du Seuil, 1977.

————. *Revolution in Poetic Language*. New York: Columbia University Press, 1984.

————. *Sémeiotikè: recherches pour une sémanalyse*. Paris: Editions du Seuil, 1968.

Kroll, W., and A. Flaker, eds. *Literaturtheoretische Modelle und kommunikatives System. Zur aktuellen Diskussion in der polnischen Literaturwissenschaft*. Kronberg: Scriptor-Verlag, 1974.

Kürschner, J. *Conrad Ekhofs Leben und Wirken*. Vienna: Hartleben's Verlag, 1872.

Kutschera, F. von. *Wissenschaftstheorie*. 2 vols. Munich: Fink, 1972.

La Barre, W. "Paralinguistics, Kinesics and Cultural Anthropology." In *Approaches to Semiotics*, Sebeok, Hayes, and Bateson, eds. The Hague: Mouton, 1964, 191–200.

Laban, R. *Principles of Dance and Movement Notation*. London: Macdonald and Evans, 1956.

Lang, F. *Abhandlung über die Schauspielkunst*. Alexander Rudin, ed. and trans. Bern and Munich: Francke, 1975.

Larthomas, P. *Le langage dramatique*. Paris: Colin, 1972.

Lasker, M. D. "The Pause in the Moving Structure of Dance." *Semiotica* 22, no. 1–2 (1978): 107–126.

Lavater, J. C. *Physiognomic Sketches*. London, 1802.

Laver, J. *Costume in the Theatre*. London: Harrap, 1964.

Leach, E. R. "Magical Hair." *Journal of the Royal Anthropological Institute* 88 (1958): 147–64.

Leibnitiana. *Elementa philosophiae arcanae*. J. Jagodinsky, ed. Russia: Kazan, 1913.

Leibniz, G. *Die philosophischen Schriften*. 7 vols. C. J. Gerhardt, ed. Berlin: Weidmann, 1875–90.

————. *Sämtliche Schriften und Briefe*. Darmstadt: Preuss Akad. d. Wiss., 1923.

Leiris, M. *Die eigene und die fremde Kultur*. Frankfurt am Main: Syndikat, 1977.

Leroi-Gourhan, A. *Le geste et la parole*. 2 vols. Paris: Michel, 1965.

Lessing, G. E. *Gotthold Ephraim Lessings sämtliche Schriften*. 23 vols. K. Lachmann, ed. 3rd rev. edition by R. Muncker. Stuttgart, Berlin and Leipzig: Vereinigg. wissensch. Verleger, 1886–1924.

————. *Werke*. Herbert G. Göpfert, ed. Vols. 1–8. Munich: Hanser, 1970–79.

Lévi-Strauss, C. *The Raw and the Cooked*. J. and D. Weightman, trans. Harmondsworth: Penguin, 1986.

————. *Structural Anthropology*. C. Joacobson and B. G. Schoepf, trans. New York and London, 1963.

de Levita, David J. *The Concept of Identity*. The Hague and Paris: Mouton, 1965.

Levy, M. "Sur le problème de la definition des unités musicales." *Semiotica* 15, no. 1 (1976): 8–27.

Lichtenberg, G. C. *Schriften und Briefe*. Wolfgang Promies, ed. Vols. 1–4. Munich: Hanser, 1967–74.

Caroli Linnaei. *Systema naturae sistens in regna tria naturae, in classes et ordines, genera et species redacta, tabulisque aenis illustrate*. Leyden, 1756.

Linné, C. von. *Philosophie botanique*. Paris: Cailleau, 1788.

Lippe, R. *Naturbeherrschung am Menschen*.
I: *Körpererfahrung als Entfaltung von Sinnen und Beziehungen in der Ara des italienischen Kaufmannskapitals*.
II: *Geometrisierung des Menschen und Repräsentation des Privaten im französischen Absolutismus*. Frankfurt am Main: Suhrkamp, 1974.

Lissa, Z. "Czy muzyka jest sztuka asemantyczna." *Kwartalnik muzyczny* 25 (1949): 120–38.

————. Über das Wesen des Musikwerkes." In his *Neue Aufsätze zur Musikästhetik*. Wilhelmshaven: Heinrichshofen, 1975, 1–54.

Litzmann, B. *Friedrich Ludwig Schröder: Ein Betrag zur deutschen Literatur- und Theatergeschichte*. 2 vols. Hamburg and Leipzig: Voss, 1880–94.

————. *Der Grosse Schröder.* Berlin and Leipzig: Schuster and Loeffler, 1904.

Locke, J. *An Essay Concerning Human Understanding.* B. Rand, ed. Cambridge: Harvard University Press, 1931.

Lohr, G. "Körpertext. Historische Semiotik der komische Praxis—vom Cinquecento bis zur Mitte des 18. Jahrhunderts." Dissertation. Frankfurt am Main, 1979.

Lotman, Y. M. *Aufsätze zur Theorie und Methodologie der Literatur und Kultur.* Kronberg: Scriptor-Verlag, 1974.

————. *The Structure of Aesthetic Texts.* G. Lenhoff and R. Vroon, trans. Ann Arbor: University of Michigan Press, 1977.

————. *Die Struktur literarischer Texte.* Munich, 1972.

————. *Vorlesungen zu einer strukturalen Poetik.* Munich: Fink, 1972.

Maletzke, G. *Psychologie der Massenkommunikation.* Hamburg: Verlag Hans Bredow Institut, 1963.

Martinet, A. "Accents et tons." *Miscellanea Phonetica* 2 (1954): 13–24.

Martino, A. *Geschichte der dramatischen Theorien in Deutschland im 18. Jahrhundert.* I: *Die Dramaturgie der Aufklärung (1730–1780).* Tübingen: Niemeyer, 1972.

Martinson, S. D. *On Imitation, Imagination and Beauty.* Bonn: Bouvier, 1977.

Maser, S. *Numerische Ästhetik.* Stuttgart, 1971.

Matejka, L., and J. R. Titunic, eds. *Semiotics of Art. Prague School Contributions.* Cambridge: MIT Press, 1976.

Mattenklott, G., and H. Peitsch. "Das 'Allgemeinmenschliche' im Konzept des bürgerlichen Nationaltheaters: G. E. Lessings Mitleidstheorie." In *Westberliner Projekt: Grundkurs 18. Jahrhundert. Die Funktion der Literatur bei der Formierung der bürgerlichen Klasse Deutschlands im 18. Jahrhundert,* G. Mattenklott and K. Scherpe, eds. Kronberg: Scriptor-Verlag, 1974, 147–88.

Mattenklott, G., and K. Scherpe. "Aspekte einer sozialgeschichtlich fundierten Literaturgeschichte am Beispiel von Lessings Mitleidstheorie." In *Historizität in Sprach- und Literaturwissenschaft: Vorträge und Berichte der Stuttgarter Germanistentagung 1972,* W. Müller-Seidel, ed. Munich: Fink, 1974, 247–58.

Mauss, M. "Die Techniken des Körpers." In his *Soziologie und Anthropologie.* 2 vols. Munich: Hanser, 1975, 197–217.

Mead, G. H. *Geist, Identität und Gesellschaft.* Frankfurt am Main: Suhrkamp, 1973.

————, *Mind, Self and Society.* Chicago: Chicago University Press, 1934.

Mehren, G. "Sinn und Gestalt der Maske." *Antaios* 11, no. 2 (1969): 136–53.

Mendelssohn, M. *Moses Mendelssohn's gesammelte Schriften.* 7 vols. G. D. Mendelssohn, ed. Leipzig: Brockhaus, 1843–45.

"Ménestrier, La philosophie des images." Anonymous lecture, Paris (1682). In *Acta eruditotum.* Lipsiae 1683, 17f.

Messing, S. D. "The Nonverbal Language of Ethiopian Toga." *Anthropus* 55, no. 3/4 (1960): 558–61.

Meyer, F. L. W. *Friedrich Ludwig Schröder.* 2 vols. Hamburg: Hoffman and Campe, 1819.

Michelson, P. "Die Erregung des Mitleids durch die Tragödie." In "Lessings Ansichten über das Trauerspiel im Briefwechsel mit Mendelssohn und Nicolai." *DVjs* 40 (1966): 548–66.

Molino, J. "Fait musicale et sémiologie de la musique." *Musique en Jeu* 17 (1975): 37–62.

Moravia, S. *Beobachtende Vernunft: Philosophie und Anthropologie in der Aufklärung.* Frankfurt am Main, Berlin and Vienna: Ullstein, 1977.

Morris, C. W. "Foundations of a Theory of Signs." In *International Encyclopedia of Unified Science,* vol. 1, no. 2. Chicago: University of Chicago Press, 1938.

————. *Signification and Significance.* Cambridge: MIT Press, 1964.

————. *Signs, Language and Behavior.* New York: Prentice-Hall, 1946.

Mounin, G. "La communication théâtrale." In his *Introductions à la sémiologie.* Paris: Editions de Minuit, 1970, 87–94.

Mukařovský, J. *Aesthetic Function, Norm and Value as Social Facts.* M. Swino, trans. Ann Arbor: University of Michigan Press, 1979.

———. *Kapitel aus der Poetik.* Frankfurt: Suhrkamp, 1967.

———. *Studien zur strukturalistischen Ästhetik und Poetik.* Munich: Hanser, 1974.

———. "Zum heutigen Stand der Theorie des Theaters." In *Moderne Dramentheorie,* A. van Kesteren and H. Schmid, eds. Kronberg: Scriptor-Verlag, 1975, 76–95.

Nattiez, J. J. *Fondements d'une sémiologie de la musique.* Paris: Union générale d'éditions, 1976.

Niessen, C. *Das Bühnenbild: Ein kulturgeschichtlicher Atlas.* Bonn and Leipzig: F. Klopp, 1924–47.

Ninnin, G. *Maschere e costumi.* Brescia: La scuola, 1963.

Nivelle, A. *Kunst und Dichtungstheorien zwischen Aufklärung und Klassik.* Berlin: Walter de Gruyter, 1960.

Ogibenin, B. L. "Mask in the Light of Semiotics—A Functional Approach." *Semiotica* 13, no. 1 (1975): 1–9.

Osiński, Z. "O semiologii teatru." *Nurt,* no. 10, (1969): 69–70.

———. "Przekład tekstu literackiego na język teatru. (Zarys problematyki)." In *Dramat i teatr,* Jan Trzynadlovsky, ed. Wrocław, 1967, 119–56. (= *V. Konferencia Teoretycznoliteracka w Swiętej Katarzynie*).

Osmond-Smith, D. "L'iconisme formel: pour une typologie des transformations musicales." *Semiotica* 15, no. 1 (1976): 33–42.

———. "Problems of Terminology and Method in the Semiotics of Music." *Semiotica* 11 (1974): 269–94.

Osolsobě, I. *Divadlo které mluwi, zpivá a tanči. Teorie jedne komunikačni formy.* Prague, 1974.

———. "Dramatické dilo jako komunikace komunikaci o komunikaci." In *Otkazy divadla a filmu.* I. Brno, 1970, 11–46.

———. "Der vierte Strom des Theaters als Gegenstand der Wissenschaft oder Prospekt einer strukturalen Operettenwissenschaft." In *Otkazy divadla a filmu.* II. Brno, 1971.

Ostwald, P. F. *The Semiotics of Human Sound.* The Hague: Mouton, 1973.

Pagnini, M. "Per una semiologie del teatro classico." *Strumenti critici* 12 (1970): 122–40.

Pavis, P. *Languages of the Stage: Essays in the Semiotics of Theater.* Montreal: Presses de l'Université du Québec, 1976.

Peacock, R. *Criticism and Personal Taste.* Oxford: Clarendon Press, 1972.

Peirce, C. S. *Collected Papers.* Vols. I–IV. 2nd ed. C. Hartshorne and P. Weiss, eds. Cambridge: Harvard University Press, 1960.

Pfister, M. *The Drama.* London: Routledge, 1990.

Pietschmann, C. "Conrad Ekhof." Dissertation. Berlin, 1954.

Pikulik, L. *"Bürgerliches Trauerspiel" und Empfindsamkeit.* Cologne and Graz: Böhlau, 1966.

Piotrowska, E. "Teatr—sztuka autonomiczna." *Nurt* 3 (1973): 38–41.

Plessner, H. "Zur Anthropologie des Schauspielers." (1948). In his *Zwischen Philosophie und Gesellschaft* (1953). Frankfurt am Main: Suhrkamp, 1979, 205–219.

Plett, H. *Textwissenschaft und Textanalyse.* Heidelberg: Quelle und Meyer, 1975.

Poetics Today 1980. Issue dedicated to theatre, drama and performance.

Polieri, J. "Scénographie moderne." *Aujourd'hui* 42/43 (1963): 182ff.

———. *Scénographie - sémiographie.* Paris: Denoël, 1971.

Polti, G. *The Thirty-Six Dramatic Situations.* L. Ray, trans. Boston, 1944.

Posner, R., and H. P. Reinecke, eds. *Zeichenprozesse: Semiotische Forschung in den Einzelwissenschaften.* Wiesbaden: Akademische Verlagsgesellschaft Athenaion, 1977.

———. *Przestrzen—czas—ruch. Wybór prac uczonych radzieckich.* Warsaw: 1976.

Quintilian. *De institutione oratoria.* H. E. Butler, trans. New York and London: 1820–22.

Rapp, U. *Handeln und Zuschauen.* Darmstadt: Luchterhand, 1973.

Raszewski, Z. "Partytura Teatralna." *Pamiętnik Teatralny* 7, no. 3/4 (27/28) (1958): 380–412.

Revzina, O. G., and I. I. Revzin. "A Semiotic Experiment on Stage: The Violation of the Postulate of Normal Communication as a Dramatic Device." *Semiotica* 14, no. 3 (1975): 245–68.

Reynolds, R. *Beards—Their Social Standing, Religious Involvement, Decorative Possibilities and Value in Offence and Defence through the Ages*. New York: Doubleday, 1949.

Riccoboni, F. *L'art du théâtre*. (1750). G. E. Lessing, trans. G. Piens, ed. Berlin: Henschel, 1954.

Richter, H. "Zum kommunikationssoziologischen Inhalt des Medienbegriffs." In *Stilforschung und Rhetorik—Patholinguistik—Sprecherziehung*, E. W. B. Hess-Lüttich, et al., eds. Stuttgart, 1978, 37–43.

Rieck, W. *Johann Christoph Gottsched*. Berlin: Akademie-Verlag, 1972.

Rudowski, V. A. *Lessing's Aesthetica in nuce: An Analysis of the May 26, 1769, Letter to Nicolai*. Chapel Hill: University of North Carolina Press, 1971.

Ruffini, F. "Semiotica del teatro: Ricognizioni degli studi." *Biblioteca teatrale* 9 (1974).

———. *Semiotica del testo: l'esempio teatro*. Rome: Bulzoni, 1978.

Rusterholz, P. *Theatrum Vitae Humanae, Funktion und Bedeutungswandel eines poetischen Bildes*. Berlin: E. Schmidt, 1970.

Ruwet, N. *Langage, musique, poésie*. Paris: Editions du Seuil, 1972.

Saitz, R., and E. Cervenka. *Handbook of Gestures: Colombia and the United States*. The Hague: Mouton, 1972.

Sauer, J. *Symbolik des Kirchengebäudes und seiner Ausstattung in der Auffassung des Mittelalters: Mit Berücksichtigung von Honorius Augustodunensis, Sicardus und Durandus*. Freiburg: Herder, 1902.

Sauerwald, G. *Die Aporie der Diderot'schen Ästhetik*. Frankfurt am Main: Klostermann, 1975.

Saussure, F. de. *Course in General Linguistics*. R. Harris, trans. London: Duckworth, 1983.

Schaeffner, A. "Le pré-théâtre." *Polyphonie*, Paris 1947–48 I, 7–14.

Schapiro, M. "Niektóre problemy semiotyki sztuk plastycznych: Pola i nośniki znaków obrazowych." *Kultury i Społeczeństwo* 1 (1967): 101–119.

Schechner, R. "Drama, Script, Theatre and Performance." *The Drama Review* 17 (1973): 5–36.

Schechner, R., and C. Mintz. "Kinesics and Performance." *The Drama Review* 17 (1973): 102–108.

Scheflen, A. E. *Body Language and Social Order*. New York: Prentice-Hall, 1972.

———. *How Behaviour Means*. New York: Gordon and Breach, 1973.

Scherer, K. R. "Die Funktionen des nonverbalen Verhaltens im Gespräch." In *Gesprächsanalyse: Bericht zum 5. IPK-Kolloquium*. Hamburg: Buske, 1977, 273–95.

———. *Nonverbale Kommunikation: IPK-Forschungsbericht* Vol. 35. Hamburg, 1970.

Scherer, K. R., and H. G. Wallbott, eds. *Nonverbale Kommunikation: Empirische Untersuchungen zum Interaktionsverhalten*. Weinheim: Beltz, 1978.

Scherer, K. R., H. G. Wallbott, and U. Scherer. "Methoden zur Klassifikation von Bewegungsverhalten: Ein funktionaler Ansatz." *Zeitschrift für Semiotik* 1 (1979): 177–92.

Schings, H.-J. "Consolatio Tragoediae. Zur Theorie des barocken Trauerspiels." In *Deutsche Dramentheorien*, R. Grimm, ed. 2 vols. Frankfurt am Main: Athenäum-Verlag, 1973, vol. 1, 1–44.

———. *Der mitleidigste Mensch ist der beste Mensch: Poetik des Mitleids von Lessing bis Büchner*. Munich: Beck, 1980.

Schmidt, S. J. *Texttheorie*. Munich: Fink, 1973.

———. *Literaturwissenschaft als argumentierende Wissenschaft*. Munich: Fink, 1975.

Schneider, R. *Semiotik der Musik*. Munich: Fink, 1980.

———. "Zur Tätigkeit des Entwerfens in der Architektur." In *Zeichenprozesse: Semiotische*

Forschungen in den Einzelwissenschaften, R. Posner and H. P. Reinecke, eds. Wiesbaden: Akad. Verlagsgesellschaft, 1977, 49–57.

Schöne, A. *Emblematik und Drama im Zeitalter des Barock.* 2nd rev. ed. Munich: Beck, 1968.

Schraud, P. "Theater als Information." Dissertation. Vienna, 1967.

Schulte-Sasse, J. "Der Stellenwert des Briefwechsels in der Geschichte der deutschen Ästhetik." In *G. E. Lessing, Moses Mendelssohn, Friedrich Nicolai, Briefwechsel über das Trauerspiel*, J. Schulte-Sasse, ed. Munich: Winkler, 1972, 168–237.

Schweizer, N. R. *The ut pictura poiesis Controversy in Eighteenth-Century England and Germany.* Bern and Frankfurt am Main: Lang, 1972.

Scotto di Carlo, N. "Analyse sémiologique des gestes et mimiques des chanteurs d'opéra." *Semiotica* 9 (1973): 289–318.

Shallek I. *Masks.* New York: Viking, 1973.

Sicard, R.-A. C. de. *Théorie des signes pour l'instruction des sourds-muets.* 2 vols. Paris: Déterville, 1808.

Simmel. G. "Die Mode." In *Philosophische Kultur. Ges. Essais.* 2nd expanded ed. Leipzig: A. Kroner, 1919, 25–57.

———. "Zur Philosophie des Schauspielers." In his *Das individuelle Gesetz. Philosophische Exkurse.* Frankfurt am Main: Suhrkamp, 1968, 75–95.

Skwarczyńska, S. "Anmerkungen zur Semantik der theatralischen Gestik." In *Literaturtheoretische Modelle und kommunikatives System. Zur aktuellen Diskussion in der polnischen Literaturwissenschaft*, W. Kroll and A. Flaker, eds. Kronberg: Scriptor-Verlag, 1974, 328–370.

———. *Wokol teatru i literatury.* Warsaw: Institut Wydawniczy "Pax", 1970.

Sławinska, I. *Współczesna refleksja o teatrze. Ku antropologii teatru.* Krakow: Wydawnictwo Literackie, 1979.

Smith, E. B. *Architectural Symbolism of Imperial Rome and the Middle Ages.* Princeton, 1965.

———. *The Dome: A Study in the History of Ideas.* Princeton: Princeton University Press, 1950.

Souriau, E. *Les deux cent mille situations dramatiques.* Paris: Flammarion, 1950.

Sperber, D. *Rethinking Symbolism.* A. L. Morton, trans. Cambridge: Cambridge University Press, 1975.

Stange, A. *Das frühchristliche Kirchengebäude als Bild des Himmels.* Cologne: Comel, 1950.

Stanislavski, K. S. "Von den physischen Handlungen." In *Der schauspielerische Weg zur Rolle. 5 Aufsätze über K. S. Stanislawskijs Methode der physischen Handlungen.* East Berlin: Henschel, 1952.

Stegmüller, W. *Probleme und Resultate der Wissenschaftstheorie und Analytischen Philosophie.* Berlin, Heidelberg, and New York: Springer Verlag, 1969.

Steinbeck, D. *Einleitung in Theorie und Systematik der Theaterwissenschaft.* Berlin: Walter de Gruyter, 1970.

Stempel, W. D., ed. *Beiträge zur Textlinguistik.* Munich: Fink, 1971.

Stierle, K. H. *Text als Handlung.* Munich: Fink, 1975.

Stone, G. P. "Appearance and the Self." In *Human Behaviour and Social Processes: An Interactionist Approach.* London: Houghton, 1962, 86–118.

Strauss, A. *Mirrors and Masks.* Glencoe, Ill., 1959.

Sulzer, J. G. *Allgemeine Theorie der Schönen Künste in einzeln, nach alphabetischer Ordnung der Kunstwörter auf einander folgenden, Artikeln abgehandelt. Zweyther Theil.* Reprint. Hildesheim: G. Olms, 1967.

Szondi, P. *On Textual Understanding.* H. Mendelsohn, trans. Minneapolis: University of Minnesota Press, 1986.

———. *Die Theorie des bürgerlichen Trauerspiels im 18. Jahrhundert: Der Kaufmann, der*

Hausvater und der Hofmeister. Gert Mattenklott, ed. Frankfurt am Main: Suhrkamp, 1973.

Testa, A. *Discorso sulla danza e sul balletto.* Rome, 1970.

Theater von heute—Räume von gestern. Schriften der Dramaturgischen Gesellschaft. Vol. 11. Berlin, 1979.

Theatre Space. 8th World Congress, Munich 18–25 Sept. 1977/Der Raum des Theaters. J. F. Arnold, general ed. Munich: Prestel, 1977.

Thiel, E. *Geschichte des Kostüms.* Berlin: Henschel, 1960.

Titzmann, M. *Strukturale Textanalyse. Theorie und Praxis der Interpretation.* Munich: Fink, 1977.

Todorov, T. "La sémiotique de XVIII siècle." *Critique* 308 (1973): 26–39.

Tournefort, J. P. *Institutiones rei herbarii.* Paris, 1719.

Trager, G. L. "Paralanguage: A First Approximation." In *Language in Culture and Society*, Dell Hymes, ed. New York: Harper, 1964, 274–88.

Trubetzkoj, N. S. *Grundzüge der Phonologie.* Prague: Harrassowitz, 1939. Reprint. Göttingen: Vandenhoeck and Ruprecht, 1967.

Trzynadlovsky, J. *Dramat i Teatr.* Wrocław, 1967.

Ubersfeld, A. *L'école du spectateur. Lire le théâtre II.* Paris: Editions sociales, 1981.

———. *Lire le théâtre.* Paris: Editions sociales, 1978.

Uhde, H. *Conrad Ekhof.* Leipzig: Brockhaus, 1876.

Veltrusky, J. "Das Drama als literarisches Werk." In *Moderne Dramentheorie*, A. van Kesteren and H. Schmid, eds. Kronberg: Scriptor-Verlag, 1975, 96–132.

———. "Dramatic Text as a Component of Theater" (1941). In *Semiotics of Art. Prague School Contributions*, L. Matejka and J. R. Titunic, eds. Cambridge: MIT Press, 1976, 94–117.

———. "Man and Object in the Theater" (1940). In *A Prague School Reader in Esthetics, Literary Structure and Style*, Paul L. Garvin, ed. Washington, D.C., 1964, 83–91.

Wallis, M. "L'art au point de vue sémantique. Une méthode récente d'esthétique." In *Deuxième congrès international d'esthétique et de science de l'art.* I, Paris: F. Alcan, 1937, 17–21.

———. "Dzieje sztuki jako dzieje struktur semantiycznych." *Kultura i Społeczeństwo* 2 (1968): 63–75.

———. "Semantic and Symbolic Elements in Architecture: Iconology as a First Step towards an Architectural Semiotic." *Semiotica* 8, no. 3 (1973) 220–38.

———. "Świat sztuki i świat znaków." *Ruch Filozoficzny* 20 (1960–61).

Watson, O. M. *Proxemic Behaviour: A Cross-Cultural Study.* The Hague: Mouton, 1970.

Watson, O. M., and T. D. Graves. "Quantitative Research in Proxemic Behaviour." *American Anthropologist* 68 (1966): 971–85.

Weinrich, H. "Phonologie der Sprechpause." *Phonetica* 7 (1961): 4–18.

Wekwerth, M. *Theater und Wissenschaft.* Munich: Hanser, 1974.

Wellbery, D. E. "Aesthetics and Semiotics in the German Enlightenment." Dissertation, Yale University. New Haven, 1977.

Wellek, A. *Musikpsychologie und Musikästhetik: Grundriss einer systematischen Musikwissenschaft.* Bonn: Bouvier, 1975.

Widdowson, W. "Semiotic Theory and Environmental Design." *Kodikas/Code* 2 (1979): 150–64.

Winkler, P. "Notationen des Sprechausdrucks." *Zeitschrift für Semiotik* 1, no. 2/3 (1979): 211–21.

Wittig, S. "A Semiological Approach to Dramatic Criticism." *Educational Theatre Journal*, 1974.

———. "Toward a Semiotic Theory of Drama." *Educational Theatre Journal*, 1975.

Wölfel, K. "Moralische Anstalt." In *Deutschen Dramentheorien.* 2 vols. R. Grimm, ed. Frankfurt am Main: Athenäum-Verlag, 1973, Vol. 1, 45–122.

Wolff, C. *Vernünftige Gedanken von Gott, der Welt und der Seele des Menschen*. Renger Halle, 1747.

Wundt, W. "Die Gebärdensprache." In *Völkerpsychologie*. 10 vols. I: *Die Sprache*. Stuttgart, 1900. Reprint. The Hague: Mouton, 1973.

Wuthenow, R.-R. *Die erfahrene Welt: Europäische Reiseliteratur im Zeitalter der Aufklärung*. Frankfurt am Main: Insel-Verlag, 1980.

Index of Names

Index of Terms

ERIKA FISCHER-LICHTE is Director of the Institute of Theater Research at the Johannes Gutenberg Universität, Mainz.